Inclusion and Exclusion in Europe

ECPR Press

The ECPR Press is published by the European Consortium for Political Research. It publishes original research from lead-ing political scientists and the best among early career researchers in the discipline. Its scope extends to all fields of political science, international relations and political thought, without restriction in either approach or regional focus. It is also open to interdisciplinary work with a predominant political dimension.

ECPR Press Editors

Inclusion and Exclusion in Europe

Migration, Work and Employment Perspectives

Edited by
Olena Fedyuk and Paul Stewart

Published by the European Consortium for Political Research, Harbour House, 6-8 Hythe Quay, Colchester, CO2 8JF, United Kingdom

British Library Cataloguing in Publication Data
A catalogue record for this book is available from the British Library

ISBN: HB 978-1-78660-539-9 PB 978-1-78661-312-7

Library of Congress Cataloging-in-Publication Data

Names: Fedyuk, Olena, editor. | Stewart, Paul, 1956– editor.
Title: Inclusion and exclusion in Europe : migration, work and employment perspectives / edited by Olena Fedyuk and Paul Stewart.
Description: London : ECPR Press, [2017] | Includes bibliographical references and index.
Identifiers: LCCN 2017057315 (print) | LCCN 2018000179 (ebook) | ISBN 9781786605405 (Electronic) | ISBN 9781786605399 (cloth) | ISBN 9781786613127 (pbk.)
Subjects: LCSH: Foreign workers—European Union countries. | European Union countries—Emigration and immigration—Economic aspects. | Immigrants—Employment—European Union countries.
Classification: LCC HD8378.5.A2 (ebook) | LCC HD8378.5.A2 I5644 2017 (print) | DDC 331.6/2094—dc23
LC record available at https://lccn.loc.gov/2017057315

ecpr.eu/shop

Contents

Figures

Tables

Glossary

'Obra Social de la PAH': One of the PAH's campaigns, aimed at collectively squatting empty buildings owned by banks and organising communal living in them. The PAH assembly establishes the criteria to prioritise the most vulnerable households, usually those who have already been evicted and have no other housing alternative, in order to give them access to a housing unit in these buildings. The name 'Obra Social' contains an irony, as it mocks the slogan of the charitable foundation linked to a particular savings bank, La Caixa.

15-M: A social movement that emerged in Madrid, Barcelona and other Spanish cities on the 15 May 2011, as several main squares were occupied after a demonstration protesting the shortcomings of democratic representation under the economic crisis. The movement entailed a plurality of social, political and economic claims, and led to the development of several social movements and new political parties.

Assignment in payment (in Spanish dación en pago): A legal operation that entails the cancellation of debt after giving back a property to the creditor. Unlike other legislation, the Spanish mortgage law does not include this possibility: debtors are responsible for the remaining debt after the property's auction. Therefore, only some debtors are accorded the assignment in payment after putting much pressure on the bank. The acquiescence of the credit institution on a case-by-case basis is a necessary condition.

Central Hipotecaria del Inmigrante (CHI): A mortgage broking firm – disguised as an NGO – that operated in Madrid specifically with Equatorian working-class migrants that encouraged vulnerable borrowers to accept abusive loans.

Iniciativa Legislativa Popular (ILP): People's Initiative for Legislation. By collecting at least 500,000 signatures from Spanish citizens (non-nationals are therefore excluded from signing, and can only support the Initiative in a symbolic manner), social movements and other civic organisations may propose new legislation to be considered by Parliament.

***ius pecuniae* (Latin)**: right of the money.

***ius sanguinis* (Latin)**: right of blood.

***ius soli* (Latin)**: right of the soil.

Observatori DESC (Observatori dels Drets Econòmics, Socials i Culturals – Observatory for Economic, Social and Cultural Rights): An organisation based in Barcelona whose research and reports have contributed to inspiring social movements in several fields, the PAH in the housing arena among them, from a human rights viewpoint. It has also been key to the rise of the popular movement that is governing the city since May 2015, called Barcelona En Comú (Barcelona in Common), with Ada Colau, former PAH spokesperson, as mayor.

Plataforma de Afectados por la Hipoteca / Plataforma d'Afectats per la Hipoteca (PAH): The most famous anti-foreclosures movement, created in Barcelona in 2009. It has now spread to dozens of other cities and towns all over Spain. It can be translated as 'Coalition of People Affected by Mortgages'.

***sans-papier* (French)**: 'without paper', meaning undocumented migrants.

Abbreviations

A8 countries	Czech Republic, Estonia, Hungary, Latvia, Lithuania, Poland, Slovakia and Slovenia
AFBE-UK	Association for BME Engineers UK
AoM	Autonomy of Migration
BAME	Black, Asian and Minority Ethnic
CEE	Central Eastern Europe / European
CERN	European Organization for Nuclear Research
CIA	Central Intelligence Agency
CGIL	Confederazione Generale Italiana del Lavoro (Italian General Confederation of Labour)
CME	Coordinated Market Economy
COMPAS	The University of Oxford's Centre on Migration, Policy and Society
CPE	First Contract of Employment (French)
CV	Curriculum Vitae
DGB	Confederation of German Trade Unions
ECB	European Central Bank
EEA	European Economic Area
ETUC	European Trade Union Confederation
EU	European Union
Eurozone	The nineteen EU member states using the Euro currency
EWC	European Works Council
FAU	Free Workers' Union
GCSE	General Certificate of Secondary Education
GP	General Practitioner
GUF	Global Union Federation

GUS	Główny Urząd Statystyczny (Central Statistical Office of Poland)
HSMP	Highly Skilled Migrants Programme (UK high-skilled immigrant scheme in operation from 2002 to 2008)
ICTU	Irish Congress of Trade Unions
IELTS	International English Language Testing System
ILO	International Labour Organization
ISDS	Investor-State Dispute Settlement
IWU	Independent Workers Union
LME	Liberal Market Economy
MAC	Migration Advisory Committee (advisory body to the UK government on migration)
MDNS	Migrant Doctors Network in Scotland
MWRN	Migrant Workers Research Network
NBS	National Business Systems
NCDN	Nigerian Community in Diaspora Network
NHS	National Health Service
NIC ICTU	Northern Irish Committee of Irish Congress of Trade Unions
NMDS-SC	National Minimum Data Set for Social Care
N-VA	New Flemish Alliance
NVQ	National Vocational Qualification
OECD	Organization for Economic Co-operation and Development
PBS	Points-Based System (system of migrant visa regulation in the UK)
PIGS	reference to Portugal, Ireland, Greece and Spain
PFIs	Private Finance Initiatives
SME	Small- and medium-sized enterprises
SNP	Scottish National Party
TGNF	The Global Nigeria Forum
TISA	Trade in Services Agreement
TTIP	Transatlantic Trade and Investment Partnership
TUC	Trade Union Congress
UIL	Unione Italiana del Lavoro (Italian Labour Union)
UK	United Kingdom
UKBA	United Kingdom Borders Agency (replaced by UKVI in 2013)
UKVI	UK Visas and Immigration (replaced the UKBA in 2013)
US	United States
USA	United States of America
USDAW	Union of Shop, Distributive and Allied Workers
VoC	Varieties of Capitalism
WTO	World Trade Organisation

Preface

Olena Fedyuk and Paul Stewart

Over the last twenty years, the EU has been confronting a range of seemingly conflicting interests; a struggle between making its borders secure while at the same time responding to the needs of capital for an exploitable, expendable and low-cost workforce which in many sectors is increasingly represented by migrants. The EU has correspondingly multiplied its borders by pushing them both outwards and inwards in such a manner as to fragment the process of their policing into moments of bodily and identity surveillance irrespective of the geographical proximity to national borders. The so-called Global Approach to Migration most vividly marked the externalization of the borders as, in the early 2000s, the EU migration policy framework shifted its focus from strengthening its own borders towards cooperation with non-EU countries for control and management of the migratory flows that eventually lead to Europe (Casas-Cortes et al. 2015). This book considers the inward proliferation of national borders whereby borders are extended; not so much geographically or physically but to the arenas of rights, permissions and restrictions. Many of these fragmentations link directly to the work and employment status of mobile individuals. The cumulative effect of this fragmented status leading to permissions and exclusions divides mobile people into hierarchal, privilege-based systems. Often this leads to a recycling of somewhat more traditional inequalities linked to race, ethnicity, class and gender.

This book pursues a twofold agenda. One is to take the debates about inclusion and exclusion of migrants in Europe out of strictly migration debates. This requires a conceptual shift from treating migrants as a state of exception whereby rights and freedoms have varying limitations. Thus, we seek to reintroduce power relations between capital and labour and the hierarchies of race, ethnicity, gender and class into the discussion in the new context, which since 2015 has been deemed a 'migration crisis'. In this respect we argue that the 'migration crisis' should be attributed not so much to the new situation in migration flows but rather to a wider European failure to respond to it humanely. This is an ongoing European crisis of humanitarian and democratic values that includes a failure to respond to the continuous encroachment on workers' rights and the ongoing precarisation of working lives. Following this, our second objective explores the ways in which the fragmentation of migrant workers' statuses fits with other, more lengthy, transformations of labour relations in the EU. We interpret this as a shift from a system of full employment to a multiplicity of flexible, decentralised and fluid forms of underemployment integrated into a range of employment regimes.

In exploring the applicability of a range of existing research frameworks the book maps further analytical agendas for connecting labour and migration studies. Taking a cross-disciplinary perspective, the book examines both the life of institutions and individual experiential knowledge in the context of migration. This allows us to explore the possibilities for mobilisation and collective action at the intersection of migration and worker activism in a novel way. Through critical research we seek solidarity with workers in various precarious circumstances arguing that the defence of collective processes can lead to better circumstances for disadvantaged non-migrant and migrant workers alike.

Of course, the context of the so-called migration crisis is the *longue durée* of neoliberalism, and this inevitably frames the conceptual inquiry of many chapters. A number of authors pose the questions: 'What is neoliberal in the current relationship between (migrant) labour and (global) capital?' and 'What is neoliberal in the role states play in shaping capital-labour relations through employment, migration and care policies?' The state's role intricately links the inquiry about neoliberalism to an investigation of the transformations of the meaning and practices of citizenship, as discussed in the majority of the chapters.

The book concludes with an intriguing round-table debate that took place between the book's contributors and several external readers in October 2015. The discussion, addressing common themes and difficulties in the chapters, reflects collective ideas on the missing links and potential for further research on the theme of employment and mobility in Europe.

REFERENCE

Casas-Cortes M., S. Cobarriubias and J. Pickles 2015. 'Riding Routes and Itinerant Borders: Autonomy of Migration and Border Externalization'. *Antipode*, Early View (Online Version of Record published before inclusion in an issue), http://onlinelibrary.wiley.com/doi/10.1111/anti.12148/pdf (accessed 19 December 2015).

Acknowledgements

This book is an initiative that evolved out of the activities of the Theme 2 'Inclusion and Exclusion' of the Marie Curie FP7-PEOPLE-2012-ITN project 'ChangingEmployment' ('The changing nature of employment in Europe in the context of challenges, threats and opportunities for employees and employers'), no. 317321. It is led by Professor Paul Stewart, University of Strathclyde, Glasgow. The Marie Curie 'ChangingEmployment' Fellows are Karima Aziz, Ben Egan, Olena Fedyuk, Mateusz Karolak, Radosław Polkowski and Nina Sahraoui.

The editors of the book would like to thank Marek Čaněk (Multicultural Centre Prague NGO, Prague), Frances Pine (Goldsmiths, University of London) and Francesca Alice Vianello (University of Padova), the external readers of our book who committed their time and energy to discussing individual chapters and the concept of the volume as a whole.

Mateusz Karolak (Marie Curie Fellow), the author of Chapter II.4, wishes to express his gratitude to his co-supervisors Prof. Adam Mrozowicki and the book editors for their useful comments and remarks.

Ben Egan (Marie Curie Fellow), one of the co-authors of Chapter III.1, would like to formally thank his friend Salvo Leonardi, without whom much of the fieldwork would have been impossible.

Martin Lundsteen and Irene Sabaté, the authors of Chapter III.2, would like to thank the people who, going through such a traumatic experience as a home repossession process, were ready to share their stories with them. The authors are especially grateful to the eldest son of the person they have anonymised as Nelson, who let Irene into his family's concerns and hopes; to the PAH assembly in l'Hospitalet de Llobregat (Barcelona) who accepted the presence of Irene during meetings and mobilisations throughout 2012; and to the Observatori DESC, who, in the framework of their research on housing emergency in Catalonia, facilitated interviews with several members of the PAH.

Finally, we would like to thank Alexandra Segerberg of ECPR Press for her ongoing support to and encouragement of this publication and two anonymous reviewers for their helpful comments and suggestions.

Introduction

Migrants' Inclusion and Exclusion in the Context of Precarization of Working Lives in the Post-Enlargement EU

Olena Fedyuk and Paul Stewart

The spectre of migration will never become a new working class.

Papadopoulos and Tsianos (2013: 187)

The last two decades have seen the EU grappling with what seems to be a direct conflict of interests; a struggle between securitization of its external borders and the demand for an exploitable and disposable low-cost workforce which, in various sectors of the economy, is increasingly represented by migrants. During this process the EU has multiplied its borders by pushing them both outwards and inwards, fragmenting the process of their policing into moments of bodily and identity surveillance irrespective of the geographical proximity to national borders. The so-called Global Approach to Migration most vividly marked the externalization of the borders as, in the early 2000s, the EU migration policy framework shifted its focus from strengthening its own borders towards cooperation with non-EU countries for control and management of the migratory flows that eventually lead to Europe (Casas-Cortes et al. 2015). For our book, however, the inward multiplication of national borders is more interesting; it is characterized by extending borders not so much in geographical and physical spaces but to the arenas of rights, permissions, qualification, differentiated and point-based access to labour markets, social benefits, mobility and political rights (De Genova 2013; Mezzadra and Nielson 2013). Many of these fragmentations of status are linked directly to the work and employment status of mobile individuals. The cumulative outcome of the fragmented status, permissions and exclusions dividing mobile people into hierarchal, privilege-based systems, often recycle more traditional inequalities linked to race, ethnicity, class and gender.

This book pursues two interconnected objectives. One is to take the debates about inclusion and exclusion and migrants in Europe out of strictly migration debates. By this, we mean a shift from treating migrants in a certain state of exception, in which rights and freedoms have different limitations. With this we seek to reintroduce power relations between capital and labour and the hierarchies of race, ethnicity, gender and class into the discussion in the new context, which since 2015 has been deemed a 'migration crisis'. We add our voice to those arguing that the 'migration crisis' should be attributed not to so much to the new situation in migratory flows but to a failure in Europe to respond to it humanely. Specifically, this is an ongoing European crisis of humanitarian and democratic values including a failure to respond to the continuous encroachment on workers' rights and the ongoing precarization of working lives (e.g. see debates on the *FocaalBlog* by Bojadžijev and Mezzadra 2015; Rajaram 2015). To have a more focused debate from this point of view, we introduce our second objective, which is to explore the ways in which the fragmentation of migrant workers' statuses fits with other, more lengthy, transformations of labour relations in the EU. The latter we see as broadly characterized by a shift from a system of full employment in industrial society to a multiplicity of flexible, decentralized and fluid forms of underemployment integrated into a range of employment regimes (Beck 1992; Standing 2011).

This book looks at the experience of migration precisely at the intersection and overlap of these main shifts in both migration and employment regimes. On a theoretical level, we set out to investigate the applicability of the existing research frameworks and map out further analytical agendas for linking labour and migration studies. As a cross-disciplinary exercise, methodologically this book scrutinizes both the life of institutions and individual experiential knowledge about migration. We then build on both in exploring the possibilities of mobilization and collective action at the intersection of migration and worker activism, the nature of which we are still to fully recognize and comprehend. Through critical research we seek solidarity with workers in various precarious circumstances and argue that defending collective processes can lead to better circumstances for disadvantaged non-migrant and migrant workers alike.

It is no accident that we put work at the heart of the migration experience; some of the classic migration studies emphasized the centrality of labour in migration (e.g. Burawoy 1976; Sayad 2004). As this book will further elaborate, the possibility of work and working conditions determines not only migrants' daily experiences but increasingly chances for transnational mobility and the scope of rights that accompany it. To move beyond the perspective that situates migrants' exclusion and inclusion solely in migration processes, we contextualize migration in the larger transformations of the local, national and transnational labour markets and relations that point to the ongoing processes of precarization of working lives. As Wills et al. (2010) point out, today's immigration is taking place against the background of a sufficient native labour force, ongoing crumbling of the welfare states' provisions, and austerity measures that increasingly remove European job security, pushing further flexibilization of contracts and precarization of employment and life. Unemployment also can be seen as a critical part of this new complex of insecurity. These trends, Wills argues, 'have thus placed the migrant at the centre of the contemporary labour process. While subcontracting is now the paradigmatic form of employment across the world, the migrant is the world's paradigmatic worker. … Even those who cross borders legally find themselves politically disenfranchised' (2010: 6).

In the EU context the connection between migration and labour was made explicit as citizens of East European expansion in 2004 and 2007 accepted limitations to labour market participation in several pre-2004 EU countries in exchange for freedom of movement within the expanded EU. Some of these limitations were removed after almost a decade. This effectively pushed many new European citizens towards irregular and substandard employment. This connection gains new significance in the light of the 2016 Brexit vote. While this book is not directly concerned with the consequences of Britain's decision to leave the European Union (EU) on the mobility of people within the EU, or on those seeking entry to it, nevertheless we feel it necessary to state our position on migration and the so-called migration crisis given the febrile context in which we write. In this regard we would agree with the argument made by Teresa Hayter at the turn of twenty-first century that immigration controls represent an attack on a person's right of movement, on their freedom, with all the consequences this brings. She writes,

> By far the most important reason for opposing immigration controls is that they impose harsh suffering and injustice on those who attempt to migrate, or to flee for their lives and liberty. (2000: 7)

Through focusing on intra-EU mobility (seven out of nine core chapters in this book), we hope to tackle other lines of fragmentation central to migration experience but not limited to it, that is, flexible and low protection level contracts (including the posted workers programme and temporary agency workers) and differentiated access to welfare, intra-sectoral job hierarchies of high- and low-skill profile jobs. By no means does this suggest that experiences of intra-EU and non-EU migrants are the same. However, we seek to explore fragmentations in migration status that go beyond this division situating it further at the intersection of race, gender and class. This book brings forward results of original qualitative research carried out in Germany,

Poland, Spain and the UK, with Poland standing out as a sending country. We thus want to emphasize that the sending country context is crucial for understanding migrants' trajectories and, in particular, opportunities for organized resistance, as sending countries often come out as the forerunners of what Woolfson and Sommers describe as a new economic logic and a political structure promoting labour migration (2008: 56).

The distinctions between migrants' statuses are of importance for our discussion about inclusion and exclusion to the extent that it serves the purpose of the state to differentiate, divide and legitimize control over the right to freedom of movement. (Ir)regularity, (il)legality and (non-)citizenship in European migration policies have been continuously portrayed as black-and-white issues to effectively produce and sustain an analytical, political and practical divide that obscures 'shadowy, publicly unacknowledged or disavowed, obscene supplement: the large-scale recruitment of illegalized migrants as legally vulnerable, precarious, and thus tractable labour' (De Genova 2013: 2). The policies construct irregular migrants as 'unskilled', 'poor' and 'unwanted' and often criminalize them, while they construct the category of 'skilled' migrants as 'good' and 'wanted', granting them distinct access to rights and benefits (De Somer 2012). The EU's acknowledged priority for high-skilled labour (which found its reflection in the EU Blue Card Directive) is shadowed by the escalation of the posted workers programmes (Lillie 2014), deskilling of certain sectors (e.g. care and social work) and further privatization of formerly public sector jobs, which often enables hiring deskilled migrant workers through private companies (e.g. PIQUE 2009; Lutz and Palenga-Möllenbeck 2011). All these trends reinforce the principle of cataloguing migrants by their skills, nationality, age, gender and, ultimately, ability to generate income. This principle has not only widened the gap between the 'good' (high-skilled and prosperous migrants) and 'poor' (unwanted migrants) (De Somer 2012; De Genova 2013) but also effectively legitimized intensification of control over various labour flows justifying the differential provisions for migrants, such as prospects for long-term residence, renewal of contracts, family reunification, prospects for studying and career advancement, and access to social benefits. These processes not only point to a distinct paradigm of inclusion and exclusion, or the categories of insider/outsider, but also hint at the intriguing changes in the role nation states reinvent for themselves in neoliberal economies.

A range of literature on the nature of the migrant labour demand in the EU (Ruhs and Anderson 2010; Wills et al. 2010) conceptualizes a utilitarian approach to migration (manifested in objectification of migrants through skilled/unskilled labels including deskilling) as a part of mechanisms devaluing it with the purpose of excluding people who deliver work and services from equal pay and rights. In their *Global Cities at Work* (2010) Wills et al.

consider similar mechanisms connecting labour deregulation and the ways of managing international migration, and offer a valuable Marxist reading of what happens to the reserve army of labour if we add international migrant labour flows into the equation. Their contextualization of migration in the uneven global geography of wages and welfare is then backed up by a number of qualitative research-based exemplars from various sites of migrant employment in London. Indeed, there is a strong temptation to draw an equation between migrant labour and an increasingly precarious workforce, as 'migrant labour becomes increasingly precarised (especially after the 2008 economic crisis) and precarious labour becomes increasingly mobile' (2013: 189). However, rather than a rise of solidarity movements what we see is the growth in populist anti-immigrant sentiment across Europe. Papadopoulos and Tsianos (2013) warn against making hasty comparisons as they argue that it would take much more for migrant precarious workers to rise as a mobilized collective, or a class: 'The forms of political action that migrants engage [sic] cannot be confused with a mobilization that resembles the action of a collective historical or political subject. The very conditions of current migration defy the possibility of constructing a viable intentional and permanent subjectivity' (2013: 187). In this case, how are we to make sense of the growing similarity and discord between the precarious and migrant work forces?

Specifically, this book looks at the inclusion of the migrant labour and exclusion of migrants through a system of differentiated and limited rights. On a more subtle level we explore spaces, tools of mobilization and identifications arising from the selective inclusion and exclusion of migrants, often through work practices and employment. In the context of an existing debate in migration literature, we interpret 'inclusion' not in a binary whose opposite is 'exclusion', but as a process within an endless range of practices, experiences and fragmentations of legal statuses. In this sense the selective or fragmented inclusion of migrants becomes a form of their disciplining, control and exclusion from rights and solidarities of and with non-immigrant workers. Following De Genova's conceptualization of 'inclusion through exclusion', we see that immigrants' 'incorporation is permanently beleaguered with the kinds of exclusionary and commonly racist campaigns that ensure that this inclusion is itself, precisely, a form of subjugation. What is at stake, then, is a larger socio-political (and legal) process of inclusion through exclusion' (De Genova 2013: 5).

Responding to the analytical challenge of the book, the conceptual inquiry of many of the chapters is closely linked to the question of the nature of neoliberalism (as an ideology and practice that transforms the relationship between labour and capital) and citizenship (as open to interpretation or formal membership that often sets aside migrant and non-migrant workers). Peck (2013: 153) argues that we should approach neoliberalism not as 'a substitute for explanation' but as 'an *occasion* for explanation'. Thus many of the authors in this book pose the questions: 'What is neoliberal in the current relationship between (migrant) labour and (global) capital?' and 'What is neoliberal in the role states play in shaping labour-capital relations through employment, migration and care policies?' The state's role intricately links the inquiry about neoliberalism to an investigation of the transformations of the meaning and practices of citizenship, as discussed from various perspectives in the majority of chapters in this book.

To map the connections between ideology, policies, states and individual migrants' decisions, we found Vicki Squire's (2011) notion of the *politics of mobility* a sound analytical starting point. Squire argues that while the state is actively engaged in the politics of control, migrating individuals are engaged in the politics of mobility, and in order to grasp the fluid and ever-changing picture of the lived practice of migration we need to look at the point of collision of these two types of politics. The distinction is indeed an analytically useful one, as it allows us to step aside from the perspective of migrants, as being passive subjects of the state's politics and ideological shifts, and opens up space for the necessary investigation of the motives that guide migrants in their choices and practices. It also transcends the simplified perspective of migrants as free will agents operating within a fully informed and deterministic mindset. Instead the politics of mobility offers a more politicised and egalitarian frame in which states are involved in a politics of control and migrants as exercising the politics of mobility. This paradigm opens up a sharper perspective on individual experiences and dynamics as a part of collective, ever-changing migratory flows and practices.

Squire's framework reflects an important turning point in migration studies, known as 'autonomy of migration (AoM)', which significantly redirects debate around migrants' subjectivities from the narrow liberal perspective of the 'free will individual' to the 'constituent powers of migrant journeys' (Casas-Cortes et al. 2015: 2). AoM offers an analytical shift from the 'apparatuses of control to the multiple and diverse ways in which migration responds to, operates independently from, and in turn shapes those apparatuses and their corresponding institutions and practices' (Casas-Cortes et al. 2015: 2). Together with 'border as method' (Mezzadra and Nielson 2013), it enters a methodological debate that is particularly close to our book: how are we to understand the active role a mobile individual takes in migration, as well as to grasp the possibilities and forms of shifting collective actions or solidarities emerging out of migratory flows and experiences across borders and statuses? Papadopoulos and Tsianos (2013) warn us that first and foremost we need to deconstruct our own understanding of the political, in order to catch the politics of 'migrants' practices which neither attempt to integrate people into an existing polity nor to systematically resist this polity: 'Migrants' politics are in this sense *non-politics* (that is, they are not seen as representable in the dominant existing polity) (2013: 188). In dialogue with these debates this volume's contributions explore subtle, often 'non-political' politics of everyday migrants' practices of compliance and subversion of existing migratory and work regimes. However, we also seek various forms of collective response, directed at challenging the hegemony of migration and employment regimes through the transformations of trade unions or the collaboration of various grassroots organizations and other groups.

STRUCTURE OF THE BOOK

Looking at the multifaceted processes of inclusion through exclusion at the level of national policies, individual practices and collective actions methodologically mean that we seek not only to contextualize individual ethnographically documented experiences of mobile individuals in the larger transformations of 'global capital – local labour' relationships, but also to understand the emerging forms of the political in these relationships. Thus, our book is set up to explore collective responses and contestations emerging in these reconfiguring contexts. In other words, if we talk about a transnational workforce, where can we trace transnational collective responses and, although possibly fleeting, but always emerging, acts of solidarity? Like most transnational practices, such forms of solidarity would take very specific local manifestations and mobilize allies and forms relevant to the local context. These localized contexts and emergence of alliances across migration, employment and social statuses, are where we seek new optimism for collective struggle in response to the rising precarization of the working lives of both migrants and non-migrants.

The book has three sections: the first looks at the macro-level political economy to contextualize the changes in employment and migration regimes with all three chapters paying attention to the reconfiguration of the role of the state in these changes. The second section takes a close look at case studies of individuals making sense of their mobility, in terms of both migration and employment. The third section brings back the collective perspective by focusing on the case studies of collective responses to growing precarity among migrants and non-migrants. All chapters are thus not only guided by the leitmotif of the book, but form a dialogue with all three sections as they contextualize their contribution at the macro, meso and micro levels of inquiry.

The first section sets the political economy background of recent transformations in the relevant EU and national employment and migration regimes by looking at changes in national policy-making, migration and employment regulations. Several studies have noted that the unevenness of the global geography of wages, welfare provisions and consumption levels have 'reconfigured the geography of the reserve army of labour' (Wills et al. 2010: 7) transforming immigration into a lucrative business for the state. The role of nation states in running such a business has been a prominent and an intriguing one. By introducing a great variety of immigration systems that justify objectification and further stratification of immigrants by their perceived contribution, states have been claiming the legitimacy to exercise control over the conditions and price of immigrant labour. In exercising immigration controls, state immigration policies act as an instrumental feature of capital. This is a 'political dimension' (De Genova 2013: 9) favouring its own interests that increasingly strengthens employers' bargaining power over the local labour force.

Chapter I.1, by Jamie Woodcock, provides background to the main developments and debates relating to changes in the role of the state in the liberalization of employment policies, as well as in shaping national immigration priorities. The analysis focuses on the public sector and service work, where the state remains a major employer, albeit introducing fragmentation of work and outsourcing to (multinational) agencies that, in turn, often incorporate migrant labour. This intersection allows us to explore the impact of state reconfigurations, the changing position of trade unions and the specific pathway to precarization of labour. The main argument, that is, that the state is not retreating under neoliberalism, but rather reconfiguring its role to deregulate capital and employment policies while attempting to manage migration for employment, sets the background for most of the following contributions. Building on this discussion, Chapter I.2, by Ben Egan, is concerned with making sense of a contradiction at the heart of debates in Europe – economic systems that seek migrant labour within political systems that reject migrants themselves. It poses the question, 'What would constitute migration employment relations in Europe, if we are to theorise such relations?', and develops a model of the way in which institutions at various levels have the potential to affect outcomes with regard to employment relations at the point at which they intersect with migration. Making an exercise of applying institutional analysis that has underpinned much of the employment relations literature in Europe to institutions structuring labour migration, the chapter links developments in migration with the broader weakening of employment stability associated with neoliberal reforms. In particular, it sees migration as a new frontier of the precarization of employment per se. Chapter I.3, by Nina Shahraoui, Radosław Polkowski and Mateusz Karolak, shifts the focus to the regulation of migration by nation states and at the EU level. Drawing on the analysis of the utilitarian and market logics of formal polarization of EU versus non-EU migrants, the authors highlight the latent pitfalls of intra-EU mobility regulations and the practical limitations of EU citizenship. Specifically, they look at the connection between the expansion of the EU and border closures to non-EU migrants and the rise of various precarious forms of employment resulting in the fragmentation of workers' statuses (e.g. differential access to social security for the members of the new accession states or the rise of the posted workers programmes). Finally, the chapter challenges another common binary in migration literature in rejecting the notion of citizens versus non-citizens, proposing instead an understanding of citizenship as a continuum of rights written into global inequalities.

The second section of the book comprises ethnographic case studies from Poland and the UK. It looks at the micro level of personal experiences and challenges in employment and labour relations triggered by individual mobility embedded within transnational employment, migration and care regimes. The qualitative methods applied by the authors in this section (such as biographic narrative and life story interviews) bring out migrants' voices in relation to the role employment and work play in shaping the sense of success or shame, self-esteem, exclusion, satisfaction or disillusionment with mobility. In line with the focus of the book, this section explores how neoliberal ideals of the self-sustaining, independent individual intertwine migrants' motivations and reasoning. Many respondents embrace these ideals as a moving force of their migration, while others feel betrayed by the promise of such self-sufficiency. The section broadly asks, 'What is neoliberal about the new striving after the supposed self-made character through migration?' For answers, it turns to sites of employment and work.

The chapters in this section focus on four case studies, dealing with a range of gendered experiences in various sectors of migrants' employment. Chapter II.1, by Radosław Polkowski, explores a new paradigm for discussing the role of the sending country (Poland) by looking at how its economy and ideologies shape and affect migrants' choices and practices. Behind many stories of successful (i.e. in economic terms) lives abroad lie 'structures of feeling' (Williams 1961) characterized by hidden injuries such as shame and fear of social failure, which the author traces through migrants' narratives. The chapter offers an interdisciplinary approach to migration by bringing in concepts not just from migration studies but also cultural and literary studies in addition to the psychology and sociology of emotions which are then linked to the macro-structural context on the new role of the state, that is the state as a 'community of value' (Anderson 2013). In Chapter II.2, Nina Sahraoui brings to the fore the importance of care regimes along with employment and migration. In her analysis of migrant workers' experiences in for-profit private elderly care in Greater London she explores the links between the rise of the demand for care workers and the construction of care as unskilled labour that channels into the sector a gendered and racialized workforce. The care sector's reliance on migrant labour, argues Sahraoui, engenders structural pressures to maintain low labour costs while deskilling workers in the context of the commodification of care. Gendered understanding of care work leads to further barriers created by the articulation of migration and employment policies for workers' lives and employment trajectories. Karima Aziz, in Chapter II.3, explores work trajectories of female Polish migrant workers in the UK within the dynamics of changing employment in Europe. Ten years after the accession to the EU, female Polish migrants in the UK are not merely low-paid, low-skilled workers, but are now represented in a variety of sectors and occupations. Employing biographical narrative interviews conducted among Polish women in the UK and those who have returned to Poland, the author uncovers the relevant gendered and migrant employment patterns, as well as the agency these women seek and how they enact agency in their narratives of migration and work trajectories. While many respondents are happy with the chance of free movement in the EU that European citizenship provides, they feel the limitations of the implicit exclusion based on the gendered division of work resulting from the conceptualization of the mobile European citizen as a productive worker. This chapter examines the construction of Polish women and generational dynamics that affect the way women engage with their migration and work experience. Chapter II.4, by Mateusz Karolak, argues that mobility should not be seen as a unidirectional straight line, as he assesses the labour market experience of return migrants from the UK to Poland and double return migrants back to the UK. Challenging the assumptions about employment as an indicator of return migrants' 'reintegration' back home this chapter draws a dynamic picture of mobile Poles' experiences in the sphere of work and employment, against the background of the changing employment patterns and flexibilization of work in both countries. By comparing experiences of work abroad and in Poland, individuals try to make rational decisions about their mobility choices, while the author proposes a four-type classification of coping strategies employed by return migrants facing distress. The latter results from the perceived discrepancies between employment standards: re-emigration, activism, adaptation and/or entrepreneurship.

The third section considers migrants' collective responses to precarization of their working lives. Particularly, we want to explore what alliances and solidarities are possible beyond the status of the 'migrant'. We are interested in initiatives that seek to bridge the gap between migrant and non-migrant workers, thus creating the possibility for wide-ranging solidarity. This section steps away from the discussion of individual practices and experiences focusing rather on collective responses by posing the question: can collective experiences of precarization give rise to collective responses across the divisions of legal status, ethnicity, race, gender and class?

We open the section with a coauthored chapter that looks into a more traditional site of workers' organization – trade unions. Chapter III.1, by Aziz, Egan and Polkowski, analyses how well trade unions are prepared to meet the challenge of post-Fordist transformations linked to flexibilization of labour and increasing privatization and fragmentation of workplaces. This is, moreover, linked to the politics of infusion of migrant labour into certain sectors and jobs. The authors draw upon semi-structured interviews with migrant workers and trade union officials in Italy, the north of Ireland and England to examine how trade union organization, broadly conceived, impacts outcomes for migrant workers. Historicizing their inquiry, they argue that various traditions and cultures of European trade union movements, separated by borders, history, language and confederal structure, lead to inevitable differences in strategies, attitudes and outcomes in relation to all members (and non-members), inclusive of migrants and other groups of workers seen as under-represented in workplaces. The authors suggest a return to an examination of class as crucial to understanding the ways in which unions define the boundaries of what representation actually means. Chapter III.2, by Martin Lundsteen and Irene Sabaté, expands the scope of possible solidarity actions between migrants and non-migrants by looking into the anti-repossessions movement, PAH, in Catalonia. This movement, through different actions of disobedience and protest actions in the franchises of specific financial institutions, has gained a broad legitimacy and strong support, mobilizing otherwise excluded groups around a common identity of victims of mortgage fraud (as opposed to any kind of ethno-national identification). The research focuses on the work of the movement assessing to what extent it overcomes the usual divide between native and foreigner while nonetheless stopping short of an overall critique of racist structuring and class divisions that exist between the different participants.

As Raia Apostolova highlights in Chapter III.3, some of the EU open-border principles serve to reduce the possibility of solidarity in the face of fragmentation. By looking into the cases of the struggles of Bulgarian-day labourers in Munich and Romanian construction workers in Berlin, she points to the difficulties of collective responses to overexploitation as they emerge in the context of freedom of movement. The author looks at the very heart of the EU principle of freedom of movement in order to analyse its inherent contradictions while reclaiming some of its political potential. Chibuzo Ejiogu's Chapter III.4 looks into what seems to be the other end of the migration spectrum, that is, high-skilled migration of non-EU nationals. Drawing on his ethnographic and participatory research conducted with several networks of skilled Black, Asian and Ethnic Minority (BAME) doctors in the UK, the chapter analyses how the most recent changes to the UK regulations on high-skilled migration fragment the status of these workers in their workplaces, despite their high-skilled positions. The author argues that high-skilled migrant workers experience a precarious migrant status that is socially and legally constructed by employment and immigration policies resulting in the institutionalization of uncertainty and a range of non-citizenship restrictions imposed on their status. The author then assesses the role of migrant networks in both resisting and reproducing the precarity experienced by high-skilled migrants as well as the role of networks in articulating the collective voice of migrant labour in the context of recent changes to UK immigration policy.

The third section explores the way in which various collective actions aimed at bridging migrant/non-migrant divides are far from being harmonious or egalitarian; various groups pursue their interests dictated by political, economic and social struggles that often leave such actions fruitless, or, temporary and febrile, lacking genuine solidarity. However, we see solidarity actions (even if they are temporary) as important political manifestations in the imagining of alternative forms of struggle against deepening neoliberal transformations in both employment and migration regimes.

Following a short concluding section that ties together the threads of all three sections and highlights the impact of an integrated approach to the issues of migration and collective workers' struggles, we close the book with the transcript of a round-table debate that took place between the book's contributors and several external readers in October 2015. The discussion, addressing common themes and difficulties in the chapters, was recorded, transcribed and written up by the editors with the aim of reflecting collective ideas on the missing links and potential for further research around the theme of employment and mobility in Europe. We hope that this last contribution will reflect the ongoing discussions among the authors beyond the contributions in their chapters shedding light on their own political positions on these issues.

REFERENCES

Anderson, B. 2013. *Us and Them? The Dangerous Politics of Immigration Control*. Oxford: Oxford Scholarship Online.

Beck, U. 1992. *Risk Society: Towards a New Modernity*. London: Sage.

Bojadžijev, M. and S. Mezzadra. 2015. '"Refugee crisis" or crisis of European migration policies?' *FocaalBlog, Focaal: Journal of Global and Historical Anthropology*, 12 November 2015. http://www.focaalblog.com/2015/11/12/manuela-bojadzijev-and-sandro-mezzadra-refugee-crisis-or-crisis-of-european-migration-policies (accessed 2 November 2016).

Burawoy, M. 1976. 'The functions and reproduction of migrant labour: Comparative material from southern Africa and the United States'. *American Journal of Sociology* 81 (5): 1050–1080.

Casas-Cortes, M., S. Cobarriubias and J. Pickles. 2015. 'Riding routes and itinerant borders: Autonomy of migration and border externalization'. *Antipode* Early View (Online Version of Record published before inclusion in an issue). http://onlinelibrary.wiley.com/doi/10.1111/anti.12148/pdf (accessed 19 December 2015).

De Genova, N. 2013. 'Spectacles of migrant "illegality": The scene of exclusion, the obscene of inclusion'. *Ethnic and Racial Studies* 36 (7): 1–19. https:/doi.org/10.1080/01419870.2013.783710

De Somer, M. 2012. 'Trends and gaps in the academic literature on EU labour migration policies'. *NEUJOBS*: state of the art report no. 5. http://www.neujobs.eu/sites/default/files/publication/2012/12/NEUJOBS%20D.18.1.pdf (accessed 6 February 2015).

Lutz, H. and E. Palenga-Möllenbeck. 2011. 'Care, gender and migration: Towards a theory of transnational domestic work migration in Europe'. *Journal of Contemporary European Studies* 19 (3): 349–364. https://doi.org/10.1080/14782804.2011.610605

Mezzadra, S. and B. Neilson. 2013. *Border as Method, or, the Multiplication of Labor*. Durham, NC: Duke University Press.

Papadopoulos, D. and V. Tsianos. 2013. 'After citizenship: Autonomy of migration, organisational ontology, and mobile commons'. *Citizenship Studies* 17 (2): 178–196.

Peck, J. 2013. 'Explaining (with) Neoliberalism'. *Territory, Politics, Governance* 1 (2): 132–157.

PIQUE Summary Report. 2009. 'Summary report of the project "Privatisation of Public Services and the Impact on Quality, Employment and Productivity" (PIQUE)'. European Commission's 6th Framework Programme (Contract No. CIT5-2006-028478) Vienna. http://www.pique.at/reports/pubs/PIQUE_SummaryReport_Download_May2009.pdf (accessed 19 December 2015).

Rajaram, P. K. 2015. 'Beyond crisis: Rethinking the population movements at Europe's border'. *FocaalBlog, Focaal: Journal of Global and Historical Anthropology,* 19 October 2015. http://www.focaalblog.com/2015/10/19/prem-kumar-rajaram-beyond-crisis/ (accessed 15 December 2015).

Ruhs, M. and B. Anderson, eds. 2010. *Who Needs Migrant Workers? Labour Shortages, Immigration, and Public Policy*. Oxford: Oxford University Press.

Sayad, Abdelmalek. 2004. *The Suffering of the Immigrant*. Cambridge, UK: Polity Press.

Squire, V. 2011. 'Politicising mobility'. In *The Contested Politics of Mobility: Borderzones and Irregularity*, edited by Vicki Squire, 1–16. Routledge Advances in International Relations and Global Politics. Abingdon: Routledge.

Standing, G. 2011. *Precariat. The New Dangerous Class*. London and New York: Bloomsbury Academic.

Wills J., K. Datta, Y. Evans, J. Herbert, J. May and C. McIlwaine. 2010. *Global Cities at Work: New Migrant Divisions of Labour*. London: Pluto Press.

Williams, R. 1961. *The Long Revolution*. London: Chatto and Windus.

Woolfson, C. and J. Sommers. 2008. 'Trajectories of entropy and "the labour question". The political economy of post-communist migration in the New Europe'. *Debatte* 16 (1): 53–69.

Section I

CHANGES IN EMPLOYMENT AND MIGRATION TO THE EU

Chapter I.1

Changes in Employment

The Role of the State and Its Reconfiguration in the Liberalisation of Employment Policies

Jamie Woodcock

In order to address the role of the state and its reconfiguration in the liberalisation of employment policies it is first necessary to situate the dynamics involved both temporally and geographically. The countries that are the subject of this chapter can be broadly divided into three groups: first, the UK, a member of the European Union (EU) with its own currency that has been at the forefront of implementing neoliberal policies. The second is France, Spain and Germany, EU member states that use the single currency. While there are of course important differences between the three, the membership of a monetary union introduces a number of common dynamics. The last is Poland, a more recent EU member state that had undergone a rapid transition from being a so-called member of the communist bloc to the free market with its own currency. The chapter begins by discussing the emergence and development of neoliberalism, before moving on to discuss migration. The example of the UK will be examined, focusing on the role of the state and new employment policies. The next part will discuss France, Spain and Germany while considering the trends in the Eurozone more generally. Finally, the last section considers the trajectory of Poland, before drawing overall conclusions.

An important starting point for understanding neoliberalism is provided by David Harvey (2005: 2). He argues that it is 'in the first instance a theory of political economic practices that propose that human well-being can best be advanced by liberating individual entrepreneurial freedoms and skills within an institutional framework characterized by strong private property rights, free markets, and free trade'. These practices have achieved a relatively hegemonic position since the 1970s, resulting in the state implementing programmes of 'deregulation, privatization, and withdrawal of the state from many areas of social provision' (Harvey 2005: 3). It is for this reason that the chapter will predominantly focus on the public sector. Not only does the state remain a major employer, both directly and indirectly, but the three areas identified by Harvey have a significant effect on workers in this sector. Harvey (2003: 157) reformulates Marx's (1990: 915) notion of primitive accumulation, arguing for its continued importance today as 'accumulation by dispossession', of which privatisation forms 'the cutting edge'. However, it is not sufficient to merely cite the process of neoliberalism in analysis. As Peck (2013: 153) argues, this must not become 'a substitute for explanation'; rather, it 'should be an *occasion* for explanation', interrogating the specificities of the processes that are unfolding. Thus, while neoliberalism – in general terms – has become a target for even mainstream economic critics, Lapavitsas (2005: 39) argues this analysis still tends to 'avoid recognising the implications of capitalist class divisions and power'. As a consequence, 'they are incapable of providing effective support to those engaged in opposing capitalist exploitation and oppression'. This is the challenge that the subsequent sections of this chapter will attempt to take up.

The subject matter of this chapter requires a deep discussion of what neoliberalism has entailed in practice. It is a term, after all, that has risen to ascendancy in contemporary analysis in ways that can be problematic. As Peck (2013: 133) has argued, 'neoliberalism has always been an unloved, rascal concept, mainly deployed with pejorative intent, yet at the same time apparently increasingly promiscuous in application'. The important question is distinguishing what is *new* that is being referred to when the term is deployed. Does neoliberalism imply a novel mutation of capitalism or is it an intensification of the exploitative dynamics at the core of capitalism? Is neoliberalism the problem or is it a symptom of something more systemic? Therefore, when attempting to address the question of changes in employment, the relationship between labour and capital requires interrogation. This relation is complicated by the role of the state and employment policies, acting in different ways to mediate between labour and capital. Although anti-state rhetoric permeates much neoliberal discourse, this chapter will detail the ways in which the state continues to play an important role.

THE DEVELOPMENT OF NEOLIBERALISM

In order to understand employment relations today there are three important moments to consider. The first is the transformation of capitalism that took place at the end of the 1970s and start of the 1980s. In the broadest terms, this entailed a shift from the preceding 'Keynesian compromise' of Fordist capitalism. In Western Europe and North America this had entailed a period of high growth rates and low levels of unemployment. For workers – although limited predominantly to white men – this meant an expectation of continuous and secure employment and increased consumption of mass-produced commodities. In addition to this there was the proliferation of welfare provision: education, healthcare, pensions and so on. This compromise did not last. The world economy entered a 'structural crisis' in the 1970s, precipitated by the falling rate of profit and punctuated with energy crises. The result was stagflation: growth rates declined while unemployment and inflation soared. It is out of this context that 'a new social order' emerged: neoliberalism (Duménil & Lévy 2005: 9).

The first instance of experimentation with the neoliberal project can be traced to the 1973 military coup in Chile. The 'Chicago Boys' – economists trained in the USA who returned to Chile – established a radical right-wing programme of reforms following the CIA-backed overthrow of the democratically elected socialist government of Salvador Allende. The programme has been described as an instance of the 'shock doctrine' (Klein 2008), exploiting a crisis to implement widespread reforms. After this test of neoliberal reforms – which it should be remembered involved thousands of deaths, tens of thousands tortured and hundreds of thousands exiled – it took on a more 'established form' within a decade with the election of Margaret Thatcher in the UK and Ronald Reagan in the USA shortly after. The employment reforms that followed were unprecedented: the 'labour market was to be "deregulated" and labour made more "flexible"'. These terms are somewhat euphemistic, yet they are helpfully clarified by Munke's (2005: 62) further explanation that it would involve the restoration of 'management's "right to manage" . . . in all its splendour' and that the 'market would not be allowed to suffer from "political" constraints'. This articulates the class-based nature of the project: increasing the exploitation of labour in various ways. The state withdrew or reduced employment regulations, freeing capital to take the initiative. Clearly these 'paths towards neoliberalism were diverse', with different historical circumstances and political contexts, but by 'the end of the 1980s it had become remarkably hegemonic' (Munke 2005: 62).

The second moment of neoliberalism started in the 1990s. From a position of relative power there was a shift towards a more active approach. This involved 'a "roll out" of new policies rather than just a "roll back" of the state'. The preceding process that extended 'the logic of the market through liberalisation and commodification was no longer sufficient'; therefore, new aggressive policies were introduced that aimed to reach into the 'social domain with issues such as welfare reform, penal policy, urban regeneration and asylum seekers coming to the fore' (Munke 2005: 63). In the UK this could be seen with the election of Tony Blair in 1997; having previously ditched Clause 4 of the Labour Party constitution that referred to public ownership, it heralded a new wave of neoliberalisation.

The third moment is the shift in policies that has occurred since the 2008 financial crisis. The widespread adoption of austerity measures by different countries has involved both continuity and change. The same principles are still guiding state policies – lowering taxes, deregulation, privatisation and the reduction of public spending – yet they are now 'being pursued in an even more sternly necessitarian fashion than before' (Peck 2013: 134). In a sense it is remarkable that the neoliberal doctrine was able to survive the banking collapse and subsequent bailout from the state. As Peck (2013: 135) argues, at one point 'even Keynes was exhumed, if not entirely rehabilitated, as a justification for once again saving capitalism from the capitalists'. In the process 'the "system"' was 'duly saved, almost entirely at public expense and with hardly any strings attached'. The remarkable part of this is that the bailout and its implications were quickly forgotten, and 'it was not long before business was being conducted almost as usual' again.

The development and acceleration of neoliberal policies covers an increasingly broad reach and so it is important to identify those that have a specific impact on employment. The theoretical basis of neoliberalism contends that 'factors of production – labour and capital – get paid what they are worth'. Therefore wage levels and income distribution will be resolved effectively by the market. When considering 'aggregate employment determination' it is asserted that 'free markets will not let valuable factors of production – including labour – go to waste'. It is argued that prices will change and all factors will become employed, treating labour like any other factor. This claim is the basis of Chicago School monetarism that 'economies automatically self-adjust to full employment', so there is no need to intervene to raise employment as it will only cause inflation (Palley 2005: 20). This provides the theoretical justification for a number of employment policies. First, if the market itself results in labour being paid a wage according to its worth, there is no role for other institutions. Trade unions in particular are identified as problematic in this process. By this understanding, 'policy interventions to increase employment either cause inflation or raise unemployment, by destabilising the market process' (Palley 2005: 23).

Yet this does not mean the complete withdrawal of the state from the workings of the market economy, something that can often be misunderstood. The state remains important for 'remedying market failure', as 'a provider of essential services related to education and health', and furthermore 'plays a critical role in stabilising the business cycle through fiscal and monetary policy'. At the most basic level the 'government is integral to the working of private markets, through its provision of a legal system that supports the use of contracts' (Palley 2005: 27). So despite the anti-state rhetoric throughout neoliberal discourse, it remains an essential component – both as a driving force and support – for organising society as a free market. As Munke (2005: 62) has also argued, 'Government intervention was crucial to the making of markets, yet neoliberalism has as a central tenet the seemingly contradictory missions of "driving back" state intervention'.

MIGRATION AND THE NEOLIBERAL STATE

The contradictory role of the neoliberal state in the EU can be seen clearly in the development of migration policies. The management of nation states and EU borders has been fundamentally restructured since the early 2000s. The rise of so-called Fortress Europe has seen a tightening of restrictions, particularly as 'wall jumps in Ceuta and Melilla' – the Spanish pene-exclaves in North Africa – 'increased and boat interceptions in the Atlantic and Mediterranean became commonplace' (Casas-Cortes et al. 2015: 2). A shipwreck in the Mediterranean in April 2015 saw almost a thousand migrants die – four months into 2015 the number of deaths was already thirty times that of 2014 (Kingsley et al. 2015). The scale of these numbers highlights how debates over migration policies have concrete and horrifying outcomes. Rather than retreating under neoliberalism, the state is undergoing a process of reconfiguration. In particular, this has involved an increase in the role of the state in deregulating capital and employment policies and the pressure to manage migration for employment.

The neoliberalisation of the state has two interrelated ramifications for migrant workers. The first is that while there remains a high demand for migrant workers within Europe, processes of social exclusion are increasing (both for migrants and other low-paid workers). These 'European Others' therefore face 'contemporary practices of social exclusion [that] are indisputably tinged by *racialization* or *ethnification*' (Schierup et al. 2006: 2). This reduces the social security safety net, forcing migrants into more precarious employment conditions. This is greatly exacerbated by the second factor that these neoliberal policies 'tend to be publicly rationalized and legitimized in ethnic, racial, and cultural terms' (Schierup et al. 2006: 2). Therefore, it can be argued that neoliberalism creates conditions of state-led racism at the top of society, which provides the space for the widespread growth of far-right populism and fascism. As will be discussed later, in Poland there has been a significant rise of the far-right, while there are also notable examples in the UK, France and elsewhere in Europe. This means that migrants can face racist policies and also risk street violence, a combination that has been incubated in the deregulation of the neoliberal state. These increases in nationalist, conservative and even outwardly fascist movements come into conflict with state policies that while they take an anti-immigrant rhetoric do not seek the same aims. However, like that of employment policies discussed before, there is a similar risk that structural forces are overemphasised in a way that obscures the agency or resistance of migrants themselves.

One approach to investigating migration has been proposed by Casas-Cortes et al. (2015: 2). They argue that two components are required to understand contemporary migration in Europe. The first is 'border externalisation'. This is the process by which the management of territory has shifted from the geographic limits of the state. As Raeymaekers (2014: 168, quoted in Casas-Cortes et al. 2015: 2) puts it, the shift from the 'stable ground of national checkpoints and territorial lines on maps to make them part of a more fluid landscape built on overlapping, and often contradictory, histories of mobility and exchange'. The second is 'AoM', referring to the way in which the 'focus has shifted from the apparatuses of control to the multiple and diverse ways in which migration responds to, operates independently from, and in turn shapes those apparatuses and their corresponding institutions and practices' (Casas-Cortes et al. 2015: 2). This important theoretical shift is analogous to that of Italian Workerism, which Tronti (1971: 89) explains as having to 'invert the problem', rather than starting with capital, to 'change direction, and start from the beginning – and the beginning is working-class struggle'.

While this chapter focuses on the macro-level structural changes taking place in Europe, particularly examining employment, the notion of the AoM – and indeed of labour – is an important consideration to keep in mind. In the context of neoliberalism and austerity programmes in which labour is facing a sustained attack there is a risk to minimise both worker and migrant agency. The role of migrant labour across the EU is significant yet varied. Casas-Cortes et al. (2015: 3) suggest that Moulier-Boutang's (1998) contribution to migration – only available in French and less well known than his work on cognitive capitalism (see Moulier-Boutang 2011) – indicates an important way forward. The AoM highlights the 'primacy of mobility in the history of capitalist development'. So rather than casting migrants as passive victims, it is important to understand the role that they play in Europe, in terms of both employment and resistance. This chapter seeks to outline the structural forces at work in a range of countries and across the EU more generally, the task of uncovering the agency of workers and migrants on a micro (Section II of this book) and collective (Section III) level is left to subsequent chapters. It is, however, important to first map out the conditions, both as a result of these struggles and as the context from which new struggles will emerge.

NEOLIBERAL EMPLOYMENT POLICIES IN THE UK

The UK – along with the USA – has led the way in introducing neoliberal policies and the restructuring of both the state and society. The period from

Thatcher to Blair has seen an iterative process of changes that, while many of them began in the UK and USA, are increasingly adopted elsewhere. It is therefore possible, particularly in the context of the EU, to discuss the UK as a testing ground where policies are developed. The watchful eye of capital and the ruling elite in different countries can take inspiration from these experiments and even the less attentive will be compelled to do so through competitive pressures. This section therefore discusses neoliberal employment policies with specific reference to the UK, before moving on to discuss France, Spain and Germany, followed by Poland.

The processes of neoliberalism have undergone a significant intensification in the wake of the 2008 financial crisis. The coalition government that took power in 2010 in the UK promptly embarked on a far-reaching programme of reforms. This involved abandoning measures to address employment that the previous Labour government had introduced, for example, removing 'an employment subsidy scheme and a scheme that "guaranteed" young workers access to work, education or training'. In addition to the abandonment of individual policies, the proposed assault on the public sector would by the government's 'own estimate . . . lead to the loss of up to half a million public sector jobs'. University tuition fees were tripled to over £9,000 per year, while the Educational Maintenance Allowance – a grant for young people from low-income families to continue education – was stopped. In addition to these attacks on further and higher education, it was also proposed to stop the Train to Gain scheme for training at work. A wide range of welfare benefits were frozen or cut, with a drive to reclassify those receiving incapacity benefits as unemployed. Access to unemployment benefits became contingent on accepting job offers, forcing people to accept low-paid work and typically non-unionised work. The combinations of these 'measures imply a substantial reduction in security and opportunities for "lifelong learning", weaker labour market and social mobility and a deepening of social divisions' (Heyes 2011: 654). The resistance to austerity in the UK had a promising beginning. There were mass mobilisations of students following national strike days called by trade unions. However, the lack of coherent alternatives and a general acceptance of the framework of the reforms significantly hampered the official trade union movement.

The neoliberal transformation of the state has involved specific changes in employment policies related to the question of unemployment. MacGregor (2005: 144) argues that there has been 'a general move away from the full employment goal towards *activation policies*'. This has entailed policies like the 'use of unemployment benefit to ensure compulsory training or redeployment, combined with support for low-paid work'. This policy shift relating to benefits requires support, something that the government attempted to achieve, as Jones (2012: 11) argues, by 'blaming its users' in the UK. There has been a constant stream of articles demonising people receiving benefits, particularly found in the 'tabloid caricature of the slobbish single mother who milks the benefit system by having lots of children', despite the lack of any empirical evidence to support this. This has gone hand in hand with whipping up anti-immigration rhetoric: the oft-repeated story that immigrants are coming to take jobs, housing, benefits and so on. A particularly telling example took place on New Year's Day 2014. Both 'politicians and journalists' claimed that the lifting of immigration restrictions would result in 'the arrival of millions of unemployed Romanians' and although they were 'desperately waiting' for this at the airport on the day, they were 'greeted by two new entrants, both of whom already had jobs' (Syal 2014). The demonization of the unemployed and immigrants is an attempt to shift responsibility for the crisis and justify various policy interventions. This is a dual attack on already marginalised groups like migrants in society: not only are they being blamed for causing the crisis, they are also being forced to pay the cost.

The attacks on marginalised groups take place in a context with two important defining characteristics. The first is a trade union movement that does not seem to have recovered from the defeats of Thatcherism, nor has it come to terms with the second feature: the reorganisation of post-Fordist work. As Beck has previously argued, there has been

> a transition from a uniform system of lifelong full-time work organized in a single industrial location, with the radical alternative of unemployment, to a *risk-fraught system of flexible, pluralized, decentralized underemployment, which, however, will possibly no longer raise the problem of unemployment in the sense of being completely without a paid job.* In this system, unemployment in the guise of various forms of underemployment is 'integrated' into the employment system, but in exchange for a *generalization of employment insecurity* that was not known in the 'old' uniform of full-employment system of industrial society. (Beck 1992: 144)

Too often casualised work is treated as a problem at the margins of the labour market and challenges from trade unions are limited to protecting the core membership from its reach. The levels of trade union membership are continuing to fall in the UK and the failure to successfully oppose neoliberal employment reforms has had directly tangible effects. In 2012/2013, 52 per cent of households were receiving more in benefits than they paid in taxes (Memon & Knox 2015). However, this does not reflect the prevalence of the tabloid caricature, rather that the reforms have created 'a layer of low-paid workers on the margins of the labour market, dependent for their living standard on state benefits' (MacGregor 2005: 144). The state is therefore subsidising the low wages paid by private companies. This has a disproportionate effect on migrants who face stigmatisation, economic compulsion and furthermore 'are often excluded from welfare entitlements' (MacGregor 2005: 147), thus lacking the same access subsidisation for low wages.

There has been a significant increase in casual work across the EU since 2008. In 2012 the share of temporary hiring had grown to 71 per cent for elementary occupations and was becoming widespread in skilled occupations too. The prevalence of temporary work has also involved the rise of new forms such as 'on-call work'. In the UK there is increasing use of 'zero-hour contracts'. This is a particularly precarious arrangement, in which the worker must be constantly available, yet receives no guarantee of any work (Eurofound 2015: 46). Therefore, capital need only purchase labour time when required, eliminating any non-profitable moments. There is legal ambiguity surrounding zero-hour contracts in the UK, as well as a difficulty in ascertaining the exact total number of workers they affect. For example, the UK Labour Force Survey estimated that there were 250,000 people on these contracts in 2012, the Office for National Statistics estimated that during a two-week period there were 1.4 million active and 1.3 million inactive contracts, whereas the trade union Unite puts the figure at 22 per cent in the private sector (quoted in Eurofound 2015: 59–60). In the fast food industry and other service occupations it has become the norm, and there is also now widespread use of the contracts in care work in the NHS and local authorities (Eurofound 2015: 60–62). This relation between labour and capital is proving successful and becoming generalised further. For example, a UK company called Slivers of Time 'provides technology that enables its clients to build and manage talent pools to meet short-term fluctuations in staffing' and in somewhat dystopian terms 'it operates in real time' (Eurofound 2015: 47).

Privatisation has a number of implications for employment. However, before considering these it is necessary to distinguish between the two main forms that privatisation has taken. The first is the more straightforward form: 'the sale of publicly owned assets', the transferral of ownership into the private sector. This has a clear potential to negatively impact on the terms and conditions of workers. The new owners buy these assets to make money, often this can involve driving down the pay and conditions of workers, restructuring the organisation and the introduction of the profit motive. The second type of privatisation is the 'more creeping form under the heading of the private finance initiatives [PFIs]' a 'part of public private partnerships' (Arestis & Sawyer 2005: 199). This involves the 'shift away from the "in-house" provision of goods and services (and particularly the latter) by the public sector and towards the contracting out of services to be provided by the private sector' (Arestis & Sawyer 2005: 200). For example, in the UK this process can be seen clearly in healthcare and education. Private companies were contracted to build hospitals and schools which they are then paid to operate, often taking over the contracts of workers who were previously public sector employees. There have been over 700 PFI contracts for new schools, hospitals and other public facilities with a total capital value of £54.7bn, yet it is estimated that by the end of the contracts these will have cost the UK government £301bn overall (Campbell et al. 2012). This represents a vast transferral of public money into private hands. The change in employer – or indeed shift to multiple employers – can result in 'weakening the power of trade unions in public-sector wage bargaining' (Arestis & Sawyer 2005: 200). Although the state as an employer is increasingly hostile to trade unions, for now at least, it does not prevent workplace organisation in the more aggressive ways found in the private sector. Particularly in healthcare, outsourced services are increasingly being delivered with the use of zero-hour contracts, partly because the 'local authority pays only for the working time actually spent with clients' (Eurofound 2015: 65), and partly as a drive to make these services profitable.

THE EUROPEAN UNION AND NEOLIBERAL EMPLOYMENT POLICIES

The EU and its constituent member states include a range of different experiences, yet the common trajectory has been towards the adoption of neoliberal policies. The European institutions have played an important role in the convergence of these policies, but distinct national contexts complicate the overall picture. In a similar way to the processes described before, there has been a concerted move towards neoliberalism in most European countries since the late 1970s. It is important to note that these policies have not only been pushed by the centre or right-wing parties in Europe. As Milios explains:

> Centre-left governments persist in not prioritising the reduction of unemployment or the promotion of growth by public spending. Instead, they prioritise price stabilisation, the reduction of public deficits, the promotion of 'labour-market flexibility' and the privatisation of public enterprises . . . the persistence of neoliberal policies and ideas has been achieved through policies officially aiming at the promotion of economic, monetary, and political unity among EU states. (Milios 2005: 209)

This widespread acceptance of neoliberal policies was famously summed up in the acronym TINA – There Is No Alternative – and while it is possible to theorise various alternatives, European politics has so far been relatively bereft of these in practice. The recent emergence of Podemos in Spain could represent a break from the status quo, but is still far from a European-wide rejection of austerity and the neoliberal policies of the last thirty or so years.

Across Europe there have been pressures to achieve low inflation and reduce public deficits, spurred by the Maastricht Treaty and later the adoption of the single currency. Thus in Europe it is not only the national state that has developed employment policies; these are also influenced by the European Commission and common monetary policy rules (Heyes 2011: 645). The most recent changes to employment in Europe have followed in the wake of the economic crisis in 2008. The overall rate of unemployment in Europe jumped from 7.1 per cent in 2007 to just below 9 per cent in 2009. For younger people aged under 25 in the EU-27, the rate of unemployment increased from 15.3 per cent in 2007 to almost 20 per cent in 2009 (European Commission 2010: 165, quoted in Heyes 2011: 642). The response from the European Commission (2008) was to introduce a Europe Economic Recovery Plan, which 'emphasized that in addressing the labour market dimensions of the crisis, EU member states should develop measures within a policy framework informed by the principles of "flexicurity"' (Heyes 2011: 643). The European Commission (2007: 10, quoted in Heyes 2011: 643) defined the principles as an 'integrated strategy to enhance, at the same time, flexibility and security in the labour market'. Heyes (2011: 643) concludes that despite the discussion of 'flexicurity', 'the dominant trend has instead been towards less security'.

The success in changing to the terms and conditions of established core workers makes it much easier to force changes on to workers at the margins. The increasingly precarious position of workers in the EU labour market can be seen in the rise of temporary and agency work. Policy changes have resulted in fewer restrictions on these kinds of contractual arrangements and in this less-regulated environment they have expanded. In 2006, before the economic crisis, almost 15 per cent of workers in the EU-15 had a temporary employment contract, increasing from 12 per cent in 1996. However, in France, before the economic crisis, half of the total employment growth from 1991 to 2001 was as a result of new temporary jobs (Heyes 2011: 647). Seven years after the crisis, 'intermittent work' has become a much more common phenomenon across Europe (Eurofound 2015: 46). For example, in France intermittent work contracts known as '*intermittents du spectacle*' and categorised as 'custom short-term contracts (*CDD d'usage*)' (Eurofound 2015: 54) have been formally introduced. While workers retain various employment rights, it nevertheless represents the normalisation of short-term employment contracts. Similarly, in Spain and Germany there has been an increase of ICT-based mobile work (Eurofound 2015: 75). If these become profitable arrangements for capital, there is likely to be the imperative to generalise these out into further sectors.

In France, the relatively high proportion of public sector workers means that the impact of a shrinking or restructured public sector is particularly significant. Before the economic crisis, the state attempted to implement the CPE (or First Contract of Employment) law for under-26s. This aimed to remove employment protections for younger workers, for example, allowing them to be dismissed without reason. There was a mass mobilisation against the law by students and trade unionists, which included protests, strikes and occupations. This forced the French government to withdraw the CPE law. In 2010 there was 'the attack on retirement', an attempt to raise the retirement age and the full state pension age by two years. As Simon (2011) argued, it was 'an expression on the French level of the world-wide tendency to ward off the global fall in the rate of profit by both increasing productivity and cutting labor costs'. Pensions have been a focus of reform across various countries, and Simon (2011) notes how 'the crisis has accentuated these tendencies'. For workers they represent deferred wages, yet for capital they present two problems: they are becoming more expensive because workers are living longer (something which should in fact be a cause for celebration) and they are a commitment that poses a major obstacle to privatisation. The costs of pensions make public services less profitable, therefore driving down the cost can be a prelude to further privatisation, seen, for example, with the recent reforms of the pension scheme for academics in the UK. The response from the French trade union federations was militant but complicated. Official union membership is less than 10 per cent with 'seven "recognized" national federations'. Part of the problem, Simon (2011) argues, is that the 'unions had no intent of promoting large-scale actions, knowing well the reform will be adapted in the end' and that 'the government will only let them demand adjustment in details'. So despite mass protests the changes were made and further reforms implemented in 2013.

Spain is an example of three important phenomena in Europe. The first is being a representative of the offensive acronym the PIGS – Portugal, Ireland, Greece and Spain, countries that have stagnated under post-crisis austerity. The crushing of the public sector has combined with staggering unemployment levels; for example, in Spain unemployment is at almost 26 per cent. This includes 5.5 million people not receiving unemployment insurance while youth unemployment was estimated to be 57.5 per cent in 2014 (Seguín 2014). The second is the increasing tension of separatist movements across Europe. The movement for Catalonian independence has been growing, with Spain refusing the possibility of a binding referendum. The possibilities of Scottish independence, the breakup of Belgium, the rise of other separatist movements and the withdrawal of the UK (with or without Scotland) from the EU has the potential to redraw national boundaries across the continent. The third – and potentially most optimistic – is the rise of left in Spain. The

15-M – or indignados – Movement started in the spring of 2011 with mass demonstrations and occupations of public spaces across the country. This movement has been channelled, in part, by Podemos and led to recent electoral successes, mounting a popular challenge to austerity.

The experience of Germany is different to both France and Spain. Austerity has had an impact in Germany, particularly with the implementation of work and welfare reforms. These began with the Hartz Commission in 2002. Peter Hartz, who was the personnel director for Volkswagen, was appointed to propose reforms which were duly implemented. Like in the UK, the involvement of the private sector in planning and carrying out neoliberal reforms predated contemporary austerity programmes (Heyes 2011: 648). The important difference with Germany lies in its structural position within the EU. The Eurozone has created significant benefits for the German economy: in particular it has provided markets for German exports within a single currency zone. This, along with internal reforms, has allowed Germany to restore profitability and mitigate the effects of the economic crisis. However, with the collapse of the Greek economy the contradictions of the Eurozone have come to the forefront. The ideological attempt to blame the peripheral EU countries masks the benefits that Germany has reaped from the arrangement. The direction and the continuation of the EU is therefore dependent on the outcome of contestation at various levels in different locations.

THE TRANSFORMATION OF POLAND

The historical context in Poland is markedly different to the UK, France, Spain or Germany. The early 1980s saw the emergence of Solidarity, which while it 'began as a "free trade union", went on to demand elements of worker control of industry, developed the demand for a "Self-Governing Republic"'. Although there was a revolutionary crisis in Poland at the time, it was not workers' demands that would be successful in defeating totalitarianism, as martial law was imposed in 1981 (Barker 2002: 213). It would take until the late 1980s for the Communist Party to lose its grip on state power in Poland. This turbulent period saw the fall of the Berlin Wall and the collapse of the Soviet Union. Following these events there has been a concerted attempt to incorporate states in Eastern Europe into the EU.

The demands from the early 1980s have not been the driving force behind the changes in Poland. As Shields (2003: 225) argues, 'Solidarity failed in its historic mission to create a self-governing republic in 1989'. Although there have been different experiences across Eastern Europe, in general it has not been the 'embedded neoliberalism' of the existing EU member states, but there has been the 'export of a much more "market-radical" variant of neoliberalism' (Bohle 2006: 58). Bohle (2006: 61–64) has argued that the expansion of the EU can be best understood through a neo-Gramscian analysis that focuses on the role of hegemony at various levels. The first requires an understanding of the 'sphere of production' and the shifting social relations that have accompanied the 'dissolution of Fordism'. A crucial component of the project of European integration has been the attempt to restore global competitiveness. Gramsci's (1971: 106) notion of 'passive revolution' is therefore used by Bohle (2006: 75) to denote 'a situation of radical change pushed by elites whose ideas do not stem from the domestic context, but rather reflect international developments'. Thus, the integration of Poland into the EU has been spurred by the needs of capital in Europe and implemented to the benefit of the local elite.

The crisis of Fordism was addressed with widespread restructuring in Western Europe, serving to restore profitability – if only temporarily. However, in Eastern Europe the economy 'stagnated over the 1980s' and then 'experienced [the] total breakdown of its system'. The fall of the Soviet Union presented the opportunity to put into practice the 'shock doctrine' that Klein (2008) discusses, yet Shields (2003: 238) argues that, 'in a sense, "Shock Therapy" should have been impossible; change in socio-economic systems surely requires longer-term internalisation of new forms of behaviour'. Despite this, there was 'radical systemic change in Poland' which 'created the foundations of a new system in a matter of years'. This led to an 18 per cent unemployment rate by the start of 2002, meaning 3.2 million people without work, of which 80 per cent were not receiving benefits from the state. The trade union movement was significantly weakened in the 1990s, with falling levels of unionisation and a failure to organise in new or emerging industries. In a similar way to trade unions in the UK, France, Spain and Germany there has been a failure to 'define a counter-position to the dominant project of Europeanisation and neoliberal restructuring'. This is complicated by the 'legacy of both communism and anti-communism' and has resulted in 'nationalist and xenophobic forces' offering populist resistance (Bohle 2006: 77).

The processes taking place in Poland intensified with accession to the EU in 2004. The enlargement brought Poland – along with Cyprus, the Czech Republic, Estonia, Hungary, Latvia, Lithuania, Malta, Slovakia and Slovenia – into the EU, moving the borders eastward to include over 70 million more people. In the run-up to accession and since then there have been significant changes in employment in Poland. Large transnational temporary staffing agencies began to expand into central and Eastern Europe (CEE), supported by changes in employment legislation at both the national and EU level (Coe et al. 2008). These agencies flourished with the legalisation of temporary employment in 2004, operating in a context of high unemployment and a significantly smaller public service sector than any of the previous countries' examples. There were further reforms in 2009 and 2010 to increase labour market flexibility, including changes to the structure of unemployment benefits and other initiatives funded by the EU. Over the past ten years the number of workers on 'a fixed-term contract, mandate contract and contracts for specific work has increased from 19.4 per cent to 26.9 per cent', the highest level of any country in the EU (Kałużyńska et al. 2014: 192). Since 2005 onward Poland has had right-wing conservative and liberal-conservative coalition governments. They have continued the integration with the EU with plans to join the single currency eventually. The effects of neoliberal restructuring have become increasingly clear: high unemployment, rising inequality, the transfer of wealth to a small minority and sweeping changes in the organisation of work. The rise of the far-right 'reflects the inability of the dominant forces to offer solutions to' these 'burning social problems' (Bohle 2006: 78). The recent history of Poland has involved successive defeats of labour and the rise of a new elite. At this point in time 'societal polarisation and continuous restructuring requirements . . . threaten to widen the gap within' society further (Bohle 2006: 78).

CONCLUSION

This chapter has sought to discuss the changes in employment in the UK, France, Spain, Germany and Poland. This has involved an understanding of the changing role of the state and the implementation of new employment policies. Across Europe there has been a concerted drive toward 'flexicurity'; however, the evidence indicates increasing precarity with no attendant benefit for workers. The overarching context within which the analysis takes place is one of neoliberal dominance. There is a vagueness with which the term neoliberalism is often deployed; in this case, it is taken to mean a class-based project to restore the profitability of capitalism. It has important ideological components and specific policy outcomes aimed at increasing profitability. In the broadest terms these have involved the breakdown of Fordism, while more specifically this has meant an end to secure and long-term employment. The two most important examples discussed in this chapter have been the privatisation and reorganisation of the public sector and the prevalence of new casual forms of work. The first directly exposes a relatively large group of workers to the pressures of capital accumulation – that might not have been the same before – while the second represents a significant shift in the balance of power from labour to capital.

There are specific implications for migrant workers in this context. It has become popular for governments and the media to blame the economic crisis on immigration. For example, in the UK all of the mainstream parties have taken the position that there is some kind of problem with immigration. Migrants therefore face multiple barriers when seeking to work in Europe: the official racism of the state that discriminates with visas and other entry restrictions, the exclusion from benefits and other protections from the state, the exploitation of informal work arrangements, and the racism in society in general (often whipped up by the state and the media). The failure of the left and the trade union movement in general in this period has allowed other forces to articulate anger against the economic crisis and state response. The increasingly popularity of right-wing populist and fascist parties across Europe is a trend that has serious implications for the position of migrant workers, in terms of not only exploitation in the workplace but also the threat of street violence.

Although the current situation may seem unremittingly bleak, there remain possibilities for resistance to neoliberalism, capital and the state. The failure of contemporary trade unionism to challenge or contest the dominant logic in a national or European context is severely problematic. However, this does not mean that resistance is not taking place. The labour/capital relation remains necessarily antagonistic, pushing workers into conflict with supervisors and bosses, whether they are trade union members or not, and regardless of the machinations at the top of the trade unions or within parliamentary politics. The explosions of struggle in the UK in 2010, France in 2006/2010 and Spain more recently point to a potential future direction. The historic failure of Solidarity in Poland has made open struggle harder to find but certainly has not eliminated it. The rise of Podemos, while it does not offer a solution to the crisis of neoliberalism, is a popular and tentative step towards an alternative. This should be considered with reference to the rise of the far-right; there is a pressing need to put forward an alternative Europe, not one dictated by the Troika of unelected European institutions, but by workers across the continent – whether they were born here or not.

REFERENCES

Arestis, P. and M. Sawyer. 2005. 'The neoliberal experience of the United Kingdom'. In *Neoliberalism: A Critical Reader*, edited by A. Saad-Filho and D. Johnston. London: Pluto Press.

Barker, C. 2002. 'Poland 1980-81: The self-limiting revolution'. In *Revolutionary Rehearsals,* edited by C. Barker. Chicago, IL: Haymarket Books.

Beck, U. 1992. *Risk Society: Towards a New Modernity*. London: Sage.

Bohle, D. 2006. 'Neoliberal hegemony, transnational capital and the terms of the EU's eastward expansion'. *Capital & Class* 30 (1): 57–86.

Campbell, D., J. Ball and S. Rogers. 2012. 'PFI will ultimately cost £300bn'. *The Guardian*, 5 July 2012. http://www.theguardian.com/politics/2012/jul/05/pfi-cost-300bn (accessed 2 March 2015).

Casas-Cortes, M., S. Cobarriubias and J. Pickles. 2015. 'Riding routes and itinerant borders: Autonomy of migration and border externalization'. *Antipode* Early View (Online Version of Record published before inclusion in an issue) http://onlinelibrary.wiley.com/doi/10.1111/anti.12148/pdf

Coe, M. N., J. Johns and K. Ward. 2008. 'Flexibility in action: The temporary staffing industry in the Czech Republic and Poland'. *Environment and Planning A* 40 (6): 1391–1415.

Duménil, G. and D. Lévy. 2005. 'The neoliberal (counter-)revolution'. In *Neoliberalism: A Critical Reader*, edited by A. Saad-Filho and D. Johnston. London: Pluto Press.

Eurofound. 2015. *New Forms of Employment*. Luxembourg: Publications Office of the European Union.

European Commission. 2007. *Towards Common Principles of Flexicurity: More and Better Jobs through Flexibility and Security*. Luxembourg: Office for Official Publications of the European Communities.

European Commission. 2008. *Communication from the Commission to the European Council: A European Economic Recovery Plan*. Brussels: Commission of the European Communities.

European Commission. 2010. *Employment in Europe 2010*. Luxembourg: Publications Office of the European Union.

Gramsci, A. 1971. *Selections from the Prison Notebooks*. New York: International Publishers.

Harvey, D. 2003. *The New Imperialism*. Oxford: Oxford University Press.

Harvey, D. 2005. *A Brief History of Neoliberalism*. Oxford: Oxford University Press.

Heyes, J. 2011. 'Flexicurity, employment protection and the jobs crisis'. *Work, Employment and Society* 25 (4): 642–657.

Jones, O. 2012. *Chavs: The Demonization of the Working Class*. London: Verso Books.

Kałużyńska, M., P. Karbownik, W. Burkiewicz, K. Janiak and M. Jatczak, eds. 2014. *Poland's 10 Years in the European Union*. Warszawa: Ministry of Foreign Affairs.

Kingsley, P., A. Bonomolo and S. Kirchgaessner. 2015. '700 Migrants Feared Dead in Mediterranean shipwreck'. *The Guardian*, 19 April 2015. http://www.theguardian.com/world/2015/apr/19/700-migrants-feared-dead-mediterranean-shipwreck-worst-yet (accessed 2 March 2015).

Klein, N. 2008. *The Shock Doctrine*. London: Penguin Books.

Lapavitsas, C. 2005. 'Mainstream economics in the neoliberal era'. In *Neoliberalism: A Critical Reader*, edited by A. Saad-Filho and D. Johnston. London: Pluto Press.

MacGregor, S. 2005. 'The welfare state and neoliberalism'. In *Neoliberalism: A Critical Reader*, edited by A. Saad-Filho and D. Johnston. London: Pluto Press.

Marx, K. 1990. *Capital: Critique of Political Economy, Volume 1*. London: Penguin.

Memon, A. and T. Knox. 2015. 'Welfare dependency and the size of the state'. *Centre for Policy Studies* 52.

Milios, J. 2005. 'European integration as a vehicle of neoliberal hegemony'. In *Neoliberalism: A Critical Reader*, edited by A. Saad-Filho and D. Johnston. London: Pluto Press.

Moulier-Boutang, Y. 1998. *De l'esclavage au salariat: économie historique du salariat bridé.* Paris: Presses Universitaires de France.

Moulier-Boutang, Y. 2011. *Cognitive Capitalism.* Cambridge: Polity Press.

Munke, R. 2005. 'Neoliberalism and politics, and the politics of neoliberalism'. In *Neoliberalism: A Critical Reader*, edited by A. Saad-Filho and D. Johnston. London: Pluto Press.

Palley, T. I. 2005. 'From keynesianism to neoliberalism: Shifting paradigms in economics'. In *Neoliberalism: A Critical Reader*, edited by A. Saad-Filho and D. Johnston. London: Pluto Press.

Peck, J. 2013. 'Explaining (with) neoliberalism'. *Territory, Politics, Governance* 1 (2): 132–157.

Schierup, C.-U., P. Hansen and S. Castles. 2006. *Migration, Citizenship, and the European Welfare State*. Oxford: Oxford University Press.

Seguín, B. 2014 'The syriza of Spain'. *Jacobin* 25 July 2014. https://www.jacobinmag.com/2014/07/the-syriza-of-spain/ (accessed 2 March 2015).

Shields, S. 2003. 'The "Charge of the Right Brigade": Transnational social forces and the neoliberal configuration in Poland'. *New Political Economy* 8 (2): 225–244.

Simon, H. 2011. 'How the French pension system works'. *Insurgent Notes* 3.

Syal, R. 2014. 'Romanian ambassador mocks MPs and media waiting for immigrants'. *The Guardian*, 2 January 2014. http://www.theguardian.com/uk-news/2014/jan/02/romania-ambassador-jinga-mps-migrants-airports-godot (accessed 2 March 2015).

Tronti, M. 1971. *Operai E Capitale*. Turin: Einaudi.

Chapter I.2

The Political Economy of an Ongoing Crisis

How Institutional Evolution Is Shaping Employment and Migration in Europe

Ben Egan

Migrant workers face specific and additional challenges in European labour markets. This chapter therefore explores the shifting institutional landscape in Europe in relation to both migration and employment – and specifically the intersection of the two – to identify models of employment relations, as they relate to migrant workers in Europe today. It develops the multilevelled governance analysis that has been articulated by Keune and Marginson (2013) regarding industrial relations to make the case that there are further distinct institutional challenges faced by migrants which must also be integrated into the approach if we are to gain a deeper understanding of how such workers are included or excluded from European labour markets.

Institutional frameworks are responsible for creating opportunities and challenges for actors in a whole range of social and economic activities. From nation states (Bojadžijev and Karakayali 2010) to citizenship notions to collective bargaining regimes (Thelen 2001), institutions shape options and influence the decision-making of actors. Glenn Morgan has likened institutions to the available equipment in a gymnasium: the end results are dependent on whether and how actors make use of them, and how they adopt or adapt them to suit desired outcomes (Morgan 2015). Recent contributions to institutional literature have developed sophisticated analyses of how institutions are shaped by actors in certain circumstances – including during crises – in line with actor-objectives as well as many other factors relating to path-dependency and culture (Morgan and Hauptmeier 2014; Wilkinson, Wood and Deeg 2014).

In this contribution, I develop the idea of 'migrational employment relations', which is strongly influenced by a contradiction at the heart of the debate in Europe: namely, economic systems that seek migrant *labour* to function alongside political systems that reject denizen migrants themselves. I propose that this equates to a paradox at the heart of the European debates on labour mobility as *economic and political imperatives point in opposing directions*. This creates the institutional space for exploitation. The case made here is that the countries of Europe are members of a political and economic union which is distinct and unique: the most integrated trading bloc in the world today, while also changing rapidly under the pressures imposed by the multifaceted crises that are spread very unevenly across its constituent nations. The economic and social settlements therefore remain contested.

From both an employment relations and social dialogue perspective, as well as those relating to migration, the institutional terrain of each nation state has a distinct heritage. In addition, the areas of both public discourse and policy have been heavily influenced by the establishment and expansion of the single market. Developing a detailed conceptual understanding of how the various institutional dynamics that are presently in place in these countries interact, change and serve to support or undermine the role of actors is essential for framing empirical findings found elsewhere in this book and beyond. It is not only viable answers that are ruled in or out by given institutional arrangements but in many cases what questions can even be posed. These challenges are addressed by identifying the changes in the political-economic institutions that traditionally govern employment relations and integrating them with an analysis that also includes the institutions implied in the regulation of migration. This highlights the discrepancy between migrants' roles as labour, on the one hand, and denizens, on the other. Two questions supporting the initial proposition regarding the relationship are therefore essential to developing this understanding. What is the role that institutions play in influencing the outcomes in the spheres of employment relations and migration patterns? And furthermore, how are the frameworks that govern both these important areas of social affairs changing?

The chapter proceeds by first proposing a model of 'migrational employment relations' which seeks to integrate an analysis of migration into one of neoliberalising employment relations. This introductory section also details *why* it is important to integrate migration into an analysis of the institutions governing employment relations. It will first sketch the debates around distinct models of capitalism within the single market. I will then propose a way of understanding these developments in the specific European setting by setting them in a multilevelled governance analysis addressing the political, economic and social pressures, as well as the power dynamics that impact on these transitions: global; European institutional; national and local bargaining. Each of these is clearly subject to institutional fluidity and the power relations that actors can impose in each of the national contexts. To aid this, the chapter develops a model of how the institutions at the various levels have the potential to affect outcomes with regard to employment relations at the point at which it intersects with the weakening of employment stability associated with neoliberal reforms. The different levels emphasise a second, vertical, dimension in the analysis that fuels the chaotic outcome of economic rights to work without commensurate rights to social protection. The chapter then concludes by highlighting the 'double isolation' that the separation of the economic and the social imposes on migrants.

MIGRATIONAL EMPLOYMENT RELATIONS IN THE MODERN EUROPEAN ECONOMY

It is enlightening to integrate migration into an analysis of the institutions governing employment relations for many reasons, not least because of the increasing prevalence of both migration and economics in the public discourse. Trans-European politics have now been dominated by the coordination of responses to economic and migrant crises for several years. But more significantly, both speak to the issue of vulnerability and of people (actors) having their ability to exercise autonomy over their lives diminished by developments in the political-economic settlement (institutions). This is not necessarily new. Throughout history the mobility of labour has often been contested – indeed, according to the 'AoM' thesis it is mobility itself that enabled capitalism to emerge as the first 'workers' fled feudal bondage (Bojadžijev and Karakayali 2010). It is the processes of globalisation and, more than any other one single factor, the relentless dismantling of borders in relation to the mobility of capital that makes the contradiction at the heart of the migration debates more pronounced. Borders for capital movement come down just as those for human beings are fortified. Lest we forget that Fortress Europe is celebrated as the world's largest market.

In the case of migration, the institutional analysis that has underpinned much employment relations literature in Europe (or more commonly nations *within* Europe) is underdeveloped, particularly when understood at the European level and as a multilevelled interaction. The argument here is that the interactions between such institutions – both horizontally and vertically – lead to differentiated outcomes for the actors involved, most notably for migrant workers. Horizontally in the sense that different nation states are evolved from distinct social and economic models and therefore have arrived at comparably different institutional settlements with regard to the regulation of migration and economic relations; and vertically in the sense that the pressures of globalisation and EU economic and political integration make it increasingly necessary to be aware of the many levels that influence these outcomes. For example, global capital flows and geopolitical instability both impact on models of capitalism and migration management systems. These are manifest in local communities and workplaces, via the national level which remains sovereign. It is therefore critical to develop some understanding of how both the horizontal and the vertical interact. This is explored in more detail later in the chapter where the institutions implied are integrated into a multi-levelled model.

The political and economic crises in Greece of recent years demonstrate starkly the way that economic and migratory aspects of policy interact. The discourse around providing 'humanitarian assistance' to Greece had she refused austerity and therefore fallen out of the single currency during the 2015 refinancing negotiations and the hundreds of thousands of young educated citizens that have left that country, as in Spain, Portugal and other 'peripheral' member states, demonstrates one way that the two are linked as economic opportunity drives migration. Decline in living standards and an exodus of talented young workers to the more prosperous parts of the EU go hand in hand as opportunity seeking has always driven migration. The free movement of labour around the EU and the insistence of its key decision-makers that austerity programmes be adopted have consequently become decisive factors in the decline of the standing of the EU in the national politics of many member states, benefitting anti-European parties from both left and right.[1]

In addition, the historic development 'the market' is a stronger force for change than in the earlier decades of the European project. Market considerations are now more influential in guiding policy. The admittance of migrants

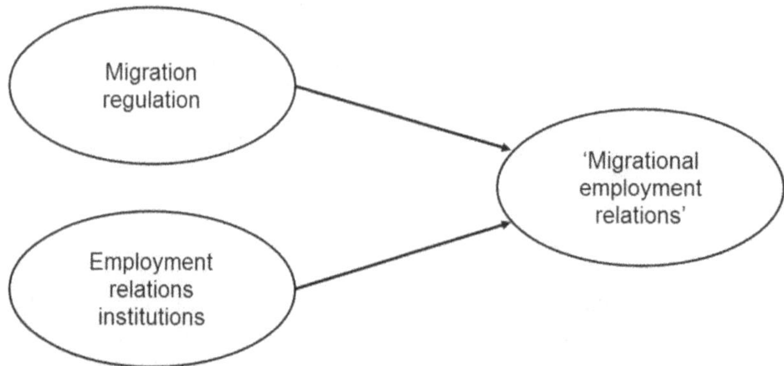

Figure I.2.1 The Integration of Employment Relations Institutions and a Migration Analysis to Develop 'Migrational Employment Relations'. This is author's own construction/graphic.

to various European countries has been driven by labour market demands, such as the guest worker schemes in Germany from the 1960s through to that country's relatively open policy in relation to the ongoing European refugee crisis. This is well established in employment relations, with Commons's (1909) proposition over a century ago that unions were more successful when they were designed to reflect the markets in which their members were employed. Many unions continue to pursue this approach, as explored in Chapter III.1 of this book.

INSTITUTIONS MATTER IN EMPLOYMENT RELATIONS

Before developing a framework incorporating employment and migration, it is important to first be clear where we currently are in relation to the institutions that govern economies and those that impact on employment relations more specifically. Institutions are the arrangements by which employment relations are governed. These include legal frameworks in the form of statutory responsibilities and any collective agreements. Institutions are the arrangements with which actors must engage to achieve their objectives. In the case of institutional economics there has been a great deal of progress in developing an understanding of these institutions and how they are changing in the last decade or so. This gives great insight into the questions at hand in this chapter to furnish the proposition that there is a fundamental contradiction in the economic and social approaches to migration in Europe.

The search for theoretical explanations of institutional variation across different countries has a rich history which has nevertheless tended toward a concentration around two dominant typologies: the *Varieties of Capitalism (VoC)* (Hall and Soskice 2001) and *National Business Systems* (Whitley 1999). Both seek to offer insight into the 'comparative institutional advantage' that given institutional arrangements afford actors operating in distinct institutional environments. At the heart of these analyses of institutional variation is the query that has arguably more pertinence for countries inside the EU than anywhere else in the world. Namely, why is it that there continues to be significant variation despite the powerful pressures of globalisation and – in the case of EU member states – ever closer economic and political union? The role of institutions in the coordination and regulation of employment relations and business development has also received greater attention in recent years. There have been many insightful contributions from different theoretical perspectives on making sense of the present state of advanced capitalist economies (Dimaggio and Powell 1983; Powell and Dimaggio 1991; Whitley 1999; Culpepper 2001; Morgan and Kristensen 2006; Morgan 2007; Hall and Gingerich 2009).

Central to these considerations are the institutional arrangements and the logics which they both inspire and reinforce. In other words, the ways in which institutions and organisations (or, more accurately, the actors within them) interact with one another – understood as institutional 'coherence' when referring to structures and 'complementarity' when we consider the actual outcomes they precipitate (Höpner 2005). Opportunities and challenges for policy and practice transfer in the management-focused analysis of multinationals (including human resource management) are deeply affected by the various institutional environments in which actors operate – or indeed *seek* to operate, as actors change institutions too. This is especially pressing in the case of migration because the contradiction between coherence and complementarity is more vivid. As I propose, these arrangements are specifically designed to be the former but not the latter – that is to say, migration arrangements are designed to be coherent in restricting migration but lack complementarity in never achieving it because this places pressure on migrants as economic agents. Firms that employ migrant labour therefore have an interest in maintaining this system and so institutional analysis must account for the role of firms in developing given institutional frameworks.

Perhaps the most widely cited, the *VoC* framework situates companies as the most important actors in capitalist economies – contrary to many citations of the model in which the institutions themselves seem to acquire various degrees of sentient agency. It is actor centred (i.e. a 'relational view of the firm'), as it is the way in which each company interacts with other actors – both internally and externally – that is most telling. The unique role of migrants in a system that is explicitly relational is initially unexplored. Employment, migration and inclusion/exclusion factors are all highly dependent on institutional frameworks and so understanding them allows us to shine a light on outcomes for actors – most notably in this case for migrant workers and their advocates.

The original model provides for two ideal types: *liberal market economies*, on the one hand, and *coordinated market economies*, on the other, with a gradual spectrum in between on which countries can be situated in accordance to how companies operating in the country are able to manage relationships and overcome coordination challenges in five key spheres:

1. *Industrial relations,* in which bargaining coordination is influenced by factors such as labour market participation and productivity rates as well as trade union structures.
2. *Vocational training and education,* in which broader societal expectations on the part of both workers and employers in relation to skills and education investment and maintenance come to the fore.

3. *Corporate governance,* whereby the need for a company to secure lines of finance is influenced by the expectations of investors and regulators in a given jurisdiction.
4. *Inter-firm relations,* including standard setting, technology transfer, and collaborative research and development with supplier- and customer-firms in order to maintain competitiveness and sustain the industry.
5. *Employee coordination,* which relates to the highly specific knowledge, skills and information that employees will possess which will be differentiated across types in terms of subsidiaries, organisational roles and demographic profile. This final sphere relates to the coordination of employees as people, rather than the first sphere, which is more closely associated with institutional and bureaucratic administration.

The most prominent alternative to the *VoC* analysis in contemporary political economy is that of *national business systems (NBS)* which has been developed by Whitley (particularly 1999) and others over the last couple of decades. *NBS* was arguably more global in its outlook from the start with more categories within the typology that explicitly accounted for the institutional specificities of, for example, the advanced capitalist economies of East Asia. *NBS* is also more sociological in origin and perspective than *VoC*, as opposed to the political scientists and economists more prevalent in *VoC*. From even the earlier works the focus in *NBS* literature has been less on the firm itself and more on the way in which cultural and institutional legacies intervene in actor relations, rather than assuming that market competition 'will, in some mysterious way, select the most efficient pattern of economic organisation' (Whitley 1992: 6).

The distinction between *VoC* and *NBS* can seem somewhat artificial, with notable scholars publishing in volumes associated with either school. Furthermore, there has recently been an increasing acknowledgement among scholars in the industrial relations/employment relations/human resource management fields that nationally based typologies are of diminishing value in globalising employment relations (Lakhani et al. 2013). The most important aspects of the developing sophistication of institutional analyses in relation to research presented in this book are twofold. First, the focus being based broadly around employment issues and migration among several EU member states makes it necessary to be conscious of the role of the EU institutions in affecting the national differences that may be predicted by *VoC*, *NBS* and indeed any other analyses of national political economy. Secondly, and related to the Europeanisation question, is to be aware that any categorisations that can be made in relation to each of the countries included remain highly contested. They are not static but ever-shifting, particularly so in such periods of crisis.

DEVELOPING A MULTILEVELLED UNDERSTANDING OF MIGRATIONAL EMPLOYMENT RELATIONS

What then are the different levels that interact in migrational employment relations and how are they changing? The pressures of globalisation have seen the role of the nation state in recent years shift from regulation of the economy and markets towards their facilitation, particularly in its relationship with transnational capital. This is even more pronounced in sensitive sectors that are vulnerable to competition from lower wage economies, including manufacturing industries and those involved in some logistical business support; it has been described a shift from the welfare state to the competition state (Cerny, Menz and Soederberg 2005). The increasing power of multinational companies and supranational trade bodies, facilitated by the very sovereignties that they usurp (national governments), continues to preface profound shifts in power dynamics that bleed into institutional environments in which actors operate. This has coincided with a fundamental shift away from the national level as the key (sovereign) level at which decisions are taken as capital goes global yet bargaining units are fragmenting ever more to the local. When the migratory aspect is also integrated, we find an institutional settlement that is increasingly chaotic with employment and migration torn in different directions at different times and at different levels.

This new landscape of the 'multilevelled governance' of industrial relations has recently been developed by Keune and Marginson (2013), who highlight that it represents both an outcome of European integration of employment regimes as well as an intervening variable (476). The multilevelled analysis of industrial relations builds on similar accounts of the broader political changes in European countries that have been brought about by the 'ever closer union' of the EU project (Bache and Flinders 2004), in particular developments in policy and implementation. The levels that a multilevel governance approach implies have both vertical and horizontal dimensions: vertical due to the increasing interdependencies between governance mechanisms at the different levels, from the global to the local; and horizontal in the sense of a concurrent growing interdependence between actors across the public and private spheres. For this reason, the present contribution is enriched further by integrating the migration aspect into industrial relations as this draws into focus a whole new range of institutions that support and contradict one another – hence the thesis that migration and employment regimes often pull in opposite directions; that they lack institutional complementarity.

The neoliberal turn from the European Commission, which has accelerated in the last dozen years or so, has put the needs of business at the centre of these (multi-)levels of governance, which presents clear problems for organised labour, including migrant labour as collective bargaining has been curtailed. Furthermore, the subsequent role of large multinational firms within this paradigm has been shown to be explicitly political. Indeed, the role that they played in establishing the current manifestation of the EU with the completion of the single market in 1992, for example, is often overlooked. This, according to Streeck (1993: 96), was

> concluded essentially among national political elites and large European countries with organized labor excluded. At its core it involved business support for a collective effort by West European nation states to recover some measure of external sovereignty in a turbulent, deinstitutionalized world economy by pooling their individual sovereignties. In exchange, business received a commitment of the emerging European polity to a largely deregulated political economy ('a single market without a single state'). (quoted in Rubery and Grimshaw 2003: 198)

The influence of the various 'levels' that together make up employment relations or the broader economic environment – and therefore affect the increasing precaritisation of work – is uniquely configured in recent European developments. The establishment of the single currency, alluded to by Streeck, has inevitably led to a more assertive form of decision-making at 'the European level' – a term which is itself increasingly problematic, due to the increasing distinction between being a member of the EU-28(27) and the nineteen-member Eurozone. The levels that affect employment outcomes within and across European countries are in many cases becoming, on the one hand, ever more transnational, yet, on the other, more localised. The pressure towards the levels below the national can be seen by the breakdown of nationally oriented collective bargaining mechanisms to political threats to the nation state itself – as is seen in the rise of secessionist movements in Belgium, Spain, the UK and elsewhere. This is indicative of a system in which there is no *shared vision* across the levels of how the governance arrangements should work (Keune and Marginson 2013: 480).

Here I propose a new way of looking at the various levels from the global to the local, as they impact on employment *and* migration outcomes in EU countries (see Table I.2.1). This includes a proposed primary mechanism for governance and opportunities for employees to have an input, most commonly via their trade unions, as well as for regulating migration. The interaction between business and trade regulations at each level and the opportunities for employment relations dialogue are put side by side because the institutional settlements that facilitate the latter are most commonly negotiated by the former. That is to say that transnational agreements are facilitated by a desire to improve (i.e. liberalise) trade dynamics as a priority, though this in some cases does provide opportunities for labour voice.

Table I.2.1 Proposed New Levels of Employment Relations and Migration in Europe

Level	*Traditional Employment Relations*		*Migration Aspect*
	Primary Mechanism	*Primary Dialogue Opportunity*	*Primary Regulation of Migration*
Global	Transnational trade agreements	International framework agreements	None
Economic bloc	ECB and Commission regulation	European Works Councils	Weak – e.g. failed integration of asylum policy, patchy enforcement of posted workers and Blue Card
National	Government policy and budgets	Social dialogue	Very dominant level: exclusive sovereignty for policy on non-EU and interpretation on EU rights
Subnational	Regional strategy	Collective bargaining arrangements	None
Local	Local government and plant decisions	Workplace/local organising	Workplace documentation checks

Global

From the perspective of trade, truly global agreements remain surprisingly elusive. Since the founding (or renaming) of the World Trade Organisation (WTO) in 1995, several rounds of negotiations have under-delivered – according to their own terms – on stated ambitions of removing tariffs and other restrictions on global trade. The last twenty years, for example, have seen ten regional trade deals a year but only one global WTO one in the shape of the 2013 Bali package (Economist 2015). The regulation of employment has, however, seen much greater progress (in theory) with International Labour Organisation (ILO) core standards operating for the best part of a century, though enforcement is notoriously patchy, and certainly not the preferred recourse in the relatively advanced democracies of Europe. More significant has been the emergence of International Framework Agreements, of which there are now well over a hundred (Global Unions 2015). These agreements (sometimes referred to as Global Framework Agreements) are between global union federations (GUFs) and multinational companies and act as quasi-union-recognition agreements for the GUFs' affiliates. There are no significant global institutional frameworks for regulating migration, as demonstrated by the current refugee crisis emanating from the Middle East and North Africa.

Those that do exist, such as the relevant articles of the Universal Declaration on Human Rights, are notoriously difficult to enforce in the absence of widespread (national) political will to do so.

Economic Bloc

With the proliferation of regional trade deals, it is the level of the 'economic bloc' that has attained prominence in recent years in relation to economic policy. In Europe, which is undoubtedly the most advanced and sophisticated example of such a supranational bloc, the scope and sheer volume of intervention has escalated in response to the Eurozone crises. It is also at this level that we begin to see widespread concerns about 'democratic deficits'. The issue of an executive branch of the EU (the Commission) that is not directly elected is a long-established problem but this has been compounded in the last decade by both the expansion of its work into new areas and countries and the increasingly codified nature of its economic agenda. The Fiscal Pact, for example, legally codifies debt and annualised fiscal deficit limits on member states of 60 per cent[2] and 3 per cent of gross domestic product, respectively (European Commission 2011). This naturally has profound implications for the role of democracy at both this level and the national level below as it restricts future elected governments of Eurozone member states from implementing an economic programme that contravenes this austerity agenda.

The European Commission's representative role to outside nations and economic blocs has also come under question recently; in particular, its role as the negotiator of trade deals, such as the Transatlantic Trade and Investment Partnership (TTIP) and Trade in Services Agreement (TISA). Between these two agreements was the explicit intentions of liberalising two-thirds of the global trade in services (Sinclair and Mertins-Kirkwood 2014: 5) as well as empowering private businesses to effectively sue democratic governments via the controversial 'investor-state dispute settlement' (ISDS) mechanism if political decisions are taken that are seen to undermine business strategies (Bieler and Erne 2015). This means that political decision-making, which has long been heavily influenced by the need to attract corporate investment, is increasingly restricted by the interests of those investors. The scale of the use of these ISDSs in the new treaties was unprecedented, though they had been used in previous multi- and bi-lateral trade agreements. Some of the more egregious examples of their deployment include tobacco companies claiming hundreds of millions of dollars in damages from the governments of Australia and Uruguay for introducing new cigarette packaging restrictions as part of public health initiatives, and their use by foreign investors during periods of economic crisis:

> When Argentina froze utility rates (energy, water, etc.) and devalued its currency in response to its 2001-2002 financial crisis, it was hit by over 40 lawsuits from big companies including CMS Energy (US), Suez and Vivendi (France), Anglian Water (UK) and Aguas de Barcelona (Spain). By the end of 2008, awards against the country had reached a total of US$1.15 billion. In May 2013, Slovak and Cypriot investors brought an investor-state lawsuit against Greece, for the debt swap which Athens had to negotiate with its creditors in 2012 to get bailout money from the EU and the International Monetary Fund (IMF). Both the UN and the IMF have warned that investment agreements can severely curb states' abilities to fight financial and economic crises. (Bizzarri 2013: 24)

Both issues suggest that austerity and a neoliberal approach to governance as the technocratic management of public policy so as to enable markets to flourish – with social cost increasingly marginalised – show no sign of abating in the short to medium term.

Likewise, employment relations have seen significant change since the 1990s. Debates around the 'Europeanisation' of industrial relations versus regime competition became necessarily more complex as the bloc expanded from fifteen to twenty-eight member states within a decade. This tension of competition between an increasingly diverse set of national institutional arrangements and attempts to provide common frameworks for a newly integrating economic bloc was partly responsible for a second major change in European employment relations: the 'propelling of European Works Councils (EWCs) onto the statute book' (Marginson 2006: 19). Since the introduction of the right to EWCs, more than one thousand have been established, including in many of the major contracting firms that are active in delivery of public services. Clearly, these bodies create an opportunity for transnational social dialogue, though, as one would expect, there have been mixed results in terms of delivering employee protection, both within companies for different groups of workers and across companies, as some function far more efficiently than others (Pulignano 2006; Contrepois and Jefferys 2010). For trade unions, the opportunities for engagement at the level of the economic bloc have been dominated by the EWCs, although it must be noted that there has been an upturn in transnational action through political campaigning work in response to the austerity agenda pursued by the Commission. These have included several 'European Day of Action' demonstrations in Brussels coordinated by the European Trade Union Confederation. Increased union coordination has also been seen in the progression of the anti-TTIP campaign (ChangingEmployment 2015) but while the level of cooperation between unions and other civil society groupings on a transnational basis on this issue represents marked progress, it is highly uneven. Many trade unions in Europe are ambivalent on TTIP and other trade deals, while some support them.

On migration, the EU level has a distinct and peculiar challenge in that the free movement of people is one of the four principle freedoms of the European single market (along with that of goods, capital and services). However, on the other hand, and indeed influenced by this free movement *within* Europe, there is the idea of Fortress Europe to keep people from beyond the borders of Europe out. This dichotomy has been clouded by the apparent inability of existing institutional frameworks to cope. Nevertheless, the idea of Fortress Europe has been vividly demonstrated as insufficient for the new reality of the recent refugee crisis as hundreds of thousands of refugees have been able to enter Europe and initially move relatively easily within its territory thereafter. The existence of the Schengen area and the long-standing lack of a coherent and enforceable asylum policy are both implicated as individual nation states take very different approaches to the crisis. It is in this context and at this level that we can most clearly see evidence of the proposition at the centre of this chapter: Europe has policies and provisions for migrants as *labour* (economic agents) which are lacking in the social sphere. The key issue in this regard remains the effectiveness of EU-wide legislation at two levels. First, in gaining agreement across all member states around policy, and then secondly in their enforcement across the different legal regimes with widely varying employment protections. Opt-outs are significant for the former, as has been observed with the EU Blue Card – an example of where some members like the UK, Ireland and Denmark have stayed outside (Eisele 2013). This represents the continuation of a theme as the UK and Ireland have also stayed outside Schengen and were among only three countries (along with Sweden this time) to not impose restrictions following the 2004 accessions; an incoherence that demonstrates the challenge of 'migrational employment relations': the open invitation of cheaper labour from CEE without the commitment to fair (or equal) treatment. This is demonstrated by the second level: enforcement of regulation that does exists. Here the issue of posted workers is instructive and the gaps in policing such agreements even in relatively highly coordinated economies like Germany where significant undercutting of pay and conditions has been identified (ETUC 2015).

National

The national level comprises the traditional basis of any economic governance and dialogue but it is declining unevenly. The pushing up of economic regulation to the economic bloc and the pushing down of dialogue through the fragmentation of collective bargaining are widely recognised, leading to the hollowing out of the national. Nevertheless, the nation state remains sovereign; the level at which governments are elected, frameworks developed and, for the most part, where identities coalesce. It is important not to exaggerate the death of the national level, while recognising the shifting power resources at other levels. From an employment relations perspective, the national level remains of crucial importance in many countries, primarily via sectoral-level negotiations, particularly in more coordinated economies like Germany and France. Germany has, however, seen moves to gradually fragment collective bargaining mechanisms outside key industries of union strength. France continues to maintain a highly regulated bargaining system with extremely high levels of collective bargaining, in contrast to membership levels. This is not the case in either liberal economies, such as the UK, or those in much of CEE. Furthermore, through taking a multilevel governance approach to assessing employment regimes it becomes clear how ambiguous the national can be, in relation to vertical and horizontal integration. For example, the wealthier and more powerful countries in the EU are able to gain competitive advantage over other countries (horizontally) by mobilising power resources at the economic bloc level rather than directly.

Migration policies, attitudes and outcomes vary widely within Europe. In relation to extra-EU inward migration nation states maintain significant autonomy and in fact this is the dominant level at which migration institutional frameworks have been developed. Again, responses to the ongoing refugee crisis are instructive, with Germany the most generous in offering asylum and many other countries (particularly in CEE countries) resisting any mandatory obligations. The sovereignty issue also means that governments are responsible for interpreting the directives and so on that emanate from the economic bloc level so even in areas that are not *national* we see significant autonomy. This is as a result of the 'organised decentralisation' that characterises EU decision-making (Traxler 1995).

Subnational

The subnational level has seen significant political disruption recently, particularly in the UK. This is the level below the *nation state*. It is not best described as 'regional', as in cases like the UK and even Belgium recent changes relate to national identities, rather than regional ones. Upturns in these 'nationalisms' are reshaping their traditional political settlements at all levels, but most notably in its relationship with the national government. In the case of Scotland, it is difficult to overstate the impact that the Scottish National Party (SNP) has had of late following the independence referendum of September 2014 and the record electoral swing it received from Labour in the subsequent 2015 UK general election. Though less sudden, the federal election of 2014 in Belgium saw the first national government led by Flemish nationalists whose ultimate aim is secession. In reality, the Belgian

New Flemish Alliance (N-VA) and the SNP have achieved this via opposing strategies (attacking established parties from the right and left, respectively), which has clear implications for outlooks on trade, investment and, ultimately, experiences of employment.

In other European countries, the subnational distinction is different again. Levels of prosperity in the former East Germany, for example, continue to lag behind those of the West. Increasing autonomy of various kinds at the subnational level has prompted a recent interest in the institutional frameworks that businesses encounter in resource allocation decision-making (Crouch, Schröder and Voelzkow 2009; Miller 2010; Ferner, Edwards and Tempel 2012). This is even foreseen in the current trade agreements involving the EU and the US, where the role of states in the US – referred to as the 'subfederal' in the documents – is explicitly recognised by the EU as providing impetus to delegating to the 'subnational' in members states of the EU when devising treaty frameworks (European Union 2014: 1). The opportunities and restrictions that these frameworks afford firms are generally understood in terms of regulation and resources in the employment relations literature. There are no significant institutional implications at this level in relation to migration beyond narrative and discourse building – for example, the Scottish approach to the refugee crisis.

Local

The local level encompasses all that comes beneath the subnational, ranging from the small workplace to the local or provincial authority. It is the level that is most prominent for dialogue and agreement in less coordinated economies. It is the level at which an investment in organising workers through practical networking activity leads to the strongest returns. As with the subnational – with which it can have an ambiguous relationship in terms of where one ends and the other begins – it is a level that often takes on an increased role as traditional bargaining mechanisms fragment. However, it is in *outcomes* where the local is most profound, in line with the strong employment relations sociological tradition. It is at the local level where the interchanging dynamics outlined above reach management and workers in their daily interactions. That is not to say that the local level is completely at the mercy of the global, national and so on, but to merely recognise that the dominant macro-institutional perspective(s) needs to be complemented by a micro perspective of how plant-level relations in particular reach their outcomes in relations to the actors involved (Pulignano and Stewart 2012).

Although the local level remains contentious for migration with employment, housing, public services and so on cited as sources of social tension, the regulation and institutional frameworks at this level are limited. In several

European countries (e.g. the UK) this is becoming more influential as workplaces are obliged to check the migration status of staff. Indeed, the UK government has now extended this to landlords with £3,000 fine for those who do not check their tenants adequately. This again weakens the bargaining power of a vulnerable group of workers, even when not in the workplace. The precaritisation of work spreads to all areas of life.

DISCUSSION AND CONCLUSIONS

How then are the employment relations and migration aspects connected? What is the added value that is integrating migration into the institutional analysis of employment relations? To see this, it is essential to refer back to the latter in order to identify the *institutional disparity* that created the earlier hypothesis that economic and political imperatives are pulling in opposing directions. This means towards the local in employment as bargaining fragments but remaining national in relation to migration, though with increasing efforts at the level of the economic bloc. This creates the institutional space for the exploitation of migrant labour, as shown in Figure I.2.2: the institutional complementarity that I described above.

In developing theoretical understanding on this institutional disparity, it is helpful to refer to the institutional literature on employment relations. This is in part because the dominant levels at which regimes are regulated are not static but subject to manipulation by actors. The key to understanding what

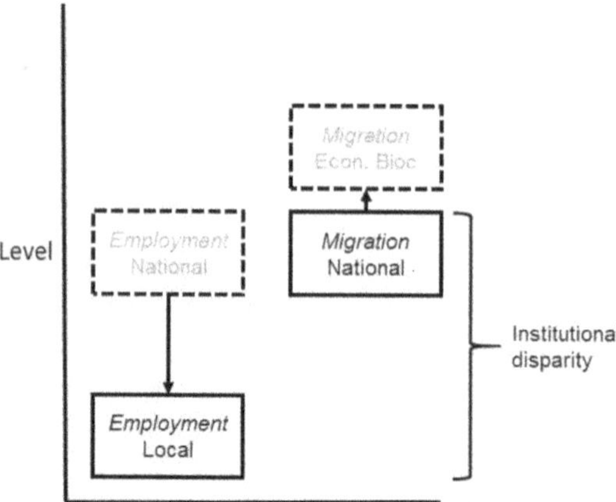

Figure I.2.2 Multilevelled Institutional Disparity Between Employment and Migration Regimes.

drives this distinction between LMEs and CMEs in the *VoC* framework, for example, is that they are not binary, and neither are they devoid of the influences of regional or sectoral institutional dynamics. Rather, they simply see the national as the most significant source of differentiation between the firm and other actors. These relationships are coordinated primarily by the maintenance of competitive market forces in LMEs and by more mutually reliant 'strategic interaction' in the case of CMEs – in which game theory is highly implicated in accounting for the 'deliberative proceedings' of companies and other actors in relation to the outlined five spheres (Hall and Soskice 2001: 11).

This has direct implications for the development of migrational employment relations because the workplace is the local level at which employment relations outcomes are felt by workers – as is the case for migration. Political antipathy towards migration is typically couched in *local* services/culture rather than any recognition of international push-and-pull factors. In addition, the grouping of countries in ideal types is closely correlated to those with relatively higher or lower levels of migration as most coordinated markets have the higher levels (with the notable exception of the UK). This thought must be noted with the caveat that headline figures on migration statistics do not account for the very different nature and lived experiences of different migrant categories. The relationship that extra-EU asylum seekers have with the institutions of host countries is very different to that for intra-EU economic migrants, for example.

Hall and Soskice do cover the role of institutional complementarity but more sophisticated explanations have been provided by others (Crouch et al. 2005; Höpner 2005). Perhaps the most important theoretical value that is added by institutional complementarity to developing migrational employment relations comes from the fact that it embeds findings into a broader context by asking whether the institutional landscape in its entirety is first coherent and secondly delivers on stated goals. Are actors able to challenge and manipulate these in the complex world of shifting employment relations and migration? This is particularly crucial if we are integrating a migration analysis because migrants themselves also have agency; they too are actors, though actors who are overlooked in much of the existing debate. Understanding these ambiguities through a broader understanding of context and *how* these institutions and actors relate to one another is a great help in advancing our understanding. How, for example, are migrants (and their advocates in organised labour and so on) specifically able to adapt employment relations?

It is beyond dispute that the global financial crises that have shaped Europe in profound ways since 2008 continue to impact on the way people live and work. Fundamental shifts in long-established political, economic and social norms have taken place, with no end in sight as to when 'normal service' might be resumed. From the widespread attacks on collective bargaining mechanisms in earlier phases of the crises and a spate of unscheduled changes of government (including the installation of unelected governments in Italy and Greece) to the adoption of the European Fiscal Pact, an increased deterioration of democratic accountability can be observed. Add opaque negotiations around the highly ambitious TTIP and TISA, and what we can see is a further hardening of the rules of the game – towards capital and away from democratic accountability.

Migration from *anywhere* remains a politically contentious issue and has influenced the national discourse of many member states, which has placed the core freedom of movement of people under strain as many countries seek to limit access to similar levels of social security, for example, than those afforded to citizens. While not explicitly forbidding intra-EU migration, it does nonetheless undermine the labour market by creating a more vulnerable segment that can lack the tools with which to fight this exploitation. Of course, there are notable examples where this has been successfully challenged both inside and outside of the trade union movement but taken in totality the downward pressure is unmistakeable.

As this chapter has shown, there is a fundamental contradiction at the heart of approaches to employment and migration: the desire for capital to utilise migrant labour without the implied social commitment. Consequently, the institutional frameworks that govern employment relations, on the one hand, and migration, on the other, are diverging to create an unstructured environment in which this unsatisfactory compromise can survive. This divergence is both horizontal and vertical. Horizontal in the sense that we can observe different settlements in different countries and vertical in the sense that even this discrepancy is being further complicated by shifts in influence away from the national level that dominates in the case of migration. Financial and economic decisions are increasingly taken at the global and European levels while employment relations – or, more specifically, collective bargaining – are pushed down to the local as bargaining units fragment.

As bargaining between capital and labour is pushed every closer to the individual worker, it is migrant workers who are doubly isolated with their inferior access to the social rights of many other workers. Developing a theoretical understanding of the role that institutions play in challenging or reinforcing decisions of economic *and social* management – particularly in times of crisis – empowers researchers to be brave in how we address the questions we wish to ask. Understanding how modern societies and their economies function, which questions are being asked and which are not, is a vital first step to improving them.

NOTES

1. The decision of the June 2016 UK referendum to leave the EU is the biggest indication of this, at the time of writing.
2. The wording of the treaty in fact states that it should be 'significantly below' this figure (European Commission 2011: 12).

REFERENCES

Bache, I. and M. Flinders, eds. 2004. *Multi-Level Governance*. Oxford: Oxford University Press.

Bieler, A. and R. Erne. 2015. 'Transnational solidarity? The European working class in the Eurozone crisis'. *Socialist Register*.

Bizzarri, K. 2013. *Report: A Brave New Transatlantic Partnership*. Seattle to Brussels Network.

Bojadžijev, M. and S. Karakayali. 2010. 'Recuperating the sideshows of capitalism: The autonomy of migration today'. *E-flux Journal* June–August (17).

Cerny, P. G., G. Menz and S. Soederberg. 2005. 'Different roads to globalization: Neoliberalism, the competition state, and politics in a more open world'. In *Internalizing Globalization: The Rise of Neoliberalism and the Decline of National Varieties of Capitalism*, edited by S. Soederberg, G. Menz and P. G. Cerny. Basingstoke: Palgrave Macmillan.

Commons, J. 1909. 'American shoemakers 1648–1895: A sketch of industrial evolution'. *Quarterly Journal of Economics* 24: 38–83.

Contrepois, S. and S. Jefferys. 2010. 'European works councils in Central and Eastern Europe: Varieties of institution building among French service sector multinationals'. *Industrial Relations Journal* 41: 584–602. https://doi.org/10.1111/j.1468-2338.2010.00587.x

Crouch, C., M. Schröder and H. Voelzkow. 2009. 'Regional and sectoral varieties of capitalism'. *Economy and Society* 38 (4): 654–678. https://doi.org/10.1080/03085140903190383

Crouch, C., W. Streeck, R. Boyer, B. Amable, P. A. Hall and G. Jackson. 2005. 'Dialogue on "Institutional complementarity and political economy" Three meanings of complementarity'. *Socio-Economic Review* 3 (2): 359–382.

Culpepper, P. D. 2001. 'Employers, public policy and the politics of decentralized co-operation in France and Germany'. In *Varieties of Capitalism: The Institutional Foundations of Comparative Advantage*, edited by P. A. Hall and D. Soskice, 275–306. Oxford: Oxford University Press.

Dimaggio, P. J. and W. W. Powel. 1983. 'The iron cage revisited: Institutional isomorphism and collective rationality in organizational fields'. *American Sociological Review* 48 (2): 147–160.

Economist. 2015. 'Free exchange: Game of zones'. *The Economist* 19 March 2015. Available at: http://www.economist.com/news/finance-and-economics/21646772-regional-trade-deals-arent-good-global-ones-they-are-still (accessed 19 April 2015).

Eisele, K. 2013. *Why Come Here if I Can Go There? Assessing the 'Attractiveness' of the EU's Blue Card Directive for 'Highly Qualified' Immigrants*. Brussels: Centre for European Policy Studies.

ETUC. 2015. *Free Movement YES! Social Dumping NO!* Brussels: European Trade Union Confederation.

European Commission. 2011. *Treaty on Stability, Coordination and Governance in the Economic and Monetary Union*. Brussels: European Commission.

European Union. 2014. 'Trade in services and investment: Schedule of specific commitments and reservations'. Brussels: European Commission.

Ferner, A., T. Edwards and A. Tempel. 2012. 'Power, institutions and the cross-national transfer of employment practices in multinationals'. *Human Relations* 65 (2): 163–187. https://doi.org/10.1177/0018726711429494

Global Unions. 2015. *Framework Agreements – Global Unions*. Available at: http://www.global-unions.org/+-framework-agreements-+.html (accessed 19 April 2015).

Hall, P. A. and D. W. Gingerich. 2009. 'Varieties of capitalism and institutional complementarities in the political economy: An empirical analysis'. *British Journal of Political Science*. https://doi.org/10.1017/S0007123409000672

Hall, P. A. and D. Soskice, eds. 2001. *Varieties of Capitalism: The Institutional Foundations of Comparative Advantage*. Oxford: Oxford University Press.

Höpner, M. 2005. 'What connects industrial relations and corporate governance? Explaining institutional complementarity'. *Socio-Economic Review* 3 (2): 331–358.

Keune, M. and P. Marginson. 2013. 'Transnational Industrial Relations as Multi-Level Governance: Interdependencies in European Social Dialogue'. *British Journal of Industrial Relations* 51 (3): 473–497. https://doi.org/10.1111/bjir.12005

Marginson, P. 2006. *Between Europeanisation and Regime Competition: Labour Market Regulation Following EU enlargement*. Coventry: Warwick Papers in Industrial Relations, Number 79.

Miller, V. 2010. 'How much legislation comes from Europe?' *Economic Indicators* (July 1988): 1–52. Available at: http://www.parliament.uk/briefing-papers/RP10-62.pdf

Morgan, G. 2007. 'National business systems research: Progress and prospects'. *Scandinavian Journal of Management* 23: 127–145.

Morgan, G. 2015. *SASE Presidential Address*. London: Society for the Advancement of Socio-Economics.

Morgan, G. and M. Hauptmeier. 2014. 'Varieties of institutional theory in comparative employment relations'. In *The Oxford Handbook of Employment Relations*, edited by A. Wilkinson, G. Wood and R. Deeg, 1–23. Oxford: Oxford University Press. https://doi.org/10.1093/oxfordhb/9780199695096.013.009

Morgan, G. and P. H. Kristensen. 2006. 'The contested space of multinationals: Varieties of institutionalism, varieties of capitalism'. *Human Relations* 59 (11): 1467–1490. https://doi.org/10.1177/0018726706072866

Powell, W. and P. Dimaggio. 1991. *The New Insitutionalism and Organizational Analysis*. Chicago: University of Chicago Press.

Pulignano, V. 2006. 'Still "Regime Competition"?' *Relations Industrielles* 61 (4): 615. https://doi.org/10.7202/014763ar

Pulignano, V. and P. Stewart. 2012. 'The management of change. Local union responses to company-level restructuring in France and Ireland – A study between and within countries'. *Transfer: European Review of Labour and Research* 18 (4): 411–427. https://doi.org/10.1177/1024258912458867

Rubery, J. and D. Grimshaw. 2003. *The Organisation of Employment: An International Perspective*. London: Palgrave Macmillan.

Sinclair, S. and H. Mertins-kirkwood. 2014. *TISA versus Public Services*. Geneva: Public Services International.

Thelen, K. 2001. 'Varieties of labor politics in the developed democracies'. In *Varieties of Capitalism: The Institutional Foundations of Comparative Advantage*, edited by P. A. Hall and Soskice, 71–103. Oxford: Oxford University Press.

Traxler, F. 1995. 'Farewell to Labor Market Associations? Organized versus disorganized decentralization as a map for industrial relations'. In *Organized Industrial Relations in Europe: What Future?* edited by C. Crouch and F. Traxler. Aldershot: Avebury.

Whitley, R., ed. 1992. *European Business Systems*. London: Sage.

Whitley, R. 1999. *Divergent Capitalisms: The Social Structuring and Change of Business Systems*. Oxford: Oxford University Press.

Wilkinson, A., G. Wood and R. Deeg. 2014. 'Comparative employment systems'. In *The Oxford Handbook of Employment Relations*, edited by, A. Wilkinson, G. Wood, and R. Deeg, 1–14. Oxford: Oxford University Press. https://doi.org/10.1093/oxfordhb/9780199695096.013.001

Chapter I.3

Migration Policies and Their Underlying Threats

Going Beyond the Polarization of EU Versus Non-EU Migration Policies

Nina Sahraoui, Radosław Polkowski and Mateusz Karolak

In the political discourse over the last decade various countries of the EU as well as the Union itself have been facing different 'migration crises'. Just to mention a few: the unexpected significant intra-EU mobility of citizens from the newly accepted CEE countries; repeated riots in deprived suburbs often inhabited by the second- or third-generation descendants of migrants; the illegal expulsion of EU citizens, mostly of Roma origin; or recently increased inflow of asylum seekers, welcomed by some states and expelled by others. The 'crises' are not an exception but normality inscribed into the migration process. Most importantly, however, in this chapter, we argue that all these constantly emerging tensions reveal something more fundamental about contemporary states as well as citizenship and rights not just with regard to migrants but, indeed, for all of us.

More specifically, we see these 'crises' as part and parcel of long-standing processes of 'displacement of noncontractual principles of solidaristic social provisions by those of market and contract' (Somers 2008: 11) and the resultant utilitarian logic that permeates political discourses and policymaking. The 'market fundamentalism' associated with neoliberal philosophy and policies unearths the notions of deservingness and un-deservingness typical of the Victorian era's classical liberalism. In this way, the flipside of tensions over migrations are tensions over rights of those formally called citizens as will be illustrated with numerous examples in this chapter. Thus, building on Anderson's (2013) argument that migration policies are just as much about 'us' as they are about 'them', the chapter redefines the binary constructions of citizens versus non-citizens commonly present in migration literature and proposes an understanding of citizenship as a continuum of rights written into global and existential inequalities (Therborn 2013).

Taking the UK, Poland, France and Spain as examples, while also drawing on EU-level migration policies, we start with the analysis of how utilitarian and market logics lead to the latent pitfalls of intra-EU mobility regulations and practical limitations of EU citizenship. Next, we show that similar logics shape policies for non-EU migrants; however, in their case it is implemented explicitly. The pragmatic selection of 'legal' and 'illegal' migrants combined with the emphasis on the temporary nature of migration eventually facilitates the disciplining of labour through labour market segmentation. We acknowledge, however, that migrants should not be perceived solely as passive victims of such policies, and they mount resistance not only in institutionalized forms but also in their everyday practices (Papadopoulos and Tsianos 2013). Finally, we highlight that the utilitarian limitation of migrants' social, economic and political rights reflects broader societal changes, in particular the commodification of citizenship and its detachment from community, as well as the ongoing process of the dismantling of the welfare state and an emphasis on solely individual responsibilities. In this way, migrants' experiences might be seen as a harbinger of a new era of common denizenship – an era in which full rights might only be enjoyed by a privileged few.

CITIZENSHIP AND MULTIPLE BORDERS IN A BORDERLESS EUROPEAN UNION

Citizenship is a concept with a relatively short history in social theory. As noted by Joppke (2010: 9), among the classics of social theory 'only Marx produced a memorable entry on citizenship', for whom citizenship was nothing more than a tool of masking class inequalities in capitalist societies. However, the most recognisable conceptualization of citizenship was developed by T. H. Marshall who perceived citizenship as a 'peace formula that reconciled workers to capitalism'. Marshall (1950) conceived of citizenship as composed of three types of rights: civil, political and social. The latter (i.e. social rights) became a particularly influential concept in that it was the first formulation of access to economic resources being an individual right for which the political community is collectively responsible. Although seemingly progressive and having potential for developing a more socially inclusive politics, the concept may also be utilized by reactionary politics that lead to social exclusion. This argument rests on the observation that was perhaps first made by Brubaker (1992), who said that citizenship necessarily involves social closure; that is, it draws 'legally consequential and ideologically charged distinction between citizens and foreigners' excluding the latter group from rights (Brubaker 1992: 21). Despite the hopes and calls for the formation of postnational, universal rights (Bauböck 1994; Soysal 1994; Kymlicka 1995), which were supposed to come closer to fruition with the introduction of European citizenship, the concept of citizenship seems to remain firmly rooted in nation states. As will be shown further in this chapter, recent political developments in Europe, where calls have been heard for reducing social rights to non-citizens, including EU migrants, indicate that the exclusionary feature of citizenship is becoming stronger rather than weaker.

Despite the narrative of a 'borderless Europe', EU policies regarding migration became an ephemeral mix of approaches, based on the proliferation of legal and practical divisions between countries, people and their statuses (Mezzadra and Neilson 2013). Whereas, due to the Schengen agreement, many of the EU internal borders became invisible and deterritorialized, their presence is still sensed and experienced by millions of migrants. Established by the Maastricht Treaty, European citizenship was aimed at guaranteeing equal rights to the nationals of EU member states residing in other member states. There is, arguably, little doubt that the opening of labour markets to citizens of the new member states from CEE expanded their scope of freedom and gave them more agency (for a critique of the 'freedom of movement' within the EU, see Apostolova 2018, Chapter III.3 in this book). First, it secured widely available exit options for both workers dissatisfied with their working conditions, as in case of Poland, and ethnic minorities discriminated in the national states (e.g. for Russians in Latvia or Roma in Romania and Bulgaria) (Meardi 2012). Secondly, it resulted in the regularization of many workers from CEE countries who had already worked in the EU-15 (Favell 2008). Finally, it allowed migrant workers from the new member states to break the dependence on employer-sponsored schemes.

However, as noted by Boswell and Geddes (2010: 188), the list of these rights was 'rather limited' and 'excluded some of the most important socio-economic rights achieved for EU nationals over the previous decades'. Insights into intra-European migration illustrate this point. The most obvious advantage of EU citizenship is the possibility to travel freely within the Schengen zone. The common view on freedom of movement is that all EU citizens with their family members are free to move and settle in any member state. However, in accordance with Directive 2004/38/EC of the European Parliament, this right is valid only for a three-month time period, unless the mobile EU citizens (who are no longer termed 'migrants') 'are workers or self-employed persons in the host Member State or have sufficient resources for themselves and their family members not to become a burden on the social assistance system of the host Member State during their period of residence' (European Union 2004). In other words, EU citizens are free to move within the EU as long as they are employed, actively looking for jobs, or pursuing education in order to find employment; and only then they are entitled to take with them their spouses and dependent children. Importantly, work is understood narrowly as paid labour and does not account for any reproductive or non-marketized work. This presupposition strengthens female formal dependence on the male breadwinner, since the labour market activity rate of women in CEECs is over a dozen percentage points lower than those of men (e.g. in Poland 64.7 per cent for men and 48.3 per cent for women) (Central Statistical Office 2015). Furthermore, none of the new member states allows same-sex marriage, which can effectively restrict EU citizens from CEE countries from being accompanied by their non-employed same-sex partners.

In practice these legal restrictions often remain a dead letter, since not all municipalities require registration and those that do, do not means-test newcomers. Moreover, as observed from the AoM perspective (Papadopoulos and Tsianos 2013), migrants themselves, both legalized and illegalized, do not stick to the formal rules and avoid sovereign control of their mobility; control which responds to their activity. They share and circulate among each other knowledge about life on the move and after settlement; and thus create 'mobile commons', which escape the logic of the market. However, the very fact that such laws exist opens a legal path for an exceptional (since contrary to the pervading practice) and selective treatment of undesirable EU citizens. This has already happened in the case of Roma people, who are EU citizens from Bulgaria and Romania, but were expelled from France as well as from Denmark, Italy and Belgium. Despite the severe condemnation which came from various institutions including the European Commission and European Parliament, France between 2009 and 2013 evicted and expelled around twenty thousand EU citizens of Romani origin. French authorities justified these acute actions by claiming that Roma people in France became an 'unreasonable burden on the French social security system' as well as a 'threat to public policy and to public security' by illegal occupation of settlements or 'stealing in landfills' (Maslowski 2015). However, many of the expelled migrants, allegedly ballasting the security system, stayed in France for less than three months and were not even 'entitled' to any social assistance. Others were maintaining themselves for less than the minimum amount required by the French law, what also excluded them from accessing benefits. Moreover, the argument that illegal occupation of a property constitutes a threat to public order was rejected by both the European Court of Justice and even French appeal courts (Maslowski 2015; see also Carrera 2014). This example shows that the selective application of the legal framework still enables member states to act upon EU internal migration flows, assessing migrants' utility for the host societies.

Furthermore, CEE migrants have been more affected by labour market segmentation than non-migrants, in spite of formal equality. According to Ciupijus (2011), who analysed the case of the UK, labour migrants from the new member states are characterized by the diverging trajectories of spatial and labour market mobility. Since the recent EU enlargement, spatial mobility has increased significantly leading to the intensification of labour migration, while labour market mobility has taken the form of a downward occupational mobility. Despite the lack of institutional settings (e.g. guest workers schemes or 'employer sponsorship') explicitly forcing CEE migrants to take a certain job or at least to work in a certain branch of economy, they still tend to work in the low-paid, insecure jobs characterized by a high level of numerical flexibility (Currie 2007; Favell 2008; Ciupijus 2011). Intra-EU migrants often encounter practical problems with the recognition of their formal qualifications, which contributes to other structural and individual factors, channelling them towards the secondary labour market and work below their level of qualification (Trevena 2013).

Most importantly, the assumption that all EU citizens have access to equal social rights is undermined by one of the most characteristic features of recent East–West migration – its temporariness. Most of the EU countries introduced the minimum working or residency period necessary to obtain access to social benefits. In the UK, for instance, citizens of the EU-8 need to have at least twelve months of uninterrupted employment in order to become entitled to jobseekers allowance. Taking into consideration intra-EU migrants' high numerical flexibility as well as the fact that many of them plan to return to their home country[1] in less than a year, their practical access to the unemployment benefits abroad remains limited. Furthermore, as discussed elsewhere (see Karolak 2018, Chapter II.4 in this book), many migrants returning from other EU countries find it difficult to integrate into their domestic labour market and falling into the 'migratory trap' (Iglicka 2010), eventually decide to re-emigrate. This in turn often leads to the formal 'zeroing' of their previous work experience. In many cases intra-EU migrant workers, despite being prized by the official discourse on mobile EU citizens, in practice seem to be institutionally punished for their higher mobility.

This section has highlighted that beyond the appearance of a borderless EU, utilitarian principles are present in the rights granted to European citizens. These are to be found in the limitations of rights based upon the idea that citizenship rights need to relate to paid employment. Even though these limitations are not systematically applied, and migrants often overcame them informally, this breach has been used by EU governments against groups of EU citizens most affected by othering processes such as those directed at Roma people. These insights into intra-European migration herald most fundamental features of EU migration policies towards people the Union designates as 'third country nationals'. The following section looks at how European overarching migration policies interact with national migration regimes towards non-EU migrants, notably through the examples of the UK, Spain and Poland.

THE PITFALLS OF THE UTILITARIAN ASSUMPTIONS GOVERNING EU MIGRATION POLICIES TOWARDS TCNS

The 1999 Tampere European Council launched a body of regulations in the field of migration management (Collett 2014). With regard to labour migration, the EU's approach focuses on the highly skilled, given that migration policies remain nation states' prerogative and that there exists no consensus among European countries on policies that relate to non-EU 'low-skilled' migration (Kofman 2008). In this context, a European directive was adopted in 2009 that created the EU Blue Card aimed at appealing to highly skilled workers. Applicants for an EU Blue Card need to have secured a job deemed highly skilled prior to migration. To attract these sought-after individuals, highly skilled migrants are allowed to migrate with their families (spouse, partner or children). This scheme illustrates the EU's will to join the 'race for talents' and align its objectives to those of countries like Australia and Canada. In practice, the EU Blue Card so far constitutes a hollow shell and EU member states continue to rely on national schemes to manage labour migration. Germany was the sole country to use the EU Blue Card to any significant extent, issuing 14,000 cards in 2013, that is, 93 per cent of all Blue Cards issued that year (European Commission 2014).

National migration policies implemented by individual European countries follow this underpinning logic: non-EU labour migration tends to be facilitated for the 'highly skilled' with paths to permanent migration, whereas 'low-skilled' migration is strictly limited, sector-specific and temporary (Stasiulis 2008). This overarching outlook reproduces a gendered understanding of what constitutes a 'skill' in that it labels as unskilled all social reproduction-related work, notably care and paid household activities. The scarcity of legal routes available to non-EU migrants for work-related purposes is reflected in the distribution of entry categories, as illustrated by Figure I.3.1 for a selection of EU countries. Family reunification constitutes a more common type of entry to the EU than work-related visas for most European countries.

This point should not conceal, however, that the category of entry is only indicative of administrative categories created by migration policies: non-EU migrants who are in employment might have come through a variety of

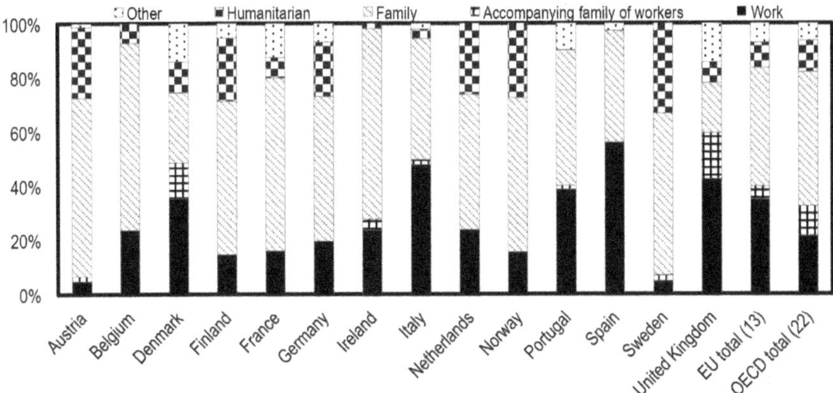

Figure I.3.1 Permanent Migrants' Categories of Entry. *Source*: OECD data 2015, Selection of countries, figures without intra-EU free movement.

routes. Those who came through family reunification or as asylum seekers are likely to be employed in 'low-skilled' sectors of the economy. The need for 'low-skilled' labour is, however, continuously played down (Kofman 2008), and the trend is to further restrict legal routes of entry to the EU other than those targeting the 'highly skilled'. Since migrants who are not perceived as 'highly skilled' do not abandon their search for a 'better life' they often choose to try informal routes of entry to the EU, risking their lives and eventually ending in shadow economies, being subjected to even greater exploitation. Restrictive policies might flatter policy makers' appetite for a hands-on 'pick and choose' management as well as politicians' temptation to adopt xenophobic positions. However, due to the limitation of rights upon which these policies rely, they produce vulnerable workers and construct a hierarchy of desirable to non-desirable migrants. Illustrative of this trend is the tightening of family reunification possibilities (Kofman 2008). In France, in the 2000s under Nicolas Sarkozy, first in the Home Office and later as president, additional requirements for family reunification were introduced (in relation to the longer stay required prior to an application, the shorter resident permit granted to the spouse, language tests and resource thresholds). The initial wording even contained a controversial proposal for DNA testing to prove the family relationship, a proposition eventually withdrawn. In the UK, the Home Office's £18,600 minimum income threshold for family reunification (only for a spouse, the threshold increases with children) was upheld by the Court of Appeal in July 2015 (BBC 2014a).

This logic of economic utilitarianism in a context of generalized economic competition has created the incentives for assimilating citizenship rights with economic assets. European citizenship, perceived as a harbinger of the postnational, or denationalized citizenship, is still attached to national citizenship: one cannot become solely an EU citizen, as was confirmed by recent rulings by the European Court of Justice (case C-135).[2] Since member states have the exclusive competence of granting or denying national and thus EU citizenship, this led to the emergence of a lucrative market for citizenship. Countries compete for 'investors', luring them with an EU passport, residence rights for families, short minimum residency requirements, but most of all with the minimum investment amount, necessary to receive special treatment.[3] For example, in the UK, the more one invests in 'UK government bonds, share capital or loan capital in active and trading UK registered companies',[4] the less one needs to wait in order to apply for UK permanent residency (from five years for a £2 million investment to three years for £5 million, to two years for £10 million). Moreover, and unlike other applicants, 'the investors' do not need to provide proof of knowledge of English. In Malta, until 2014, no minimal residency period was required for wealthy foreigners investing around £1 million and wishing to obtain a Maltese passport and thus EU citizenship (BBC 2014b). Recent pressure from the European Commission led to the introduction of the requirement of twelve months of residence. In Spain, where the construction sector collapsed with the economic downturn in the late 2000s, the government used its sovereign power to issue residency permits hoping to slow down the drop in prices affecting the Spanish real estate business. The law passed in 2013 offers permanent residency to buyers of properties worth over €500,000. The initial project mentioned an amount of €160,000, a sum deemed too low by the European Commission, which wanted Spain to have comparable legislation to Portugal (Cabrerizo 2013). Current national legislation is, however, far from homogenized and the market for citizenship mentioned above ushered in a market of intermediaries supporting potential wealthy clients in obtaining the so-called golden visas. The company 'Golden Visas by La Vida' offers for instance counselling services so that clients' investments match their visa needs (residency for family members, work permit, future citizenship, etc.).[5] Capital became the guarantor of citizenship. *Ius sanguinis* and *ius soli* gave way to *ius pecuniae* (cf. Dzankic 2012). *Ius pecuniae* reveals how race, gender and class intersect in the construction of migration policies. If non-EU migrants face increasingly tightened EU migration policies, the latter reproduce intersectional inequalities. Financial capital and thus class belonging can effectively buy one's way out of the racialization produced by EU migration policies. If high qualifications apparently operate similarly by facilitating one's immigration into the EU, empirical evidence shows nevertheless how the logic of the border affects highly skilled migrants in the long run.

Indeed one of the most worrying consequences of migration management in EU countries is the systematic deskilling that affects non-EU migrants as a result of the non-recognition of qualifications completed outside of the EU, as pointed out by the European Commission itself in May 2015 (European Commission 2015). This leads to the paradox of targeting highly skilled workers while not having facilitated the recognition of their qualifications, which is the very first condition for migrant workers to be able to make use of their skills. Often migrant workers need to invest time and money in studies again after migration, as they do not benefit from schemes that could facilitate this process. They consequently might need to take up a job deemed 'unskilled' or 'low skilled', even when they enter the EU as a highly skilled migrant. Figure I.3.2 presents OECD data on over-qualification for a selection of countries. Over-qualification is defined here as 'the share of people with tertiary-level qualifications who work in a job that is classified as low or

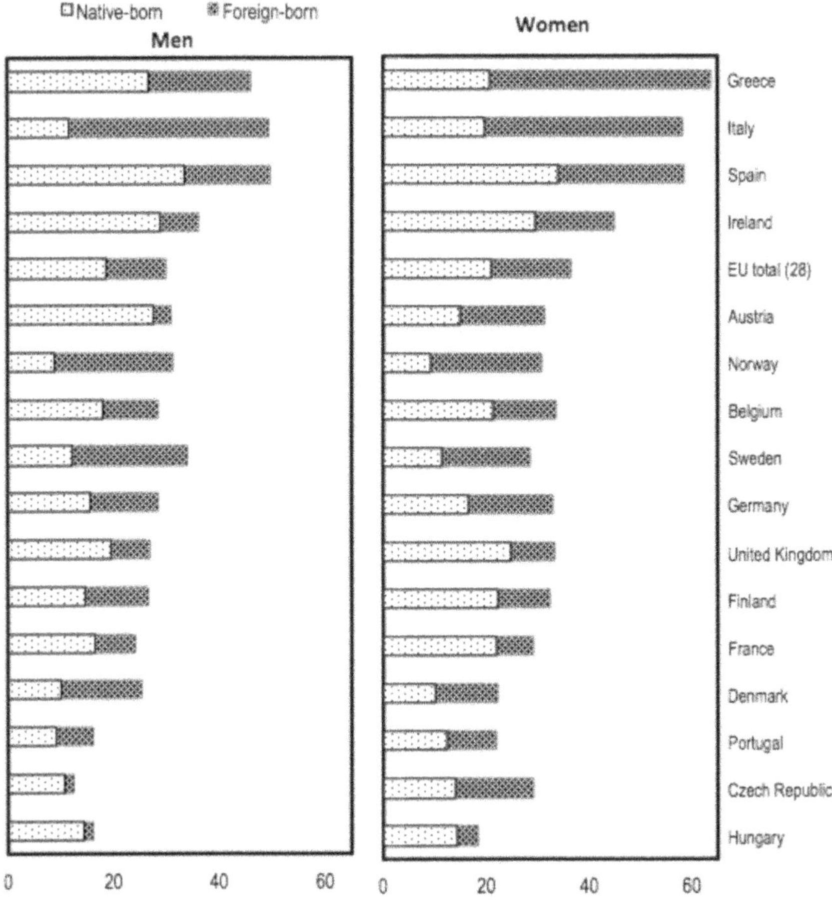

Figure I.3.2 Over-qualification Among Highly Educated Employed Persons Aged 15–64, 2012–2013. *Source*: OECD data 2015, Selection of countries, authors' compilation.

medium skilled by the International Standard Classification of Occupations' (OECD/European Union, 2015). On average, the over-qualification rate for foreign-born workers is 30 per cent in the EU-28 versus 18.6 per cent for the native-born.

Finally, it appears that EU governments use rights as a means to bargain temporariness for 'low-skilled' workers. Menz and Caviedes (2010) have argued that migration policies have come to be increasingly shaped by non-state actors and notably employers' organizations. There exists indeed a business case for more migration to answer these labour needs. Acknowledging these needs, however, challenges populist and xenophobic electoral strategies. In this context, reiterating post-war projections over migration, governments aspire to 'import labour but not people' (Castles 2006: 742), as already highlighted half a century ago by Max Frisch's famous phrase 'We called for labour and people came instead'. This pattern of migration is viewed as part of the response to sector-specific shortages (Fargues 2008) while minimising the social impact of immigration (McLoughlin and Münz 2011). To ensure that workers only come for pre-established periods of time, rights of temporary workers are limited. Rights to reside and work depend strictly on employment and employer-sponsored visa schemes limit the possibility for workers to change employers. According to Stasiulis (2008: 107), 'Eligibility to change status to permanent residence and the right to family reunification are the two rights that most clearly bleed particular temporary worker schemes into long-term resident migration'. For instance, in the UK, non-EU migrant domestic workers cannot change employers[6] and their stay is limited to six months,[7] exposing workers to abuse and exploitation, as highlighted for years by NGOs (Sloan 2015) such as Kalayaan. Anderson (2010) sheds light on how migration policies interact with labour market segmentation, notably for non-EU migrants:

> Through the creation of categories of entrant, the imposition of employment relations and the construction of institutionalised uncertainty, immigration controls work to form types of labour with particular relations to employers and to labour markets. They combine with less formalised migratory processes to help produce 'precarious workers' that cluster in particular jobs and segments of the labour market. (2010: 301)

Indeed, labour market segmentation relies upon socially constructed barriers that entrap workers in specific segments. In this regard, Castles raises the question: 'Is it acceptable to trade off workers' rights for economic gains?' (2006: 749). Employer-sponsored schemes create a space of arbitrariness and exacerbate the power of employers over employees which renders exploitation and abuse possible. Subordinating entirely workers' rights to their economic contribution based upon a manifest criterion of nationality and a latent criterion of gender serves employers' interests in that it creates the figure of the 'good and disciplined' worker/employee. This happens, however, at the cost of hierarchising rights and turning workers into disposable units of labour on the pretext of ensuring they do not lay down roots in the EU. Given that for two decades the increase in total population in the EU is largely due to international migration[8] and that the demographic forecasts predict an increasing reliance upon migration, the economic justifications of this temporariness mantra are questionable. As Castles (2006: 759) puts it, 'Can temporary worker programs meet the future labour needs of the EU, if these are not temporary in nature, but rather the result of long-term shifts in demographic and economic structures?' Not only are these policies arguably inadequate to answer the demographic, and thus economic challenges of the EU, it is implemented by creating 'denizens' (Standing 2011; De Genova 2013) and fragmenting the workforce, which is politically particularly easy to achieve given that nation states rely on the exclusion of the Other as embodied by individuals of other nationalities. The temporariness of workers provides the conditions for labour market dualization, since more often than not it takes time for migrant workers to be able to better their working and employment conditions because of the institutional barriers they face (Meardi 2012).

EU migration policies illustrate the willingness of EU governments to only take in investors and highly skilled individuals. Recent national and EU migration policies have exacerbated this economic utilitarianism, as illustrated by the absence of legal routes for so-called low-skilled workers, increasing restrictions on family reunification throughout the EU and most revealingly the emergence of *ius pecuniae*. Insights into three European migration regimes in the following section illustrate how these underpinning dynamics are extended by national policies but also how migration regimes are multilayered thus presenting significant differences.

NATIONAL EXAMPLES: THE UK, SPAIN AND POLAND

Focusing on the European level renders visible a limited space of consensus and some general trends, it does not account, however, for significant differences among migration regimes as shaped by national legislation. British, Spanish and Polish migration regimes are briefly described to offer insights into how nation states forge multilayered migration regimes in the framework of shared utilitarian assumptions.

The British points-based immigration system selects migrants on the basis of their potential economic contribution. Arguably, there already exists a mismatch between the perceived need and the actual need given that it is assumed that 'low-skilled' labour needs will be filled in by intra-European migration. In the care sector, for instance, where labour shortages are chronic, intra-EU migration makes up around one quarter of the migrant workforce (Cangiano 2014: 141): while significant, three quarters nonetheless come from outside of the EU. However, there exists no direct legal route for non-EU migrants to move to the UK to work in the care sector. Workers in the sector are thus overwhelmingly overqualified and some of them are students (see Sahraoui 2018, Chapter II.2 in this book). Highly skilled migrants cannot access the labour market opportunities for which they are qualified and are effectively deskilled through institutional and social barriers and must thus join the labour market at its lower end. Intended to serve the British economy, the points-based immigration system produces both a brain drain and a brain waste.

While the Spanish migration regime combines utilitarian hypotheses with cultural assumptions, it also produces entrapment and discrimination for non-EU migrant workers. The structural reliance of certain sectors of the Spanish economy on undocumented workers (e.g. the care sector) is well researched (IMERSO 2005; Rodriguez 2012). Somers argues that 'the political economy of migration and undeclared employment involves a "malign neglect" whereby states ensure adequate numbers of undocumented migrant workers for undeclared employment' (2008: 212). The Spanish migration regime is furthermore strongly determined by postcolonial preferences that define rights according to nationality of origin. For instance, the general rule requires ten years of legal residence before one is allowed to apply for Spanish citizenship. Some countries are nevertheless exempted from this rule and the required period of time is reduced to two years: Latin American countries, Andorra, the Philippines, Equatorial Guinea, Portugal and people of Sephardi origins.[9] This creates significant differences between migrant communities in terms of rights and reflects broader racialization processes that enshrine in law assumptions related to colonial history, language and religion.

The utilitarian underpinnings of EU migration policies are well reflected in Polish immigration policy since 1989 as it has been based on copying solutions developed in Western Europe and, from the late 1990s when the country started accession negotiations, directly shaped by the EU. One of the key aspects for the EU was to ensure tight control of Poland's eastern borders which were to become the EU's longest eastern frontiers. Not coincidentally, with the accession of Poland to the EU in 2004, the EU's border control agency, called Frontex, was established in Warsaw. As Poland gradually began to shift from a country of emigration to the transition country of significant inward and outward migrations, the Polish government, pressed with complaints by low-wage employers in finding workers in sectors like agriculture – partly due to migration of many Poles to Western Europe – began to take a more strategic approach to migration. This was reflected in the document 'Migration policy of Poland – current situation and recommendations' approved by the government on the 31 July 2012. The document explicitly calls for simplifying procedures for immigration with a focus on categories of migrants which are seen as particularly important from the viewpoint of the state's interests, more specifically its economic competitiveness.

Apart from recommending policies aimed at facilitating temporary migration in agriculture and construction sectors from Poland's eastern neighbours, the document designates students, scientists and graduates of Polish universities, people who run their own businesses, especially if they create jobs, and delegates of foreign employers categories of migrants that ought to be prioritised in the order as enumerated above. Moreover, there is a clear preference for people of Polish origin or those considered as culturally similar, as this category occupies the first place on the aforementioned priority list. The justification explicitly offered in the document is a supposedly hassle-free integration of culturally and ethnically close individuals. In line with this, a few years ago the government created a special program which granted asylum to Christian but not Muslim Syrian refugees (Reuters 2015). Arguably, this indicates how management of migration through economic utility is accompanied by management through fear which treats non-Christian, and in particular Muslim refugees, as not just economic but also a cultural threat.

The utilitarian principles which underlie the national migration regimes discussed above do not only limit workers' rights but they can also obstruct the supply of an adequate volume of labour. The analysis demonstrated also how the cost-benefit mantra was often imbued with racialization as illustrated by criteria for citizenship applications in Spain or the Polish government's preference for Christians. The arguments developed above are analysed from a different angle in the following section. More specifically, it is argued below that the analysis of the increasing restrictions applied to migrants cannot be detached from analysis of how neoliberalism impacts understandings of citizenship.

AREN'T WE ALL IN THE SAME BOAT? WHAT MIGRATION POLICIES REVEAL ABOUT NEOLIBERAL GOVERNMENTALITY

In the discussion thus far, we have shown how immigration policies rooted in utilitarian principles and focused more on economic competitiveness than the rights of workers disadvantage different groups of migrants in the EU. However, we also propose that these migration policies reveal much more fundamental processes that endanger the rights of migrants and non-migrants (i.e. those having citizenship in a legal sense) alike. More specifically, the shape that migration policies have taken in many European countries seems to reflect a larger neoliberal transformation of the state that goes beyond migration policies and which puts citizens and non-citizens in the same 'sinking' boat. Obviously, the situation of those in the latter group is usually relatively worse than those in the former, yet we argue that despite differences between and among citizens and non-citizens, the general tendency is the systematic deprivation of various rights as a result of the dismantling of the welfare state. According to David Harvey (2005: 3), the 'withdrawal of the state from many areas of social provision' is, alongside deregulation and privatization, the key characteristic of neoliberal political-economic guidelines and practices. Despite the widely acknowledged neoliberal hegemony, there is still considerable institutionalized and non-institutionalized resistance to the ongoing reforms of state functions (see Chapters III.1 and III.2 in this book). Yet one could argue that in order to pursue the neoliberal agenda and gradually dismantle the welfare state, social resistance is often bypassed by shifting the focus away from class cleavages and breaking class solidarity. It contributes to the fragmentation of the working class, whose members are played off against each other.

This is related to not only the already broadly described opposition between natives (citizens) and migrants (non-citizens)[10] but also to conflicts arising between 'deserving' and 'non-deserving' citizens as well as clashes among migrants, who clearly do not constitute a unified group. Indeed, as shown elsewhere (see Polkowski 2018, Chapter II.1 in this book), migrants distance themselves from other migrants and some citizens whom they perceive as 'benefit tourists' or 'benefit scroungers', respectively. The lines of conflict run in multiple directions, depending on the country and its type of capitalism, as well as on the group of migrants considered. First, there is a general shift from the welfare to the workfare state, meaning that access to social rights is increasingly restricted to those who are formally employed or follow strict labour office requirements (Standing 2011: 143). Such an approach excludes from the remaining safety net – with the approval of workers still entitled to benefits – all those citizens and non-citizens who are not formally employed (for instance, those who do reproductive labour). Although it leads to this outcome when it is compounded by the renewal of a nationalist discourse which advocates restricting access of non-citizens to social rights, regardless of their individual 'contribution' perceived from the utilitarian perspective. A good example of this are recent discussions in the UK. Before the referendum on the withdrawal of the UK from the EU, the British prime minister, David Cameron, negotiated with the EU seven years of 'emergency break' enabling his government to suspend the EU laws on freedom of movement and to 'restrict the EU migrants' access to in-work benefits for the four years' (Helm 2016). After the 'Brexit' vote, Theresa May, who succeeded David Camron in the position of Prime Minister, strengthened the anti-migrant rhetoric even further and pursued policy solutions that were discriminatory of EU migrants.

The essence of such state transformation was also captured by Anderson's (2013: 2) argument that 'modern states portray themselves not as arbitrary collections of people hung together by a common legal status but as a community of value, composed of people who share common ideals and (exemplary) patterns of behaviour expressed through ethnicity, religion, culture, or language – that is, its members have shared values'. The boundaries of such a community of value are defined from within by the figure of a 'failed citizen' and from the outside by the figure of a migrant, both of which are discursively set against that of a 'good citizen'. Migrants are 'tolerated citizens'; on the one hand, they may reaffirm values that the state and public discourses project (e.g. economic utility) by acting like 'good citizens'. Indeed, Anderson (2013) suggests that, in the quest for justifying their presence, they migrants often become guardians of those values by, for example, proving their exceptionally hard-working attitude. On the other hand, they can be also labelled as 'benefit tourists' who failed in living up to the ideal of self-authoring, enterprising subjects who are proactive in securing their economic well-being by means of waged labour. This differential labelling of migrants can be spotted in contrasting and changing discourses surrounding CEE migrants in the UK who are at times praised for their work ethics and at other times accused of welfare tourism. Labelling them 'benefit tourists' can be seen as part of the Conservative government's strategy to limit social rights for this category of workers. Indeed, since 2014, the government has introduced tighter eligibility criteria for CEE migrant workers to claim state support (Wintour 2014). This policy puts those in precarious employment.

However, not only the rights of migrants are at stake. While CEE migrants have been labelled benefit tourists, the 'failed citizens' who do not live up to the ideal of a 'good citizen' are labelled 'benefit scroungers', free-riders with no economic utility. As illustrated earlier, EU migrants who are judged as an economic burden can be expelled from a member state and although the state cannot apply the same measure to its citizens, Anderson (2013: 5) argues that for failed citizens 'the promise of formal citizenship is largely reduced to the bare toleration of their presence on state territory'. Moreover, she also illustrates that even citizens of white British descent become racialized in public debates as 'degenerate whites' who do not live up to the standards and values associated with their skin pigmentation and thus do not deserve social and possibly also political rights.

This indicates that citizens are not unaffected by the utilitarian logic which, as this chapter has illustrated, also underlies immigration policies. The plight of both migrants and citizens is part of the ongoing process of contractualization of citizenship, which means turning citizens from bearers of rights into participants in a market exchange in which 'social inclusion and moral worth [are] no longer inherent rights but rather earned privileges that are wholly conditional upon the ability to exchange something of equal value' (Somers 2008: 3). In the nineteenth century, the UK state used coercive measures to promote the value of economic utility: whipping the idle poor through the streets or taking them into workhouses where they would be taught the value of paid employment. Nowadays, contractual methods like workfare are used for the same purpose and they make access to social rights, for which post-war governments in Europe took responsibility through a policy of full employment, increasingly conditional on individual qualities and attitudes, and, above all, one's economic utility.

In turn, the contractualization of citizenship is, according to Somers (2008), part and parcel of a process of marketization that has been taking place in Western countries since the 1980s and which refers to the shifting balance of power between markets, state, and civil society in favour of the first of these three. This, argues Somers (2008: 11), has brought about 'displacement of non-contractual principles of solidaristic social provisions'. Utilitarian migration policies are thus just one of the cognates of this marketization trend which, as we saw, endangers rights of citizens, too. Importantly, not just social but also political and civil rights are at stake. This in turn carries a threat of turning the clock back when it comes to the well-known Marshallian progression of civil, political and social rights. For example, some politicians, including a former member of the UK parliament, have voiced arguments that the unemployed should be stripped of their political rights because they do not contribute. Although such voices can be dismissed as marginal, they nevertheless can also be seen as an outcome of a dangerous logic associated with marketization and contractualization of citizenship that considers certain individuals morally less worthy. As an illustration of this, Somers (2008), through her case study of New Orleanians affected by Hurricane Katrina, argues that these formally US citizens have been turned into a 'rightless, stateless, and expandable population deemed unworthy of the mutual recognition due moral equal' and posits that this outcome can be traced back to the long-term transformations of citizenship described above. The key issue appears to be that these processes and accompanying discourses shift 'responsibility and blame for social problems from structural conditions to alleged defects of individual moral character such as dependency, indolence, irresponsibility, lack of initiative, promiscuity, parasitism' (Somers 2008: 3). In this way, those facing social problems can be deemed as morally deficient and thus unworthy of recognition as moral equals. This is in essence the denial of the prerequisite of citizenship and other substantive rights that come with it, that is, 'the right to have rights' (Arendt 1951) which means the right to be treated as a moral equal. This is the right that, according to Arendt's (1951) analysis, Jews in Nazi Germany were stripped of as they were made stateless and consequently dehumanized, 'unrecognisable as fellow humans', and then denied equal rights (Somers 2008: 7). Although this came about in different way (i.e. outright racist discourse), there is a similar tendency behind utilitarian logic, that is, undermining one's value and worthiness followed by the undermining of rights, as the examples above illustrate.

The effects of contractualization of citizenship on both non-citizen migrants and citizens can be compared to the similarly threatening effect posed by 'governing through fear' (e.g. Huysmans 2006). Following 9/11 in the US and several terrorist attacks in Western Europe, tighter migration policies have often been justified by the need to protect citizens from terrorist threats. But apart from affecting migrants, fear of terrorism has been also used to justify the increasing encroachment of the state on many civil liberties of citizens in Europe. As noted by Somers (2008: 2), the emerging 'surveillance society' did not start but surely intensified the trend towards narrowing down the 'continuum of rights' for migrants and non-migrants alike.

These somewhat prophetic observations alludes also to an important point which is that citizenship is not simply the matter of having or not having it but, instead, can be better conceptualized as a continuum of rights that are available to citizens and migrants alike but to different degrees. Such formulation of the concept posits that citizenship is not a zero-sum game where a citizen takes it all at the expense of a migrant or, for that matter, in the reverse configuration as is often claimed in populist discourses. Moreover, if we place this continuum within the context of global capitalism which reshaped the meaning and the role of citizenship, making the legal status 'less attestation of citizenship, let alone loyalty to a protective state, than of claims to participation in labour markets' (Anderson 1994: 323–324), we get a picture of a continuum of citizenship. Thus, at one end, in place of legal citizens, there are affluent migrants, or the flexible citizens, as Ong (2006) called them. They take advantage of the global neoliberal economy and *ius pecuniae* as they 'shop' for passports as a means of advancing their economic gain and political security. At the other end of this global distribution of citizenship are the stateless, deprived of all rights, vulnerable with a 'bare life' and unwanted *sans papiers* over whom European leaders argue about whose responsibility they are but who nevertheless exercise their agency beyond the institutionalized structures by resisting sovereign control. The flexible citizens and other 'good migrants' can enjoy a much broader scope of rights than average working- or middle-class citizens in a developed country of Western Europe owing to their economic capital that allows them to navigate through global geographies of citizenship.

In this way, immigration policies in Europe reveal also a rather grim fact about the current condition of citizenship. For example, in reference to the UK, Anderson (2013) poses a provocative question: 'if the amount of money deemed necessary for non-EU nationals' "sufficient participation in everyday life" is set at a rate substantially higher than either benefits or the minimum wage, indeed, higher than that earned by half of the working population, what does this tell us about the participation in everyday life of citizens on benefits and low wages?' First, it tells us just how limited access to social, political and civil rights is among large sections of the population, including those who are citizens in legal terms. In fact, their opportunities to exercise citizenship are much more limited than those available to affluent migrants who can 'purchase' a passport and rights associated with it. Secondly, since these citizens appear technically not able to 'sufficiently participate in everyday life', what justification is there for their political or even civil rights in the context where these rights, as explained earlier, are no longer inherent but have to be individually negotiated? This is the kind of question that one day in the future a member of a parliament may ask and it illustrates the fragility of contractual rights underpinned by utilitarian values of which migration policies are a vivid reflection.

The aforementioned developments in European politics and discourse suggest that the assumingly inclusionary and progressive notion of social rights might have become a tool of exclusionary politics, which is frequently utilized by populist, anti-immigrant parties across Europe. Although undeniably these parties have capitalized on the sense of a cultural threat (Thorleifsson 2016) and a fear that has spread across the continent with regard to the changing composition of the local populations and neighbourhoods (Card, Dustman and Preston 2012), the notion of the threat to social rights posed by immigrants has also been on the agenda of these parties. This narrative has successfully tapped into actual concerns shared by many in Europe (ibid.). However, considering that the empirical evidence gives little substance to the claim that giving social rights to migrants has a negative impact on the access to such rights for citizens, it can be argued that the notion of defending the social rights of the latter group frequently voiced by populist parties has become a tool for antagonizing workers who have citizenship in a legal sense and those who do not have it (i.e. migrants). In line with what was argued previously, such breaking of potential solidarity among workers can open the door for policies that may threaten the social rights of established citizens too. Thus, one could reformulate Marx's entry on citizenship mentioned previously in this chapter by saying that citizenship can act as a tool for masking a larger project: namely that of neoliberal restructuring.[11]

NOTES

1. For example, in the case of Polish nationals, who constitute the biggest group of the post-accession migrants, one third of them plan to return to Poland (Drinkwater and Garapich 2013) and almost half of them have already returned (Karolak 2016: 5).

2. http://ec.europa.eu/dgs/legal_service/arrets/08c135_en.pdf (accessed 11 November 2016).

3. See, for example: www.best-citizenships.com (accessed 11 November 2016).

4. See: https://www.gov.uk/tier-1-investor/overview (accessed 11 November 2016).

5. See: http://www.goldenvisas.com/portugal/ (accessed 11 November 2016).

6. See: https://www.gov.uk/domestic-workers-in-a-private-household-visa (accessed 11 November 2016).

7. See: https://www.gov.uk/government/uploads/system/uploads/attachment_data/file/422047/ODW_v12_0.pdf (accessed 11 November 2016).

8. Eurostats statistics: http://ec.europa.eu/eurostat/statistics-explained/index.php/File:Population_change_by_component_(annual_crude_rates),_EU-28,_1960–2014_(1)_(per_1_000_persons)_YB15_II.png.

9. Source: http://www.mjusticia.gob.es/cs/Satellite/Portal/es/ciudadanos/tramites-gestiones-personales/nacionalidad-residencia (accessed 13 November 2016).

10. Interestingly enough, among natives and employers there is also a clear hierarchy of desirable or at least accepted migrants. Their position in this hierarchy depends not so much on their formal level of skills but rather on their country of origin, religion and ethnicity. (For the UK, see, for example, Ford 2011; McCollum and Findlay 2015.)

11. Empirical studies on whether the parties that attack migrants' social rights in the name of protecting citizens' social rights actually implement policies that benefit citizens in terms of their social citizenship, especially in the long run, could help to validate this claim.

REFERENCES

Anderson, B. 1994. 'Exodus'. *Cultural Inquiry* 20 (2): 314–327.

Anderson, B. 2010. 'Migration, immigration controls and the fashioning of precarious workers'. *Work, Employment & Society* 24 (2): 300–317.

Anderson, B. 2013. *Us and Them? The Dangerous Politics of Immigration Control.* Oxford: Oxford Scholarship Online.

Arendt, H. 1951. *The Origins of Totalitarianism.* New York, London: Harvest Book Harcourt Brace & Company.

Bauböck, R. 1994. *From aliens to citizens: Redefining the status of immigrants in Europe.* Aldershot: Avebury.

BBC. 2014a. 'Appeal court backs spouse visa change'. http://www.bbc.com/news/uk-28267305 (accessed 11 November 2016).

BBC. 2014b. 'Malta tightens passport sale terms under EU pressure'. http://www.bbc.com/news/world-europe-25959458 (accessed 11 November 2016).

Brubaker, R. 1992. *Citizenship and Nationhood in France and Germany*. Cambridge and London: Harvard University Press.

Cabrerizo M. 2013. 'El Gobierno eleva a 500.000 euros la inversión para obtener la residencia'. *elEconomista*, 29 April 2013. http://www.eleconomista.es/espana/noticias/4784979/04/13/El-Gobierno-eleva-a-500000-euros-la-inversion-para-obtener-la-residencia.html (accessed 11 November 2016).

Cangiano, A. 2014. 'Elder care and migrant labor in Europe: A demographic outlook'. *Population And Development Review* 40 (1): 131–154.

Card, D., C. Dustman and I. Preston. 2012. 'Immigration, wages, and compositional amenities'. *Norface Migration Discussion Paper* No. 2012–13.

Carrera, S. 2014. 'The framing of the Roma as abnormal EU citizens: Assessing European politics on Roma evictions and expulsions in France'. In *The Reconceptualization of European Union Citizenship*, edited by E. Guild, 33–63. Leiden: Brill Nijhoff.

Castles S. 2006. 'Guestworkers in Europe: A resurrection?' *International Migration Review* 40 (4): 741–766.

Central Statistical Office. 2015. 'Labour Force Survey in Poland – I Quarter 2015'. Warsaw: https://stat.gov.pl/files/gfx/portalinformacyjny/pl/defaultaktualnosci/5475/4/16/1/aktywnosc_ekonomiczna_ludnosci_polski_ikw_2015.pdf (accessed 11 November 2016).

Ciupijus, Z. 2011. 'Mobile Central Eastern Europeans in Britain: Successful European Union citizens and disadvantaged labour migrants?' *Work, Employment & Society* 25 (3): 540–550.

Collett E. 2014. *Future EU policy Development on Immigration and Asylum: Understanding the Challenge*. Brussels: Migration Policy Institute Europe.

Currie, S. 2007. 'De-skilled and devalued: The labour market experience of polish migrants in the UK following EU enlargement'. *The International Journal of Comparative Labour Law and Industrial Relations* 23 (1): 83–116.

De Genova, N. 2013. 'Spectacles of migrant "illegality": The scene of exclusion, the obscene of inclusion'. *Ethnic and Racial Studies* 36 (7): 1180–1198.

Drinkwater, S. and M. P. Garapich. 2013. 'Migration plans and strategies of recent polish migrants to England and Wales: Do they have any and how do they change?' *Norface Migration Discussion Paper* No. 2013–23. London.

Dzankic, J. 2012. 'The pros and cons of Ius Pecuniae: Investor citizenship in comparative perspective'. RSCAS 2012/14. EUO Working Papers. Florence.

European Commission. 2014. 'Communication from the Commission to the European Parliament and the Council on the implementation of Directive 2009/50/EC on the conditions of entry and residence of third-country nationals for the purpose of highly qualified employment'. Brussels: http://www.europarl.europa.eu/meetdocs/2014_2019/documents/com/com_com(2014)0287_/com_com(2014)0287_en.pdf (accessed 11 November 2016).

European Commission. 2015. 'Communication from the Commission to the European Parliament, the Council, the European Economic and Social Committee and the Committee of the Regions. A European agenda on migration'. Brussels: http://ec.europa.eu/dgs/home-affairs/what-we-do/policies/european-agenda-migration/

background-information/docs/communication_on_the_european_agenda_on_migration_en.pdf (accessed 11 November 2016).

European Union. 2004. 'Directive 2004/38/EC of the European Parliament and of the Council on the Right of Citizens of the Union and their family members to move and reside freely within the territory of the member states'. *Official Journal of the European Union* 158: 77–123.

Favell, A. 2008. 'The new face of east–west migration in Europe'. *Journal of Ethnic and Migration Studies* 34 (5): 701–716.

Ford, R. 2011. 'Acceptable and unacceptable immigrants: How opposition to immigration in Britain is affected by migrants' region of origin'. *Journal of Ethnic and Migration Studies* 37 (7): 1017–1037.

Harvey, D. 2005. *A Brief History of Neoliberalism.* Oxford: Oxford University Press.

Helm, T. 2016. 'Brexit: EU considers migration "emergency brake" for UK for up to seven years'. *The Guardian*, 24 July 2016. https://www.theguardian.com/world/2016/jul/24/brexit-deal-free-movement-exemption-seven-years (accessed 11 November 2016).

Huysmans, J. 2006. *The Politics of Insecurity: Fear, Migration and Asylum in the EU.* London: Routledge.

Iglicka, K. 2010. *Powroty Polaków po 2004 roku: w pętli pułapki migracji.* Warszawa: Wydawnictwo Naukowe Scholar.

IMERSO, Instituto de Mayores y Servicios Sociales. 2005. *Cuidado a la dependencia e Inmigracion, Informe de Resultados.* Coleccion Estudios Serie Dependencia.

Joppke, C. 2010. *Citizenship and Immigration.* Cambridge: Polity Press.

Karolak, M. 2016. 'From potential to actual social remittances? Exploring how polish return migrants cope with difficult employment conditions'. *Central and Eastern Migration Review* 5 (2): 21–39.

Kofman, E. 2008. 'Managing migration and citizenship in Europe: Towards an overarching framework'. In *Governing International Labour Migration: Current Issues, Challenges and Dilemmas*, edited by C. Gabriel and H. Pellerin, 13–26. New York: Routledge.

Kymlicka, W. 1995. *Multicultural Citizenship: A Liberal Theory of Minority Rights.* Oxford and New York: Oxford University Press.

Marshall, H. T. 1950. *Citizenship and Social Class and Other Essays.* Cambridge: University Press.

Maslowski, S. 2015. 'The expulsion of European Union citizens from the Host Member State: Legal grounds and practice'. *Central and Eastern European Migration Review* (June): 1–25.

McCollum, D. and A. Findlay. 2015. '"Flexible" workers for "flexible" jobs? The labour market function of A8 migrant labour in the UK'. *Work, Employment & Society* 29 (3): 427–443.

McLoughlin, S. and R. Münz. 2011. 'Temporary and circular migration: opportunities and challenges'. Working Paper No. 35. Brussels: European Policy Center.

Meardi, G. 2012. *Social Failures of EU Enlargement: A Case of Workers Voting with Their Feet.* New York: Routledge.

Menz, G. and A. Caviedes. 2010. *Labour Migration in Europe*. London: Palgrave Macmillan.

Mezzadra, S. and B. Neilson. 2013. *Border as Method or the Multiplication of Labor*. Durham and London: Duke University Press.

OECD/European Union. 2015. *Indicators of Immigrant Integration 2015: Settling In*. Paris: OECD Publishing.

Ong, A. 2006. *Neoliberalism as Exception: Mutations in Citizenship and Sovereignty*. Durham, NC and London: Duke University Press.

Papadopoulos, D. and S. V. Tsianos. 2013. 'After Citizenship: Autonomy of Migration, Organisational Ontology and Mobile commons'. *Citizenship Studies* 17 (2): 178–196.

Rodríguez, V. R. 2012. *Inmigración y cuidados de mayores en la Comunidad de Madrid*. Madrid: Fundacion BBVA.

Reuters. 2015. 'Poland to take 60 Syrian Christian families-PM'. http://www.reuters.com/article/mideast-crisis-poland-christians-idUSW8N0XX02R20150526 (accessed 11 November 2016).

Sloan, A. 2015. 'UK tied visa system "turning domestic workers into modern-day slaves"'. *The Guardian,* 17 March 2015. https://www.theguardian.com/world/2015/mar/17/uk-tied-visa-system-turning-domestic-workers-into-modern-day-slaves (accessed 11 November 2016).

Somers, M. 2008. *Genealogies of Citizenship: Knowledge, Markets, and the Right to Have Rights*. Cambridge: Cambridge University Press.

Soysal, Y. N. 1994. *Limits of Citizenship: Migrants and Postnational Membership in Europe*. Chicago: University of Chicago Press.

Standing, G. 2011. *The Precariat: The New Dangerous Class*. London and New York: Bloomsbury Academic.

Stasiulis, D. 2008. 'Revisiting the permanent-temporary labour migration dichotomy'. In *Governing International Labour Migration: Current Issues, Challenges and Dilemmas,* edited by C. Gabriel C. and H. Pellerin, 95–111. New York: Routledge.

Therborn, G. 2013. *The Killing Fields of Inequality*. Cambridge and Malden: Polity Press.

Thorleifsson, C. 2016. Migrasjonskrisen: Høyeradikale responser. *Internatjonal Politic* 7 (2): 1–9.

Trevena, P. 2013. 'Why do highly educated migrants go for low-skilled jobs? A case study of Polish graduates working in London'. In *Mobility in Transition: Migration Patterns after EU Enlargement,* edited by B. Glorius, I. Grabowska-Lusińska and A. Kuvik, 169–190. Amsterdam: Amsterdam University Press.

Wintour, P. 2014. 'EU migrants face new barrier to accessing UK state benefits'. *The Guardian,* 19 February 2014. https://www.theguardian.com/uk-news/2014/feb/19/eu-migrants-welfare-benefits-earnings (accessed 11 November 2016).

Section II

SPECTRUM OF MIGRANTS' INCLUSION AND EXCLUSION

Chapter II.1

'Hidden Injuries' of Migration From CEE

Polish Workers in the UK

Radosław Polkowski

Following the 2004 EU enlargement, a large number of citizens from the new accession states have exercised their rights to reside and work in another member state. On the one hand, these migrants may appear to be successful EU citizens who, without hesitation, took advantage of the freedoms newly available to them (Ciupijus 2011). However, recent literature has also argued that behind their mobility lies the plight created by 'low-road' neoliberalism so that, in essence, this migration can be linked as much to the loss of social and employment rights as to the acquisition of new rights as European citizens (Woolfson and Sommers 2008). This argument is succinctly captured by the notion of *austeriat* used by Anuska and Woolfson (2014) to denote workers from the Baltic States who migrated as a result of austerity policies implemented since 2007 in their own countries.

The following discussion contributes to these debates on the link between neoliberalism, citizenship and migration. It does so by reconceptualising the notion of citizenship in terms proposed by Anderson (2013): namely, as membership of a community of value. This concept was briefly introduced in the previous chapter (I.3) and is elaborated on below where it is argued that it indicates an important social process, namely, one in which states include and exclude individuals through unequal allocations of autonomy, recognition and respect; a situation which Therborn (2013) referred to as 'existential inequality'. The chapter looks at these experiences of inclusion and exclusion in a neoliberal state from the subject-centred perspective and, drawing on Williams's (1961) cultural and literary theory, conceives of them as a structure of feeling.

FACETS OF CITIZENSHIP

A standard way of conceptualising citizenship is to equate it with a legal status that binds individuals together in a polity and gives them a range of substantive rights. The best-known conceptualisation in this respect is Marshall's (1950) civic, political and social citizenship. However, recent conceptual and empirical developments in migration studies invite a reconceptualisation of this idea. As proposed in the previous chapter of this book, 'modern states portray themselves not as arbitrary collections of people hung together by a common legal status but as a community of value, composed of people who share common ideals and (exemplary) patterns of behaviour' (Anderson 2013: 2). Such a reconceptualisation of states from political communities to communities of value prompts also a reconceptualisation of the notion of citizenship. Hence Anderson (2013: 4) argued that in modern states 'immigration and citizenship are not simply about legal status, but fundamentally about status in the sense of worth and honour' (Anderson 2013: 4) and that states include and exclude individuals based on how far they live up to certain normative ideals. This makes the distinction between citizens and non-citizens somewhat obscure, in that those included in a legal sense of citizenship can be excluded in a discursive sense as 'failed citizens' (Anderson 2013) and have access to fewer rights than non-citizens who are included as 'good migrants' (Ong 2006: 6–7).

This formulation of citizenship touches upon the subtle forms of exclusion and marginalisation that Therborn (2013) refers to as existential inequality, which is concerned with allocations of autonomy, recognition and respect, as opposed to material or vital inequality, which refers to the distribution of material resources. It also resonates with Arendt's (1951) notion of citizenship as 'the right to have rights', which means a right to be treated as a moral equal. In Anderson's (2013) framework, social recognition and respect are connected to the notions of 'good citizen' and 'failed citizen', which states manifest through policies and discourses (Anderson 2013).

It has been proposed that nowadays citizens' 'worth, value, and inclusion are accordingly determined by contractual successes or failures in relationship to utility' (Somers 2008: 41). This, in turn, is seen to stem from what has commonly been referred to as neoliberalism. For example, it has been suggested that those who exhibit neoliberal ethics – the self-propulsive and self-governed individuals (Ong 2006: 16) – are rewarded by state policies and state discourses, whereas those who are deemed 'lacking in neoliberal potential may be treated as less-worthy subjects' and 'are constructed as excludable populations' (Ong 2006: 16). With regard to CEE, literature has documented the 'proselytizing of a rhetoric of responsibility, self-help, flexibility, and choice' and the manufacturing of the new ideal of a 'good citizen' who is self-authoring, enterprising and proactive in securing his or her economic well-being and, as such, is juxtaposed against 'a passive individual coddled by the paternalism of socialism' (Makovicky 2014: 2). Particularly illustrative of these normative transformations is Dunn's study (2004) of the formerly state-owned enterprise that after the collapse of state socialism in Poland was acquired by a US-based corporation. Through her exploration of new management techniques introduced by the private owner, the author unpacks fundamental transformations, which accompanied the Polish journey to capitalism, in the conception of what it means to be a person. Specifically, she documents the construction of an ideal of a privatised individual or asocial monad who acts like a scaled-down version of a corporation.

Certainly, such normative images are contested by individuals. The typology proposed by Williams (1961) neatly illustrates this by showing different positions that a person can take in relation to normative ideals and social ethics, ranging from complete internalisation (servant), through pragmatic obedience without internalisation for the purpose of maintaining one's social and possibly economic existence (subject), up to their complete rejection (exile and vagrant), or active struggle against them (rebel). Nevertheless, whatever the strategy used, individuals position themselves in relation to the normative ideal in one way or another. They can pursue other ways of living but at severe material and emotional cost. In terms of the latter type of cost, a recent psychological study indicates that, whatever our personal values, self-worth flows mostly from living up to prevailing social values (Becker and Vignoles 2014). Consequently, even the 'vagrants' and 'rebels' who reject the normative prescriptions of neoliberalism will remain affected by them.

This observation opens a whole array of questions about the effects of neoliberalism on individuals' emotional experiences. These experiences can be conceptualised in terms of structure of feeling, a concept coined by Williams (1961) that can be best explained by comparing it to the previously invoked notion of a 'good citizen'. While the concept of 'good citizen' deals with public ideals, a structure of feeling 'has to deal not only with the public ideals but with their omissions and consequences, as lived' (Williams 1961: 80); the former conveys a valued system of behaviour and attitudes that 'is taught formally and informally' (Williams 1961: 63), whereas a structure of feeling is the 'actual experience through which these are lived' (Williams 1961: 64). The 'good citizen', or a related concept of a social character, is about the ethic of a society, whereas a structure of feeling is about the deepest feelings about the experience of this ethic (Williams 1961: 85). It is 'a particular community of experience hardly needing expression, through which the characteristics of our way of life that an external analyst could describe are in some way passed, giving them a particular and characteristic colour' (Williams 1961: 64). In short, a structure of feeling should be understood as the individual but collectively shared lived experience of values, ideals and ethics conveyed by states through discourses and policies.

While Williams (1961) used his concept chiefly in literary studies, he understood literature as just one of the 'articulate records' of structures of feeling, thus suggesting that his concept has a more general application. One example of a structure of feeling that can be identified outside literary work is the notion of hidden injuries coined by Sennett and Cobb (1972), who observed a certain emotional quality to the lives of working-class people which, in turn, was directly related to a broader value system of American society at that time. This emotional quality was characterised in Scheff's (2000: 9) interpretation as chronic feelings of shame. The example of Sennett and Cobb's (1972) study is particularly useful in that it also explicates the key question about Williams's concept: why 'structures' and not just 'feelings'? The notion of structure is used to distinguish these feelings and emotions from personal and everyday experiences that are more ad hoc and felt under specific circumstances or stimuli. In contrast, structures of feelings are continuous or, as explained by Scheff (2000), chronic; they underlie long-term motivations and choices in people's lives. Moreover, they form persistent relationships with social systems and social structures. As a result, a structure of feeling is 'as firm and definite as "structure" suggests, yet it operates in the most delicate and least tangible parts of our activity' (Williams 1961: 64).

All in all, while Anderson's (2013) approach is concerned primarily with how modern states include and exclude individuals in terms of recognition and respect, the present chapter looks at how individuals experience such inclusion and exclusion and whether that can influence their migration decisions. The chapter is particularly interested in the effects of neoliberal discourses and ethics because, according to the literature introduced above, they occupy a prominent place in modern states.

Viewed in this light, the focus on Polish migrants in this chapter is motivated not only by the fact that they are the largest migrant group from 2004 accession countries; they are also migrants from a country which has been at the forefront of neoliberal reforms in the region, as captured by the notion of 'shock therapy' and reflected in key labour market indicators (Trappman 2011). The major recipient of Polish post-accession migrants has been the UK – the country which has also been in the driver's seat when it comes to implementing privatisation, deregulation and welfare retrenchment policies that characterise neoliberalism. The study draws on interviews from two places in the UK: the north of Ireland and Scotland. However, despite differences between them in terms of context of reception, the present article focuses specifically on similarities in interviewees' narratives in the two destinations and links them with the political economy of migrants' country of origin. The data comes from thirty-nine semi-structured interviews with a purposive sample of interviewees, who were reached through personal contacts and the snowball technique. The interviews were conducted in 2013 with follow-ups in 2014. All interviews were conducted in Polish, transcribed, translated into English, and analysed by coding that was initially performed 'closely to the data' (Charmaz 2006: 47), and then informed by theoretical concepts that made it possible to take the analysis to a more abstract level.

The data analysis discussed in the following section shows that the ideal of a self-propulsive, self-governed, self-made, freely choosing and independent individual oriented on economic success – an ideal that in the literature introduced above was associated with neoliberalism – occupies an important place in people's narratives on migration and seems to underline their migration decisions, in particular those regarding settlement in the UK. It is argued that migration is a response to the structure of feeling characterised by a sense of shame which emerges from a failure of these subjects to live up to the ideal of a neoliberal subject. However, the latter part of the chapter also shows how migration can involve reinterpretation of these ideals and result in a person becoming a 'vagrant' or a 'rebel' in opposition to the neoliberal ethic.

THE MAKING OF A NEOLIBERAL CITIZEN THROUGH MIGRATION

The data analysis suggested that, apart from providing better income and employment conditions, work abroad enabled many Polish migrants to exercise modes of agency and subjectivity that were relevant to them and which derived from the political economy of their place of origin. This theme appeared to a greater or a lesser degree, and in different forms, in all interviews conducted for the present study but it can be best illustrated with a few cases presented in this section. Starting with the case of Monika, a 28-year-old woman from a medium-sized town in southern Poland who worked part-time as a waitress to earn a living during her time at university, we can observe the significance of the ideal of the self-propulsive, self-maintaining, independent and self-made citizen. Monika went to the UK in 2005 for a summer job only but, after prolonging her stay repeatedly, she eventually decided to drop her studies and settle there. She started with a number of low-skilled jobs found through temporary work agencies, as well as informal part-time positions, until she was eventually able to obtain a full-time contract in a factory. When asked when she started to feel that Scotland was her permanent home, she referred to that low-paid, manual but still stable, full-time, secure job:

> Probably when I worked in [anonymised company] because it was a permanent job. ... So I felt confident. ... I felt that I was coping well. I could earn a

> living together with my partner and we were self-sufficient. … we felt that we stood up on our feet. … That we are now responsible for ourselves. That we are not dependent on our parents but that we work for ourselves. It depends on us whether we have money to pay bills and so on. So we felt stronger. And it probably also was the reason why we decided to settle here. I mean, to treat this place more like a home even though there was no such a permanent place at that time yet. (Monika, 28 years old, clerical worker)

Monika's explanation of the source of her emotional citizenship is marked with recurring themes of self-sufficiency, independence, being on one's own and being in charge of one's life. In a way, Monika's migration is a story of transition into adulthood. However, this adulthood is not a neutral category; instead, it is an ideal of personhood with significant ideological charge, and it can also be linked with a notion of citizenship. In classical liberal thought, adulthood is vested with ideals of self-maintenance, self-governance, and self-discipline which give people the right to participate in the public sphere. On the other hand, those deemed as lacking such qualities might be assigned to the private sphere, which is what historically happened to women and also men without property, who were formerly excluded from many political rights, or were even stigmatised and incarcerated, as were the poor, the 'idle', and the mentally ill in Europe's history. Sennett (2003: 107) describes the connection between dependency and citizenship through a rather graphic metaphor:

> Of all those who have invoked the shame of dependency, it could justly be said that they have a horror of the primal maternal scene: the infant suckling at the mother's breast. They fear that through force or desire, adult men will continue to suckle; the mother's breast becomes the state. What's distinctive about liberalism is its view of the man who disengages his lips; he becomes a citizen.

According to Sennett (2003: 101), dependence is nowadays the major threat to a sense of worth: 'in the public realm dependence appears shameful'. This might be even more relevant with regard to CEE, where the figure of the passive citizen relying on the state can be associated with the discredited state-socialist model, thus becoming persona non grata in the brave new world of neoliberalism. What emerges from Sennett's (2003) argument is that the liberal discourses that place a value on independence and self-maintenance affect individuals' access to social recognition and respect or, in other words, their citizenship as 'status in the sense of worth and honour' (Anderson 2013: 4). This resonates with the pride Monika derives from the narrative of her migration in which she presents herself as a brave person who took destiny into her own hands and just went abroad. In contrast, her projected self-perception from the viewpoint of the generalised other in Poland is marked with anticipation of social failure and shame encapsulated in the figure of a 'loser':

> If we returned they would treat you more like a loser than a person who was brave enough to pack her suitcase and go. … You would be perceived more as a loser … people [in Poland] are already thirty years old but sometimes they still live with parents and they are practically so tied up that they can't leave home because their earnings do not let them do so. Despite the fact that they work in their field and are graduates, and they do doctorates or they already finished doctorates, they are still tied up. (Monika, 28 years old, clerical worker)

The same pursuit of independence, self-governance and self-maintenance was associated with Judyta's decision not to return to Poland. Interestingly, having graduated from her doctoral course in Poland and still being unable to sustain an independent adult life, she epitomises the example provided by Monika in the quote above:

> In Poland I would have to live at my mum's because I would not have been able to afford to rent a flat on my own. I just wasn't interested in this kind of life … Later when my mum came here I lived with her. But I didn't live with her really – she lived with me. And this is how it is at the moment too. Mum lives with me. This makes a big difference … it's a different balance of power. (Judyta, 36 years old, self-employed professional worker)

The above experience was not exclusive to female interviewees. For example, Marek, a 35-year-old manufacturing labourer, felt that in Poland he wasn't able to realise the ideal of an adult citizen, or that, to use Sennett's (2003) terminology, he became infantilised by having to 'keep sucking on mother's breast':

> I moved out from parent's house only once in Poland but it was only for half a year or so. I tried, you know, when I was a sales representative as I mentioned earlier. I wanted to see what life on your own would be like. Independently. But I realized that it didn't make sense. Expenses were higher than earnings. … So you see, here in the UK when I wanted to move out I already had the basis for doing so. As I'm saying, I could afford to live freely on my own. (Marek, 35 years old, manufacturing labourer)

The turning point of such narratives is the contrast between being independent, self-sufficient, and free in one place vis-à-vis being tied up and dependent in the other place. In Sennett's (2003) terms, it is a contrast between the social character of a liberal adult citizen and that of an infantilised, dependent social loser. What these migrants fear is falling back on the mercy of social institutions, whether the family or the state. This fear is visible in the recurring narratives in which migrants portrayed themselves as economically active and contributing citizens by distancing themselves from the passive individuals who rely on the state – 'benefit tourists' and the native 'benefit scroungers' – thus drawing upon neoliberal discourses of self-maintenance, economic independence and economic utility. For example, in the following quote, Tadeusz and Irena distanced themselves from the image of 'benefit tourists' by enacting the neoliberal discourse of individual effort, self-making and self-propulsion:

Tadeusz: You can't deny that people come here and take advantage of everything.
Irena: Coming here, taking benefits. We've never used benefits, somehow we managed on our own. We have two healthy hands, legs and we manage somehow. But if someone comes just to wheedle out money, then really … you keep someone like this at arm's length.
Tadeusz: We don't need this. I will find a job but the other person will wheedle out … no, you have to call things as they are. One day this country has to do something, right? Because this benefits system, really.
(Tadeusz and Irena, 34 and 31 years old, cleaners)

Adrianna in the quote below draws on a similar discourse when calling on David Cameron to eventually fix this negative aspect of the country:

> I'm not fond of this 'benefit immigration' which people talk about a lot here. That we come and steal local jobs, take benefits for nothing and get flats. I can understand their frustration because I also pay taxes but I've never made use of any social assistance. People who get this social assistance don't really deserve it. Besides this, Poles are crafty people. It's their national feature. If there's some easy money available, they would take it. So I absolutely agree with Cameron. (Adrianna, 33 years old, Scotland)

The importance of proving one's worth through employment and hard work surfaced vividly and strongly in Marek's narrative, when he recollected the advice he had received from his friend just before leaving Poland:

> The most important is that you know the basics of the language, know when to say no, to be polite. But above all – and excuse my language – to work your ass off. Cause that's exactly what he told me. To prove your worth and that you are not a pussy who came here to be a slacker, not working. (Marek, 35 years old, manufacturing labourer)

Migrants also talked negatively of British citizens who rely on state help but there is no space to quote it here. What matters is that these narratives are consistent with Anderson's (2013) argument that migrants become guardians of a community of value in the receiving country in an attempt to justify their presence. Moreover, they claim their rights to citizenship and belonging by drawing on the neoliberal discourses of economic independence from the state and economic utility through employment, as can be illustrated with a brief quote from Monika, whose case was introduced earlier: 'Besides the language, nothing really sets us apart from other people. You know, we pay taxes, we work, and we don't rely on the state. We are like every other citizen'.

The fear of social failure and thus a looming sense of shame that underlies the neoliberal ethics of self-making conveyed in these narratives can also be seen in the frequent narratives about pressure to work and study in order to succeed, which are connected with the persistent feeling of being inadequate:

> The Poles are full of complexes because since they are young they are inculcated with messages that: 'If you don't study, you will end up with a shovel! If you don't achieve this, you will be this and that! If you don't get a degree …' You know, you always get a whipping. … There's been always: 'You have to! Have to! Have to!' … And you will always feel inadequate. (Monika, 28 years old, clerical worker)
>
> It's always been: study otherwise you gonna be a street cleaner. Study so that you have a better … work hard now so that later you can have it easy. Whipping, you know … In Poland everyone has a MA title before surname. (Aneta, 34 years old, waitress)

On the one hand, migration may appear as an escape from the pressure of social expectations that these people subjectively connect chiefly with Poland. On the other hand, once in the UK, Monika, like other interviewees (with the exception of Aneta whose case is unique and is discussed later in this chapter), made consistent and substantial efforts to improve her status by pursuing further education, polishing up her portfolio, and gaining carefully chosen experience which led her to a respectable white-collar job. Therefore, her migration is not the rejection of but, rather, is written into the ethic of self-making through hard work and individual effort, which she explicitly disavowed and which caused her suffering by making her feel inadequate.

The narrative exemplified above might encapsulate the experiences common to this generation of young people in post-socialist Poland for whom the free market economy opened up new opportunities for social mobility, additionally aided by unprecedented freedom of geographical mobility, while at the same time exposing them to a highly competitive environment where discourses of individual responsibility and success in the emerging knowledge economy, underlined by belief in complete, unconstrained self-enterprise, created anxieties about social failure and a sense of shame. These feelings can be thought of as 'hidden injuries' in that they are similar in character to the emotional suffering experienced by the subjects of the study by Sennett and Cobb (1972). Inasmuch as they emerge from the experience of a certain ethic and certain ideals, they can be conceived of as a particular structure of feeling. The cult of employment and economic utility conveyed in these narratives was first instilled in Poland under state socialism, with its policy of responsibility to work, and its propagandistic championing of the figure of the waged labourer. It was then reaffirmed, in a different fashion, by neoliberal capitalism.

The hidden injuries of a neoliberal subject (i.e. the one driven by the ideals of self-enterprise, self-sufficiency, self-propulsion and independence) can also be vividly illustrated with the case of Grzegorz – a 39-year-old high-skilled professional from Poland. His labour market trajectory was very different from the cases discussed so far whose subjects, while in Poland, struggled with low incomes or insecure employment, or, for that matter, with both of these predicaments. Not only did he hold a well-paid position in the UK, but he also had a rather privileged situation in Poland in that he had always worked in his profession and later, discouraged by the way his boss treated him, started his own very profitable company. However, he felt that his entrepreneurial skills and freedoms were stifled by the overwhelming, uninhibited bureaucracy:

> It is something that has to be mentioned here … that the way one runs a company in Poland, that virtually the very moment you register the company, with some kind of invisible pen your name is written down on a list of potential thieves who want to rob the state budget. During the five years of running this company I had two controls from state officials. They didn't look exactly like from the Uklad Zamkniety[1] but you get the idea. (Grzegorz, 39 years old, professional worker)

Grzegorz's narrative manifests Poland as a country that does not live up to modern standards and where the unrestrained powers of the state stifle the expression of his entrepreneurial spirit. He contrasted this with his admiration for the British ability to 'squeeze out' individual talents, thus constructing Britain as a community of value more suitable to the social character of neoliberal times, as this short excerpt from a much longer quote illustrates: 'What I admire Brits for in general is the British labour market. The way they can squeeze – maybe it's a bad word but still – squeeze out from a person what one is good at'.

Grzegorz, in his narrative about the sense of home, retrospectively describes himself in terms of an ideal of a self-driven, rational *Homo economicus* who crosses borders in the pursuit of self-interest and individual success ('my home is where my wallet is'), but we can also sense that there is more to his emotional citizenship than money:

> I found my little homeland in Belfast. And although some time ago I used to say that my homeland is where my wallet is, now I can frankly say that absolutely it is not just about it. That's not all. Here I can really say that I anchored in this city.

When asked what caused this change from purely financial motivation to emotional attachment to the place, he replied with a very illustrative metaphor that is worth quoting at length:

> Let me use one of my favourite though rather brutal metaphors. Poland for me is like an alcoholic mother: I love her because she gave birth to me. She has always had the best feelings for me and so on but she drinks now. … So now there is a question: what should I do? I am not able to be next to her cause she doesn't even want me to be there. But, on the other hand, it is a mother. She gave me life and so on. These are the kind of dilemmas. Of course, I am not able to be next to her cause she doesn't even want me to be there. … On the other hand, Belfast is a distant, distant aunt who loves me as much as she can. … So I would say that if I was to honestly, without being influenced by emotions but just consider everything with a paper and a calculator and say which one of these mothers – in inverted commas – gave me more, I would say that, well, the aunt.

In a way, he again manifests himself as a rational decision-maker ('without being influenced by emotions', 'consider everything with a pen and a calculator'), but we see that his narrative is loaded with emotion as he brings in the language of intimate family relations, comparing one country to an 'alcoholic mother' and the other to a 'loving aunt' who gives him attention and recognition, possibly through the labour market that he praised earlier. Therefore, looking into Grzegorz's narrative, his decision to migrate and settle in the UK appears to be driven, at least to some extent, by feelings of misrecognition and a sense of shame in one place and the opposite feelings of recognition and pride in another place. Apparently, even in the case of this affluent, high-skilled worker, the self-entrepreneurial move of a rational *Homo economicus* is accompanied by 'hidden injuries'.

Another impact that neoliberal capitalism in Poland had in the sphere of values was through the growth of the importance of consumption and the unleashing of consumerist aspirations (Sowa 2012), which, as argued by Ziółkowski (1999), became essential to issues of social belonging and identity. Tadeusz and Irena's account of their decision to settle in the UK is underlined by exactly these values and is illustrative of a total of thirteen interviewees in the sample:

Irena: We have something that holds us here. Here we have something that we achieved ourselves. Because in Poland we have completely nothing. Besides

family [laughter] we have nothing so. …
Interviewer: What have you achieved?
Irena: A house, a car.
Tadeusz: These are materialistic things.
Irena: Materialistic. Because generally you feel confident here cause you've got something. In Poland over the same period of time you would probably not have achieved this. Maybe we would build a house but whether we would be able to finish it – I doubt it. This is the reality. … It makes us happy that we didn't ask parents for anything. Neither of them. We try to do everything by ourselves.
(Tadeusz and Irena, 34 and 31 years old, cleaners)

The institution of family, which they mention followed by a brief laugh, is not a source of their sense of belonging. Instead, like Monika, they also invoke notions of individualism, independence and individual success, especially in the concluding sentence. But what is most striking is their outspokenness about materialistic considerations. However, what appears on the surface to be a materialistic value orientation (Kazimierska et al. 2011) can be read as a reflection of more fundamental and socially constructed individual yearnings for existential equality (Therborn 2013) and for citizenship as 'status in a sense of worth and honour' (Anderson 2013: 4). Marek's account of his decision to settle in the UK is also framed within the notion of having and not having, as the two contrasting worlds in his biography that influence his perception of the UK (specifically Northern Ireland) as his home and, hence, the decision to settle here:

> It's hard to explain how I felt at that time. You see, I had two different worlds: in one world I had nothing, completely nothing. In Poland I didn't have a job, I didn't have anything. Whereas suddenly: bang! Completely different world: Ireland. I have money, I have everything, I have a roof above my head, I have … I bought a car maybe after three months of being here ... After two months I could afford a car. Ireland for me is my home. (Marek, 35 years old, manufacturing labourer)

SELF-MANAGEMENT OF A NEOLIBERAL CITIZEN THROUGH MIGRATION

What emerges from the discussion above is that for CEE workers going abroad is not necessarily a positive, self-entrepreneurial move of a rational *Homo economicus* but, in a way, an escape underpinned by emotional rather than purely rational factors. Behind their stories of successful lives abroad lies a structure of feeling characterised by 'hidden injuries' in the form of feelings of shame and fear of social failure. While 'naive empiricism' would take such narratives of success through work abroad at face value as a positive case for migration, the term 'hidden injuries' helps to bring out a more complex picture. Specifically, it indicates that stories of successful life abroad are perhaps just an ointment that covers the underlying injuries, consisting of feelings of shame and a fear of social failure, that these people experienced in their home countries and which persist even many years after migration. Indeed, data analysis identified these feelings in interviews with people who had lived in the UK for at least five years and in most cases longer than this. Therefore, it seems that there is some baggage that migrants continue to carry with them, which persistently influences the way they interpret and experience their country of destination. In turn, this experience of migration continuously shapes their migration choices, specifically the choices of whether to return or to stay.

Therefore, such a structure of feeling may play a role in self-management of these migrants. Elias (1978) suggested that shame acted as a tool of social control through self-discipline. In his analysis of the Enlightenment, he traced the process of increased emphasis on self-regulation of individuals which, despite the period's emphasis on rationality, is not achieved through rational means but, instead, through the emotion of shame. Sennett (1980) also hypothesised shame as a tool of control, in this case by managers over workers. Similarly, we can observe the disciplining power of shame influencing choices regarding migration, return and settlement.

In this way, the structure of feeling characterised by shame appears also to have certain implications for social change or social reproduction. Based on psychological and sociological studies, Scheff (2002) argued that there are two pathways to unacknowledged shame: hostility/conflict and withdrawal/silence. What emerges from the analysis thus far is that migration can also be a strategy of dealing with a sense of shame, in that it allows one to escape the context that caused the feelings and to forge narratives of individual achievement through individual effort and hard work abroad. It also allows one to mask shame with consumption or hostility towards 'benefit scroungers'. Consequently, the ethic which created the 'hidden injuries' remains intact. However, the next section suggests that migration can also have the opposite impact: leading an individual to reject the ethics and ideals which caused his or her suffering.

THE UNMAKING OF A NEOLIBERAL CITIZEN

The structure of feeling characterised by a sense of shame and other anxieties have at times culminated in radical re-evaluation of one's valued ways of living, leading people to become close to what Williams (1961) describes as exiles, vagrants or rebels against the neoliberal ethic. For example, Aneta – a 34-year-old waitress living in Scotland – experienced the same sense of pressure to succeed through individual effort and hard work as Monika did, as exemplified in their nearly identical quotes discussed previously in this chapter. However, while Monika appeared to pursue the ideal of a self-made (wo)man in the UK, Aneta challenged it:

> At one point I realized that it's all bullshit. That it doesn't have to be this way. … That you don't have to do as the system tells you, that I don't have to study, I don't have to be a super-educated individual and have lots of money to be happy. (Aneta, 34 years old, waitress)

Unlike Monika, she did not pursue further education and upskilling in the UK and, instead, remained employed in casual, low-skilled settings like serving in coffee shops. In a way, her migration was an exile from one community of value (i.e. that of imagined Poland). At the same time, however, she was a vagrant with no strong sense of belonging either in Poland or in the UK, one who disavowed the consumerist and materialistic values of both societies. Interestingly, she used the term *emigracz* to describe herself. It is a made-up word that is a combination of Polish words *emigrant* and *gracz* (player), or 'emi-player' in English: a free spirit who migrates but is not embedded in any of the places.

Another challenge to neoliberal ideals and ethics is visible in the case of Roman, 35 years old, who after graduating in business studies, quickly achieved a high-status and well-paid position in Poland, working as manager in a large corporation, thus seizing the opportunities for rapid career advancement created by newly unleashed market forces during the neoliberal transformation. This success in his working life was accompanied by 'success' in a dimension of private life which at some level was an extension of his corporate life. It consisted of affluence and social status anchored in an engagement to an aspiring lawyer whose father assumed the role of a benevolent manager by offering Roman materialistic perks – for example, a house that he bought for the couple – but, in return, demanded a subordination that Roman found increasingly hard to deal with. This life was accompanied by what he describes as 'internal conflicts' which culminated in a dramatic reappraisal of his values facilitated by the experience of migration. While his extended narrative of this transformation cannot be quoted at length, chosen excerpts from it are used by way of illustration:

> I had a lot of money … listen, here I don't earn more than I used to in Poland. So income doesn't matter. … It was different in Poland cause personally I'm a good person inside and in Poland internal conflicts arouse inside of me. … I demanded a lot from myself and the same from employees subordinate to

> me … I thought that one has to have money, status, a car, a house, a family … you know, a stereotypical Polish way of thinking. … So you keep shaking like a fish caught in a net and you feel as if you were in a cup and someone was swirling this cup and you just swirl in it like a ball. … I was very young, stubborn, loyal, unhealthily ambitious and disciplined or, in other words, young and stupid. … I was programmed to possess, succeed, compete. (Roman, 35 years old, shop assistant)

The internal conflicts he talks about can be read as the 'hidden injuries' of a subject who, in a Faustian bargain offered by unfolding capitalism, enjoyed economic prosperity and a sense of power and status enabled by impressive consumption capabilities, but, paradoxically, sensed a loss of control, clearly captured in his metaphor of feeling like 'a ball in a cup that somebody else swirls'. As in the narratives of previous interviewees, in his account one can also notice the motif of becoming an adult. But here it takes on a different character: it is not associated with becoming economically independent and self-sufficient; instead, it is about reaching some new level of awareness about life and the values important in it.

With his extended criticism of the ills of modern life, quoted below in brief excerpts, he appears to embody Williams's (1961) rebel. However, rather than a progressive orientation towards a better future, his rebellion signifies a nostalgic retreat to the idealised past, captured in the memory of his parents' relationship, in contrast with his own business-like one: 'I have wonderful parents and I really liked their relationship. They lived peacefully all their life and I really liked it', explained Roman. His internal conflicts might have emerged from a clash between idealised ways of living that he remembers from his years of growing up in Poland, and the onset of free market reforms and neoliberal competitiveness in the 1990s which coincide with his adult life. His migration is not just an act of geographical mobility but also an ascetic retreat to stability and peace anchored in conservative values of the traditional family, communitarianism and anti-materialistic orientations:

> I threw everything into the bin. I don't read newspapers, I don't watch TV. … I shun politics … I have a simple model of phone and at home I have the standard equipment one needs. … For me the family and family values are the most important. … You should also give something from yourself. So I've been keen on participating in some social events, I've been helping and doing a lot of things for free.

The coming of neoliberal policies to Poland was accompanied by ideological efforts to promote lifestyles of uncritical consumers and workers: Marcuse's one-dimensional men who serve to reproduce the system (Sowa 2010). In a sense, Roman (as well as Aneta) is the antithesis of this image, as he becomes very aware of the ideological machine which tried to instil certain values in him:

> When I came here I had adverts milling around my mind. When I closed my eyes I would see adverts, photos and magazines. The media that shape your values and lifestyle and you take it as your own. But in reality it's not yours.

Roman's migration cannot be easily accounted for by approaches rooted in classical economics. If they were, we would expect him to return to Poland or not leave in the first place since his economic and labour market situation was better there. Nor can it be seen as an escape from the material circumstances of low-road neoliberalism (Woolfson and Sommers 2008), since he occupied a rather privileged position in that system. Instead, his migration appears to be an escape from the lived experience of the ethic of this system; in other words, it is an outcome of a specific structure of feeling that is characterised by 'hidden injuries' in the form of psychological suffering caused by a sense of lack of autonomy and control.

DISCUSSION

The framework drafted in this chapter gives a new dimension to the role of the sending country and how its economy and ideologies shape and affect migrants' choices. To recollect, Woolfson and Sommers (2008) pointed to low-road neoliberalism in CEE, characterised by poor labour standards and low incomes, as a force driving its people outwards to Western Europe. Ciupijus (2013) has called for further exploration of the effects on migration of neoliberal policies in post-socialist countries. This chapter responded to this call by suggesting that this migration is shaped not only by the material circumstances created by neoliberalism but also by the normative ideals that it champions. If not driven by values of individual success, self-maintenance, independence, consumerism and self-enterprise; these migrants might instead have stayed in their homeland, keeping their heads down and accepting poor pay and labour conditions, while surviving with the help of some welfare provisions. Alternatively, they might have engaged in collective strategies of coping with these social problems. Instead, they chose an individualistic strategy of pursuing their life goals abroad. Moreover, once in the new country, they tended to reproduce the neoliberal discourses of self-making, self-sufficiency and economic utility. In a way, we can see these CEE migrants as ideal neoliberal subjects: they didn't procrastinate in exercising their newly acquired mobility rights but left their communities and families behind to realise the ideal of the proactive, individualised self-entrepreneur: the hero of the epoch.

The reason why they have chosen individualistic strategies rather than collective ones may be partly explained by looking at the emotional level of the structure of feeling that characterises the subjects of this study: the 'hidden injuries' of shame. According to Scheff's (2002) thesis, acknowledging these feelings could help in articulating the problem at the heart of the situation and channelling the focus away from individual failures to systemic failures. It could redirect people from the search for individual ways of suppressing shame towards newly encouraged participation in governance (Scheff 2002). Instead, for many people migration appears to play a role more like that of a metaphorical Empire as seen in Williams's (1961) study of British literature in the 1840s – the exact period when liberal capitalism was at its height, replacing mercantilism with free trade and the laissez-faire orientation, along with the ethic of self-help. In the literary works of this period, 'characters whose destinies could not be worked out within the system as given were simply put on the boat, a simpler way of resolving the conflict between ethic and experience than any radical questioning of the ethic' (Williams 1961: 83). The 'black sheep' were rendered invisible from the storyline by being transferred to the Empire (i.e. British colonies), although they might return later with miraculously acquired fortunes. In this way migration to the Empire was an escape route: 'the weak of every kind could be transferred to it, to make a new life' (Williams 1961: 83). This made liberal capitalism viable in at least three ways: first, it reaffirmed its ethic inasmuch as 'going out to the new lands could be seen as self-help and enterprise of the purest kinds'; secondly, it was consistent with the belief 'that there could be no general solution to the social problems of the time; there could be only individual solutions'; thirdly, there was a need for labourers in the Empire (Williams 1961: 83–84).

In the same way, we can look at the cases discussed in this chapter as representing a solution to the conflict between the ethic and the actual experience of neoliberal capitalism in CEE, a solution that makes neoliberalism more viable in both the sending and the receiving country. To unpack this assertion, it can be argued that, on the one hand, neoliberalism advocates a certain social character, while, on the other hand, the policies it champions (e.g. labour market deregulation) undermine the material circumstances necessary to realise this ideal. Indeed, interviewees referred to income and employment precariousness as obstacles to becoming independent liberal adult citizens. This clash between ethics and experience is revealed in migrants' experiences, but the ethic is not challenged in that the 'black sheep' are rendered invisible as a result of their migration. They reappear every now and then through their contacts with family and acquaintances in Poland who may see the success and wealth that they have acquired abroad as a confirmation of the ethic of self-making. Consequently, the neoliberal ethic remains unquestioned. The UK comes to resemble the literary Empire: it needs labourers but it also provides a solution to working-class problems in Poland, thus making the ethics of neoliberalism viable. In addition, these labourers, as we can see, become guardians of neoliberal ideals in the UK.

However, the last part of the present chapter also indicated that at times the 'hidden injuries' accompanying the neoliberal ethic can provoke radical re-evaluation of one's valued ways of living. In line with existing knowledge, 'shame has the potential to separate the actor from hegemonic ideals and become "queering"' (Ray 2014: 122). Therefore, 'hidden injuries' carry the potential for mobilisation. The key question then is: to what extent is this potential utilised, and where is it channelled – towards individual efforts at masking it or towards collective efforts that could produce systemic changes?

NOTE

1. Eng. *Closed Circuit* – a Polish movie from 2013 about three entrepreneurs who have been accused of criminal activities. The film is the critique of the legal system, corruption and uninhibited power of bureaucracy in post-1989 Poland.

REFERENCES

Anderson, B. 2013. *Us and Them? The Dangerous Politics of Immigration Control.* Oxford: Oxford Scholarship Online.

Arendt, H. 1951. *The Origins of Totalitarianism.* New York and London: Harvest Book Harcourt Brace & Company.

Arunas, J. and C. Woolfson. 2014. 'Migration and the new austeriat: the Baltic model and the socioeconomic costs of the new austerity'. In *The Contradictions of Austerity: The Socio-Economic Costs of the Neoliberal Baltic Model*, edited by C. Woolfson and J. Sommers, 87–117. New York: Routledge.

Becker, M. and V. Vignoles. 2014. 'Cultural bases for self-evaluation – Seeing oneself positively in different cultural contexts'. *Social Psychology Bulletin* 40 (5): 657–675.

Charmaz, K. 2006. *Constructing Grounded Theory: A Practical Guide Through Qualitative Analysis.* London, Thousand Oaks and New Delhi: Sage Publications.

Ciupijus, Z. 2011. 'Mobile central eastern Europeans in Britain: Successful European Union citizens and disadvantaged labour migrants?' *Work, Employment and Society* 25 (3): 540–550.

Dunn, E. 2004. *Privatizing Poland: Baby Food, Big Business, and the Remaking of Labour.* Ithaca and London: Cornell University Press.

Elias, N. 1978. *The Civilizing Process: The History of Manners*. New York: Urizen Books.
Kazimierska, K., A. Piotrowski and K. Waniek. 2011. 'Biographical consequences of working abroad in the context of European mental space construction'. *Sociological Review* 60 (1): 139–158.
Makovicky, N. 2014. *Neoliberalism, Personhood, and Postsocialism: Enterprising Selves in Changing Economies*. Surrey: Ashgate.
Marshall, T.H. 1950. *Citizenship and Social Class and Other Essays*. Cambridge: University Press.
Ong, A. 2006. *Neoliberalism as Exception: Mutations in Citizenship and Sovereignty*. Durham, NC: Duke University Press.
Ray, L. 2014. 'Shame and the City – "Looting", Emotions and Social Structure'. *The Sociological Review* 62 (1): 117–136.
Scheff, T. 2000. 'Shame and the social bond: A sociological theory'. *Sociological Theory* 18 (1): 84–99.
Scheff, T. 2002. 'Working class emotions and relationships: Secondary analysis of classic texts by Sennett and Cobb, and Willis'. In *Toward a sociological imagination: Bridging specialized fields*, edited by B. Phillips, H. Mc. Kinnon and T. Scheff. Lanham, MD: University Press of America.
Sennett, R. 1980. *Authority*. London: Secker & Warburg Limited.
Sennett, R. 2003. *Respect in a World of Inequality*. New York: W.W. Norton.
Sennett, R. and Cobb, J. 1972. *The Hidden Injuries of Class*. Cambridge, London and Melbourne: Syndics of Cambridge University Press.
Somers, M. 2008. *Geneaologies of Citizenship: Knowledge, Markets, and the Right to Have Rights*. Cambridge: Cambridge University Press.
Sowa, J. 2003. 'Dezerterzy społeczeństwa konsumpcji'. In *Frustracja: młodzi o Nowym Wspaniałym Świecie*, edited by P. Marecki and J. Sowa. Kraków: Wydawnictwo Rabid.
Sowa, J. 2012. 'An unexpected twist of ideology. Neoliberalism and the collapse of the Soviet Bloc'. *Praktyka Teoretyczna* 5: 154–180.
Therborn, G. 2013. *The Killing Fields of Inequality*. Cambridge: Polity Press.
Trappman, V. 2011. 'Precarious employment in Poland – A legacy of transition or an effect of European integration?' *Emecon* 1: 1–22.
Williams, R. 1961. *The Long Revolution*. Peterborough: Broadview Press.
Woolfson, C. and J. Sommers. 2008. 'Trajectories of entropy and "the labour question". The political economy of post-communist migration in the New Europe'. *Debatte* 16 (1): 53–69.
Ziółkowski, M. 1999. 'O imitacyjnej modernizacji społeczeństwa polskiego'. In *Imponderabilia wielkiej zmiany: mentalność, wartości i więzi społeczne czasów transformacji*, edited by P. Sztompka. Warszawa and Krakow: PWN.

Chapter II.2

Non-EU Migrant Workers in For-profit Older-age Care Facilities in London

Capital's Use of Multiple Borders for the Extension of Its Own Frontiers

Nina Sahraoui

A STRUCTURAL RELIANCE ON MIGRANT LABOUR FOR OLDER-AGE CARE IN LONDON

In the UK, one in five care workers in older-age care is a migrant worker (Cangiano et al. 2009: 58). This proportion rises with a combination of factors: in larger urban areas, in the private sector and in adult social care (in comparison with the rest of the care sectors). Furthermore, the share of migrant care workers in the sector is significantly growing with an increase of 112 per cent between 2003 and 2008 compared to 16 per cent growth for UK-born carers (Cangiano et al. 2009). In London, 68 per cent of care workers are estimated to be non-UK born (Gould 2008 in Hussein, Manthorpe and Stevens 2011). This chapter looks at non-EU migrant workers' experiences in older-age care within for-profit private facilities in Greater London.

Building upon the collective argument developed in this edited book as to the necessity of analysing migration within the broader political economy of changing employment regimes, this chapter analyses migrant workers' experiences in private older-age care taking into account their perceptions of their employment trajectories. In this regard, processes of privatization and precarization foster workforce fragmentation through the recruitment of workers with limited rights, embodied here by non-EU migrant workers. The type of work available to them is shaped by a series of characteristics inter alia nationality, gender and age. Some of these characteristics are corporeally inscribed.

Until recently the number of publications addressing the specific experiences of migrant care workers in the UK was relatively limited. A pioneering report, published by COMPAS researchers in 2009, sketches out the contribution of migrant care workers to the sector exploring qualitatively and quantitatively their working experiences (Cangiano et al. 2009). In addition, a series of publications funded by the Department of Health analyses the relative position of minority ethnic and migrant care workers in the sector, looking at care assistants, senior care workers and nurses (Hussein, Manthorpe and Stevens 2011; Stevens, Hussein and Manthorpe 2011; Hussein, Manthorpe and Ismail 2014). Cuban's (2013) volume looks more specifically into the deskilling of both EU and non-EU migrants and offers an ethnographic insight into domiciliary and residential care. Most recently, a book edited by Anderson and Shutes provides key insights into the intersection of migration and care regimes (Anderson and Shutes 2014). Earlier publications tended to be more limited in their scope, and contributed to knowledge about specific groups – for instance, McGregor's study of Zimbabwean care workers (McGregor 2007). Aiming to contribute to this literature and to discuss its findings, this chapter analyses how a gendered and racialized workforce is channelled into the sector by addressing the following questions: What are the profiles and trajectories of non-EU migrant workers entering the older-age care sector? Does the care job constitute a stepping stone or an entrapment?

These questions serve the purpose of revealing what processes lead to labour market segmentation, on the one hand, and the consequent social implications for non-EU migrant workers, on the other. After a brief presentation of the methods followed for fieldwork, the first section presents how an approach in terms of transnational political economy allows for an intersectional analysis of labour market segmentation via gender, migration and racialization. In a second section, the systematic over-qualification of non-EU migrant workers in older-age care is accounted for through an analysis of the barriers that migrant workers encounter on their journey into employment. In this regard, the concept of 'proliferation of borders' (Mezzadra and Neilson 2013) encourages an analysis of how borders penetrate all aspects of migrants' lives. Finally, in an attempt to assess if the care job constitutes a stepping stone or entrapment, the third section looks into the role of professionalization, the impact of gaining citizenship and the meanings of aspirations in this regard.

A JOURNEY INTO PRIVATE OLDER-AGE CARE FACILITIES

The analysis presented here is based upon fieldwork conducted in Greater London between December 2013 and April 2014. I visited several care homes and relied on the snowballing method to conduct in total twenty-three semi-structured interviews with migrant care workers coming from outside the EU, five interviews with migrant nurses on supervisory positions and three with care home managers. Interviews took place in coffee shops as well as at work, mostly behind closed doors, and on rare occasions in a lounge where residents were present at a distance. I usually spent several hours in a home on each visit and was immersed into the workplace atmosphere, observing daily working routines in the lounges and corridors. All interviews were recorded and transcribed at length. I coded the data collected using software for qualitative data analysis and conducted a thematic analysis.

The average age of the care workers interviewed was thirty-eight. Nine migrated from the Philippines, two from Mauritius, two from Somalia, two from Bangladesh, two from Uganda, and one respectively from India, Sierra Leone, Nigeria, Ghana, Rwanda and China. Regarding the migration status of the respondents, ten had acquired British citizenship at the time of the interview. On average migrant carers in this research had been in the UK for eight and a half years, the duration of stay ranging from eighteen months to eighteen years. Carers holding British citizenship had been in the UK for twelve years on average. All but two of the respondents worked in residential and nursing homes belonging to large private care providers in the UK.

A TRANSNATIONAL POLITICAL ECONOMY OF NON-EU MIGRANTS' ROUTES INTO CARE

The theoretical starting point in this chapter for the analysis of migrant workers' trajectories to and within the care sector is the acknowledgement that these are shaped simultaneously by social care, migration and employment policies. This approach draws upon Williams's writings on the transnational political economy of care and her claim that 'a country's care regime intersects with its migration regime and its employment regime which provides the institutional context that shapes the experiences of both migrant women employed in domestic/care work and their employers, as well as the patterns of migrant care work to be found in different countries' (Williams quoted in Anderson and Shutes 2014: 17, emphasis in original). The study of the relationships between the state, the labour market as well as individual and collective social actors is then applied to various policy sectors so as to produce an understanding of different regimes. To begin with the migration regime and following Williams, it is here understood as including 'immigration rules, residency, settlement and naturalisation rules, as well as national norms and practices governing relationships between majority and minority groups' (Williams 2012: 371). Second, the care regime requires looking into what forms of care are provided and how they are financed. In her study of different European care regimes, Simonazzi offers a helpful definition: 'Each country/society defines the minimum rights to care, and the minimum obligations of family/society, doing so either explicitly through regulation, or implicitly by defining the scope of policy provision' (2009: 212). Of utmost importance here is also the employment regime, and notably the specificities of employment in the care sector as a segmented section of the labour market. It supposes looking at 'existing labour market divisions in terms of gender, ethnicity, migration and nationality and at the impact of deregulation in shaping precarious employment in the migrant care labour market' (Williams 2012: 371). In addition to the migration, care and employment regimes, the feminization of the workforce and its implications cannot be understood without being attentive to what Lutz and Palenga-Möllenbeck term the 'gender regime'. They argue that 'household and care work organization can be seen as the expression of a specifically gendered cultural script in which tasks and responsibilities are coded as either feminine or masculine' (Lutz and Palenga-Möllenbeck 2011: 350).

Looking into the intersection of various regimes also requires being attentive to how the above-mentioned social categories of nationality, gender, 'race/ethnicity' and age intersect. Intersectionality is born out of the claim that multiple forms of oppression are not additive but mutually constitutive. Following Anthias (2013: 126): 'Intersectionality posits that different social divisions interrelate in terms of the production of social relations and in terms of people's lives and they are seen as "mutually constitutive" in terms of experience and practices'. This approach has been put forward historically by black feminists who argued that their oppression was experienced differently because 'race', gender and class are not at the roots of separate systems of oppression but of intersecting ones that transform the oppression itself (Choo and Ferree 2010).

Against the Background of Privatization and Precarization

Policy choices regarding how care is financed have shaped different care regimes (Simonazzi 2009). The UK represents a case of extended privatization through the contracting out of services and the implementation of cash allowances, with the share of the public sector being significantly reduced since the 1980s (Simonazzi 2009). Expanding privatization concerns both home care and residential care, with 76 per cent of residential care being owned by for-profit organizations in England (Simonazzi 2009). The privatization of care services provision is being carried out in a context of sustained growth of care needs. Indeed it is estimated that the social care workforce caring for older people needs to increase by 79 per cent by 2032 (Wittenburg et al. 2010: 15 in Shutes 2011).

In parallel, care work remains one of the lowest paid sectors of the labour market (Low Pay Commission 2014). The gendered understanding of care work and the consequent devaluation of care-related skills underpin the precarious employment terms and working conditions that characterise the sector. Earnings can even fall below the National Minimum Wage in domiciliary care when travelling times are not compensated for.[1] In my research, respondents in full-time employment earned on average £854 net monthly, which was slightly below the national average for the sector and represented 47 per cent of the average income in 2014 (after deducting taxes from the average gross income).

The Construction of the Workforce as Unskilled, Gendered and Racialized: Characteristics Attached to Workers' Bodies

Care work is gendered in that it remains associated in contemporary European societies with women's work and with a labour of love (Folbre 2012). Feminist sociologists have attempted to de-construct the public/private divide and reflected upon its function in patriarchal and capitalist societies, uncovering its gendered implications. Reproductive labour has historically been women's responsibility and the feminization of the labour market in the twentieth century left men's lack of commitment to household work and caring duties mostly unaffected. Rather, the burden was placed on other women as pointed out by the literature on global care chains (Hochschild 2000) or the international division of reproductive labour (Parreñas 2000). The emancipation of middle-class women is indeed indebted to the subordination

Table II.2.1 Level of Earnings Compared to Average Earnings in the Country

Category of Earnings	*Amounts and Per cent*
Respondents average earnings in this research	£854 net monthly
Average earnings of care workers in the UK in older age care	Average annual pay: £12,319 (NMDS-SC online)[1] Estimation of £962 net monthly[2]
National statistics:	£27,200 gross income annually (ONS, 2014)[3]
Average earnings whole of workforce (all sectors)	Estimation of £1,787 net monthly income[4]
Average wage in this research as per cent of average earnings in the UK	47
Average wage in this research as per cent of average wage in the sector in the UK	89

Source: Own elaboration with national statistics and data from own research.
[1]https://www.nmds-sc-online.org.uk/reportengine/GuestDashboard.aspx?type=Medianannualpay (last accessed November 2016).
[2]http://www.thesalarycalculator.co.uk/salary.php (last accessed November 2016).
[3]http://www.ons.gov.uk/ons/rel/ashe/annual-survey-of-hours-and-earnings/2014-provisional-results/stb-ashe-statistical-bulletin-2014.html (last accessed November 2016).
[4]http://www.thesalarycalculator.co.uk/salary.php (last accessed November 2016).

of working class and migrant women. Migration and paid care work in European capitalist economies thus tend to be increasingly connected in the context of ageing populations, increasing female labour market participation, greater geographical mobility, social care policies that foster greater private provision of care services and most importantly global inequalities.

The naturalization of care as women's work shapes professional hierarchies with significant implications for women on the move. The homogenization and essentialization of South American, African and Asian cultures bears additional consequences for the entry of racialized women in the labour market. The figure of the 'caring' and 'disciplined' Ecuadorian or Senegalese woman constructs imaginaries that disqualify migrant women from the primary labour market (Scrinzi 2013); migration policies and labour market intermediaries further enact these stereotypes. In the UK, the points-based immigration system constructs a hierarchy of skills whose underlying logics are deeply gendered. Table II.2.1 presents respondents' earnings in comparison with average earnings in the sector and in the UK. In schematic terms, the greater assimilation of a role to reproductive labour, the less value it holds in the current labour market. Care work falls to the bottom of this latent hierarchy, and institutional care is placed slightly above domestic work in terms of pay and conditions. Working bodies are categorized in a way that reflects these hierarchies: undocumented workers tend to be found in domestic work in the informal economy and documented workers, often with unrecognized qualifications, in various types of formal employment within the care industry. As the second section points out, most women in this study held a degree obtained in their country of origin and some acquired a qualification in the UK. Professional hierarchies, and the devaluation of care work within these, impacted negatively on migrant care workers in that it limited the type of statuses they could access as well as their rights.

The migration regime defines who is allowed to enter the national territory and under what conditions; it also determines migrants' rights in the country of residency through which the proliferation of borders in migrants' lives takes place long after the crossing of the border (Mezzadra and Neilson 2013). The British points-based immigration system introduced in 2008 defines migrants' rights according to their alleged economic utility based upon the labour needs identified at a given time. As a consequence of this policy, non-EU migrants are not eligible for economic immigration for occupations deemed 'unskilled' and can only qualify for skilled and highly skilled jobs whose definition further depends on the 'shortage occupation list' elaborated by the Migration Advisory Committee (MAC). Illustrative of this logic was the introduction of a £35,000 salary threshold after six years of residency for non-EU migrant workers as of April 2016.[2] The Royal College of Nursing has warned against the threat this created to thousands of non-EU migrant nurses being able to remain in the UK[3]; obviously non-EU migrant care workers' wages do not reach this threshold either. Defining migrants' rights according to their supposed economic contribution is conducted on the basis of biased assumptions (i.e. only highly skilled workers are needed) and gendered stereotypes (i.e. care work is unskilled). One of the consequences observed in this study was that several respondents needed to study and pay fees in order to be able to renew their student visas, even when they had worked for several years in the care sector. Though often holding a degree in a different field, they were not able to obtain a visa on the basis of their qualifications and skills. The EU/non-EU divide adds a layer of discrimination in the current migration regime that bears material implications for migrant workers at the workplace level as skills are not recognized in the same way and paths for promotion tend to differ. These stratifications create groups of workers with different rights and exacerbate workforce fragmentation.

The construction of the workforce as unskilled, gendered and racialized therefore produces specific positionalities for migrant care workers in that the essentialization of caring skills for women and for non-EU women follow differentiated patterns. Intersectionality encourages in this regard a reflection around the use of social categories and its implications. Simien highlights that intersectional approaches 'contend that no social group is homogenous' (2007: 267). In this perspective Bedolla assigns to intersectional analysis the task of deconstructing the 'conceptual practices of power' at discursive and empirical levels in order to avoid reifying the very categorizations that intersectionality questions, which means that these categories might change during the process of the research (2007: 238).

An Overwhelming Over-qualification of Non-EU Migrant Workers in Older-age Care

Migrant workers, and especially recent migrants, tend to be more affected by vulnerable employment than the rest of the working population. In a large quantitative study, Jayaweera, Anderson and Phil (2008) demonstrated that migrants are disproportionately affected by vulnerable employment in relation to factors such as pay below the national minimum wage, unpaid overtime and insecurity; for instance, lack of contracts or unfair dismissals (Jayaweera, Anderson and Phil 2008). Being one of the sectors with the lowest levels of pay coupled with high turnover, it comes as no surprise that migrants constitute a significant share of the workforce in older-age care. One mechanism that contributes to this inequality is the non-recognition of skills acquired by migrants in any space other than the national labour market that they seek to enter after migration. The frequent over-qualification of migrant workers has been pointed out in the literature (Datta et al. 2006; McGregor 2007; Cangiano et al. 2009). This section analyses the extent of over-qualification found in this research; it accounts for labour market discrimination of migrant workers and illustrates how labour market segmentation happens on the ground.

For the purpose of the analysis, two main 'pathways' are presented in Figure II.2.1 to describe migrant workers' routes into the older-age care sector. The first group is constituted by twelve overqualified workers (i.e. over half of respondents in this study) in fields non-related to care. Most of them possess qualifications and work experience acquired back home and several obtained degrees in the UK in careers such as business administration, law and accounting. To all in this category, the care job came up as an unforeseen job opportunity. The second group concerns seven respondents (i.e. one third of the interviewees) and is constituted by those who held a nursing degree from their country of origin, some of whom worked as nurses before migrating to the UK. On the whole, out of every ten respondents eight were overqualified.

Individuals in both groups face barriers that effectively extend the materiality of borders into their daily lives. The concept of 'proliferation of borders' appears in this regard to be helpful for the analysis of migrant workers' employment trajectories. Mezzadra and Neilson argue that beyond the focus on material borders the study of a wide range of conceptual borders, among these temporal borders, is key to our understanding of the changing relations between labour, state and capital, as well as to an apprehension of the internal transformations that affect these entities. The authors make the point that 'borders, far from serving simply to block or obstruct global flows, have become essential devices for their articulation' (2013: 3). Most importantly, they argue that this proliferation of borders 'cuts across the composition of living labor, graduating

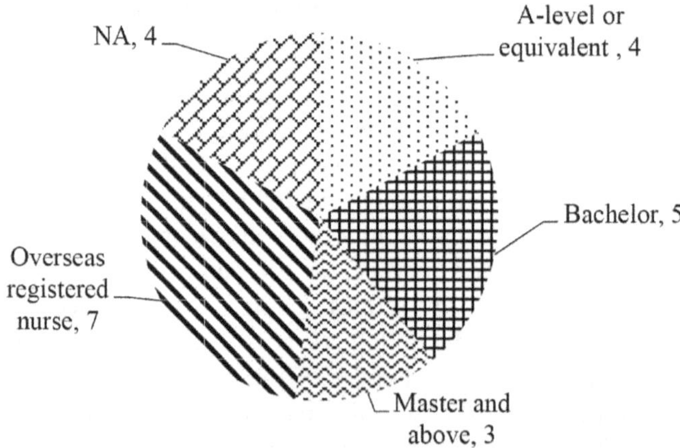

Figure II.2.1 Qualifications Held by Respondents in This Research. *Source*: Own data and elaboration.

and diffusing its subordination to capital in a wide variety of forms and to different degrees' (2013: 123). The following sections illustrate this point in that they describe how migrant workers are channelled into the positions of care assistants in spite of their qualifications, first in relation to those qualified in a different sector and secondly in relation to nurses who qualified overseas.

The 'Unskilling' of Skilled Labour: A Consequence of the British Points-based Immigration System?

This research confirms what a previous study has highlighted regarding Zimbabwean care workers: 'The decision to enter care work was defined not as a "choice" but as a "need", being a source of employment and income' (Cangiano et al. 2009: 107). In this research, this held true for virtually all respondents. Non-EU migrant workers took up a care job because this was one of the few opportunities that was available to them. Moreover, the recruitment phase can be described as a 'fast hiring process' (England and Dyck 2012), which partly explains why migrant workers are 'attracted' to the care sector. Most of the respondents heard about the possibility of getting a job in a particular care home through friends or family, while others would spontaneously apply online or enter a care home and ask for vacancies. For instance, Julie, who came to the UK fourteen years ago from Ghana, where she worked as a teacher, explained that her cousin, who had resided longer in the UK than her, introduced her to the idea of working in the care sector:

> I was looking for a job but I didn't know anything about care but I was reading the paper as I told you and one of my cousin was talking about this and she is here for a long time so she explained it to me.

The relative accessibility of the sector is reflected in the interviewees' perception of the recruitment procedures. Care jobs were among the ones available to migrant workers upon arrival because no previous experience or qualification is required. Adam, a 29-year-old Indian man who studied business administration in the UK, explained how quickly he found the job:

> I saw a care home so I just came in and asked for it, can I have a job, like a vacancy. It was Cheryl [the deputy manager] who was here, so she said – what job? I said: 'any job, I don't mind doing any job'. … He [the manager] doesn't look up for person who has got a lot of experience or anything, he looks for people who have got good attitude towards work. … I was fortunate enough that I got the job and I couldn't even believe it. I came in 2009 December 16th, the 21st I started working here.

Adam's narrative is also illustrative of the gendered dimension of recruitment processes to which male care workers in this research hinted at: male workers were particularly sought after by employers because of the heavy work older-age care involves. Intersectionality provides in this regard a framework to study what Walby names 'complex inequalities' in which both difference and inequality are entailed (Walby 2009), or in other terms both disadvantage and privilege. It appears indeed that the intersection of gender and migration accounts here for the significant presence of male migrant care workers in this feminized sector of the labour market. Cangiano and colleagues found in their elaboration of Labour Force Survey data that men accounted for 31 per cent of recent migrants employed in the care sector (by recent migrants, the authors mean those who arrived in the UK since 1998) versus 13 per cent of UK-born carers in 2007/2008 (Cangiano et al. 2009: 67). According to the NMDS-SC database mentioned above, male workers represented 13.6 per cent of the workforce in London in older-age care in 2015.[4] Among respondents in this research six were men, which corresponds to a quarter of respondents. It appears therefore that male migrant workers found themselves in a different position to female migrant care workers, which in terms of recruitment worked to their advantage in spite of a gendered essentialization of cultures at work in the channelling of migrant workers into care.

The migration regime and the temporal borders implied by immigration rules play here a crucial role both for men and women. While Adam worked in the care home waiting to enter the Tesco management programme, Fadila sought a care job because of the limitations imposed by her student visa. Fadila came to the UK from Bangladesh four years ago and completed a master's degree in business law, she explained:

> I tried different jobs but I couldn't find anything, they told me if you want to work it has to be full-time but I was not allowed to do full-time because that time I was student. So one of my friend, he used to work in [care home name], he told me you cannot find any job but if you are interested you can work in the care sector, there are some vacancies for part-time workers. That time I said okay that's fine.

In addition to possessing unrecognized qualifications, many came with substantial work experience acquired back home that was not taken into account in the British labour market. For instance, Isabel, a 37-year-old Filipina care worker, was in an office job for several years in the Philippines; and Mike, a 55-year-old male care worker from Nigeria, was a chemistry teacher before he migrated:

> Back home, I was doing office work so it's really different you know shifting to another kind of environment like a care home it's difficult but as the days go by I'm used to it already. After one month or two month or three months maximum I've learned to love the job. (Isabel)

> I was a teacher, I read chemistry from university, I had my first degree in chemistry. From university … in Nigeria, I was a teacher, that's why I can talk! I was a teacher back home but when I came here, I couldn't teach because I don't have the proper orientation about how to teach here and at the time I wanted to apply for it, they said they would train me for about three months before I become a teacher, they asked me to bring £1500, it's a lot of money. I am sitting here, I don't have one tenth of that money, the salary comes in, the salary goes into family commitment. There is no proper savings. (Mike)

Another specific group is constituted by those who possessed degrees obtained in the UK and thus did not intend to stay in their current care job but did not necessarily have the resources to move up the social ladder as the British degree did not translate into better labour market opportunities. The care job, in these cases, was often conceptualized as a temporary stage in the professional career, although this temporality tended to turn into longer periods. Cuban demonstrates indeed in her research that 'the longer participants stayed as care assistants, the less likely they were to find work as professionals' (2013: 149). Fadila, whom I quoted above, had been working as a care assistant for three and a half years at the time of the interview and her post-study visa was coming to an end. She thus applied for an entrepreneur visa and hoped it could improve her employment situation:

> Because it's more relevant to my field, if you get that visa you can do your own business, you can do whatever you want so I think it's a scope for me to do something related to my field. I have marketing experience and I'm a business graduate. I know the business law if I start my own business maybe I can utilise all my experience for my own thing, I don't have to give any explanation to anybody, I am my own boss I can do whatever I want so that's why I applied.

In most cases the care sector was not a positive choice, it was rather the result of migrant workers' confrontation with the labour market and the gendered and racialized dynamics at work within it. As the concentration of overqualified migrant workers in older-age care illustrates, there is an obvious mismatch between the shortages identified by the state and actual needs of the labour market. The gap identified here seems to rely partly on the construction of a hierarchy of more or less desirable migrants, with non-EU migrants no longer welcome in 'low-skilled' jobs in the wake of EU enlargement. The NMDS-SC data[5] provides an interesting insight into adult social care in London: 42 per cent of the workforce hold a non-EEA passport while 11 per cent hold an EEA passport. With the significant presence of non-EU migrants in older-age care, the assumption according to which intra-European migration provides for employers' needs in low-skilled labour proves to be an oversimplification. The reliance on migrant labour, and more particularly on migrants coming from outside the EU, has specific implications in the context of the transfer of an expanding share of socio-economic risks from employers to employees. For instance, the privatization and the consequent pressure on labour costs worsens the tendency for nurses who qualified overseas to find themselves entrapped, as presented in the following section.

The Specific Case of Nures from Outside the EU: A 'Proliferation of Borders'?

One third of care assistants and senior carers interviewed held nursing degrees obtained in the country of origin, most frequently in the Philippines. Workers in this situation sometimes stayed in care jobs for many years and thus the following questions arise: Why do overseas registered nurses remain in lower caring positions? What kind of 'borders' do they face? The reasons that emerged from the interviews pointed to a combination of institutional barriers at the intersection of migration and employment policies. The requirements and costs involved in the recognition procedures appeared to be increasingly discouraging for migrant workers. These constraints were strong enough to deter overseas registered nurses from engaging in the process and kept them in positions in which their salary was among the lowest in the professional hierarchy. Reasons mentioned frequently referred to the lack of time and money in relation to caring responsibilities at home or for families back home in need of financial support. For instance, Marissa explained her decision not to pursue the recognition of her degree due to her age; she was sixty at the time of the interview and she had already been working in the UK for eleven years. She referred to the opportunity structure and the general difficulty of finding a workplace willing to provide adaptation programmes:

> Before it's easy to do adaptation now it's very hard because there were so many changes in the policy that you should do before doing your practising nursing here. Before we were loads of nursing homes and hospitals having adaptation but now it's very rare, it's very hard so I said … because I'm already 60, I don't want to practice anymore as a nurse that's it.

Restrictions on entering the National Health Service for non-EEA workers and reforms in the nursing adaptation programmes limit the possibility to work in the NHS (Shutes in Anderson and Shutes, 2014). The manager of a home (that belongs to the care provider that the above cited care assistant is employed by) confirmed that there had been a shift in the company's policy regarding the nursing adaptation programmes as the latter were no longer organised within the company:

> We don't offer that as a company. Some other companies do but we don't any more. So then they would shadow nurses, they would be trained up by nurses, they'd have to go through various different courses to become qualified as a nurse. And this is something they can do externally as well, and they can approach universities and say look, these are the qualifications that I have, what further modules do I need to do to become a registered nurse in this country?

Going through this process externally, as suggested by the quotation above, however, represents a financial cost and requires time off work, a concession that many could not make in the context of pressing financial needs. Family responsibilities and consequent difficulties in finding a 'work-care-life balance', to use Datta et al.'s terminology (2006), indeed constituted a key element given the structural barriers for the recognition of qualifications. To illustrate this point, Alma, a 41-year-old Filipina care assistant, argued:

> In the Philippines I'm a nursing graduate. But I can't work as a nurse because I need to do adaptation and everything and I don't have time for that yet with the children and all.

These difficulties in finding a 'work-care-life' balance were also salient when the dependents were still in the country of origin. Karen, a Filipina senior care assistant, explained that she could not afford any income reduction, which is what would have happened had she decided to work towards recognition of her qualification:

> At the moment I'm not doing it yet because I'm helping my family back home. Because they explained it to me if you are doing that they just give you small money that's my worry that's why I am not doing it. But in the future I want to do it as well.

Rosa, a Chinese female care worker, found herself in a similar situation. She came to the UK with an agency, through which she and her friends began English classes. In her case, most of her classmates continued studying to obtain recognized qualifications, but she was unable to do so because of the urgent need to send money home:

> Because before I came here I have English class, the English class through agency they send you to university. But for me I have family, I have children, just to work I don't want to spend that money I need to make money for my family. So I chose to work and not go to university. If you can go it's okay most of my classmates chose to go to Uni to study two years, three years and then pass the IELTS examination and register as a nurse but I gave up.

Indeed, many respondents considered that the IELTS (International English Language Testing System) exam mentioned by Rosa constituted a very significant barrier, especially since the required pass level rose from 6.5 to 7 in 2007. Sitting such a written exam was therefore perceived as very time-consuming due to the preparation required, something that migrant care workers with caring responsibilities in the domestic sphere could not cope with. Joyce, a 30-year-old Indian nurse and mother of an 18-month-old boy, perceived the IELTS exam as the main barrier to the recognition of her diploma, despite a good level of spoken English:

> A problem in UK if you want to work as a nurse, you have to do the IELTS exam, that's quite difficult and until now I didn't give my exam, for if I pass that exam I can work as a staff nurse here. I didn't try really, I don't get time to go for the school or training you know.

Given that this requirement applies only to non-EU nurses and that migrant nurses from A8 countries do not have to pass this test, it further divided the workforce and was perceived as deeply discriminatory. It seemed all the more unfair to the migrant workers interviewed that they were working with care workers from East European countries and observed that their levels of English varied greatly, with many having what they considered to be a rather weak command of the language. These institutional barriers provide an example of how migration policies create, on the one hand, inequalities between citizens and non-citizens and, on the other hand, between various categories of non-citizens, in this case between EU and non-EU migrants. The trajectories of these women reveal how borders materially impact their lives long after non-EU migrants enter the EU. An analysis in terms of 'proliferation of borders' presents the advantage of drawing our attention to the global implications of the multiplication of borders and their temporal dimension. The lengthening of the time required to obtain recognition of a nursing degree, through the tightening of opportunities and the increase of its cost, forge a significant temporal border that keeps nurses outside the labour market that corresponds to their skills. It is worth citing at length Mezzadra and Neilson's words:

> The control of international borders involved in such efforts also has marked effects on establishing internal administrative borders and categories that divide labor markets, separate migrant groups beyond and within the boundaries of ethnicity, and provide parameters within which individual migrants negotiate their biographies. (2013: 138)

Overseas graduated nurses, who work as care assistants, are caught up in a series of constraints embedded in privatization processes, migration policies as well as gender roles. The externalization of the cost of adaptation programmes by private companies constitute a significant barrier; however, its implications need to be understood alongside additional elements such as the IELTS exam that is required for non-EU workers. This points ultimately at UK migration policies, as well as gender roles, as in the case of Alma, whose caring responsibilities at home would not allow her to dedicate sufficient time to achieve the recognition of her qualifications. What McCall names 'anti-categorical complexity', 'intracategorical complexity' and 'intercategorical complexity' reveal the debates within the literature on intersectionality around the use of socially constructed categories (McCall 2005). The complexities entailed in the trajectories narrated by migrant care workers in this research similarly stress the changing meanings of these categorizations in space/time and within specific intersections of inequalities. In the case of overseas registered nurses coming to the UK from outside the EU, several layers of disadvantage shaped their trajectories. If their migrant status determined an initial inequality through the non-recognition of their qualifications and work experience, the temporal borders that prevented many of them from obtaining the recognition of their qualifications relate to broader social care policies and companies' practices. Finally, how migrant care workers navigated these spaces was also shaped by their decisions and perceptions, notably as to their position in the 'global care chain' (Hochschild 2000). The following section questions the possibilities for social mobility for non-EU migrant workers employed in older-age care. It scrutinises the possibilities available to them through three types of indicators: the professionalisation of the care occupation, access to citizenship and the analysis of their aspirations.

BARRIERS AND ENABLERS OF SOCIAL MOBILITY

The Devaluation of Care Through the Absence of Professionalisation

The devaluation of care work underpins the segmentation of this sector of the labour market in that it limits workers' professional mobility. In the UK, there is no prerequisite for care workers to start in the position of 'care assistant' in a care home or in domiciliary care. There exists only a duty for employers to ensure that at least 50 per cent of their workforce attains National Vocational Qualification (NVQ) level 2 (Smith and Mackintosh 2007). However, as quoted by Smith and Mackintosh 'by early 2004, only 48% of homes met even these minimum levels of qualifications and less than half were doing any staff training' (2218). Furthermore, these qualifications are not embedded into a clear career path for care workers, and completing NVQ levels serves above all to fulfil employers' duties in terms of workforce training. The completion of these NVQs does not translate into better labour market opportunities for workers given that no prior training is formally required for the position of care assistant and that wages are kept low throughout the industry. Jenny, manager of a care home, confirmed the absence of any specific requirements regarding qualifications or previous experience; she considered that on-the-job training covered all training needs:

> I don't require previous qualifications here, or previous experience, it goes on the general demeanour of the person when they are on interview. So if they've never worked in the care sector before … it wouldn't be an issue to us, we provide a full training package to ensure that all of our carers have the standards and are aware of policies and procedures to maintain safe working. So yes it does vary much from down to attitude and their presentation on interview.

As a consequence, incentives for workers to engage in training remained limited. There was little scope for promotion apart from senior carer positions, and in this regard there is no homogenously defined criteria in terms of access and level of salary; the position itself did not exist in all the care homes visited for this study. Training provided by employers did not bear additional financial cost for workers, but often no time was dedicated to that training and workers were compelled to complete it in their personal time, as described by Amal, a 24-year-old Somalian care assistant:

NS: Can you manage to do it [the online training] during your working time?
Amal: You cannot do it during the working, especially this unit I am working in, the residents keep ringing the bell so I don't really think you have time for that because you are only two staff as well, you can't just go and do your e-learning, then the other person gets fed up with you … but sometimes if we have a day off we are allowed to come and just do our e-learning if the Internet is not working in my house I can just come here and do the e-learning.

On the whole, the lack of training reinforces the essentialisation of care skills and entraps workers into a very segmented section of the labour market without formal bridges and paths to build a career. The absence of formal training effectively renders care skills invisible and creates the conditions for the marginalization of the care workforce through the low level of wages and precarious employment arrangements. Given that the reliance on migrant workers stems precisely from these structural conditions, the question emerges: what gains does acquiring British citizenship bring about? The following section addresses this question through the analysis of respondents' discourses and trajectories.

Enduring Borders: The Limited Impact of Gaining Citizenship

The path to citizenship represents a 'temporal border' in itself: in this research those who acquired British citizenship were in the UK for an average of twelve years whereas those who depended on various temporary migration statuses resided in the UK for an average time of five years. Ten respondents possessed British citizenship at the time of the interview and twelve relied on various migration statuses. Among respondents in this study, non-EU migrants who became British citizens earned on average £950 net income per month whereas the average earnings of those with temporary migration statuses amounted to £802.72 net income per month. Given that workers holding British citizenship were also in the UK on average seven years longer than the rest of respondents, it is not possible to establish a straightforward correlation between the level of earning and the acquisition of British citizenship. Nevertheless acquiring British citizenship offers the advantage of being protected from changing migration rules that increasingly commodify migrant workers by turning individuals into units of production with a minimal requirement of 'productivity' as illustrated by the new earnings threshold of £35,000 mentioned above.

It appears nevertheless that in spite of ten respondents out of twenty-three holding British citizenship in this study fifteen were overqualified. Indeed, the trajectories of non-EU migrants demonstrate that a strictly legal perspective cannot account for lasting forms of disadvantage. The French sociologist Guillaumin wrote several decades ago: 'Each individual who used to be foreigner, alienated, condemned, always bears the scars of it, and his/her status of integration and conformism always remains ambiguous and submitted to a form good will that constitutes tolerance or the silence of the majority'[6] (Guillaumin 1972: 247). The Bourdieusian concept of cultural capital is here helpful to account for these enduring patterns of marginalization beyond formal barriers and requirements. Bourdieu distinguishes between embodied, objectified and institutionalized cultural capital (Bourdieu 1979). It is the latter that is of most relevance here: the process of institutionalization through collective recognition based upon conventional values establishes cultural capital (Bourdieu 1979). Erel (2010: 648) argues that the notion of institutionalized cultural capital helps explaining 'how educational and professional institutions exercise nationally-based protectionism by not recognizing qualifications acquired abroad'. Furthermore, institutionalized cultural capital is intrinsically related to embodied cultural capital. Here, in spite of the significant share of respondents benefitting formally from the same status as non-migrants, it appears that labour market opportunities of those who gained citizenship remained to a great extent shaped by latent social processes that easily take precedence over formal equality. Racialisation processes precisely deny migrants' ability to embody the dominant cultural capital, attached to criteria of nationality and physical appearance in latent or manifest forms. Pervasive labour market discrimination thus impedes some of those who obtained recognition or completed their studies in the UK from making use of their qualifications. Migration and racialisation intersect here in that non-EU migrants from the so-called Global South experience the British labour market on different terms to EU migrants, on the one hand, and minority ethnic workers, on the other. Their specific position in these relations of inequality results from this intersection and is shaped by additional elements such as time spent in the country.

The following section offers an insight into non-EU migrant care workers' aspirations and future professional plans. These are interpreted here as indicative of their perceptions of social mobility.

No Aspirations in the Care Sector: A Reflection of Entrapment?

Not surprisingly, eight respondents (i.e. over one third) hoped to achieve professional mobility within the sector by becoming a nurse, given that half of the individuals in this group already held nursing degrees obtained in their country of origin. As summarised in the Table II.2.2, the same proportion of respondents envisioned their professional future outside of the care sector.

Table II.2.2 Schematic Description of Respondents' Aspirations

Professional Aspirations	*LONDON*
Advancement in care	8
Including overseas trained nurses	4
Continuity in care	2
Out of care	8
Return	3

Source: Own data and elaboration.

The extract below from my interview with Fadila is illustrative of the position in which highly qualified migrants find themselves while working as care assistants, awaiting professional opportunities more in line with their qualifications:

> Actually, I don't have high ambitions regarding the care sector because I'm very happy with what I'm doing now but if I get a relevant job related to law or business definitely I will switch. Until I get this opportunity I'm very happy with what I am doing. I don't want to be like a deputy manager or a manager but of course if I get any scope to work in administration in a care home I don't mind

> I will be happy to do that because it's related to my experience I will be happy but for now it's okay. But I look for scope to enhance my professional career instead of being a care worker.

Similarly, Sonia, a 33-year-old care assistant from Mauritius, was waiting for an opportunity to leave the care sector. She graduated in Business Administration in the UK and had been working as a care assistant for nine years at the time of the interview:

> Well, because I like numbers I like to be an accountant so maybe I will go to a different field. I haven't decided anything yet I am just waiting for my immigration to clear and I will decide after that what to do.

Conceiving care as a temporary job was all the more common given that the majority of respondents were either highly skilled in a different sector or felt compelled to take up a job as care assistant. For the group of respondents who were on student visas (14%), the limitations that were imposed regarding the number of hours that they could work contributed to creating a perception of temporariness. Some were on a post-study work visa and found themselves in the contradictory position of being employed but not in a job that could secure the extension of their visa. Finally, a small group of respondents planned on returning to their home country. This project illustrates a perception of return as ensuring an upward mobility that is not foreseeable in the UK. Isabel, for instance, planned on going back to the Philippines and on opening her own business:

NS: How do you envisage your professional future?
Isabel: Actually, I'm just waiting for that visa but I think once I've got money I'll just go back home it is better to live there you know. You own your time, you are with your family, you are in your own place. … that's our long-term plan to just go back home and start a small business there.

Together, respondents who envisaged their future either out of the care sector or planned on returning to their home country represented over half of respondents. This reflects the mismatch of skills described in the second section and it hints also at a certain sense of entrapment due to the lack of advancement opportunities exacerbated by the very weak professionalisation of the occupation of care assistant. In her research, Cuban also highlighted the importance of the processes of deskilling of migrant workers and she identified three ways of coping with these situations: 'refocusing on family relationships and making a new home', 'finding deeper meaning in care assistant work' and 'seeing care assistant work as a temporary situation' (2013: 146–147). Given that only two respondents in this research envisaged remaining in their current position and that most of them wanted to leave the care sector altogether, perceiving the care assistant job as temporary was a widely shared feeling, even if respondents had been in their current job for a period of five years on average.

CONCLUSION

Neoliberal capitalism has extended market forces to the care sector hoping for new horizons of profitability. This logic appears to contradict the pursuit of higher standards of care. It denies the value of emotional labour so that care is constructed as unskilled and offers few career prospects. The underlying conceptualization of care as an extension of women's domestic work creates a gendered sector, characterized by precarious employment terms and working conditions, that ultimately leads to a reliance on migrant labour in large urban centres such as Greater London. The 'proliferation of borders', that turns highly skilled individuals into gendered and racialized bodies, weakens the bargaining power of migrant labour and simultaneously limits migrant workers' agency. However, this needs to be understood taking into account the implications that migration policies have on these workers' lives including the ways in which they experience employment regimes. The long-lasting effects of the marginalization created by migration policies and the lack of professionalisation of the care sector are reflected in respondents' aspirations. The intersectional lenses used in the analysis have furthermore illustrated Anthias's argument for an 'intersectional framing' rather than theory, given that intersectionality works best as a 'heuristic device for understanding boundaries and hierarchies of social life' (Anthias 2012: 4). Finally, it is argued here that all aspects of care, including non-EU migrant carers' working conditions, training and professional trajectories, need to be given more attention to ensure that policies aiming at improving the quality of care take into account this inherent interdependency.

NOTES

1. https://www.unison.org.uk/content/uploads/2013/11/On-line-Catalogue220152.pdf (last accessed November 2016).

2. https://www.gov.uk/government/uploads/system/uploads/attachment_data/file/420536/20150406_immigration_rules_appendix_i_final.pdf (last accessed November 2016).

3. http://www.bbc.com/news/health-33201189 (last accessed November 2016).

4. https://www.nmds-sc-online.org.uk/reportengine/GuestDashboard.aspx?type=Gender (last accessed November 2016).

5. The database was consulted on 21 and 25 March 2014.

6. Original text: '*Tout individu qui a été étranger, aliéné, condamné, porte la marque, et son statut d'intégration et de conformité reste toujours ambigu et soumis à la forme de bon vouloir que représente la tolérance ou le silence des majoritaires*'.

REFERENCES

Anderson, B. and I. Shutes. 2014. *Migration and Care Labour Theory, Policy and Politics*. Palgrave Macmillan.

Anthias, F. 2012. 'Intersectional what? Social divisions, intersectionality and levels of analysis'. *Ethnicities* 13 (1): 3–19.

Anthias, F. 2013. 'Hierarchies of social location, class and intersectionality: Towards a translocational frame'. *International Sociology* 28: 121.

Bedolla, L. G. 2007. 'Intersections of inequality: Understanding marginalization and privilege in the post-civil rights era'. *Politics & Gender* 3 (2): 232–248..

Bourdieu, P. 1979. 'Les trois états du capital culturel'. Actes de la recherche en sciences sociales. 30 (Novembre): 3–6. L'institution scolaire.

Cangiano, A., I. Shutes, S. Spencer and G. Leeson. 2009. *Migrant care workers in ageing societies: Research findings in the United Kingdom*. Report on Research Findings in the UK (Vol. 44).

Choo, H. Y. and M. M. Ferree. 2010. 'Practicing intersectionality in sociological research: A critical analysis of inclusions, interactions, and institutions in the study of inequalities'. *Sociological Theory* 28: 129–149.

Cuban, S. 2013. *Deskilling Migrant Women in the Global Care Industry*. London: Palgrave Macmillan.

Datta, K., C. Mcilwaine, Y. Evans, J. Herbert, J. May and J. Wills. 2006. 'Work, care and life among low-paid migrant workers in London: Towards a migrant ethic of care' (pp. 1–37).

England, K. and I. Dyck. 2012. 'Migrant workers in home care: Routes, responsibilities, and respect'. *Annals of the Association of American Geographers* 102 (5): 1076–1083.

Erel, U. 2010. 'Migrating cultural capital: Bourdieu in migration studies'. *Sociology* 44 (4): 642–660.

Folbre, N. 2012. 'Should women care less? Intrinsic motivation and gender inequality'. *British Journal of Industrial Relations* 50 (4): 597–619.

Hochschild, A. R. 2000. 'Global care chains and emotional surplus value'. In *On the Edge: Living with Global Capitalism*, edited by A. Giddens and W. Hutton, 130–146. UK: Jonathan Cape.

Hussein, S., J. Manthorpe and M. Stevens. 2011. 'Social care as first work experience in England: A secondary analysis of the profile of a national sample of migrant workers'. *Health & Social Care in the Community* 19 (1): 89–97.

Hussein, S., J. Manthorpe and M. Ismail. 2014. 'Ethnicity at work: The case of British minority workers in the long-term care sector'. *Equality, Diversity and Inclusion: An International Journal* 33 (2): 177–192.

Jayaweera, H., B. Anderson and D. Phil. 2008. 'Migrant workers and vulnerable employment: A review of existing data' (pp. 1–49).

Low Pay Commission. 2014. National Minimum Wage, Report 2014.

Lutz, H. and E. Palenga-Möllenbeck. 2011. 'Care, gender and migration: Towards a theory of transnational domestic work migration in Europe'. *Journal of Contemporary European Studies* 19 (3): 349–364.

McCall, L. 2005. 'The complexity of intersectionality'. *Journal of Women and Culture in Society* 30 (3): 1771–1800.

McGregor, J. 2007. '"Joining the BBC (British Bottom Cleaners)": Zimbabwean migrants and the UK care industry'. *Journal of Ethnic and Migration Studies* 33 (5): 801–824.

Mezzadra, S. and B. Neilson. 2013. *Border as method, or, the multiplication of labor*. Durham: Duke University Press.

Parreñas, R. S. 2000. 'Migrant Filipina domestic workers and the international division of reproductive labor'. *Gender & Society* 14 (4): 560–580.

Scrinzi, F. 2013. *Genre, migrations et emplois domestiques en France et en Italie*. Paris: Editions Petra.

Shutes, I. 2011. Social care for older people and demand for migrant workers. (pp. 1–9).

Simien, E. M. 2007. 'Doing Intersectionality Research: From Conceptual Issues to Practical Examples'. *Politics & Gender* 3 (2): 264–271.

Simonazzi, A. 2009. 'Care regimes and national employment models'. *Cambridge Journal of Economics* 33 (2): 211–232.

Smith P. and M. Mackintosh. 2007. 'Profession, market and class: nurse migration and the remaking of division and disadvantage'. *Journal of Clinical Nursing* 16: 2213–2220.

Stevens, M., S. Hussein and J. Manthorpe. 2011. 'Experiences of racism and discrimination among migrant care workers in England: Findings from a mixed-methods research project'. *Ethnic and Racial Studies* (March): 1–22.

Walby, S. 2009. *Globalization and Inequalities: Complexity and Contested Modernities*. London: Sage.

Williams, F. 2012. 'Converging variations in migrant care work in Europe'. *Journal of European Social Policy* 22 (4): 363–376.

Chapter II.3

Female Migrants' Agency

Work Trajectories of Polish Women in the UK

Karima Aziz

With the emergence of debates around the feminisation of migration, female migrants have attracted increasing attention in migration research (Moch 2005). They have either been framed as oppressed and disadvantaged subjects in a world full of structural constraints characterised by gender regimes, migration regimes and economic systems; or as active agents in their origin and destination countries full of agentic capabilities to confront and change structural constraints (Moch 2005). The core difference between the perspectives these studies offer, reflecting the tension within sociological studies at large, lies in the structure–agency debate (Bakewell 2010). 'The challenge taken up by many social theorists is how to acknowledge the importance of social structures in understanding social action … while leaving room for agency and providing an adequate account of social change' (Bakewell 2010: 1965). When applying Giddens' structuration theory (1984) or Archer's critical realist or morphogenetic approach (2003), there is a kind of agreement in that structure and agency are interrelated and influence one another.

While Giddens (1984) conceptualises this as the duality of structure, in which structure and agency are inseparable and agency reproduces and transforms structures, Archer (2003) promoted the dualism of the two as co-constitutive elements separated by time. In her morphogenetic approach 'the consequences of past actions contribute to structural conditions that have a causal influence over subsequent social interaction. While action may be structurally conditioned, it is not structurally determined, as actors come with their own agency' (Bakewell 2010: 1696–1697). There is a kind of consensus in that agency (the capacity of a person to take action) is conditioned by structures and structures – as patterns of social, political and economic relations – can be transformed by agency (King 2010). While this chapter is not able to solve this long-standing theoretical debate, it strives to add an account of a specific case of female migrants' agency with the example of work trajectories of Polish women in the UK. This analysis uncovers, on one hand, the structures active in transnational spaces, which are often defined by gendered and migrant employment patterns, and, on the other hand, what agency women seek for themselves and how they enact agency in their narratives of migration and work trajectories. The chapter focuses on how structure and agency come into play in migrant work trajectories and gender roles, thereby limiting the analysis to these aspects leaving other sites of agency enactment such as social networks, leisure, local integration and collective agency beyond the scope of this analysis.

As European citizens, female Polish migrant workers enjoy freedom of movement but often start out working in low-paid, as well as gendered, employment because of the gendered segmentation of the UK labour market and institutionalised inequality of migrants. While some women are able to overcome barriers and progress professionally, others can experience occupational stagnation in disadvantaged positions. This chapter examines how the possible dynamics of work trajectories can be mediated by different strategies found in the experiences of female migrant workers. These patterns emerge in the background of the conditions of post-accession Polish migration to the UK and established gender regimes.

This context has changed the dynamics of female Polish migration from an informal, short-term pattern influenced by household decision-making to a formalised movement including younger, single women. The recent migration is characterised by generational dynamics of different gendered expectations. This leads women with caring responsibilities to comply with family decisions and thereby at times sacrifice their own aspirations, while women without dependants sometimes contest or postpone their origin societies' gender roles. The research question therefore asked is: how established gender roles, individual agency and different work trajectories are interrelated in the experiences of female Polish migrant workers in the UK labour market? In order to answer this question biographical narrative interviews were conducted with the group in question in the UK, as well as with female Polish return migrants from the UK, and then analysed. This qualitative data is examined in the light of changes in employment and migration regimes, where liberalisation, flexibilisation and precarisation of labour spread out and migration has been conceptualised as part of those transformations.

FEMALE POLISH MIGRATION TO THE UK

Migration from Poland to the UK has a long and diverse history, which has been described as a continuum and as separate events at the same time: on one hand, representing a long social process and, on the other hand, marked by different motivations and conditions (Düvell and Garapich 2011). Two major changes were identified in the development of this migration. First, migration before the mid-1980s was mainly due to political circumstances resulting from the post-war order, while later migration was related to economic and social disadvantages. Secondly, there has been a transformation of Polish migration from previously permanent to increasingly temporary (Düvell and Garapich 2011). An interrelation between migration from Poland and the labour market imbalances as a consequence of the process of restructuring from socialism to capitalism has been suggested (Kurekova 2011). In this context Polish women have made use of the new East–West 'migratory space', which emerged following the end of the socialist system, and have often served as cheap and flexible labour in the informal economy of Western Europe (Morokvasić et al. 2008). These destination labour markets have taken advantage of the cheap and flexible migrant labour force in their pursuit of flexibilisation and liberalisation (Lutz 2007). The economic and political transformation in Poland affected women in a specific way. While economic activity and labour market participation decreased and unemployment increased, women were also disadvantaged by the discontinuation of public services rendering them not only unemployed but also less able to combine work and family responsibilities. Furthermore, there was a backlash in women's rights promoted by the new political structure and the influence of the Catholic Church following the top-down ideology of gender equality during socialist times (Coyle 2007).

The transformation process in Poland and political change in Europe led to a new politico-institutional context. Poland, alongside seven other CEE countries, joined the EU in 2004 and citizens from these countries were allowed access to the UK labour market (Ciupijus 2011). The UK labour market made use of the opportunity of cheap migrant work by opening up the market and adapting recruitment and employment arrangements. This led to the regularisation of the formerly mostly irregular migration from Poland to the UK and the new conceptualisation of these migrants as European citizens or mobile Europeans (Ciupijus 2011). However, these conditions are gendered and need to be investigated taking into account the female experience.

The 2011 census was the first large-scale data set to mirror the outcomes of Polish post-accession migration to the UK. The census data showed for England and Wales a Polish-born population of 579,000 or 1 per cent of the total population; Poland thereby constituted the top country of citizenship of foreign citizens, the second country of birth for foreign-born and Polish was the second most spoken language (Migration Observatory 2012; Rienzo and Vargas-Silva 2012; Booth 2013). Because of this numerical significance and the changed politico-institutional framework, this phenomenon has attracted a broad variety of interest from academia as well as local, regional and national authorities, and public and media debates (Burrell 2010). Its significance was highlighted by Favell (2008), who referred to the regularisation of intra-EU mobility and the rise in East–West migration as the new migration system in Europe. This migrant group has been characterised as rather young and often highly educated (Eade, Drinkwater and Garapich 2006; White 2010). While the main migration drivers have been identified as economic and Polish migrants have been generally conceptualised as migrant workers (Drinkwater et al. 2006; Burrell 2010), there have been many other motivations and migration patterns observed taking into consideration social and cultural capital (Burrell 2009).

The economic crisis further transformed the context of East–West migration, as receiving and sending countries were differently affected. The emigration numbers from Poland to the UK decreased from 2008 to 2009 by a substantial 47 per cent (Kaczmarczyk 2011: 22). While there has been return migration, especially of Polish migrants from the UK and Ireland, as well as lower numbers of immigrants following the economic crisis (Galgóczi et al. 2012), this cannot be simply seen as the end of East–West migration or the mobility of these individuals. At the same time restrictions in other EU member states came to an end and evidence collected by research rather suggests ongoing mobility (Krings et al. 2009). The effects of the financial and economic crisis have been varied throughout the EU, as have their effects on migration (Fix et al. 2009). The simplistic idea of migrants leaving when times are difficult has proven to be misleading in research on Polish migrants in Ireland (Krings et al. 2009). While freedom of movement and the adopted temporary and circular migration patterns offer opportunities for migrants to move on, Krings et al. (2009) found many Polish migrants in Ireland intending to stay. The explanation for this was that a majority had remained in employment and some welfare state arrangements were in place for those who did lose their jobs; moreover, social networks were important for sustaining the migration process relatively independently of the economic downturn.

This again illustrates that it is not only economic considerations that play a role in migration decisions, but, for example, family situations and children's education can also be factors in the decision to stay in the UK despite an economic downturn (White 2011). At the same time the data for this chapter shows that the preparedness of women without dependants to take risks led to a high level of mobility within the UK and other countries, as well as across sectors. As Engbersen et al. (2010) put it, it is almost impossible to predict anything in this context due to migration patterns such as circulation, incomplete or liquid migration, mobility and a lasting temporariness.

Polish Women in the UK Labour Market

The diversity of this migrant group is also reflected in the quantitative data available on Polish migrant workers in the UK. One limit of quantitative data, however, lies in taking account of changing social contexts such as not being able to effectively account for temporary and circular migration. Others include difficulties in definitions of categories and limited sample sizes for individual migrant groups especially when trying to include gendered differentiations. The most reliable large-scale data set on the topic is therefore the British census of 2011, which unfortunately can only provide an idea of the situation at a certain point in time. The Polish-born population in England and Wales in 2011 consisted of 51 per cent women and 49 per cent men; a detailed breakdown by age and sex in shown in Figure II.3.1.

In relation to economic activity the data in Table II.3.1 shows that Polish-born women are mostly employed full-time. Their rates of part-time employment, self-employment and in the gendered category of 'looking after home or family' show a gendered structure of their economic activity. This gendered dynamic is conspicuous despite their high full-time employment and low levels of economic inactivity such as being retired or a student, which characterise them as migrant workers. The biggest group of female Polish-born population is aged 20–29 years and has the highest full-time employment at 55 per cent. The older-age groups still have high full-time employment and higher part-time employment rates. This suggests that when family and caring responsibilities increase, Polish-born women combine their reproductive work more and more with part-time employment. Polish-born women also engage in more self-employment the older they are. This could be conceptualised as a way of confronting structural constraints in the labour market (Cook et al. 2011). The impression that women in the age group of 30–39 years carry the highest caring responsibilities is implied by their higher

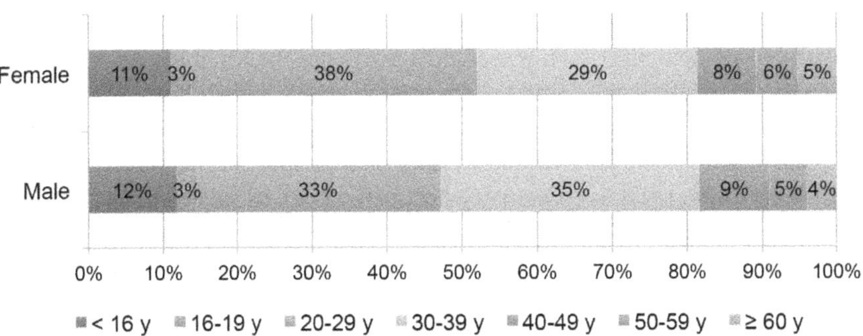

Figure II.3.1 Polish-born Population by Age and Sex in England and Wales. *Source*: Own elaboration based on the 2011 census for England and Wales.

Table II.3.1 Economic Activity of Female Polish-born Population by Age in England and Wales

Age	*16–19 years*	*20–29 years*	*30–39 years*	*40–49 years*	*50–59 years*	*60–74 years*	*> 74 years*
Total	7,811	111,980	86,016	22,754	16,408	7,516	7,640
Part-time employees (%)	4	15	19	18	18	10	2
Full-time employees (%)	9	55	47	50	47	12	2
Self-employed (%)	1	7	11	13	13	8	1
Unemployed (%)	3	4	4	4	4	1	0
Students (%)	76	8	3	2	1	1	0
Retired (%)	0	0	0	0	3	60	89
Looking after home or family (%)	3	9	11	7	7	3	1
Other economically inactive (%)	3	3	3	4	8	6	5

Source: Own elaboration on basis of the 2011 census for England and Wales.

share of 'looking after home or family' alongside their lower full-time and higher part-time employment rates. The markers of studying and retirement are likely to be biased by age and therefore have little effect on the main characterisation of the female Polish-born population as active migrant workers engaged in gendered economic activity.

The heterogeneity of the Polish-born population in the UK labour market is reflected in their industries and occupations as shown by the 2011 census for England and Wales. The main industries for Polish-born women are manufacturing, wholesale and retail trade, and accommodation and food service with 15 per cent employed in each of these industries. These sectors are also relevant for Polish-born men, as they are typical employment fields for migrant workers. The construction sector as a 'male and migrant' industry appears to be important for Polish-born men, while the female Polish-born population is also employed in more gendered work such as in health and social work, administrative and support services, and education. While the Polish-born population is represented on all occupational levels, there are differences between the genders observable. Both Polish-born women and men are most frequently employed in elementary occupations; however, 37 per cent of Polish-born women work in these, while only 27 per cent of men do. On the same level as elementary occupations are skilled trade occupations for men, which is not the case for women. Polish-born women's second most important category of employment is feminised occupations in caring, leisure and other services; this is insignificant for Polish-born men, comparable to the dynamic present in the administrative and secretarial occupations. As the level of the female Polish-born population employed in manufacturing shows, their relevance in process, plant and machine operatives is noteworthy for female workers, yet it is not surprising for migrant workers and they are still employed in the industry at a lower level than their male counterparts.

The data thus provides an insight into the position of Polish women as migrant workers in the UK following the accession of Poland to the EU as well as the generational dynamics in terms of economic activity. While regularisation has enabled migrant women to take part in the formal labour market, the dynamics of a gendered segmentation of the UK labour market (Anderson 2000) as well as existing gender roles shape their participation.

THE INTERRELATION OF GENDER, WORK TRAJECTORIES AND AGENCY: EXPERIENCES OF FEMALE POLISH MIGRANT WORKERS IN THE UK

The discussed development of Polish migration to the UK and the position of Polish women in the UK labour market provide the context for the analysis of the interrelation between gender, work trajectories and female migrants' agency. While important for understanding the background, the quantitative data available is nevertheless unable to offer information on work trajectories, how they are connected to gender roles and how women approach different opportunities. Therefore, qualitative data collected through biographical narrative interviews (Schütze 1983) is the basis for the following analysis in order to investigate how gender, work trajectories and female agency interact in the experiences of Polish women in the UK. The different forms and patterns of this interrelation are scrutinised through the structural forces of European citizenship, labour markets and gender constructions and the different ways in which women dealt with them.

The biographical narrative interview helps to avoid influencing interviewees with the formulation of interview questions and this approach can also provide insights into the changing dynamics of gender, work and migration in a life course (Apitzsch and Siouti 2007). This chapter benefits from thirty-one biographical narrative interviews conducted with female Polish migrant workers in the UK and twenty-two such interviews with female Polish return migrants from the UK in Poland. The interviewees in the UK were mainly employed in manufacturing, public administration, health, education, hotels and restaurants, and banking and finances. Furthermore, the returnees had experiences in the informal economy in the UK as waitresses, au pairs and nannies. The sample is diverse in demographic characteristics such as age, ranging from 20 to 54 years old; educational background, which includes various combinations of interrupted secondary education in Poland, GCSEs in the UK, secondary education in Poland, college in the UK, vocational training in Poland, interrupted university studies in Poland and university degrees in

Poland or in the UK; the length of stay stretches from a little less than a year to 14 years, with the majority staying 5–9 years; mobility in the interviewees' lives is in some cases one-time and in many other cases a multiple occurrence. Further diverse markers are relationship status, family situation, citizenship and ethnicity of partners, geographical location in the UK and Poland, work experience in Poland and trade union membership status of the interviewees in the UK. The sample in Poland consisting of return migrants sometimes with and sometimes without ideas of further migration helps to overcome the boundaries of a one-way understanding of migration and expands the experiences of the interrelation between gender, work and agency to show how this dynamic can lead to return or further mobility. The biographical narrative interviews, which were conducted between October 2013 and February 2015 and took between one and a half and four hours, were transcribed and the analysis was facilitated by the use of the computer-assisted qualitative data analysis software NVivo. In addition to the biographical narrative interviews with respondents, there were semi-structured expert interviews for further insights conducted in Poland and the UK with academic experts, trade union officers, community activists and Polish public institutions.

Regularisation and European Citizenship

In the context of Polish post-accession migration to the UK the EU provides the dominant structural force with the regularisation of this movement through European citizenship rights. The main right provided by European citizenship to its citizens is the freedom of movement; however, this concept has (besides its explicit exclusion of all non-EU citizens) a more implicit inclusion–exclusion dynamic based on the gendered division of work (Askola 2012). The interviewees had very often undertaken previous migration, which was mostly short-term and before the movement following enlargement. In their current post-accession migration experiences the respondents would either take up formal employment in contrast to their previous migrant work experiences or use their established networks to find informal work before returning to Poland. The freedom of movement eased the pressure of informal work and it was only accepted as a short-term solution before return or as an entrance point to the labour market. One of the respondents, 38-year-old Edyta, benefitted from her stay and work, becoming regularised. Before 2004 she was already living and working in a large city in the UK, first on a tourist visa and working informally, then with 'bogus' self-employment by registering a business. This form of regularising work was a common practice for Polish workers at the time. Here 'bogus' means that in practice the migrants were working for and depended on only one employer in contrast to conventional self-employment and they themselves took on the burden of unstable work arrangements.

> He didn't pay taxes and paid me in the hand. … It was a risk for him and for me. I had a couple of situations, that when I was returning home and saw a police car in front of the house I was so scared. I was convinced that someone informed them about me. (Edyta, 38 years old)

Edyta was scared of being found out and even avoided going home to Poland for visits because of fears that she would not be allowed back into the UK.

Many respondents also planned their move as short-term or open-ended actively making use of their citizenship rights. These were young women that left Poland right after taking their *matura*, the Polish equivalent of A-levels, or after receiving their academic degree in order to get their first work experience abroad. Liliana, for example, only planned to work in the UK for two months to earn some money after she finished her university studies and achieved some distance from an emotional breakup. However, she worked through an agency, which, on the one hand, offered work quickly but, on the other hand, often only provided work for a week or two.

> It varied – there were days when I worked twelve hours, and there were days – towards the end – when I worked only four hours a day, because it turned out that there was no work. I worked through an agency, which a friend of mine had organised. She said from one day to the other, that I will be going to work. (Liliana, 25 years old)

This forced her to extend her stay several times in order to be able to pay for her living expenses in the UK. In the end the 25-year-old stayed for almost a year and worked mostly in a warehouse in order to pay her expenses and to try to handle the precariousness and instability of her stay and work. Back in Poland she could not therefore benefit from any substantial savings from her migrant work and was now struggling to find her first employment in the field of her studies. She rationalised her migration as a means to overcome the separation from her partner and acquire work and life experience. While her work and financial difficulties made her time in the UK stressful, she did not perceive it as a personal, financial or professional risk but as an opportunity to be taken by a young, independent European woman.

Gender in European Citizenship, Work and Migrant Families

The construction of gender as a structural force influences the position of Polish women in the labour market of Poland and the UK, as European citizens as well as on the household and partnership level. Migrant women try to combine their paid and unpaid work in the context of the feminisation and gendered segmentation of the labour market as well as the gendered division of reproductive and gainful work (Aufhauser 2000). Therefore, they are faced with different forms of intersecting inequalities by being a woman and a migrant worker with European citizenship (McCall 2005; Lutz 2007). The segregation and segmentation of the labour market institutionalise gendered patterns of work connected to class and nationality. These dynamics socialise migrants differently 'depending on their position within racial hierarchies, gender, class background and income/consumption patterns both in their own country and in the country of immigration' (McDowell 2008: 496). Mobility can impact greatly on the opportunities of paid and reproductive work (Coyle 2007; Cyrus 2008; Morokvasić et al. 2008), and in the context of European mobility research has found that while gender and ethnicity continue to be influential factors, the migration experience and life in the UK can offer ways to mediate structural constraints and renegotiate gendered expectations (Cook et al. 2011: 73). This renegotiation can be observed in Agata's division of caring responsibilities. While the 29-year-old came from a conservative Catholic family background in rural Poland and still reflected these values in her belief system, she and her husband shared the care duties for their three-year-old son because of the necessity for both to work in their jobs in a store and a restaurant to make a living and the absence of close relatives who could have helped. In Poland they were not able to live as a young couple in a separate household from their family, because of their low income. While this would have provided them with the family's support in childminding, they preferred the self-reliance that accompanied higher earnings.

> After three months he decided to suggest to me to come to him, so I came here in order to work together for a while and go back to Poland. And I liked my studies. … He said that I will not lose this and that I can always take a gap year from studies in Poland. (Agata, 29 years old)

On the one hand, Agata gave up her higher education in Poland for her husband; on the other hand, this led to a more egalitarian pattern of sharing household and child-caring responsibilities.

However, the postnational citizenship of the EU is based on the ideal of a productive man who is engaged in the public sphere, while women are assigned family responsibilities located in the private sphere leading to inequalities in the opportunities in the public sphere and potentially economic dependency (Askola 2012). Therefore, when social citizenship rights are connected to full-time employment, such as pensions, women might be denied full access to their rights because of the public–private separation of spheres and the low-valued gendered caring responsibilities (Duda-Mikulin 2013). The European citizenship has been developed beyond its initial roots as a 'market citizenship' for economically 'useful' persons, but it is still influenced by the image of its members as productive workers and offers its full set of rights to labourers rather than to people.

While Polish migrant women actively make use of the national and transnational rights that fit their needs, these needs are characterised by their gender roles and gendered expectations, which in turn can inhibit their citizenship (Duda-Mikulin 2013). The pressure of the neoliberal, often precarious, migrant job market and the lack of family and state support have led some of the respondents to share their household and caring duties more equally; however, managing the household as well as, if necessary, staying at home full-time for a period of time was still undertaken by women. Furthermore, the usage of their freedom of movement often depended on the family's situation. While respondents who were single and had no dependants were very mobile within the UK, within Europe and in their return migration making use of their rights while searching for the best employment possibilities available to them; married women with and without children would stay in the region and work despite precarious or low-paid employment with no prospects for progression. Despite shortcomings for women with caring responsibilities or low-valued skills, European citizenship has the potential to provide a benefit for female Polish migrants in re-negotiating their gender role (Coyle 2007).

The 'Migrant' Employment Sector and Downward Occupational Mobility

A further relevant limitation of European citizenship is a widely acknowledged tendency for downward occupational mobility of Polish post-accession migrants (Ciupijus 2011; Galgóczi et al. 2012). The level of female educational attainment in Poland is high, and Polish migrants to the UK are often highly educated as well; however, Polish degrees are rarely acknowledged in practice in the UK (Coyle 2007; Ciupijus 2011). The class distinction is ambivalent in relation to Polish migrants, who might be considered working class on the basis of their employment and social status but view themselves as middle class because of their education and social status in Poland (Eade et al. 2007). Thirty-nine per cent of young people entering the labour market in Poland do not work in their acquired profession either, 67 per cent of them because they were unable to find employment in their profession (GUS 2010). An acquired profession or academic degree therefore does not guarantee compatible employment in Poland either, rendering young people overqualified for the needs of the labour market. Hence prior employment in Poland is a more insightful indicator of potential downward occupational mobility.

The economic trade-off of a low-status, more lucrative position in the UK against a higher-status, less-profitable employment in Poland (Trevena 2011) was accepted by most of the interviewees. The interviewees strived to find employment in their professional fields later on, some were more successful than others, but only a few women immediately started working in their higher-status profession in the UK such as Jola, who was directly recruited from her university by a recruitment agency into a pharmacy in the UK.

> While studying I was looking for work abroad in England, it was still the time when agencies would come to the universities and recruited students, so you could either go for an internship for a couple of months first during the holidays or you could straight after finishing your diploma leave for the employer. (Jola, 30 years old)

In contrast to Jola, Mariola worked in a care home despite her degree as a food analyst. However, high educational attainment in Poland did not guarantee a well-paid job in this profession either.

> The salary in that place wasn't the best, I didn't really have anywhere to live, the situation with my parents also started to depress me. I decided that I already don't have the strength to live in Poland and there is no chance, I had sent my CV to different companies, because I had finished my studies, had done a *magister*, and I didn't find anything in my profession so I decided you know to go to Great Britain. (Mariola, 33 years old)

Now in the UK she was suffering under the work conditions such as night shifts, low pay and the emotional burden of care work, and has been trying for years to find work in her profession, but so far has not been successful. The respondents were either not able but in some cases also did not actively try to find work in their profession, either worried about their lack of English language skills or thinking that work agencies were the only route into employment for them as migrants.

The Construction of Polish Women

The specific Polish notion of gender roles and the social construction of Polish women influences female migrants' lives and interrelates with their migrant work trajectories. The image of the *Matka Polka* subordinating her own needs to those of the family and the Polish state by upholding and reproducing Polish national consciousness in the private sphere under foreign rule constructs the ideal Polish woman as self-sacrificing while at the same time characterised by a high capability to effectively deal with difficult circumstances

(Janion 1996). In Polish gender relations this is combined with the notion of 'soft patriarchy' from aristocratic times marked by chivalry while assigning women their space in the private sphere. The conceptualisation of the 'other', external enemy during the Polish partitions and socialist rule created a form of gender solidarity, which, while it had led to developments towards gender equality following Polish independence in 1918 (Pickhan 2006), has taken a different turn in a form of a backlash against women's rights after the end of the socialist era (Graff 2006; Petrowa-Wasilewicz 2006).

The socialist construction of gender roles perceived men as collectively oriented workers with strength and leadership qualities taking up the role of the head of the household and entitled to respect and obedience by his family. Whereas the ideal woman was characterised by her double role of a working mother, sharing the collectively oriented worker ideal with men while also having to fulfil her reproductive role as a woman and a mother in the private sphere (Marcus 2009). Therefore, on the one hand, specific gender roles were promoted while, on the other hand, gender inequality was not acknowledged (Rubchak 2011). The socialist state's narrative about gender inequality saw it rooted in the oppressive class structure shared with men and the in-class dependence on their men, which led to the inclusion of a commitment to equality and many achievements in women's emancipation in the socialist constitution while in practice a fraternal patriarchy persisted (Marcus 2009). The socialist state took over the role of a paternalistic caretaker providing welfare, through which the men's provider role diminished while women were still assigned their role but supported in their employment through job security and relief from caregiving. As discussed above, the transition from a planned to a market economy led to more inequality with harsh reductions in family and maternity benefits, the closing and privatisation of childcare facilities and gender discrimination in the workplace; therefore women grew more likely to be unemployed and fall under the poverty line. The role of the Catholic Church is also crucial, since a negative agenda towards women's rights was kept hidden – for example, by never mentioning the issue of abortion while at the same time supporting its opposition. Following 1989 the Church's influence on politics grew strong and they seized the moment to criminalise abortion, phase out sex education and eliminate contraceptive health insurance coverage (Mishtal 2009).

Challenging Gender Roles

Mobility entails the possibility of enabling Polish women to construct different identities and avoid the gender roles of the conservative discourse (Coyle 2007). For example, Kaja was focusing her energies on building up a business of her own. Since she started working as a care worker in the UK, she became more interested in the quality of care and different care philosophies and was now working on offering her own care services, with a colleague, incorporating these insights. In order to fulfil this idea, she separated from her long-term partner, whom she had met in the UK and moved abroad with to open up his business of hostels, and came back to the UK. Her family, from a rural area in Poland, did not understand her life choices and wanted her to settle down, get married, have children and not take the risks associated with opening up her own business.

> So I'm still, I'm not married, I don't have children, my parents ask: when will you get married, when will you have children, when this, when that? (Kaja, 34 years old)

However, Kaja resisted and did not want to fulfil these expectations.

Reinforcing Gender Roles

While some respondents, such as Kaja, were able to mediate gendered expectations, especially when they left Poland as young and single women with no dependants, others were also fulfilling their gendered roles in the tradition of a *Matka Polka*. For example, Kinga's migration and work trajectories were determined by her family situation and she sacrificed her own ambitions for the sake of the family. While she enjoyed her profession in Poland and appreciated its stability, her partner's precarious work in Poland urged him to search for better opportunities in the UK. After two years of working there, during which Kinga took care of their son alone in Poland while working full-time, he could not imagine a future living and working in Poland for him anymore and Kinga had to decide if she wanted to become a single mother in Poland or leave her job and move with her then ten-year-old to the UK. She then worked through an agency in various short-term jobs before she found longer-term employment in a food packing factory, where the work was characterised by physical strains such as the low temperature at her workplace and heavy lifting as well as low pay.

> The biggest punishment for me was to come here and lose my job. … For some years now I worked in a factory where we were packing bananas. That was physical work, I must admit, hard work. (Kinga, 35 years old)

Kinga's difficult times alone in Poland and now in her demanding work bring to mind the *Matka Polka*, who is able and willing to suffer, an idea based in Christianity and which relieved from its religious meaning was also used in socialism (Marcus 2009).

The Influence of Gender and Family on Return

The idea of the proactive woman, who is able to deal with difficult circumstances in order to sustain the Polish household, is comparable to the discourse around the Ukrainian *Berehynia*. These seemingly positive attributes, however, also serve as a patronising approach, in which compliments to the esteem and beauty of women, supposedly intended to be flattering, uphold the matriarchal ideal (Rubchak 2011). In research on Ukrainian women in Italy it was shown that the freedom from patriarchal constraints on everyday life in the origin country combined with, despite its precariousness and informality, more stable work arrangements led to the female migrants becoming more independent, building close personal relationships in their destination country and finding it difficult to reintegrate into their home community because of the stigma attached to migrant women as supposedly 'loose' women and bad mothers (Hrycak 2011). While the first insight from this research is parallel to the experiences of the present sample, the problems of reintegration due to stigma were not observable. This might be due to the fact that following EU accession less women from Poland were forced to move abroad without their partners and children. Migration rather happened, while often consecutively, still in the family context, resulting in fewer 'Euro-orphans' than through earlier movements (Urbańska 2015). In a similar vein, return migration was also connected to the family situation.

As mentioned above, in some cases emigration was intended as short-term and return was planned beforehand, especially in the case of single women without dependants; in other cases the return decision was based on familial factors. In these cases either a child was born or expected, and it was decided to raise it in Poland in order to have the family's support and to use family property in Poland for the growing family to live in, or there were other care responsibilities that the women had to take over in Poland. Both patterns were present in the case of Kasia, who is 34 years old. After working in a UK warehouse she returned to Poland to care for her mother, who was suffering from a severe illness, and her younger, disabled sister. After her mother passed away she took over the care and provider role for her sister, since her sister's father was not involved in her life. However, she was not able to sustain the two of them in Poland and arranged for her sister to live in an assisted living facility and Kasia went back to her previous work in the UK warehouse, where she then met her husband. The couple decided to have a child and move back to Poland into the house that her husband had inherited.

> My boyfriend has a house outside [a big Polish city], which he got from his dad. … It is a very nice location, quiet, peace. There were many reasons: that

> house, my studies. But despite it all I would like to go back [to the UK]. (Kasia, 34 years old)

They now lived in his home region, where he has family and friends, but she did not have many social contacts and it was far away from where her sister lives. She would have therefore prefer to re-emigrate but could not make use of this right because of her family situation. While the majority of women who returned to Poland had low-paid employment in the UK such as Kasia, some also prioritised their family decisions over their high-status jobs in the UK, like Renata, who had a managerial position and was married to a British citizen. The couple decided to move to Poland in order to make use of the support of Renata's family in raising their first child, because they lived in a very expensive city in the UK, where they would have, despite their high positions, had to work a lot. Moreover, assistance with childcare was absent because the partner's family did not live near to them.

Gender and Agency in Different Work Trajectories

In their investigation of the relevance of migration for work trajectories Grabowska-Lusińska and Jaźwińska-Motylska (2013) examine gender specific effects such as differences in the approach to and the making use of opportunity structures. These researchers found differences in the experiences of women and men, where Polish migrant women were more determined to take advantage of the opportunities available while living in a different country. Their work trajectories can be changed tremendously by the migration process, through which migration becomes a stage in their working lives, which is less dependent on their family situation. Men, on the other hand, use migration as an intermission in their career and a means to an end. The authors explain these gender-specific effects with the difficult positioning of women in the gendered labour market of their origin and destination countries, which urges greater determination from women to overcome the different challenges posed by migration. In contrast to male migrants' tendency to conform to institutional conditions, women were found to be quick in reacting to changed conditions and innovatively making use of their chances for professional development (Grabowska-Lusińska and Jaźwińska-Motylska 2013).

The migrant work trajectories that result from the interplay between structures and agency were categorised into stable or changing pathways with different levels of structural and agentic influences (Grabowska-Lusińska 2012). The stable careers were labelled as the 'fixative' and the 'project' paths, in which the latter is in need of a higher level of agency. The changing trajectories were identified as the 'coincidence' and the 'exploration' paths, where the second again calls for higher agentic initiative (Grabowska-Lusińska 2012). These insights of a greater determination of female Polish migrant workers to confront structural constraints and the significance of agency for their work trajectories are helpful in understanding the experiences reflected upon by the interviewees.

The majority of the interviewees found their first employment in the UK in low-paid work below their level of education. Some women stayed in those jobs feeling stuck and often realised their ambitions in other fields such as trade union and community activities. However, other women were able to either follow a straightforward career path within the migrant sector they had started in or pursue additional UK education and found work in those sectors afterwards. Only a few interviewees could make use of their Polish diplomas in the UK. Among the return migrants many pursued low-paid jobs in the UK and were looking for employment more adequate to their educational level in Poland or had left higher positions in the UK for non-work-related motivations or professional fulfilment that was difficult to achieve in the UK.

Agency in Pursuing One's Fulfilment

An example of the latter is the case of Ula, who held a managerial position in a shop in the UK but wanted to return to her profession of working in the culture and arts arena. In her experience this pathway was difficult to fulfil in the UK without a network in culture, so she returned to Poland, where she had worked before in the field and found her professional fulfilment as cultural attaché for a philharmonic orchestra. This can be seen as a 'project', in Grabowska-Lusińska's (2012) terms, with the migration experience as an interlude in her career path. In contrast to Ula, most women who were content with their work conditions in the UK and returned to Poland had family reasons for doing so. Most women who remained in the UK had experienced some form of occupational change over time, which were often in line with the concepts of either a 'project' or an 'exploration' (Grabowska-Lusińska 2012); however, they would refer to their successful path as luck or coincidence despite the risks and efforts they had undertaken. After having experienced exploitative and precarious working conditions, Lidia had found work in a care home, where she and her mother, with whom she emigrated right after finishing school in Poland, worked together. However, work in the care home was emotionally draining and she wanted to pursue higher education, so she agreed with her mother to work and save money for a year and then study a year full-time at college. Most women who undertook further UK education had to work and study at the same time, so respondents with caring responsibilities were usually not able to do this and afford the comparatively high costs of UK education. In Lidia's case, her mother's support for her studies was exceptional, yet relatable to her mother's providing responsibilities for her daughter reflecting the generational dynamics of both these women's trajectories.

> I made an agreement with my mum that I would work for a year and I would save all the money and I would save up enough to go to college, cause obviously I wanted to continue with my education. (Lidia, 27 years old)

Although Lidia's 'project' pathway saw her be proactive and confront difficulties such as working, saving and studying a difficult course in a foreign language (Grabowska-Lusińska 2012), she belittled her agentic role and portrayed herself as being a lucky person. Olga's work trajectory can be conceptualised as an 'exploration' (Grabowska-Lusińska 2012), because after three years of stable, well-paid employment she grew tired of the lack of possibilities for progression because of new supervisors and changed her work. She went from a secretarial position to employment in catering in a higher education institution, where she took advantage of the possibilities provided by the trade union and the institution to take different courses. Thereby she attained further qualifications and was promoted to hospitality supervisor. This progression within a typical migrant sector was often the case in the sample and shows that, while progressing professionally with support of their agency, Polish women often still just made use of the opportunity structures available to them as migrant women.

> They took me into catering and I worked in catering selling coffee, tea, that sort of thing, and in the meantime I did courses. … And after three years of work in just catering I was promoted to hospitality supervisor. (Olga, 38 years old)

Olga and Lidia both did not refer to their gender roles and had no caring responsibilities; this suggests that while they worked in gendered sectors and fulfil the gender construction in the destination country (Anderson 2000), they were able to challenge the traditional gendered expectations from their home country in the private sphere marked by their generational position.

Structural Forces Impeding Fulfilment

After working for twenty-seven years as a teacher in Poland, Beata started the migration movement for her whole family. When she left she had only intended to stay for a few months; however, her family followed one by one, and she ended up staying and working in physical labour in the food packing industry. She was discontent with her work and life in the UK but stayed because of her caring responsibilities for the whole family and her grandchildren.

> And at that moment, if I wanted to go back to Poland I would no longer be able to, because I could not leave my family here. (Beata, 54 years old)

Although she wanted to go back to Poland her agency and freedom of movement was impeded by her gendered role. Her work trajectory can be understood as 'fixative' (Grabowska-Lusińska 2012) since in Poland she had a straightforward career as a teacher and in the UK she continued the same job in which she started out; however, the migration as such brought unintended change, since it was an agreed sabbatical from work in Poland and a pre-planned short-term work and living arrangement in the UK.

> I took leave from work for that period, the headmaster had consented and after four months that I was here, my husband came for two months. … I'm still not too thrilled about England, I do not know maybe out of habit, it was such that I came to England with 47 years old, so some of these things in Poland, considering my age, I was not accustomed to a lot of other things, right? … Also, to be honest maybe I do not like it in the UK, because somehow I cannot fulfill myself professionally. (Beata, 54 years old)

In this case the 'fixative' (Grabowska-Lusińska 2012) trajectory interrelates with the ideal of the sacrificing *Matka Polka.* However, while feeling stuck in her work and in the UK, she used her agency in other fields to fulfil her aspirations. She was active in a women's group of a Polish trade union branch and prepared homemade dinners for delivery to the Polish community in her area. While her small business did not add a substantial amount of income, it served her wish for fulfilment, since she conceptualised it as a social activity, which at the same time responded to her, with her means, difficult-to-achieve dream of opening a Polish cafe or *kawiarnia.* Occupational mobility in her case was also not easy because of factors such as the industrial area where she lived and could not move away from because of her family's permanent settlement, which limited work opportunities, as well as her age and limited English proficiency.

CONCLUSION

The difficulty of determining to what extent structure and agency influence the migration experience and migrant work trajectories derives from their interrelation as co-constitutive elements (Bakewell 2010; King 2010) either as part of the duality of structure (Giddens 1984) or conceptualised as separated by time (Archer 2003). Therefore, this chapter has investigated the different forms and patterns the interrelation between gender roles, work trajectories and agency expose in the context of female Polish post-accession migration to the UK. This chapter has focused on enacted agency in relation to work trajectories and gender roles, whereas the interviewees have also exhibited agency in many other areas such as social networks, leisure, local integration and collective agency (briefly touched on but whose further investigation would have gone beyond the scope of this chapter). The analysis of interviews with female migrant workers as well as female return migrants supports the understanding of moving, staying and returning as different sides of the same migratory agency (de Haas 2014).

While European citizenship has provided Polish women with the potential benefits of free movement and the possibility to renegotiate gender roles and is actively being used in choosing and combining different possibilities of living, working and studying, the availability of all the facets of this right are often limited to single working women with no dependants. Women with caring responsibilities also make use of this right, though in a way that will satisfy their family's need and not necessarily according to their personal preferences. A significant shortcoming of European citizenship is its inability to prevent downward occupational mobility, leading to acquired Polish education and work experience remaining unused and unrecognised in the UK labour market. Many young, single women will accept this pattern, since their stay is intended to be short-term, they in some cases have not had prior work experience in Poland and they plan on fulfilling their professional aspirations back in Poland. However, those women that intend to stay often try, predominantly without success, to find work in their profession. In order to achieve professional progression they pursue additional UK education, a pathway limited to women with enough time and financial resources. These 'project' pathways as well as the 'exploration' pathways (Grabowska-Lusińska 2012) require a higher level of agency and also the ability to take risks, which sometimes leads to challenging gender roles. The agency of women with caring responsibilities, on the other hand, is impeded to a certain degree and they experience occupational stagnation or even leave beneficial employment arrangements behind, in Poland and in the UK, in order to fulfil their gendered expectations.

REFERENCES

Anderson, B. 2000. *Doing the Dirty Work? The Global Politics of Domestic Labour*. New York, London: Zed Books.

Apitzsch, U. and I. Siouti. 2007. *Biographical Analysis as an Interdisciplinary Research Perspective in the Field of Migration Studies*. Frankfurt am Main: Johann Wolfgang Goethe Universität.

Archer, M. 2003. *Structure, Agency and the Internal Conversation*. Cambridge: Cambridge University Press.

Askola, H. 2012. 'Tale of two citizenships? Citizenship, migration and care in the European Union'. *Social & Legal Studies* 21: 341–356.

Aufhauser, E. 2000. 'Migration und Geschlecht: Zur Konstruktion und Rekonstruktion von Weiblichkeit und Männlichkeit in der internationalen Migration'. In *Internationale Migration: Die globale Herausforderung des 21. Jahrhunderts?* edited by K. Husa, C. Parnreiter and I. Stacher, 97–122. Frankfurt am Main: Brandes und Apsel, Wien: Südwind.

Bakewell, O. 2010. 'Some reflections on structure and agency in migration theory'. *Journal of Ethnic and Migration Studies* 36 (10): 1689–1708.

Booth, R. 2013. 'Polish becomes England's second language'. *The Guardian*, January 30, 2013. http://www.guardian.co.uk (accessed 15 April 2015).

Burrell, K., ed. 2009. *Polish migration to the UK in the 'New' European Union: After 2004*. Surrey: Ashgate.

Burrell, K. 2010. 'Staying, returning, working and living: Key themes in current academic research undertaken in the UK on migration movements from Eastern Europe'. *Social Identities* 16 (3): 297–308.

Ciupijus, Z. 2011. 'Mobile central eastern Europeans in Britain: Successful European Union citizens and disadvantaged labour migrants?' *Work, Employment & Society* 25 (3): 540–550.

Cook, J., P. Dwyer and L. Waite. 2011. 'The Experiences of Accession 8 Migrants in England: Motivations, Work and Agency'. *International Migration* 49 (2): 54–79.

Coyle, A. 2007. 'Resistance, regulation and rights. The changing status of polish women's migration and work in the "New" Europe'. *European Journal of Women's Studies* 14 (1): 37–50.

Cyrus, N. 2008. 'Managing a mobile life: Changing attitudes among illegally employed polish household workers in Berlin'. In *Migration and Mobility in an Enlarged Europe: A Gender Perspective*, edited by S. Metz-Göckel, M. Morokvasić, and A. S. Münst, 179–202. Opladen: Barbara Budrich.

de Haas, H. 2014. 'Migration theory – Quo Vadis?' *IMI Working Papers* Paper 100.

Drinkwater, S., J. Eade and M. Garapich. 2006. *Poles Apart? EU Enlargement and the Labour Market Outcomes of Immigrants in the UK*. IZA Discussion Paper 2410, Bonn: IZA.

Duda-Mikulin, E. 2013. 'Citizenship in action? A case study of polish migrant women moving between Poland and the UK'. *Kultura i Edukacja* 6 (99): 205–224.

Düvell, F. and M. Garapich. 2011. 'Polish migration to the UK: Continuities and discontinuities'. *Centre on Migration Policy and Society Working Paper* No. 84.

Eade, J., S. Drinkwater and M. P. Garapich. 2006. *Polscy migranci w Londynie – klasa społeczna i etniczność*. Surrey: Economic and Social Research Council.

Eade, J., S. Drinkwater and M. P. Garapich. 2007. *Class and Ethnicity: Polish Migrant Workers in London: Full Research Report*. ESRC End of Award Report, RES-000-22-1294. Swindon: ESRC.

Engbersen, G., M. Okólski, R. Black and C. Panţîru. 2010. 'Introduction: Working out a way from East to West: EU enlargement and labour migration from Central and Eastern Europe'. In *A Continent Moving West? EU Enlargement and Labour Migration from Central and Eastern Europe*, edited by R. Black, G. Engbersen, M. Okólski, and C. Panţîru, 7–22. Amsterdam: Amsterdam University Press.

Favell, A. 2008. 'The new face of East West migration in Europe'. *Journal of Ethnic and Migration Studies* 34 (5): 701–716.

Fix, M., D. G. Papademetriou, J. Batalova, A. Terrazas, S. Yi-Ying Lin and M. Mittelstadt. 2009. *Migration and the Global Recession*. Washington, DC: Migration Policy Institute.

Galgóczi, B., J. Leschke and A. Watt, A. 2012. 'EU labour migration and labour markets in troubled times'. In *EU Labour Migration in Troubled Times: Skills Mismatch, Return and Policy*, edited by B. Galgóczi, J. Leschke and A. Watt, 1–10. Farnham: Ashgate.

Giddens, A. 1984. *The Constitution of Society: Outline of the Theory of Structuration*. Cambridge: Polity.

Grabowska-Lusińska, I. 2012. *Migrantów ścieżki zawodowe bez granic*. Warszawa: Wydawnictwo Naukowe Scholar.

Grabowska-Lusińska, I. and E. Jaźwińska-Motylska. 2013. 'Znaczenie migracji w życiu zawodowym kobiet i mężczyzn'. *Kultura i społeczeństwo* 3: 85–108.

Graff, A. 2006. 'Warum Frauen in Polen "nicht stören"'. In *Jahrbuch Polen 2006 Frauen*, 34–44. Wiesbaden: Deutsches Polen-Institut, Harrassowitz Verlag.

GUS. 2010. *Entry of Young People into the Labour Market in Poland in 2009*. Warszawa: ZWS.

Hrycak, A. 2011. 'Women as migrants on the margins of the European Union'. In *Mapping Difference: the Many Faces of Women in Contemporary Ukraine*, edited by M. J. Rubchak, 47–64. Berghahn Books.

Janion, M. 1996. *Kobiety i duch inności*. Warszawa: Wydawnictwo Sic!

Kaczmarczyk, P., ed. 2011. 'Recent trends in international migration in Poland. The 2010 SOPEMI report'. *CMR Working Paper* 51 (109).

King, A. 2010. 'The odd couple: Margaret Archer, Anthony Giddens and British social theory'. *British Journal of Sociology* 61: 253–260.

Krings, T., A. Bobek, E. Moriarty, J. Salamonska and J. Wickham. 2009. 'Migration and recession: Polish migrants in post-celtic Tiger Ireland'. *Sociological Research Online* 14 (2): 1–6.

Kurekova, L. 2011. 'Theories of migration: Conceptual reviews and empirical testing in the context of the EU East–West flows'. *Paper prepared for Interdisciplinary conference on Migration Economic Change, Social Challenge*, University College London.

Lutz, H. 2007. 'Die 24-Stunden-Polin – Eine intersektionelle Analyse transnationaler Dienstleistungen'. In *Achsen der Ungleichheit. Zum Verhältnis von Klasse, Geschlecht und Ethnizität*, edited by C. Klinger, G. A. Knapp, and B. Sauer, 210–234. Frankfurt and New York: Campus Verlag.

Marcus, I. 2009. 'Wife beating: Ideology and practice under State Socialism in Hungary, Poland, and Romania'. In *Gender Politics and Everyday Life in State Socialist Eastern and Central Europe*, edited by S. Penn, and J. Massino, 115–132. New York: Palgrave Macmillan.

McCall, L. 2005. 'The complexity of intersectionality'. *Journal of Women in Culture and Society* 30 (3): 1771–1800.

McDowell, L. 2008. 'Thinking through work: Complex inequalities, constructions of difference and trans-national migrants'. *Progress in Human Geography* 32 (4): 491–507.

Migration Observatory. 2012. *Pole Position – New Census Data Shows Ten-Fold Growth of England and Wales' Polish Population.* Migration Observatory commentary. Oxford: COMPAS, Oxford University.

Mishtal, J. Z. 2009. 'How the Church became the State: The Catholic regime and reproductive rights in State Socialist Poland'. In *Gender Politics and Everyday Life in State Socialist Eastern and Central Europe*, edited by S. Penn, and J. Massino, 133–150. New York: Palgrave Macmillan.

Moch, L. P. 2005. 'Gender and migration research'. In *International Migration Research. Constructions, Omissions and the Promise of Interdisciplinarity*, edited by M. Bommes and E. Morawska, 95–108. Aldershot: Ashgate.

Morokvasić, M., A. S. Münst and L. Metz-Göckel. 2008. *Migration and Mobility in an Enlarged Europe. A Gender Perspective.* Opladen: Barbara Budrich.

Petrowa-Wasilewicz, A. 2006. 'Denkmal der unbekannten Köchin oder braucht Polen den Feminismus?' In *Jahrbuch Polen 2006 Frauen*, 52–59. Wiesbaden: Deutsches Polen-Institut, Harrassowitz Verlag.

Pickhan, G. 2006. 'Frauenrollen, Geschlechterdifferenz und Nation-Building in der Geschichte Polens'. In *Jahrbuch Polen 2006 Frauen*, 7–18. Wiesbaden: Deutsches Polen-Institut, Harrassowitz Verlag.

Rienzo, C. and C. Vargas-Silva. 2012. *Migrants in the UK: An Overview.* Migration Observatory Briefing. Oxford: COMPAS, University of Oxford.

Ruchak, M. J. 2011. 'Turning oppression into opportunity: An introduction'. In *Mapping Difference: The Many Faces of Women in Contemporary Ukraine*, edited by M. J. Rubchak, 1–22. Oxford, New York: Berghahn Books.

Schütze, F. 1983. 'Biographieforschung und narratives Interview'. *Neue Praxis* 13 (3): 283–293.

Trevena, P. 2011. 'Divided by class, connected by work: Class divisions among the new wave of Polish migrants in the UK'. In *Studia Migracyjne - Przegląd Polonijny: Polacy na Wyspach (w Wielkiej Brytanii)*, edited by M. P. Garapich. Nr 1/2011: 71–96.

Urbańska, S. 2015. *Matka Polka na odległość. Z doświadczeń migracyjnych robotnic 1989–2010.* Toruń: Wydawnictwo Naukowe Uniwersytetu Mikołaja Kopernika.

White, A. 2010. 'Young people and migration from Contemporary Poland'. *Journal of Youth Studies* 13 (5): 565–580.

White, A. 2011. *Polish Families and Migration since EU Accession.* Bristol: The Policy Press.

Chapter II.4

'Once You See That It Can Be Otherwise, Then You Expect Something Else'

The Labour Experience of Polish Migrant Returnees from the UK

Mateusz Karolak

Many migration scholars implicitly assume that the migration process ends upon the moment of return.[1] However, as already shown by Alfred Schütz (1945) in his famous essay 'The Homecomer', migrants returning to their place of origin after significant time spent abroad are often only at the beginning of a long process. It consists of attempts to achieve the reconciliation of memories and expectations about the shared norms and values with the facts of the matter, which might have changed significantly. As the migrants themselves have also changed in the time spent abroad, the process of adaptation might be painful. Psychologists called this situation a reverse culture shock, and although 'the theoretical literature states no returnee is exempt from [it]' (Gaw 2000, 84), the empirical data supporting this statement is limited. Yet the researchers who acknowledged the complexity of return migration process make two another assumptions, which – as I will attempt to show in this chapter – are strongly debatable.

First, they often write about the reintegration of those who 'come back home' and perceive it analogously to the integration of the immigrants abroad. These narrations start with an imagined state of complete inclusion, which falls apart during migration and needs to be re-established after return from abroad. While it seems uncontroversial for the socio-cultural aspects of integration (since returnees already know the local language, have native friends and understand – but not necessarily share – norms and values), their structural position with the situation on the labour market as the main indicator is more debatable.

Secondly, similarly to analyses regarding immigrants, in much, mostly quantitative, research devoted to returning migrants, employment is perceived as a sufficient indicator of successful labour market integration (e.g. Saarela and Finnäs 2009). Yet, as shown elsewhere (see Egan 2018, Chapter I.1 in this book), employment patterns have changed significantly. As a result of complex economic, political and ideological processes, employment in Europe became more flexible and unstable, which led to the precarisation of workers' lives (Standing 2011).

Therefore, in order to gain a more nuanced picture of the returning migrants' situation in the labour market it is necessary to ask not only about their formal status (either employed, unemployed or inactive) but also about the subjective meaning ascribed to work by the returnees themselves as well as the paths of their occupational careers.

Challenging the above-mentioned popular assumptions, in this chapter I will examine Polish post-accession return migrants' experiences in the sphere of work and employment, against the background of changing employment patterns and flexibilisation of work. Through an examination of the returnees' life stories the chapter will investigate in what way their work experience abroad impacts on their subjective perception of employment standards after return. The main research question focuses on the return migrants responses (coping strategies) to the imagined tensions created by differing employment standards. I argue that, first, although many Polish migrants worked in precarious jobs on the peripheries of the labour market in the UK, they tend to perceive positively their previous work conditions after return; secondly, that the revealed tensions between employment experiences during and after migration might potentially bring about a social change, although its actualisation depends on the configuration of the returnees' coping strategies and structural circumstances.

The case study concerns post-accession migrants who have returned from the UK to Poland. These two countries were chosen for a variety of reasons. Poland, with its embedded neoliberal regime (Bohle and Greskovits 2012), belongs to those EU countries with the highest share of flexible employment contracts (ETUI 2015). Moreover, after 2004 it was the country with the highest, in absolute figures, migration outflow. It is estimated that eleven years after the 2004 EU enlargement, roughly 2,000,000 Poles lived in other EU countries (GUS 2016). At the same time, the UK, with its liberal market economy (Hall and Soskice 2001) and one of the most flexible labour markets in the world (Schwab 2014), became the most popular destination of Polish post-accession migrants with 720,000 Poles living in the UK at the end of 2015 (GUS 2016). Furthermore, Polish migrants in the UK, most of them being between 15–34 years old, are on average younger than those who migrated to the so-called old destination countries, for example, Germany (Kaczmarczyk 2012; Okólski and Salt 2014). This put them in double jeopardy on the labour market, since they were not only migrants but also young people, who tend to have structurally worse positions in the labour market than the middle aged (Piore 1979; Currie 2007; Ciupijus 2011; Hodder and Kretos 2015). On the other hand, Polish migrants in the UK are formally better educated than pre-accession migrants and non-migrants remaining in Poland (Trevena 2013; Okólski and Salt 2014).

Migration, however, is not always permanent. Researchers characterised the post-accession movement of people by its 'liquidity' (Grabowska-Lusińska and Okólski 2009; Engbersen, Snel and De Boom 2010) and migrants' unwillingness to pre-determine their length of stay abroad (Drinkwater and Garapich 2013), called 'intentional unpredictability' (Eade, Drinkwater and Garapich 2007). Eventually many of CEECs' migrants either return (at least temporarily) to their country of origin or move to another country (Smoliner, Förschner, Hochgerner and Nova 2011; Lang 2013). Indeed, it is estimated that at least 587,000 Polish post-accession migrants returned from the UK to their homeland (Karolak 2016). Since most of the returning migrants worked abroad, it leads to questions addressed in this chapter: namely, how (precarious) work experience from abroad impacts on the returnees' perception of employment standards after return and what returnees do about it.

The chapter starts with a review of the existing literature devoted to the specificity of post-accession migration and return migration between the UK and Poland. Next it outlines the methodological background used to obtain the research results, divided into two main parts. The first part presents selected returnees' narratives concerning the disadvantages of work in Poland as compared to the UK, whereas the second part discusses coping strategies employed by returnees facing the described discrepancies and assesses their potential for social change.

MIGRATION AND RETURN AFTER 2004

Following the enlargement of the EU in 2004, the opportunity structure for the new EU citizens changed, as labour market restrictions were gradually withdrawn and the state did not mediate anymore between migrant workers and the labour market. Despite the intra-EU migrants still experiencing legal and practical disadvantages (see Sahraoui, Polkowski and Karolak 2018, Chapter I.3 in this book), it is without a doubt that the opening of labour markets expanded their scope of freedom and gave them more agency as compared to that enjoyed before the EU enlargement.

The post-2004-accession Polish migrants in the UK differ with respect to their socio-demographic characteristics from both the pre-accession migrants and migrants to the 'old destination countries' (e.g. Germany) (Okólski and Salt 2014). First, the general trend indicates that there is an over-representation of people with tertiary education (Trevena 2009). However, despite the relatively high level of education of Poles in the UK and their high economic activity rate (85%), this does not translate into good positions in the British labour market (Currie 2007). As noted by Okólski and Salt (2014: 14), with the increase in the number of Polish migrants in the UK their occupational structure has changed, shifting towards basic and low-skilled jobs. For many young migrants, work in the UK was their first experience in the labour market. This is explained by Paulina Trevena (2013) by the combination of the structural demand on the British labour market for the migrants' low-skilled labour, the unprecedented number of young graduates in Poland, the existing migrant network and finally migrants' temporary acceptance of low-skilled jobs in exchange for relatively high earnings which allowed them to lead a certain lifestyle. Nevertheless, over time some migrants managed to climb the career ladder (Knight et al. 2014), overcoming not only the dual labour market but also gender divisions (see Aziz 2018, Chapter II.3 in this book).

This reflects the diversity of migration forms and patterns, one of the features frequently underlined by scholars of post-accession mobility. Apart from the 'incomplete', 'circular' and 'settlement' migrations, researchers noted that a new phenomenon called 'liquid migration' gained importance. It is characterised by individualisation, a lower migrant attachment to the family and temporality (Engbersen et al. 2010). '[Liquid] migrants try their luck in new and multiple countries of destination, benefiting from open borders and labour markets' (Engbersen and Snel 2013: 960–961). Characteristic to 'liquid migrants' is deviation from specific plans and the application of strategies to keep their options open. John Eade, Stephen Drinkwater and Michał Garapich (2007) coined the term 'intentional unpredictability' for this strategy. They write that '[migrants'] refusal to confine themselves to one nation-state setting underlines their adaptation to a flexible, deregulated and increasingly transnational, post-modern capitalist labour market' (Eade et al. 2007: 34). It is, however, too simplistic to perceive the flexibility of CEE migrants only as a matter of their choice and an expression of their agency. As McCollum and Findlay (2015) point out, the segmented labour market and geopolitical constraints create the constant demand for flexible migrant labour from the CEE. The permanent circulation of those migrants 'can be seen as both a cause and effect of the growth in flexible labour structures' (McCollum and Findlay 2015). Additionally, the low-wage employers tend to racialise central and Eastern Europeans as hard-working, non-demanding and flexible employees and thus in the case of certain precarious jobs they particularly seek migrants from the A10 accession countries.

Many of those 'flexible' post-accession migrants eventually decided to return to Poland. Their accomplishment of their migration aims (either spending a certain time abroad or earning a planned amount of money) appears to be the main reason for their return (Anacka and Fihel 2013: 51). The reasons declared for their return vary between those related to family and work, and they often are a combination of instrumental and non-instrumental aims, which make up the returnee's life project, revised during the course of migration (Karolak 2015).

The existing research provides mixed evidence with regard to the return migrants' situation in the labour market. Kaczmarczyk and Lesińska (2012: 31) suggest that so far the migratory experience is not perceived as an advantage in the Polish labour market, in contrast to the knowledge of foreign languages and other soft skills. Nonetheless, Budnik (as quoted in Lang 2013: 33) states that

> return migrants [from the CEECs] had around a three times higher probability of finding a job after a return to the source country than the unemployed or non-participants. If the return migrants were positively selected or if they were able to accumulate a job-relevant human capital abroad, the increase of emigration after 2004 might be seen as a factor reinforcing labour market activity foremost of those who would otherwise find it hard to enter into employment.

The discrepancies in the assessment of the return migrants' situation result from the narrow understanding of the labour market integration in the latter case. The fact of finding employment says nothing about its quality. This remark seems especially relevant in the case of migrants returning to Poland, one of the EU leaders in terms of temporary employment, the country which since the late 1990s has witnessed strong labour market dualisation and the emergence of millions of insecure and precarious jobs (Mrozowicki and Maciejewska 2016).

Another puzzling phenomenon is a very clear increase in the percentage of returnees running their own businesses. While before emigration only 1 per cent of the future migrants had their own business, after emigration this rose up to 19 per cent (Centrum Doradztwa Strategicznego 2010; Iglicka 2010; GUS 2013). Some optimistic interpretations conclude that such an increase 'clearly indicates that emigration teaches self-reliance and awakens "the spirit of the entrepreneurship"' (Centrum Doradztwa Strategicznego 2010: 56). However, the results of the census show that only 4 per cent of returnees employed somebody else, while 15 per cent were self-employed without employees (GUS 2013: 75). Taking this into consideration, it could be asked to what extent such a high rate of self-employment is an outcome of the returnees' entrepreneurship, and to what extent it is a result of the structural constraints on the Polish labour market. As shown by numerous works (e.g. Fudge, Tucker and Vosko 2002; Schmiz 2013), self-employment is one of forms of the ongoing flexibilisation and precarisation of the labour market. For many companies, pushing employees to became self-employed is a way of lowering labour costs and shifting the risk of market fluctuations on to subcontractors. It would require further and more in-depth examination to determine what motives guided return migrants to choose this form of labour market activity.

All in all, the overwhelming majority of adult returnees had worked abroad, often in precarious jobs. The divergent research results presented above point to the fact that despite the attention paid to employment of returnees the quality of jobs found by returnees was often overlooked. Therefore, the next parts of this chapter explore in what ways Polish returnees from the UK experience and perceive their employment in Poland as well as how these translate into their individual strategies in the labour market.

RESEARCH DESIGN AND METHODOLOGY

Following the methodologies established in the biographical tradition of Fritz Schütze (2007), between November 2013 and January 2015, I carried out twenty-six biographical narrative interviews with Polish returnees from the UK (fourteen) and re-emigrants to the UK (twelve).[2] All interviews were recorded and transcribed. Choosing biographical narrative interviews as a method of data collection allowed for capturing two dimensions, namely: the objective course of migrants' working experiences and the subjective perception of his/her own situation (cf. Hughes 1997), thus overcoming the narrow understanding of labour market integration as any employment. The research concerned long-term migrants, who had worked in the UK at least one year, and after returning had lived in Poland for at least six months, irrespective of their reasons for migration, return and re-emigration (if such occurred). Interviews with returnees were conducted in the Lower Silesia region of Poland and in Warsaw, while those with re-emigrants were conducted in the major cities of Scotland as well as in London. Fourteen of the interviewees were women, and twelve were men. They were from different social, economic and educational backgrounds and aged between 23 and 50, with a predominant number of those interviewed between 25 and 35 years old. The respondents were initially recruited by snowball sampling, mailing and via internet forums for migrants. During the second stage of the research the sampling became theoretical and interviewees were chosen from the established contacts database. This allowed exploration in more depth categories emerging from the collected data and was aimed at data saturation. In the interviews I raised biographical questions, explored the motives and motivations for migration, return and re-emigration, as well as addressed returnees' post-migration experience in the labour market. The interviews were analysed following procedures of the grounded theory methodology (GTM) (Glaser and Strauss 1967), including open coding and selective coding. A software programme, NVivo 10, was employed for more systematic data comparison.

RESEARCH RESULTS

Experience Trap Versus Experience Path

For a lot of young Polish migrants, employment in the UK was their first serious work experience. They left Poland just after high school, during a semester break or after graduating from university. Money was not always their only motive for migration, which was also often associated with a choice for a certain lifestyle and a search for an adventure. Planned initially for a few months, the stay in the UK was often prolonged; however, it was not considered a permanent one. Migrants' first jobs were usually obtained through social networks or work agencies and were treated as temporary, as it was, for example, in the case of Patrycja: 'I got this job in the museum so I thought it will be only for a while, such a transition job, we will see. ... The money was gone so I had to take some work' (W7). However, once Patrycja got the job, she kept it longer than she had initially expected. Besides structural factors constraining an advancement of their labour market position, migrants themselves also did not actively search for another options. As stated by Bartosz, a 30-year-old economics graduate:

> The first job [in the UK] was at a car wash [laughs] but, you know, it was something that you could got easily. And I stupidly really relished this money – you know – at that time one pound costed 7 Polish Zlotys! [laughs] So, I really enjoyed that for one day at work I earned more than in a week in Poland. (M6)

The feeling of temporariness combined with the satisfaction of higher earnings compared to those available in Poland, new work environment and colleagues – as put by another interviewee, 'a seductive comfortable life' (M2) – prevented many young migrants from actively searching for a better job, especially in the early stages of migration. This confirms findings by Paulina Trevena (2013), who called such migrants the 'drifters'. Trevena stated that some of them eventually decide to pursue (with various results) more sustainable career paths in the UK. My interviews revealed, however, that some of the 'drifters' who decided to return to Poland fell into a 'migration experience trap'. This indicates a situation in which a returning migrant, despite his/her higher education and ambitions, is unable to find employment in accordance to his/her education. Eventually, seeing no chance for other job opportunities, the returnee decides to take up low-skilled job similar to those which he/she only temporarily accepted abroad (e.g. as a waiter (W1, W2, W3) or a receptionist (M1, W5)). They get those jobs even more easily than non-migrants since Polish employers (particularly in tourism and other sectors of services requiring often and direct contact with foreigners) appreciate experience, usually reduced to good knowledge of English, of a similar post from abroad. At the same time the lack of work experience in the learned profession causes reluctance in employers looking for qualified employees.

It was, for example, in the case of Maja (W3), who, after returning from the UK, unsuccessfully searched for a job or an internship enabling her to develop professionally as a speech therapist:

> So now it's OK, even though after return to Poland I lost hope. I was quite depressed since I didn't want to be a waitress. Because I knew that the references from England will certainly give me work in Poland, because I used to work there [in England] for Hilton and Marriott. … So they employ me very willingly and I must admit that when I was looking for a job in Poland – between the fourth and fifth year of study – I finally decided to work in a hotel. I only chose where they pay better and where is closer to place where I lived. (W3)

Migrants also fell into the 'migration experience trap' when their return was motivated by reasons not directly related to work – for instance, joining the family or, on the contrary, a breakup with a partner in the UK. It seems that in contrast to the predictions of the human capital approach, in some cases migrants' precarious work experiences channel them toward precarious segments of the labour market even after returning to their home country. On the other hand, the 'experience trap' might also turn into the 'experience path'; a situation where an accidentally taken, incompatible with qualifications and low-skilled job turns into a passion developed back in Poland. For instance, Gosia, currently a 23-year-old, former student of chemical science, explains how she became involved in an experimental restaurant project in Kraków:

> Thanks to work there [in the UK] I became interested in cookery. I met chefs who know their job, I met sommeliers, who know wines. I had contact with such things that are not … things of everyday life. … I didn't practise, because I was a waitress but I peeped out cautiously, I was discussing and asking. (W2)

Redefinition of Normality

It has already been acknowledged that living in a different society might lead to the development by migrants of a new perception of normality (Rabikowska 2010; McGhee, Heath and Trevena 2012). While previous researchers explored Polish migrants' attitudes toward the material aspects of life and highlighted their satisfaction with broader possibilities of consumption (McGhee et al. 2012), as well as relative income security and different work standards abroad (Cieslik 2011), the redefinition of normality also concerns the migrants' perception of their work environment and work-related practices upon their return.

There are two groups of returnees: those who had never worked in Poland and those with work experience before their migration. The former group often treats return as a 'test' (W7) to 'see how it is' (M1). As explained by Piotr, who before returning to Poland had worked in London as an architect: 'We [with his wife] wanted to try. You know, if you don't experience something first-hand you won't know' (M7). Return was also frequently not treated as a definitive move and migrants 'did not want to burn bridges' (W8) behind them, maintaining open bank accounts and contacts with their previous employers in the UK. These returns were also combined with a search for a more prestigious occupation; however, it could end in the already-described migration experience trap.

Irrespective of their work experience before migration, all the returnees I talked to had worked in the UK. Upon return those who took up a job compared different aspects of work 'here and there', redefining what is 'normal at work'. Some returnees admitted that they 'changed their expectations' and started 'thinking in an English way' (W3). Krzysztof, a 30-year-old returnee, concluded:

> I think that once you see that it can be otherwise, then you expect something else. I think that there are dilemmas, and perhaps everyone who returns experiences such a contrast. ... I really realized that some things are not normal, and I had got used to normal. (M1)

The redefinition of normality also applies to the sphere of work. Hence this part of the chapter focuses on those aspects of work which – in comparison to what returnees experienced in the UK – appeared to them most striking, namely: enhanced earning capacity, different workplace relationships and a more harmonious work–life balance. Importantly, these are migrants' subjective representations of their experiences, which might be idealised as in the saying 'the grass is always greener on the other side'. Nevertheless, the world narrated by returnees is no less real, since the actions taken on its basis impact not only the returnees themselves but also their environment and in some cases (e.g. social movements) the whole of society.

ENHANCED EARNING CAPACITY

Since the most popular declared reason for migration was the possibility of higher earnings, it should not come as a surprise that most of the returnees pointed to the differences in incomes. Returnees underlined not so much the absolute level of income as the possibility of living a 'decent life' (W2), maintaining themselves on a single job involving relatively simple work abroad. Monika, who lived, worked and studied in Scotland for six years, describes her two-year experience following her return to Poland. It is important to note that she had not worked in Poland before her emigration at age 20.

> Every day it's just trying to make ends meet, each time it's from the first to the first [day of each month]. You never have money for a dentist or new shoes, never, never. If you compare this with the life, which in terms of ideas, organization and finances is a life in which you just overcome obstacles and swim, here I have the feeling that I'm swimming not in water but in a tar. Very, very slowly. (W8)

Monika lacked 'income security', identified by Guy Standing (2011: 10) as an 'adequate and stable income', assured not only by work itself but in case of lower paid jobs also by certain state policies such as minimum wage or progressive taxation. Returnees' income insecurity also concerned its regularity, which in turn depended on the type of employment contract. Savings brought from the UK might serve as a buffer reducing income instability, but this is a short-term solution, as described by Maria and her husband:

> You know, first of all you need to have enough money to live. And this, so to say, wasn't our strong point in Poland. All the time we have lived from our savings or from that what Piotr [the interviewee's husband] brought from this company. But he worked on different terms, he was employed on specific task contracts [*umowa o dzieło*], and each time the contract ended we were afraid there wouldn't be another one. So, there was nothing stable for us. (W10)

Maria's experience was no different from that of thousands of non-migrants, since Poland is one of the European leaders in terms of atypical employment contracts (ETUI 2015). Besides the numerous fixed-term contracts, a specific feature of the Polish labour market is the relatively high share of workers employed solely on the least secure civil-law contracts (Mrozowicki and Maciejewska 2016). However, for some returnees (for example, the previously quoted Krzysztof), the type of contract ensuring income stability was of secondary importance and only adequate income was crucial for their sense of stabilisation:

> Here you don't have a sense of stabilization like there, there you can do the worst job, but you feel secure, here you don't have this, you live a little bit like day to day. ... In the UK I could have a civil-law contract [but] I felt like I would have had to do I don't know what to lose my job. Here it is not like that, at least I don't feel it. (M1)

Krzysztof's statement illustrates an interesting paradox. Although Polish migrants in the UK are often employed in the secondary segment of the labour market and migrants are considered to be in vulnerable and precarious position (e.g. Currie 2007), they do not consider themselves as such, since they use their previous experiences as a reference point. In Poland in turn, even with a so-called typical contract, due to inadequate income the subjective sense of security is lower than those from the UK. Since young people in Poland tend to normalise work-related insecurity, the question arises whether the transfer of returnees' experiences might impact non-migrants' perception of work standards and contribute to the slowly growing protests against the precarious nature of work in Poland.

WORKPLACE RELATIONSHIPS

Income and type of contract are not, however, the only components of a worker's sense of well-being. Return migrants also underlined the differences in the way they were treated as employees. They refer to the 'professionalism', 'emotional moderation' and 'diplomacy' of their bosses in the UK. As recalled by Piotr: 'No one raises his voice, no one screams, no one tenses up, this is more a partnership approach' (M7). Polish employees in the UK felt that they were respected, which was often not the case in Poland. Moreover, being on a first name basis with all co-workers and bosses – a practice rather rare in Poland, especially between young workers and older superiors – is treated by the returnees as a sign of the modesty of the bosses. Stanisław, a 33-year-old engineer and re-emigrant, describes it as follows:

> The bosses are as if equal with you, they don't have an exalted position. People [at work] are also helpful, there is not such a competition. In Poland it is more often a rat race ... [In the UK] people trust the employee. For example, in the company in London where I used to work, quite often I worked from home. Nobody controlled me. I could just work from home, I worked on my computer, and nobody appraised what I did. (M8)

While this relatively high level of worker's autonomy is appreciated by Polish migrants, it differs widely depending on the sectors in which the migrants worked. The 'partnership approach' and trust resulting from it is perceived not only as a feature of the work environment, but more broadly as a feature of British society and institutions. Returnees complained about the lack of mutual trust in Poland and pointed out that it is also demonstrated by the state administration, which 'assumes that you are trying to cheat' (M7). On the other hand, the migrants themselves do not trust their unnamed compatriots.

In their narratives, success in Poland is often linked with fraud. For example, 31-year-old Zofia, who, after returning to Poland and six months of unsuccessful attempts to find a satisfying job, decided to re-emigrate, concludes:

> They [other Poles] need to cheat, play games. It's sad but you can't live normally and cope as a human being; you need to swindle, do monkey business. If somebody wants to live honestly, then it's rather hard or impossible. (W6)

Although returnees noticed also negative aspects of work environment in the UK, they tended to talk about it fondly. This might have several sources. On the one hand, faced with difficulties after return, migrants might feel nostalgic about the idealised past abroad. On the other hand, in the case of the re-emigrants, the emphasising of the contrast between work in Poland and the UK serves as a mean for easing the sometimes difficult transition between countries. Moreover, it might be understood as an element of the rationalisation of the re-emigration and perceiving it as a necessity. It would, however, require further examination to fully understand such attitudes.

WORK–LIFE BALANCE

Income insecurity, the low level of autonomy and the stronger hierarchy at work translate into stresses related to work. However, comparison of the work–life balance experienced in the UK and Poland differs depending on the initial aims of the migration. The so-called target earners often worked two jobs at the same time and/or took as much overtime as possible. Their sacrifice of free time was a conscious strategy aimed at maximising profits. For example, 50-year-old Andrzej recalls:

> The work was good but it was hard. Because I wanted to earn quickly I got the idea that every third week I will have only one day off. … I was totally exhausted and we had an hour-and-a-half commute to work every day, so I was at home around 8 p.m. [It was] operating at the limits. I managed somehow, but it was really tough. (M2)

Both young and middle-aged target earners 'bite the bullet' and hold out in order to achieve their initial aim. For them, their work after returning to Poland, despite some of the already-described inconveniences, was a relief, all the more valuable in that they were closer to their family. The migration as such appeared to them as a sacrifice and was perceived as a necessity rather than a choice. In contrast, those who went to the UK 'not just to earn but to live' complained upon their return to Poland about employers who expected them to work overtime, often without payment. Work in Poland was even compared to 'slavery' (M7), driven, in the returnee's opinion, by students willing to work without pay, just for the experience.

All in all, most of returnees found differences in their work experiences in the UK and Poland. Their perception of the work environment was, however, mediated by their personal situation as well as the objectives assigned to migration and return. While for some migrants return turned out to be a relief and a chance for a more prestigious but lower-paid job, for others it meant a painful farewell to youth and/or a fall into the 'migration experience trap'. Therefore, in the next section I will present four types of coping strategies applied by the returnees in order to deal with the tensions resulting from the discrepancies between their perceptions of 'how it should be at work' and 'how it is'.

STRATEGIES OF COPING WITH WORK-RELATED TENSIONS

Analysis of the interviews enabled me to distinguish four main strategies employed by return migrants facing distress resulting from the discrepancies between the employment standards experienced in the UK and in Poland. It must be noted at the outset that these strategies are ideal types which emerged from generalisations, and in certain returnees' cases they overlapped and/or shifted over time. The identified strategies are re-emigration, adaptation, activism and entrepreneurship.

Re-Emigration

The first identified strategy, re-emigration, implies leaving Poland and moving back to the UK. The lack of formal barriers constraining intra-EU mobility facilitate this decision. In addition to short-term, seasonal migrants, who deliberately engage in the back and forth migration, often earning abroad and living in Poland (Fihel and Grabowska-Lusinska 2014), there is another group consisting of those who, after long-term migration, decided to 'give Poland a chance' and treated their return as a test. When 'the test failed' these migrants – in their own words – 'return' to the UK. The interviews confirmed the process described by White (2014) as 'double return migration'. Despite the reluctance of the most of the re-emigrants to make binding declarations regarding their future, their actions – such as acquiring properties or striving to obtain qualifications recognised in the UK – indicate that their second migration to the UK might be expected to be more permanent. The decision about re-emigration was often triggered by impulse, and in almost all examined cases was preceded by contact with acquaintances, colleagues or previous employers in the UK. According to the interviewees, maintaining the transnational ties after their return to Poland gave them a greater sense of security, as they 'could always leave' again. Forty-year-old Grzegorz, currently a small entrepreneur (self-employed) in Scotland, explained how he left Poland for the second time, this time 'for good':

> It [the decision] was maturing in my mind. And it was that moment when I received my salary, a bag with coins. 360 coins – 5 Polish Zloty each, all together an enormous [ironically] amount of 1800 Polish Zloty for spending all my nights there … it was when I got this salary in coins that something again broke in myself … and I told him [the boss], 'pal, you better start looking for somebody for this evening'. Since I was working at nights and I was finishing at 8 a.m., I went to the Internet cafe and I found people going by car to Scotland in just three days. … Despite the fact that I had left [Scotland], I didn't close all doors in different small enterprises where I'd worked before. So, on Saturday I called a colleague of mine … and she told me that she would find a job for me when I came. (M4)

Interestingly, some of the interviewees felt more committed to their previous managers than the companies they used to work for. As explained by Krzysztof, who, in the course of back-and-forth migration, re-emigrated two times:

Interviewer: So, were you returning to the same place [in the UK]?
Krzysztof: Initially yes, but later we were changing places … but it wasn't because we wanted to. It was because the hotel manager moved, so each time we were leaving [Poland] everything was prepared [in the UK] and we didn't even look for a job. And today we wouldn't need to, if we wish to leave Poland again. (M1)

Re-emigration might be interpreted in terms of the 'exit option' proposed by Hirschman (1970). Exit is perceived as the easiest solution in cases of discontent with a particular sphere of one's life. Importantly in this case, the re-emigration consists of two 'exits' since migrants are leaving not only their unsatisfactory workplace but also a country. Both exits might happen simultaneously, as in the case of 25-year-old Patrycja (W7), who, after an 'unsuccessful test' in Polish labour market, immediately went back to Scotland. There could, however, be a space between both exits, as shown by the example of 31-year-old Zofia (W6), who for almost two months was looking for a new job in Poland before eventually deciding to leave the country.

Adaptation

The second observed strategy was gradual adaptation and acceptance of the standards different to those abroad. Despite the clear differences observed in the sphere of work, a portion of returnees eventually adjusted to the Polish reality. For example, Maja, after an initial period of disagreement, changed her attitude:

> You can get used to it. After one, two months in Poland, I was saying to myself: My goodness, that's simply how it is here. 'Maja, where are we?' And I answered [to myself]: 'In Poland'. So you need to put your tail between your legs [*podkulić ogon*] and be nice to the lady who is the office clerk, because she rules here. (W3)

The lower income and worse employment standards are perceived to be a result of the 'Polish mentality' and Poland's economic position, sometimes ascribed to the post-socialist legacy. Such explanations are a way of shifting responsibility on to unmanageable – even collectively – forces, often embedded in history. The returnees' conviction of their own agency is rather weak, therefore they search for an external explanation of their situation.

Adaptation was also a strategy employed by migrants who returned for reasons other than work related. They felt that if they wanted to save the family, be closer with elderly parents, or simply finish their education they needed to readjust their expectations. In the words of Andrzej:

> Maybe there [in the UK] I had more time to think everything through. And I realized there that I needed to lower the level of my expectations, so that I could also have satisfaction from a simple job. So, I returned from England … found a job, simply in the factory for eight hours a day – something I totally could not picture. Of course, there are disadvantages because you have less money, but the life is more stabilised, more calm, because I'm with the family, perhaps now I'm the most happy in my entire life. (M2)

At first glance 'adaptation' might seem easily equated with Hirschman's term 'loyalty'. Yet for Hirschman loyalty is associated with an expectation that the unfavourable conditions will eventually alter and therefore one can wait longer without undertaking action (be it exit or voice). The cases described above show that adaptation is, rather, acceptance of the status quo and resignation from the expectation of any change. Interestingly, since the adaptation might also be conditional, once the reason for being in Poland is no longer relevant, the returnee(s) might seriously consider re-emigration.

Activism

Activism is the third strategy and the one employed by the smallest group of interviewed returnees. Faced with tensions related to work they undertake action in order to improve their situation. Activism and a conscious striving for change is a strategy undertaken by returnees convinced of the high level of their agency. Their stay abroad reinforced, or even brought about, their feelings of self-esteem and self-determination. Their actions can be taken either in the workplace or more generally at the local level. Furthermore, such actions can take either an individual or a collective form. While the former is mostly aimed at improving returnees' own situation, the latter answers the needs of a broader group and could, for example, take the form of involvement in trade unionism or engagement in a political party. This strategy might be seen as resorting to voice, which is defined as 'any attempt at all to change, rather than to escape from, all objectionable states of affairs' (Hirschman 1970: 30).

Activism is the strategy most likely to contribute to change in the sphere of work. However, to understand how and why some returnees become actors of change, one needs to take into consideration 'specific institutional, political and economic conditions at home' (Cassarino 2004: 270). In the case of social remittances in the sphere of work, the crucial factor seems to be the structural position of the employee, defined in relation to other employees and, most of all, to managers. A migrant's charisma and ability to attract non-migrants is also of significance. However, the relatively low autonomy experienced by employees in Poland gives them little space for change. Krzysztof, who after returning to Poland fell into the 'experience trap' and worked in a luxury hotel, offered following analysis of the impact of his experience from abroad:

> I think that it [the work experience from the UK] doesn't matter. I mean, I'm working here [and] I used to work in various hotels … that were four, five stars hotels. It seemed to me that there were high standards and I was in some way trained, but it is not useful at all. This is not useful because coming back here, even if you wanted to implement these standards, you are alone, and in a while you start to work and behave exactly like the others. (M1)

In his case the failed attempted to 'implement British standards' led him to change his strategy to adaptation. Patrycja, mentioned already, in turn, unsuccessfully tried to fight for better working conditions:

> I wanted to negotiate at least that if we work overtime, because there is non-stop overtime work, that we could at least have some extra free time. But he [the boss] had the attitude that the work in a culture [sector] is not like work in a mine, where you have to punch a clock. It is the work with a mission and either you are a person who has a mission, or you are not suited to do this. It was such an approach that, you know, if you are simply a person with a mission, you can't have a private life, [you should] only and exclusively work. Work for seventy hours a week and you shouldn't expect more money or even a word of recognition. You know … so I just gave up on this. (W7)

The activism of returnees could be also institutionalised and directly linked with their return, as was the case of Michał, who came back to Poland because of a job offered to him by one of the British trade unions. The British union, being aware of global competition, followed the logic that supporting the organisation of Polish workers will translate into better working conditions and higher wages in Poland. This, in turn, should lower the competitive pressures on Polish companies and prevent the race to the bottom in the common EU market. Michał's involvement in trade union movements began in the UK but currently might translate into improvement of the working conditions in a certain company in Poland. However, the results of his attempts are not clear yet.

Entrepreneurship

The last distinguished strategy is entrepreneurship, which usually takes the form of self-employment. A few interviewees admitted that among the reasons that pushed them towards working for themselves was 'the fear of working for somebody in Poland' (M5). The decision was obviously also motivated by other factors, such as the desire for self-realisation, expectation of higher earnings and a need for independence; however, the returnees did not perceive these issues as problematic when they were employed in the UK. Indeed, those who eventually re-emigrated were usually employees in the UK (in one case the interviewee was formally self-employed; however, he was a subcontractor providing services on regular basis for only one company). Stanisław, already quoted above, recalls the time when he ran his business in Poland:

> Well, in running a company I liked the fact that I was my own boss. I didn't have to work for somebody else. I liked that, but it of course it also had some disadvantages. You know, most of the time bosses don't have weekends, don't have holidays but … that was fine for me. When I already had the company I thought that for sure I wouldn't like to work for somebody in Poland, so later it wasn't even an option. Well, abroad it's totally different, you know. (M8)

The self-employment of returnees might be seen as a new form of strategy in the Polish labour market which combines exit and activism. It allows the returnees to express their disappointment with the domestic labour market for employees and at the same time remain loyal to the country. Entrepreneurship is also a form of actively 'taking matters into one's own hands'. In the narratives of the self-employed returnees the prevailing discourse is that of the 'self-made man', who with his/her own work achieved a lot.

> Now I'm aware that if you work hard and you want to, you can earn more and you can live at a different level. So, it's so to say a motivation. (M5)

> Well, I wouldn't blame the employers. I see that there are a lot of shortcomings in my generation, especially with regard to the quality of qualifications. … I don't know, I think that if you really want to, if you really work hard – we need to be clear about this – you can find the job which you want. (W2)

Self-employment appears to be a strategy with a high potential for the transfer of social remittances. The combination of returnees' work autonomy with their developed sense of agency leads to attempts to implement the different work standards and solutions observed abroad. The success of these efforts, however, depends not only on returnees' will but also on the general market conditions and the 'prevailing rules of the game'. Despite some positive examples, small entrepreneurs still complained how difficult it is nowadays in Poland to be a good employer.

> We didn't want to employ anybody on the black market, we didn't want to give a starvation wage, but we just counted how much one needs to earn to maintain themselves in our city. And when we calculated that we'd need to pay all social contributions and pay somebody normally, not peanuts but not a huge sum but just normally, we found out that we couldn't afford it [laughs]. (W11)

Piotr, after two years of running a business in Poland and finally re-emigrating, sums it up as follows:

> I mean, in Poland to run a company you need to have a specific approach. You know, that all the time you want to earn as much as possible at once. There is no long-term thinking and you need to be ruthless to achieve success. And this is not exactly my feature and perhaps I'm not suitable for doing business in Poland. (M7)

In case of the self-employed, re-emigration often took place after two years of doing business, when the entrepreneurs were faced with losing their special exemption for social service contributions. Faced with high competition, they often decided to close their small enterprises and leave the country.

CONCLUSION

The aim of the chapter was twofold: first to examine the perception of post-accession return migrants about work conditions in Poland compared to their (often precarious) experiences in the UK; and second to analyse what are return migrants responses (or coping strategies) to the imagined tensions created by the differing employment standards.

The examination of the biographical narrative interviews with return migrants confirmed that due to the double frame of reference Polish migrants often prefer their work in the secondary segment of the labour market in the UK. Moreover, from the returnees' perspective the main disadvantages of work in Poland (as compared to the UK) are: 1) low earnings making it impossible to live a 'decent life'; 2) hierarchical relations at work; and 3) the fragile work–life balance. This partially confirms the findings by Cieślik (2011), who showed that Polish highly skilled migrants in the UK became aware of and dissatisfied with the differences in work and earning conditions between the two countries, which in turn contributed to their reluctance to return. My research revealed additionally that some of return migrants with no previous work experience in Poland, after return fell into the 'experience trap' and continued on a path of precarious employment in the services sector. In some cases, the migrants' relatively low status in the labour market in the UK and formally being employed in precarious conditions was not perceived as such by the migrants themselves. This observation has ambivalent consequences for organised labour. Whereas in the UK the acceptance and normalisation of precariousness by Polish migrants interferes with the already-weak potential for their unionisation; in Poland, after their return, their individual dissatisfaction with wages and work standards might be translated into organised resistance. The latter scenario depends, however, on the coping strategy employed by returnees as well as structural circumstances.

Further analysis of the interviews enabled the creation of four types of coping strategies employed by return migrants facing distress resulting from the discrepancies between employment standards. In most cases, re-emigration, activism, adaptation and/or entrepreneurship were the returnees' main responses to the encountered tensions. The first two scenarios correspond somewhat with the options described by Hirschman as exit and voice. However, in contrast to Hirschman's position, they are not mutually exclusive, can change over time, and take different forms in the transnational social field. It would require further research to determine, for example, in what ways those returnees who decided to re-emigrate (exit) might make efforts from abroad (voice) to change the situation in Poland.

NOTES

1. An earlier version of this chapter appeared in *Central and Eastern European Migration Review*, February 2016, pp. 1–19. I would like to express my gratitude to the book editors and anonymous reviewers for their useful comments.
2. All interviews are anonymous and the names are fictitious. 'M' and 'W' after quotations stand for man and women and are followed by the number of the interview.

REFERENCES

Bohle, D. and B. Greskovits. 2012. *Capitalist Diversity on Europea's Periphery.* Ithaca and London: Cornell University Press.

Cassarino, J.-P. 2004. 'Theoretising return migration: The conceptual approach to return migrants revisited'. *International Journal on Multicultural Societies* 6 (2): 253–279.

Centrum Doradztwa Strategicznego. 2010. *Warto wracać? Strategie zachowań reemigrantów i rozwiązania służące wykorzystaniu ich potencjału.* Kraków: Centrum Doradztwa Strategicznego.

Cieślik, A. 2011. 'Where do you prefer to work? How the work environment influences return migration decisions from the United Kingdom to Poland'. *Journal of Ethnic and Migration Studies* 37 (9): 1367–1383.

Ciupijus, Z. 2011. 'Mobile central eastern Europeans in Britain: Successful European Union citizens and disadvantaged labour migrants?' *Work, Employment & Society* 25 (3): 540–550.

Currie, S. 2007. 'De-skilled and devalued: The labour market experience of Polish migrants in the UK following EU enlargement'. *The International Journal of Comparative Labour Law and Industrial Relations* 23 (1): 83–116.

Drinkwater, S. and M. P. Garapich. 2013. 'Migration plans and strategies of recent Polish migrants to England and Wales: Do they have any and how do they change?' *Norface Migration Discussion Paper* No. 2013–23. London.

Eade, J., S. Drinkwater and M. P. Garapich. 2007. *Class and Ethnicity: Polish Migrant Workers in London.* Final report. http://www.surrey.ac.uk/cronem/files/POLISH_FINAL_RESEARCH_REPORT_WEB.pdf (accessed 12 November 2016).

Engbersen, G. and E. Snel. 2013. 'Dynamic and fluid patterns of post-accession migration flows'. In *Mobility in Transition. Migration Patterns after EU Enlargement*, edited by B. Glorius, I. Grabowska-Lusińska and A. Kuvik, 21–40. Amsterdam: Amsterdam University Press.

Engbersen, G., E. Snel and J. De Boom. 2010. '"A van full of poles": Liquid migration from Central and Eastern Europe'. In *A Continent Moving West? EU Enlargement and Labour Migration from Central and Eastern Europe,* edited by R. Black, G. Engbersen, M. Okólski and C. Pantîru, 115–140. Amsterdam: Amsterdam University Press.

ETUI. 2015. *Benchmarking Working Europe 2015.* Brussels: ETUI.

Fihel, A. and I. Grabowska-Lusinska. 2014. 'Labour market behaviours of back-and-forth migrants from Poland'. *International Migration* 52 (1): 22–35.

Fudge, J., E. Tucker and L. Vosko. 2002. *The Legal Concept of Employment Marginalizing Workers.* http://publications.gc.ca/collections/collection_2007/lcc-cdc/JL2-35-2002E.pdf (accessed 12 November 2016).

Gaw, K. F. 2000. 'Reverse culture shock in students returning from overseas'. *International Journal of Intercultural Relations* 24 (1): 83–104.

Grabowska-Lusińska, I. and M. Okólski. 2009. *Emigracja ostatnia?* Warszawa: Wydawnictwo Naukowe Scholar.

GUS. 2013. *Migracje zagraniczne ludności. Narodowy Spis Powszechny Ludności i Mieszkań 2011*. Warszawa: GUS.

GUS. 2016. *Informacja o rozmiarach i kierunkach emigracji z Polski w latach 2004 – 2015*. Warszawa: GUS.

Hall, P. A. and D. Soskice. 2001. *Varieties of Capitalism*. Oxford: Oxford University Press.

Hirschman, A. O. 1970. *Exit, Voice and Loyalty. Responses to Decline in Firms, Organizations and States*. Cambridge and London: Harvard University Press.

Hodder, A. and L. Kretos, eds. 2015. *Young Workers and Trade Unions. A Global View*. London and New York: Palgrave Macmillan.

Hughes, E. C. 1997. 'Careers'. *Qualitative Sociology* (20): 389–397.

Iglicka, K. 2010. *Powroty Polaków po 2004 roku: w pętli pułapki migracji*. Warszawa: Wydawnictwo Naukowe Scholar.

Kaczmarczyk, P. 2012. 'Labour market impacts of post-accession migration from Poland'. In *Free Movement of Workers and Labour Market Adjustment. Recent Experiences from OECD Countries and the European Union*, 173–196. Paris: OECD.

Kaczmarczyk, P. and M. Lesińska. 2012. 'Return migration, state policy and integration of returnees'. In *Welcome home? Challenges and Chances of Return Migration,* Policy Paper 51: 29–37. http://www.gmfus.org/file/2876/download (accessed 12 November 2016).

Karolak, M. 2015. 'Migranci powrotni z Wielkiej Brytanii do Polski – przyczyny powrotów z perspektywy biograficznej'. *Opuscula Sociologica* (2): 37–52.

Karolak, M. 2016. 'From potential to actual social remittances? Exploring how polish return migrants cope with difficult employment conditions'. *Central and Eastern Migration Review*. Early View (Online Version of Record published before inclusion in an issue): 1–21. http://www.ceemr.uw.edu.pl/sites/default/files/Karolak_From_Potential_to_Actual_Social_Remittances.pdf (accessed 12 November 2016).

Knight, J., J. Lever and A. Thompson. 2014. 'The labour market mobility of Polish migrants: A comparative study of three regions in South Wales, UK'. *Central and Eastern European Migration Review* 3 (2): 61–78.

Lang, T. 2013. *Return Migration in Central Europe: Current Trends and an Analysis of Policies Supporting Returning Migrants*. Leipzig: Leibniz-Institut für Länderkunde e.V. http://www.ssoar.info/ssoar/handle/document/35966 (accessed 12 November 2016).

McCollum, D. and A. Findlay. 2015. '"Flexible" workers for "flexible" jobs? The labour market function of A8 migrant labour in the UK'. *Work, Employment & Society* 29 (3): 427–443.

McGhee, D., S. Heath and P. Trevena. 2012. 'Dignity, happiness and being able to live a "normal life" in the UK – An examination of post-accession Polish migrants' transnational autobiographical fields'. *Social Identities* 18 (6): 711–727.

Mrozowicki, A. and M. Maciejewska. 2016. *PRECARIR: The Rise of the Dual Labour Market: Fighting Precarious Employment in the New Member States through Industrial Relations. Poland: Country Report*. Central European Labour

Studies Institute (CELSI) http://www.celsi.sk/media/research_reports/13_CELSI_RR_1.pdf (accessed 12 November 2016).

Okólski, M. and J. Salt. 2014. 'Polish Emigration to the UK after 2004, Why Did So Many Come?' *Central and Eastern European Migration Review* 3 (2): 11–37.

Piore, M. J. 1979. *Birds of Passage*. Cambridge: Cambridge University Press.

Rabikowska, M. 2010. 'Negotiation of normality and identity among migrants from Eastern Europe to the United Kingdom after 2004'. *Social Identities* 16 (3): 285–296.

Saarela, J. and F. Finnäs. 2009. 'Return migrant status and employment in Finland'. *Journal of Manpower* 30 (5): 489–506.

Schmiz, A. 2013. 'Migrant self-employment between precariousness and self-exploitation'. *Ephemera. Theory & Politics in Organization* 13 (1): 53–74.

Schütze, F. 2007. *Biography Analysis on the Empirical Base of Autobiographical Narratives: How to Analyse Autobiographical Narrative Interviews—Part I. Module B. 2.1. INVITE.* European Studies on Inequalities and Social Cohesion.

Schwab, K., ed. 2014. *The Global Competitiveness Report 2014–2015.* World Economic Forum. http://www3.weforum.org/docs/WEF_GlobalCompetitivenessReport_2014-15.pdf (accessed 12 November 2016).

Smoliner, S., M. Förschner, J. Hochgerner and J. Nova. 2011. *Comparative Report on Re-Migration Trends in Central Europe.* http://www.re-migrants.eu/download/311_Comparative_Report_on_Re_Migration_final_PP02.pdf (accessed 12 November 2016).

Standing, G. 2011. *The Precariat: The New Dangerous Class.* London: Bloomsbury Academic.

Trevena, P. 2009. *'New' Polish Migration to the UK: A Synthesis of Existing Evidence.* ESRC Centre for Population Change Working Paper Number 3. http://www.cpc.ac.uk/publications/cpc_working_papers/pdf/2009_WP3_New_Polish_Migration_to_the_UK_Trevena.pdf (accessed 12 November 2016).

Trevena, P. 2013. 'Why do highly educated migrants go for low-skilled jobs? A case study of Polish graduates working in London'. In *Mobility in Transition. Migration Patterns after EU Enlargement*, edited by B. Glorius, I. Grabowska-Lusińska and A. Kuvik, 169–190. Amsterdam: Amsterdam University Press.

White, A. 2014. 'Polish return and double return migration'. *Europe-Asia Studies*, 66 (1): 25–49.

Section III

COLLECTIVE PERSPECTIVES ON INCLUSION AND EXCLUSION

Chapter III.1

Trade Unions' Responses at the Intersection of Class and Migration

Karima Aziz, Ben Egan and Radosław Polkowski

The changing context of work and migration patterns mean that it is important to develop an understanding of the formulation of collective responses. To this end, this chapter uses union approaches to migrant workers in three countries to develop an understanding of how this can be pursued successfully. Trade unions can provide an opportunity for advancing the rights and citizenship of migrant workers while migrant workers also create opportunities for unions as institutions in a hostile environment of austerity and the transformation of the labour market that are the subject of this book. However, migration also poses a range of challenges and dilemmas for trade unions (Penninx and Roosblad 2000). With the 2004 and 2007 EU enlargements, migration became a topic of renewed interest for trade unions in many European countries including those previously unaffected by inward migration to any significant extent (Krings 2009). Yet the policy context in which trade unions have had to develop their responses to migration is arguably a more complex one compared to post-war guest worker schemes in that it draws a sharp divide between EU and non-EU migrants that results in a highly fragmented workforce and a segmented labour market.

Because 'labour processes and hierarchies vary depending on regional histories and social structure' (Stewart et al. 2013: 98), inevitable legacies remain in relation to how unions confront these challenges. This impacts on strategies, attitudes and outcomes in relation to all members (and non-members), including migrants and other groups of workers seen as 'under-represented', in the workplace and beyond. It presents existential questions for unions. Questions in which the role of class can be central in establishing whom exactly each union sees itself as representing and what the boundaries are of this representation. Where does membership end? Does a prominence for class politics in a union lead to a more inclusive environment for migrant workers? And if so, why? These are the key questions we address.

This chapter therefore contributes to the literature on migrant worker organising efforts in European trade unions by integrating a class analysis of the unions as ideological organisations (Connolly et al. 2014). In particular, it builds on the framework developed by Penninx and Roosblad (2000) to explain union responses as well as the outcomes for migrant workers. We argue that the dilemmas with which trade unions traditionally contend in relation to migrant workers are 're-experienced' as union identity politics – including the role of class politics – leads to adaptations in approaches to engagement with subsequent migration flows.

We further propose that class and identity politics are therefore important elements in shaping trade unions' approaches and outcomes for migrants. This is not saying that class and identity politics are either synonymous or contradictory but that the *result of their presence* can be a more robust union organisation in relation to including migrant workers. This argument is illustrated using qualitative data collected between 2012 and 2014 in England, Northern Ireland and Italy. Showing the divergence in outcomes between unions with different approaches to class and other elements of identity politics, we see class, and broader identity politics, as an essential feature in this analysis because without it a union is reliant upon its professional staff to 'service' the membership in strictly workplace issues (Waddington and Kerr 2009). Only through engaging activists on a broader political basis are unions able to renew and grow to include new worker types.

MIGRATION AND SHIFTING UNION STRATEGIES

Being interested in explaining unions' responses to migration, it is nearly impossible not to refer to Penninx and Roosblad's (2000) seminal work on the same topic, as it makes us sensitive to a range of factors that may shape these responses. In what follows, we critically discuss their framework and its applicability to the context of contemporary migration in Europe. In the present chapter, we are interested in the dilemmas *instrumentally,* rather than as being insightful themselves. That is to say, by identifying the dilemmas confronting unions in England, Italy and Northern Ireland, we are able to explore the factors that influence these changes – most significantly for our thesis, that of class and identity politics. Penninx and Roosblad identify three dilemmas that unions must historically go through in their engagement with migrant workers. Individual union groupings will be at different points of this dilemma structure at different times, according to several factors which we address in the following section.

THE THREE HISTORICAL DILEMMAS

The three union dilemmas can be identified as (1) resistance or cooperation; (2) inclusion or exclusion; and (3) mainstreaming or special treatment. The first relates to the attitudes of unions towards the employment of foreign workers from the outset. The authors here draw reference to several European examples in the 1960s and 1970s of a mixed approach in this regard before recognising that the restrictions placed by governments on the growing body of refugees and asylum seekers from the mid-1980s onwards largely relieved trade unions of this dilemma. They merely needed to agree with employment restrictions on these potential workers. This was the point at which undocumented migrants were 'made and kept "illegal"' (Penninx and Roosblad 2000: 8) with the consent of some trade unions, who at this point were tied into the tripartite decision-making of the post-war era. The second dilemma relates to union attitudes once migrant workers do arrive. Are they to be included or excluded from the union? This engagement can also be taken to mean both direct recruitment and representation of migrant workers as individuals as well as engagement with autonomous migrant organising groups that emerge in relation to the unique status of migrants in society or even as a response to traditional trade unions being unable or unwilling to incorporate such workers from the outset. Castles and Kosack's (1973) observation of the tipping point at which even unions that have been hostile to immigration must hold back in expressing this view if they wish not to alienate new potential immigrant members is used to back up Penninx and Roosblad's (2000) second dilemma. The third dilemma relates to the treatment of migrant workers who do join the union once they have arrived and a union has taken the approach of recruiting such workers to the union: whether to give such members special treatment or treat them as any other member. Within the now accepted view that minority groups do, to some extent, need 'special treatment' to thrive in unions, Penninx and Roosblad (2000) conceptualise a scale which at one end provides for extra, often advisory, groupings, and at the other end a more proactive agenda. This can include active anti-discrimination policies, training and activities, as opposed to a 'colour-blind' treatment, as well as employing and promoting immigrant workers within the union.

'SETTING THE CLOCK' ON MIGRANT ORGANISING

In order to assess the role of class and identity politics in unions and its connection to migrant strategies, it is necessary to be clear on how and where this influence is exerted. The transition between the dilemmas cited is influenced by several factors (outlined below) so it is within these transitions from one dilemma to the next that the roles these factors play in influencing union practices become salient. One potential problem in analysing this is that the three dilemmas debate risks overlooking the crucial importance that historical and cultural legacies impose on the countries in which our trade union case studies are situated. Not only did England, Italy and Northern Ireland experience migration upturns that were qualitatively different in character, but they also occurred at different times and so clearly no uniformity will be observed. Moreover, these national experiences engender differentiated responses: not all unions in each country react in the same manner to all migrant groupings. This can be guided by many factors from the ease of integration of arrival populations into existing union structures to the political power of certain factions over others inside the union at any given time as well as the state of the labour market. It can also be heavily influenced by the more simple preferences and actions of a small number of people in influential positions within the union, such as a charismatic leader, in either direction. The result of these various influences is that at any time the clock can be reset on migrant organising approaches.

What do we mean by 'setting the clock'? The original framework, intended to specifically apply to the period 1960–1993, seemed somewhat linear in its approach. That is to say that unions pass through the dilemmas sequentially. However, subsequent spikes in the levels of inward migration have shown employment relations scholars that as new groups arrive it cannot be taken for granted that if a union has reached dilemma three (i.e. *how* to include migrant workers in the union, rather than *whether*) that that union will stay there. New groups of arrivals can reopen debates about whether to include or exclude them (i.e. dilemma two). Therefore, the clock can go back on migrant organising approaches. Difficulties of the model in relation to more recent migration movements have in fact been acknowledged by the original authors in a recent article, ahead of the anticipated publication of an updated version of the volume (Marino et al. 2015). We propose an understanding that accounts for this reversal with a 'delinearisation' of the dilemmas, as shown in Figure III.1.1.

Most major trade union organisations in Europe today have some nominal commitment to organising migrant workers – broadly defined. It is the historical legacy of more overt public displays of racism and xenophobia from which the three dilemmas emerge, and which have informed the considerations confronting unions. Put simply, overt public exclusion of migrants is no longer a tenable position. A result of this is that all union strategies in these countries are concentrated around the third dilemma, with some at the second, but none at the first – primarily due to the restrictions governments place on migration. This is because of shifting ideas of what is 'politically acceptable' both inside unions and in broader society. This is not a one-way street,

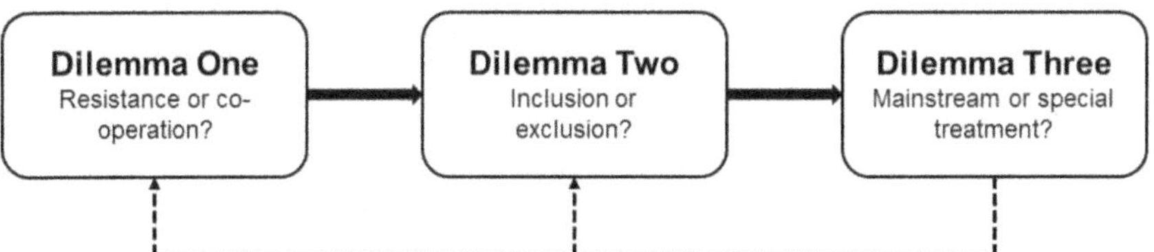

Figure III.1.1 Delinearisation of the Three Dilemmas. *Source*: Own elaboration based on Penninx and Roosblad 2000.

however, and different migrant groups and different union organisations will result in different outcomes at different times. That is to say each wave of immigration can result in moving back to earlier dilemmas – the resetting of the clock metaphor. However, it is important to be clear at this point what dilemma one actually means. The resistance or cooperation dilemma relates to unions' role in developing government policy – *not* internal union policies, or rhetoric and so on. Therefore, an observation that this union or the other is resistant to migration or migrant workers is not tantamount to dilemma one. Rather it represents most likely the latter option of dilemma two, inclusion or exclusion. The first dilemma entirely presupposes a certain level of 'social partnership' with the state for trade unions to have any impact on migration policy.

DILEMMAS IN THE THREE COUNTRIES: UNIONS AND MIGRANT WORKERS IN ENGLAND, ITALY AND NORTHERN IRELAND

The trade union landscapes of England, Italy and Northern Ireland differ significantly due to ambiguous statuses and historical legacies. Variation inevitably exists in the approaches taken by different unions and confederations in relation to a whole range of organisational challenges, not least migration with its political and social baggage. The development of Italian union structures and industrial relations mechanisms in relation to migrant organising are relatively recent, with significant numbers of migrant workers representing a new social phenomenon: before 1990 there were few migrant workers whereas today they account for more than one in eight workers. This has meant that each confederation has had to be experimental in how it approaches these new workers and potential members. Before the late 1980s, there were relatively few migrant workers and consequently union strategies in relation to the three dilemmas have emerged over the course of the last twenty-five years or so. The wide diversity of the migrant groups has pre-empted the establishment of numerous migrant organisations within the various confederations and beyond. Meanwhile, the conflictual model of industrial relations in Italy has largely ruled out any consideration of dilemma one (Regalia and Regini 1998). The current focus is on dilemma three and ways of integrating such special interest groupings into mainstream union business (Marino 2015).

Similarly, the decades-long civil conflict in Northern Ireland had for a long time insulated unions from the dilemmas of immigration. The first noteworthy inward migration began with the 2004 EU enlargement and it was indeed unprecedented in scale as in a short time Northern Ireland had one of the highest concentration of CEE workers in the UK (Department of Learning and Labour 2009). Trade unions supported freedom of movement of workers from 2004 accession states. Interestingly, however, they found themselves in a peculiar position with regard to 2007 accession states in that British trade unions were against transitional measures whereas the Irish Congress of Trade Unions (ICTU) supported them and, being the amalgamation of both, the trade union movement in Northern Ireland found itself between two contrasting stances. As explained by the representative of the Northern Irish Committee (NIC) of ICTU interviewed for this study, 'NIC-ICTU did not have a separate position on this issue' and, thus, unions in Northern Ireland were formally at odds with the rest of the UK when it came to their approach to migration from Romania and Bulgaria. In terms of the second and third dilemmas, unions developed inclusionary policies and within that special treatment was preferred to respond to what ICTU calls 'particular needs' associated with the vulnerability of migrants in the labour market, the 'knowledge gap' about employment law and trade unions or language skills, and specific needs that go beyond the workplace and include accommodation, education, welfare and other issues (Philips 2015). This approach has found its embodiment in the Migrant Workers Support Unit within ICTU, established in Belfast, as well as in the Belfast Migrant Centre, supported by ICTU and the UK-based Unison.

In the rest of the UK including England, unions started to be exposed to the migration dilemmas much earlier. Following a phase of hostility towards immigration after the Second World War, the Trade Union Congress (TUC) reacted to migration in the 1960s with rhetoric against discrimination but at the same time with a lack of policies (Castles and Kosack 1973). While in some workplaces membership was refused to black workers, others recruited actively with leaflets in other languages (Virdee 2000). During the 1970s a more positive approach towards equality and opposition to racism influenced the TUC (Fitzgerald and Hardy 2010) and trade unions started to respond to immigration by demanding the same pay and working conditions for migrants (Castles and Kosack 1973). Nowadays they are primarily concerned with dilemma three: which form of inclusion strategy should be implemented?

Also, from the early stages of the EU enlargement process, UK trade unions were in favour of opening up the labour market. However, while the general national approach of trade unions to migrant workers was characterised by the promotion of inclusion, there are certain differences in equal versus special treatment (Wrench 2004; Fitzgerald and Hardy 2010). The TUC started out with a special treatment approach by implementing a separate migrant workers strategy, which later on turned into an equal treatment policy, where migrant workers were conceptualised in the broader vulnerable workers strategy (Fitzgerald and Hardy 2010).

Noting the position of each union or confederation in relation to migrant workers, while interesting, is not the intention of this chapter. Rather, what we seek to show through the data is the role that class and identity politics play in motivating a shift through the dilemmas.

INFLUENCING UNION DILEMMAS: THE FOUR COMPLEXES OF FACTORS

The tendency for unions to proceed through the three dilemmas is contextually dependant, and how unions react to these dilemmas depends on four complexes of factors according to Penninx and Roosblad (2000). If the dilemmas can be seen as addressing the *what* in relation to unions' strategies, these are four factors that influence the *why*:

1. Power position and structure of the national trade union movement
2. Condition of the economy and labour market
3. National identity, ideology and institutions
4. Dominant perceptions and characteristics of migrant groups

As shown in Figure III.1.2, these complexes of factors influence the transition between each of the dilemmas. We contend that there is a fifth important complex of factors around union identity politics and the role of class in framing debates.

POWER POSITION AND STRUCTURE OF NATIONAL TRADE UNION MOVEMENT

While differing in character, the institutional embeddedness of trade unions into their respective national power relations in England, Italy and Northern Ireland is united by the fact that they have generally seen their institutional status diminish in recent years. This has led to the promotion of openness in

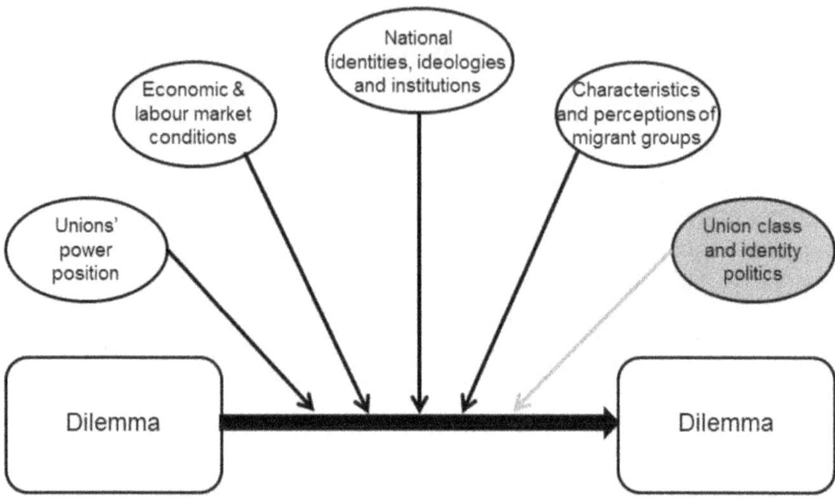

Figure III.1.2 Complex of Factors' Influence on Dilemma Transitions. *Source*: Own elaboration based on Penninx and Roosblad 2000.

unions to a diverse membership as recruitment becomes less linked to collective bargaining coverage. In Italy, despite the distinct power resources available to unions relating to 'industrial muscle', there is relative impotence in national social dialogue on the issues pertinent to migrants and their labour. Even Northern Ireland, despite still boasting a relatively high union density and collective bargaining coverage compared to England, and indeed the entire UK, has seen the proportion of workers who were in a trade union fall in the period between 1995 and 2014 (Department for Business Innovation and Skills 2015). Moreover, the relatively high union density is mainly accounted for by high unionisation in the still comparatively extensive public sector which masks the movement's actual weakness, particularly in the context of the post-1998 Keynesian settlement giving way to neoliberalism: a process that produces new categories of vulnerable workers (e.g. casual employees in the privatised welfare sector, agency workers, part-timers), many of whom are migrants (Stewart et al. 2013). Finally, the role of structural conditions is very clear in Northern Ireland as exemplified by the clash of stances between ICTU and British unions on the free movement of labour from the 2007 EU accession countries highlighted in the previous section.

CONDITION OF THE ECONOMY AND LABOUR MARKET

A second factor determining trade union responses is the macroeconomic situation at the time of the migration. Low unemployment rates and a labour shortage around 2004 led to the UK being one of the few European member states to open up its labour market to migrants from the new member states. At the same time, Northern Ireland was still characterised by Keynesian state strategies implemented as part of the 1998 settlement established in an attempt at maintaining peace (Stewart and Garvey 2015: 4). The expanded public investment, driven by the UK and the EU, accompanied by the inflow of private investment and tourists encouraged by relative stability, brought a 'golden era' to the economy of Northern Ireland. In the period 1998 to 2008, more new jobs were created here than in any other part of the UK (Department of Learning and Labour 2009). In contrast, the Italian economy has been weak for many years as it was enduring much higher levels of unemployment in the run-up to the 2004 accessions, as shown in Figure III.1.3. This clearly makes it a less attractive destination for A8/10 citizens. One prominent exception to this is in the sector of home-based care services, which is the dominant approach to elderly care in the absence of a nationally administered system in Italy and is largely staffed by migrant women. It is precisely this sector where many migrant workers are employed.

NATIONAL IDENTITY, IDEOLOGY AND INSTITUTIONS

The perception of current challenges as being linked to previous migrations and the long-established stronger support for diversity as well as the importance of anti-racism have influenced the UK trade union movement's response to post-accession migration (Fitzgerald and Hardy 2010). In turn, in justifying their formal attitudes to CEE migrants, trade union representatives in Northern Ireland have tended to appeal to notions of solidarity and empathy

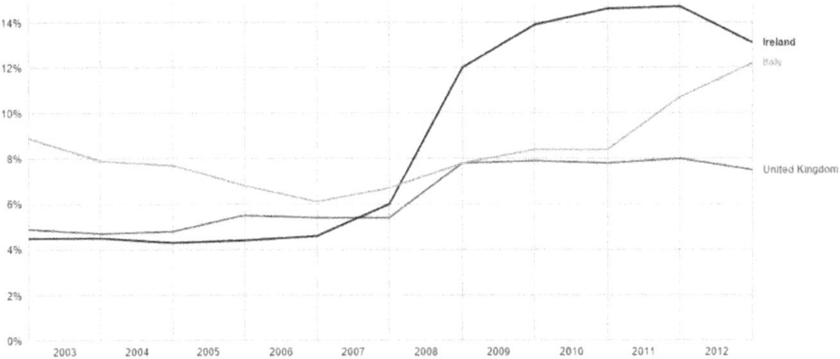

Figure III.1.3 Unemployment (%) in Ireland, Italy and the UK, 2003–2012. *Source*: World Bank.

by drawing on national narratives about the long history of emigration from Ireland (Krings 2009: 63). This role of national identities and ideologies in shaping trade union responses is also evident in Italy with its similar history of emigration, particularly to the US. In addition, the dominance of the CGIL union confederation plays a key role in the development of such narratives, with its historical association with the Italian communist party and the latter's role in resistance to fascism following its establishment by Antonio Gramsci and others in the inter-war years.

DOMINANT PERCEPTIONS OF MIGRANT GROUPS

Migrants' characteristics is the fourth complex of factors Penninx and Roosblad (2000) describe as influential. In the context of Polish post-accession migration to England trade unions have reported problems with English proficiency, trust building (because of the history and status of trade unions in Poland) and difficulties in organising because of long working hours, low pay and potential short-term stays (Fitzgerald and Hardy 2010). Given the similarity of the nationalities of the arrivals in Northern Ireland we can expect similar outcomes. The particular route to establishing migrant communities in Italy means that it lacks a clear correlation to either EU expansion (as in Northern Ireland and England) or as a legacy of empire (England). Indeed, one of the most notable characteristics of the Italian experience is the wide diversity of groups that arrived with up to 170 nationalities now present. These made up more than 7 per cent of the population by 2012 of which the highest proportions were Romanian, Albanian and Moroccan (Marino 2015).

Beyond the four complexes of factors outlined by Penninx and Roosblad (2000), it is our contention that a fifth should be added: an organisational commitment to class-oriented politics within union structures in the way that debates are framed among activists and members. These factors are useful to understand trade union responses to migration but, as Frege and Kelly (2003) argue, trade unions are not solely influenced by structural variables but have to be seen as independent organisations, whose structures and framing processes are crucial for understanding their actions.

CLASS AND IDENTITY POLITICS IN UNIONS – A FIFTH COMPLEX OF FACTORS?

Clearly times have changed, and the relationship between migrant workers and the broader societies into which they move will change accordingly. Work to advance understanding of these interactions is confronted by nuanced distinctions within the literature as to what may constitute a 'fifth complex of factors', as per our contention. It has been recognised in previous empirical work utilising Penninx and Roosblad's original framework that each of the complex of factors combine to provide explanatory value; they are not each mono-causal explanations (Krings 2009; Marino 2012; Marino et al. 2015: 10). This therefore raises the legitimate conceptual question of what exactly should constitute a new and separate complex of factors and as opposed to a variation within an existing complex – or indeed a composite of more than one. Furthermore, distinctions may be drawn *within* factors, as indeed was the case with the updated work. Here the authors incorporate their own fifth complex of factors, 'internal union dynamics', in which three key variables are identified:

> The first one, 'trade union identity', consists of the inherited tradition that shapes trade union choices (Hyman 1996). In this respect, Marino (2012) argues that the attitude of the Italian trade union federation CGIL (Confederazione Generale Italiana del Lavoro) towards migrant workers is strongly shaped by its identity as a 'general' union promoting defence of the social rights of 'disadvantaged groups' and engagement with problems not strictly related to employment. (Marino et al. 2015: 13)

Nevertheless, we make the case that the incorporation of class and identity politics does indeed constitute an additional complex of factors.

One reason for this is that, though separate from any individual formal strategy or set of policy aspirations, the fundamental question of what the union is *for* is critical to assessing how it is able to represent and involve new workers of diverse backgrounds. This is not a new phenomenon. Most notably, Richard Hyman has written extensively on the role of class in trade unions over several decades, including developing the idea of 'purpose' in relation to what the unions as organisations are seeking to achieve (Hyman 1971). More recently, his triangular 'geometry' of European trade unionism posits a triangle with the three points labelled 'society', 'market' and 'class', in which 'society' relates to the work done by unions to raise work standards generally and promote social justice; 'market' as regulators of the sector in which they organise; and 'class' as generators of activists in the class struggle (Hyman 2001).

Furthermore, identity politics are closely aligned with class, being a broader categorisation that encompasses not only class but also other ideologies that promote 'under-represented' groups in society and within unions as organisations. In a practical, lived sense class and identity politics can have a great deal of common ground even if their ideological origin is very different. This is because within the politics of a trade union both are used to mobilise power resources. These manifest in three distinct relationship types. First, they may be external bodies putting pressure on traditional union structures such as in the case of migrant organising groups, see the work of the Indian Workers Association for a good example (Josephides 1991), and organisations from within the women's movement. Secondly, they can be internal structures set up by unions to address the concerns and needs of specific groups of the membership – hence the proximity to the idea of using 'internal union dynamics' by Marino et al. (2015) as the overarching factor. Activists or officers involved with these structures must then make the case for its objectives within the wider union (mainstreaming). Thirdly, they can be a hybrid of the two, in which an organisation is autonomous yet funded by unions or their confederations. In this case the relationship is symbiotic in that the organisation can have positions that differ to those of the unions funding it, while providing for a fertile ground of organising experimentation. Examples of this include the anti-racism group Hope Not Hate in the UK as well as several anti-austerity initiatives.

The issue of identity within trade union cultures is central not only to the propensity to mobilise but also attitudes towards non-traditional core members, of which migrant workers represent a key component. However, it remains the poor relation of leadership in terms of the literature available. Cregan et al. (2009: 702) note that the field is underdeveloped as despite one major study of collectivism of individual members' impact on a mobilisation campaign, 'there has been no empirical study of mobilization that examines the impact of workers' social identification with the workplace union and local union leadership on members' collectivism'. The research the authors conducted nevertheless found that social identification acts as a 'mediator' between transformational leadership and member collectivism (Cregan et al. 2009: 714). More recently Connolly and Darlington (2012: 247), in a comparative analysis of rail worker unions in France and the UK, have demonstrated the importance of both 'left-wing' leadership and an explicit commitment to class politics in revitalising union structures in the two countries.

Conversely, the absence of broader political objectives in UK conceptions of 'the organising agenda' is conspicuous (Simms and Holgate 2010; Connolly and Darlington 2012; McIlroy 2012; Simms 2012). Simms and Holgate (2010) use the examples of three UK unions, Unite, GMB and USDAW, to demonstrate the wide variety of conceptions of 'union organising' within the UK and show that the 'turn to organising' represents more of a toolkit than a coherent renewal strategy. This demonstrates that an apolitical and rhetorical approach to organising members is insufficient to turn the fortunes of a union alone. What this means in practice is that unions are able to pursue different and indeed opposing approaches while all proclaiming to be 'organising unions'. The authors argue that the 'practice of organising' in itself exposes radically different underlying values of the 'purpose of organising' and this opens up new questions to academics and activists about why certain approaches are adopted, particularly in times of union crisis (Simms and Holgate 2010: 165–166). The insistence of the TUC from the outset of their Organising Academy in 1998 that it was not a political project is also cited, again bringing into focus the questions around the costs and benefits of an apolitical 'broad-church' confederation discussed in the previous paragraph. The absence of a coherent agenda with political elements surely risks the 'embourgeoisement of the working class' that Charles Sabel (1982) warned of thirty years ago, where unions cease to be in any way expressions of class consciousness and instead become mere tools that collections of individuals use to get what they want at the bargaining table.

It is therefore essential to consider in our analysis the role of these debates within unions as it has a direct effect on how they approach migrant workers and what their role is in representing the interests of those workers in the workplace and beyond.

FINDING CLASS IN OUR DATA: BETWEEN MIGRANT WORK AND CLASS SOLIDARITY

Field research was conducted in England, Italy and Ireland between 2012 and 2014, and consisted primarily of a series of semi-structured interviews with trade unionists, as well as observations of meetings and conferences. In the case of Northern Ireland, the data from eighteen semi-structured interviews with migrant workers from Poland was also used to inform some of the arguments made in this chapter. Likewise, semi-structured interviews with eight migrant workers and union officials from two Italian confederations were drawn upon, as well as observations of several events, including a two-day national conference in Rome entitled *Nuovi cittadini!* (New Citizens!) on organising migrant workers into the union as well as broader Italian society. Moreover, visual data in the form of still and motion pictures have been collected with two of the former included in the findings below and a series of subsequent films is available on the broader research project website (http://www.changingemployment.eu). The rich data contained in our findings suggest several variations on the expected outcomes for certain unions and migrant groups taking account of their context.

England

Most UK trade unions find themselves faced mainly with the third dilemma of which form of inclusion strategy to apply in relation to migrant workers. While many unions in the UK have based their approach to Polish migrants on the union learning strategy, community organising or activism and later on as part of the TUC's strategy under their vulnerable workers' approach; the case of the mostly Polish migrant workers' branch of the GMB in West Yorkshire was an unusual form of special treatment. Through attending branch meetings, interviewing members, activists and the branch secretary, information about its activities and structure were accessed, as its work was not otherwise published.

> On the scale of the country it is a unique trade union branch for Polish people. Before that, there was no such thing as a nationality branch. In the GMB it was understood as a form of discrimination or unequal treatment of other nationalities, so there were no such branches, it was an experimental branch. And it was a big success, because the branch consists of 400 people. (migrant workers' branch activist)

This understanding of the branch as an exception as well as a success by an activist represents the rationale in which the members, activists and the former branch secretary argued for its existence while being aware of the dilemma this caused. The GMB is the third largest union in the UK and organises members in a number of industries. This trade union had already established the first Polish migrant workers' branch consisting of up to 500 members in 2008, which, according to a former activist, was dissolved with the communicated intent to include members in existing union structures. The former activist explained that it was conceptualised as a holding branch trying to educate and organise Polish workers and build up confidence before incorporating them into existing structures. The branch was set up when the union realised that there were many workers in need of protection and information; however, this initial class solidarity could not endure the day-to-day pressure. The branch grew to have a heavy workload of individual cases in different workplaces, which was not sustainable according to its former activist. A similar branch was then set up in 2010, which at the time of conducting the fieldwork was the only migrant workers' branch with an approximately 90 per cent Polish membership. The experiences of these two branches show, on the one hand, the success in recruiting and activating migrant workers, among which women were often more engaged and even set up a women's forum within the branch; on the other hand, they illustrate the dilemma of equal versus special treatment. This union traditionally organises workplace by workplace but experienced problems in organising CEE migrants. The interviewees reported that migrant workers' lack of knowledge about trade unions and poor English competency hindered them from taking part in union structures: 'The migrant workers' branch is a part of the union which brings together Polish people, which do not speak English. Those who are able to speak fluently in English have no problems talking to anyone from the GMB' (migrant workers' branch activist).

The former branch secretary explained that there was an arrangement that where recognised workplaces existed the migrant workers would stay in those branches, but if there were workers in a non-recognised workplace they could join the migrant workers' branch, which during fieldwork counted between 300 and 400 members. Active members tried to ensure the sustainability of this branch, but this was difficult since in non-recognised workplaces they did not receive paid time off for union activities. The branch president was represented in the regional structure, but did not get paid for his union work or for taking part in the regional meetings. The branch organised through workplaces, training, language courses, community activities and word of mouth. The main commonality for members was being Polish while their identification as workers and with the union as a whole was developing. However, the union's competence to get involved in specific workplace-related issues was also limited because of the migrants being employed in mostly non-recognised workplaces. The former branch secretary identified the potential benefits of national coordination and other regional initiatives and predicted the branch could be sustainable in the future if Polish migrant workers took ownership of their branch. This former branch secretary, who was also a trade union officer at the time and as such had access to resources and support from the union, had, however, mainly driven the establishment and organisation of the branch. Since his departure, the branch struggled to organise meetings and receive sufficient support from the union and two years after the fieldwork took place its website and social media group have been discontinued. This way of responding to Polish migrant workers was unique and differed to other unions' responses in tending more towards special treatment. However, they were caught between the commitments to special treatment in the short-term and a long-term equal treatment strategy, demonstrated by the case of the prior migrant workers' branch as well as the rhetoric and recent developments around the researched branch. These difficulties in sustaining the branch, according to the former branch secretary, also derived from the discrepancy between identity formation in the migrant workers' branch and identity politics in the wider union.

Northern Ireland

In Northern Ireland, the Independent Workers Union (IWU) is an all-Ireland union that illustrates very well the role of class and broader identity politics not just in union responses to migration but indeed in the outcomes for migrant workers. The IWU sees itself as a continuation of the activist, political, anti-sectarian tradition within the Irish trade union movement. The union took an inclusionary approach to migrant workers arriving in Northern Ireland after the EU enlargements and within that we can see some elements of the special treatment approach embodied, for example, in the setting up of the Polish branch that operates from Dublin. The union initially concentrated on offering advice and help on issues specific to migrant workers that go beyond workplace concerns, but rather than merely serving their 'particular needs' through advice and top-down education, it went a step further as exemplified by the Migrant Workers Research Network (MWRN): an action research project which brings together migrant and non-migrant workers as well as community activists and academics. Thus, the MWRN is an example of a broad class-based alliance that includes not just migrant workers but also different categories of non-migrant workers that have all been affected by the precarisation of employment. As noted by Stewart et al. (2013), MWRN is an example of a creative tool for self-mobilisation of a workforce dispersed across different sectors of the labour market.

Moreover, such class-based and, importantly, anti-sectarian orientation of the IWU has made it more flexible in addressing the needs of migrant workers compared to the mainstream unions whose hands have been tied by a lack of clear political vision, pragmatism and far-reaching integration within the political establishment. These were the key issues identified by Boyd (1984) already thirty years ago in his exploration of the paradox that, despite unprecedented formal strength and the privileged position of unions in Northern Ireland, they have largely failed workers. Nowadays it seems that the same issues made unions fail in responding to migrant workers' needs, as the experience of an IWU activist suggests.

> Quite often someone comes to us and says: 'I have been a member of one of the big unions for many years and I've never had any problems. Then I had an issue with my employer and my union would not help me'. Because the big unions take calculated assessment, the prospect of success … and if they see that there is not more than 60–70 per cent chance of success they will simply tell the employee 'I'm sorry, there is not much we can do'.

The validity of this opinion was reflected in the experience of a Polish trade union activist who complained that, despite all the valuable help she gets from one of the large unions, she has the feeling that the union delegate and the employer talk together behind migrant workers' backs and the employer makes only certain concessions while the union tries not to push too far. As a result, she felt that many important issues in her workplace could not be resolved through the union. This contrasts with the more militant approach of the IWU, which has used threats of direct action more readily to advance workers' interests.

Of course, the inclusionary approach of the IWU towards migrant workers can be explained not necessarily in terms of the union's appeal to socialist and republican tradition but, more simply, in terms of sheer pragmatism. As explained by one of the activists, being a small union, the IWU saw migrant workers from CEE as a potential shot in the arm. However, there are also clear class politics underlying this pragmatism in that the very nature of migrants' employment brings them particularly close to the IWU's political agenda of challenging neoliberalism and sectarianism. This is because migrant workers in Northern Ireland have been affected by these two forces possibly to a greater extent than other groups: first of all, existing literature suggests that it was the 'low road neoliberalism' that has driven many CEE migrants to the UK (Woolfson and Sommers 2008; Woolfson and Sommers 2015); secondly, once in the UK they found themselves occupying the lowest echelons of the deregulated labour market (McCollum and Findlay 2015); and thirdly, entering and crossing the long-established landscape of divisions, they often faced issues with sectarianism in their communities and workplaces.

In contrast, sheer pragmatism unaccompanied by a political orientation among major trade unions can be a particular liability when it comes to addressing the needs of migrant workers, especially considering Northern Irish demography, thus leaving many migrant workers vulnerable.

> Outside the city, there are only really two or three major cities and settlements in Northern Ireland and outside of that you're talking about small, parochial areas that would not pay a large union to send an organiser out to recruit in small firms. So workers approach us from very small family companies where unions have not reached. (IWU representative)

According to the IWU representative quoted below, these areas are particularly tricky to organise because employers there are perceived as pillars of the community. Indeed, among eighteen Polish migrant workers interviewed in the course of this study, only those living in rural areas and working either on farms or in family-run factories reported problems of workplace exploitation and discrimination. At the same time, only one of them was actively working with a trade union organisation. This was the case of a large farm where only migrant workers were employed. In smaller factories employing both 'local' and migrant workers, no trade union organisations were present. This may be a result of the obstacles to organising in such workplaces that emerge from the paternalistic relationship between employers and 'local' workers and communities that the IWU representative described in the following way:

> The employers' tentacles are very deeply embedded in a local community … these are respectful pillars of the community … you see their sponsorship

> boards everywhere. So, workers are under the impression that it's these small firms that are holding the community together. So, anyone who challenges the employer is challenging the broader community cohesion. (IWU representative)

While the farm that gives jobs to foreigners only may not be perceived as benefiting local people and, hence, be less relevant for the local community, the 'mixed' workplaces are a completely different story. Therefore, organising trade unions in the former is less problematic than in the latter.

The situation is further complicated by a unique context of Northern Ireland in that the protestant working class has sometimes expressed feelings of being under siege: first, by local Catholics as a result of the post-1998 settlement that undermined protestant privilege in the economy and social services; and, secondly, by newly arriving migrants of whom Polish Catholics are the largest group and who are often perceived as competitors for jobs and social services. This feeling of being under siege is illustratively captured in Figure III.1.4, which was taken during the fieldwork in Northern Ireland.

In such a context it can be particularly difficult for a union to take the side of a migrant worker against a local employer as the former is seen as a threat and the latter as a pillar of a sectarian community. Moreover,

Figure III.1.4 Protestant Community in the City of Derry/Londonderry Expresses Sense of Siege Through Wall Graffiti. *Source*: Radek Polkowski.

in some SMEs cross-class paternalistic employment relations between management and 'indigenous' workers, who both come from the same 'sect', continue to operate. Some of these SMEs are run by ex-combatants and, therefore, sectarianism-driven violence is an ongoing threat (Stewart and Garvey 2015). On several occasions, the IWU was able to help workers succeed in their struggles in such workplaces but at times they had to withdraw owing to intimidation and threats by paramilitaries (Stewart et al. 2013). Nevertheless, facing such extreme conditions, it is hard to imagine more pragmatically oriented unions, which have accepted the post-1998 institutionalisation of sectarianism, to intervene at all. This can explain the absence of trade unions in family-run factories in rural areas which is something that became evident from interviews with Polish migrant workers despite the frequent accounts of exploitation and discrimination that they talked about in the interviews. Therefore, it can be argued that class politics and a clear anti-sectarian orientation that accompanies it have made the IWU more flexible in addressing the needs of the most vulnerable migrant workers in Northern Ireland.

Italy

In Italy, three sectors that are widely cited as highly dependent on migrant labour are construction, agriculture and domestic work. The latter of these is influenced by a structural specificity of Italy as the size of the labour market in domestic work has traditionally been large due to the culture of keeping elderly family members in the home and the absence of a nationally administered care sector or market (as is the case in Northern Ireland and England). One participant even referred to these workers by a special name recognised in Italy: '*badante*', which refers specifically to foreign-born female workers in Italian domestic work. This is so widespread that it can create dilemmas for unions in that the CGIL often faces the 'problem' of being involved in employment disputes between two of its own members. Many 'employers' in this context do not see themselves as employers, merely a working person paying for an elderly parent to be looked after during the day.

All participants in Italy reported detailed and specific strategies being adopted to engage migrant workers. CGIL officers, in particular, took a firm ideological line on the imperative to organise these workers as they were the most vulnerable in the labour market and therefore a priority as the rights of all workers are to be safeguarded. The idea that securing migrants' rights protected everybody's was repeatedly raised. However, a UIL officer also spelt out clear strategies including the belief within that particular confederation of the value of networks.

> We use the concept of networks of workers. It is scientifically proven in that immigrants tend to organise in a different society in networks. So, for example, the first individual immigrants often come to Italy and then the family, sons and daughters come. Using these networks you can organise people ... Albanians for example are a very closed community, almost a parallel society, but if you have an Albanian-speaking trade unionists you can gain access to this community. (UIL officer)

The priority for all participants was not perceived to be recruitment, as this was universally understood as a by-product of organic engagement. One CGIL officer, who had himself been an undocumented migrant worker in the agricultural sector for a number of years and had been helped by CGIL, explained how the union did not try to recruit irregular migrants, 'not because we don't want them, but because the priority is to have them regularised'. This officer also cited the fact that the migrant support department in which he worked assisted one million migrants each year, despite the confederation only having 400,000 migrant members. This participant also put the comparison of Italy and the UK strategies into stark contrast when he stated, 'I wouldn't be sitting here with you now if the union had taken the UK approach'. The idea of helping now and recruiting later was widespread, even beyond CGIL: 'When the worker has a good job, then they will join. And because of this system of networks they will say to other workers "I was in UIL and they treated me well"' (CGIL officer).

Other initiatives to engage particularly undocumented migrant workers included the 'trade unions on the road' campaign, which travelled around inspecting workplaces and talking to workers, a role carried out by the state in England through the poorly resourced Gangmasters' Licensing Authority. None of the Italian participants gave any indication that prioritising migrant organising was anything other than the – uncontroversial – right thing to do. Comments such as 'work joins people more than it divides them' and 'work is the way to integrate people' were common. A number of participants did, however, allude to the connection between upholding the rights of the most vulnerable workers and the rest of the working population. The general attitude was best expressed by one respondent, who said that the strategy of all trade unions needed to be to start by defending the weakest and work upwards.

The visibility of these approaches was stark in Rome on the day of a national CGIL conference on defending migrant workers' rights. Every available space around the centre of Rome was occupied with thousands of posters, as shown in Figure III.1.5, in a way not seen in the UK. These were posted by migrant worker activists from within the union and this visualisation is therefore a good representation of the ability of the union to mobilise on the issue of migrant workers' rights.

Figure III.1.5 Posters Publicising Migrant Rights Conference by CGIL. *Source*: Ben Egan.

Numerous participants in Italy referred to rapidly diminishing employment rights and the difficulties this was causing, as well as the increasing need to take collective action. A very senior officer referred to his opening speech to the conference, where he spelt out the CGIL strategy 'two paths at the same time'. This referred to political pressure to reverse attacks on rights while also concentrating on mobilisation as the greatest buttress of union power.

CONCLUSION: CLASS, COMPETITION AND THE STATE

What then can we conclude from the findings of the approaches to migrant workers of the unions investigated in this chapter, and what are the implications of their approaches to class and identity politics in shaping this? It is clear that the unions with an ideological framing that necessitates an involvement with these new worker types beyond the strict limitations of the workplace are better positioned to be relevant to these workers. This is fairly uncontroversial. What we have shown that goes beyond this observation is that there are distinct relations at work within modern European employment relations that give this a unique character and represent an opportunity for trade unions: namely, the competitive forces unleashed by class-oriented approaches to union power and the reconfiguration of the state(s) in Europe which has rendered more traditional union attitudes to migrants untenable.

Competitive Forces

Identity politics within trade unions are in many ways shaped by the historical and structural conditions which they find themselves in – as seen in our case studies. The politics of the IWU are shaped by the long-standing tradition of the class-based and anti-sectarian movements in Northern Ireland, which the IWU sees itself as a continuation of, while the CGIL maintains a semblance of ideological legacy to its foundation as a political trade union confederation, born of the resistance to fascism in the 1940s. In comparing the approaches of these unions we can see how their approaches, actions and the structures that these embed can have far-reaching effects beyond their immediate environment.

Much of this is due to competitive pressures that have taken root, which can lead in opposing directions depending on circumstances, structural challenges and design, competition between unions to grow as well as competitive pressures between different types of workers that those unions must therefore navigate. Both these aspects of competition are affected by a union's commitment to class consciousness. In the sense of solidarity between native and non-native groups of workers this was observed from the repeated insistence of interviewees that all workers were of the same working class – as may be expected. However, it is the other sense, that of unions competing with one another, that the real collective benefits of the ideology can be observed. In this data, we find clear evidence of this.

English unions' general approach to activity, servicing paid-up members who need assistance, is clearly unsuited to representing 'uninitiated' migrant workers who may face a whole multitude of problems that extend beyond the workplace. Yet one of the most common reasons given that they do not pursue such initiatives is that they have limited resources to deal with the membership issues that they already have. At its most basic, this is a calculation between income and expenditure, and therefore membership (and the subscription fees it implies) remains the primary goal of organising strategies in relation to migrants as well as other groups. The ideal member in this logic is *high paying* and *low maintenance* because there are usually several competing unions in any sector or workplace, all fighting for members within the same apolitical confederation. In this sense we see the malevolent face of competition on union strength. However, in Italy, the class-oriented approach of the CGIL caused a competitive pressure on the other unions – most notably the liberal UIL confederation – to do the same, or else risk irrelevance in the fast-growing demographic of migrant workers. The same competitive pressures as in England were managed completely differently.

In terms of generating *inter-organisational* competition (i.e. between unions) the role of class-based ideology was repeatedly raised in the Italian and Irish contexts, yet not in the English. In considering the third of Penninx and Roosblad's three dilemmas (2000: 10–12) for unions in whether and how to go about organising migrants, our findings are mixed between the philosophical underpinnings and the practical activities. The repeated insistence, particularly from CGIL officers, that they were for all workers and the various contributions highlighting how all working people were effectively the same with the same core interests gives the impression that CGIL officers continue to display higher levels of class consciousness in how they approach union activities. This is consistent with the class-based tradition of Italian trade unionism. In reality, the various special activities that are undertaken with the explicit objective of engaging migrants demonstrate a practical commitment to treat these workers quite differently to native Italians if necessary, such as the 'trade unions on the road' scheme, but this was also explicitly class-oriented.

A final essential consideration in relation to the role of class and union competition is what organising is taken to mean. Union discourses are key to developing this. 'Organising' means very different actions and strategies, with different objectives, in different unions (Simms and Holgate 2010). The data here shows that this is very different again for migrants and that unions need to think about how they can become more relevant for workers, rather than the other way around. In Italy the role of class, and more specifically class politics, as a motivation to migrant organising in unions is evident across different sectors and political backgrounds. We see a high degree of consistency in the responses of the trade unionists in Italy to many of the questions, even from different confederations, and therefore, in theory at least, different political traditions. Every participant was wholly dismissive, for example, of the notion that a unions' role is to recruit and represent members.

The Reconfigured State

A crucial change in (Western) European countries which transforms the whole established approach of unions in receiving countries is the reconfiguration of the state under neoliberal logic, shifting the interaction between it, capital and labour. This is the reason that we identify none of our unions as being involved in dilemma one. Unions play social and political roles but in the modern free market model they must increasingly be relevant to workforces that are precarious and mobile. This is further exacerbated by the growth of the EU into countries previously on the opposing side in the cold war. This has made obsolete many of the older arguments against including migrants more fully into union work. In traditional approaches unions had a more national focus and there was some joint interest between unions, business and the government in the economic and political growth of the country. This has been undermined by the growth of the EU as a sovereign body on issues relating to inward investment as well as the privatisation of many public services. Across Europe, the assets of the state have become those of private capital and so unions have had to reposition themselves in a way that is arguably more uniform than at any other time in the twentieth century. This means being more flexible to new workers' groupings and more ambitious in establishing themselves outside the fragmented workplace.

The cases analysed in this chapter indicate that even though the factors identified by Penninx and Roosblad (2000) have relatively strong explanatory power in terms of trade union responses to migration, there has also been an important role for class and identity politics when it comes to not just trade union approaches per se but especially with regard to the actual outcomes for the latter. However, in each case this has manifested itself somewhat differently depending on regional histories and social structures. In Italy, the class-based tradition of trade unionism is reflected in the repeated insistence among union officials that they were for all workers. The argument that rights of all are best secured by protecting those at the margins of the labour market helped to drive a range of practical policies, which, even though paradoxically singling out migrant workers as different to native Italian workers, had nevertheless many positive outcomes for migrant workers.

Somewhat in contrast to this approach, rather than starting with a narrative of shared class identity, the migrant workers' branch in England illustrated a way of including a specific migrant group through a special treatment approach with the potential to gradually develop a general workers' identity. While the prevalence of migrants employed in non-recognised workplaces and the potential to offer trade union events in Polish have led to a strong branch, the question remained how sustainable this exceptional form of organising could be, when it was mainly built on the Polish identity and was in the process of developing a workers' identity with its members and activists taking ownership of their branch. The case of Northern Ireland indicated that the class-based and anti-sectarian politics of the IWU, which also has to be seen within the specific historical context of the labour movement in this part of the world, has been an important factor in shaping outcomes for the most vulnerable migrant workers as well as the union itself, making it more flexible and taking it to the territories of the Northern Irish economy where pragmatically oriented mainstream trade unions did not dare to venture.

REFERENCES

Boyd, A. 1984. *Have the Unions Failed Us in the North?* Dublin: Mercier Press.

Castles, S. and G. Kosack. 1973. *Immigrant Workers and Class Structure in Western Europe*. Oxford: Oxford University Press.

Connolly, H. and R. Darlington. 2012. 'Radical political unionism in France and Britain: A comparative study of SUD-Rail and the RMT'. *European Journal of Industrial Relations* 18 (3): 235–250. Available at: http://ejd.sagepub.com/cgi/doi/10.1177/0959680112452693 (accessed 8 September 2014).

Connolly, H., S. Marino and M. M. Lucio. 2014. 'Trade union renewal and the challenges of representation: Strategies towards migrant and ethnic minority workers in the Netherlands, Spain and the United Kingdom'. *European Journal of Industrial Relations* 20 (1): 5–20.

Cregan, C., T. Bartram and P. Stanton. 2009. 'Union organizing as a mobilizing strategy: The impact of social identity and transformational leadership on the collectivism of Union Members'. *British Journal of Industrial Relations* 47 (4): 701–722.

Department for Business Innovation and Skills. 2015. 'Trade union membership 2013'. Statistical Bulletin. Available at: https://www.gov.uk/government/uploads/system/uploads/attachment_data/file/431564/Trade_Union_Membership_Statistics_2014.pdf (accessed 10 November 2016).

Department of Learning and Labour. 2009. *The Economic, Labour Market and Skills Impacts of Migrant Workers in Northern Ireland.* Lisburn: Oxford Economics. Available at: https://www.economy-ni.gov.uk/publications/economic-labour-market-and-skills-impacts-migrant-workers-northern-ireland (accessed 10 November 2016).

Fitzgerald, I. and J. Hardy. 2010. '"Thinking Outside the Box"? Trade Union organizing strategies and polish migrant workers in the United Kingdom'. *British Journal of Industrial Relations* 48 (1): 131–150.

Frege, C. M. and J. Kelly. 2003. 'Union revitalization strategies in comparative perspective'. *European Journal of Industrial Relations* 9 (1): 7–24.

Hyman, R. 1971. *The Workers' Union.* Oxford: Clarendon.

Hyman, R. 1996. 'Union identities and ideologies in Europe'. In *The Lost Perspective? Trade Unions between Ideology and Social Action in the New Europe. Volume 2: Significance of Ideology in European Trade Unionism,* edited by P. Pasture, J. Verberckmoes and H. de Witte, 60–89. Aldershot: Aveburypp.

Hyman, R. 2001. *Understanding European Trade Unionism: Between Market, Class and Society*. London: Sage.

Josephides, S. 1991. *Towards a History of the Indian Workers' Association*. Research Paper in Ethnic Relations No. 18. Coventry: Centre for Research and Ethnic Relations.

Krings, T. 2009. 'A race to the bottom? Trade Unions, EU enlargement and the free movement of labour'. *European Journal of Industrial Relations* 15 (1): 49–69.

Marino, S. 2012. 'Trade union inclusion of migrant and ethnic minority workers: Comparing Italy and the Netherlands'. *European Journal of Industrial Relations* 18 (1): 5–20.

Marino, S. 2015. 'Trade unions, special structures and the inclusion of migrant workers: On the role of union democracy'. *Work, Employment & Society* 29 (5): 826–846.

Marino, S., R. Penninx and J. Roosblad. 2015. 'Trade unions, immigration and immigrants in Europe revisited: Unions' attitudes and actions under new conditions'. *Comparative Migration Studies* 3 (1): 1–16.

McCollum, D. and A. Findlay. 2015. '"Flexible" workers for "flexible" jobs? The labour market function of A8 migrant labour in the UK'. *Work, Employment, Society* 29 (3): 427–443.

McIlroy, J. 2012. 'Radical political unionism reassessed'. *European Journal of Industrial Relations* 18 (3): 251–258.

Penninx, R. and J. Roosblad, eds. 2000. *Trade Unions, Immigration and Immigrants in Europe 1960–1993*. New York: Berghahn Books.

Philips, S. 2015. *Towards a Strategy for the Inclusion of Migrant Workers in Trade Unions*. ICTU.

Regalia, I. and M. Regini. 1998. 'Italy: The dual character of industrial relations'. In *Changing Industrial Relations in Europe*, edited by R. Hyman and A. Ferner, Oxford: Blackwell.

Sabel, C. 1982. *Work and Politics: The Division of Labour in Industry*. Cambridge: University Press.

Simms, M. 2012. 'Imagined solidarities: Where is class in union organising?' *Capital and Class* 36 (1): 97–115.

Simms, M. and J. Holgate. 2010. 'Organising for What? Where is the Debate on the Politics of Organising?' *Work, Employment & Society* 24 (1): 157–168.

Stewart, P., B. Garvey and T. McKearney. 2013. 'An alternative trade union organizing approach to migrant workers in Northern Ireland in the wake of the Good Friday Agreement'. *Warsaw Forum of Economic Sociology* 4:1 (7): 91–108.

Stewart, P. and B. Garvey. 2015. 'Migrant workers and the north of Ireland: Between neoliberalism and sectarianism'. *Work, Employment and Society* 29 (3): 1–17.

Virdee, S. 2000. 'A Marxist critique of black radical theories of Trade-Union racism'. *Sociology* 34 (3): 545–565.

Waddington, J. and A. Kerr. 2009. 'Transforming a Trade Union? An assessment of the introduction of an organizing initiative'. *British Journal of Industrial Relations* 47 (1): 27–54.

Woolfson, C. and J. Sommers. 2008. 'Trajectories of entropy and "The Labour Question". The political economy of post-communist migration in the New Europe'. *Debatte* 16 (1): 53–69.

Woolfson, C. and J. Sommers. 2015. 'Migration and the new austeriat: The Baltic model and the socioeconomic costs of the new austerity'. Working Paper Presented at Workshop on Immigration, Race, and Ethnicity, Ash Center for Democratic Governance and Innovation at the Harvard Kennedy School, February 2015.

World Bank. *Jobs data*. Available at: http://datatopics.worldbank.org/jobs/ (accessed 8 September 2014).

Wrench, J. 2004. 'Trade Union responses to immigrants and ethnic inequality in Denmark and the UK: The context of consensus and conflict'. *European Journal of Industrial Relations* 10 (1): 7–30.

Chapter III.2

The Social Articulation of the Crisis and Political Mobilisation in Spain

Some Reflections on the Shortcomings of the New Social Movements

Martin Lundsteen and Irene Sabaté

In the last decade, as a response to the social effects of the economic crisis and its political management, a whole array of new social movements have emerged in Spain. Specific to these movements is the fact that they often accomplish something left-wing movements have usually had a hard time doing: gaining broad social support and mobilising a great number of people across the usual migrant/non-migrant divide. Indeed, movements such as 15-M – the popular mobilisation that occupied the main squares of the country (Romero 2013), and later propagated to many neighbourhoods and smaller towns (Doñate 2013) – have gathered a wide variety of citizens from the middle and working classes, both with and without a migrant background. The explicit aim of 15-M was to protest against the impact of the economic crisis on ordinary people, and to resist the austerity policies that have contributed to the increasing precariousness of many people's lives.

A great example of this new tendency is the anti-repossession movement *Plataforma de Afectados por la Hipoteca* (PAH)[1], which emerged in Spain as a response to one of the political and economic impacts of the so-called crisis. A great number of home repossessions[2] have taken place as a consequence of the over-indebtedness in which many members of the Spanish middle and working classes found themselves in the aftermath of the crisis. Seeking to become homeowners, they had relied on the availability of temporary jobs and on the ever-increasing real estate prices of the housing bubble (Naredo 2009; García Montalvo 2008) in order to take out a mortgage. The actual precariousness of that situation, which would be unveiled by the dramatic decrease of household income caused by mass unemployment, among other circumstances, was overlooked, or deliberately veiled in some cases, both by mortgage debtors and by credit institutions. The Spanish economic boom, heavily based on the expansion of the building sector, had somehow entailed a promise of prosperity and upward social mobility for the working and middle classes. In the particular case of recently arrived migrants, purchasing one's home – in the context of the local consumption standards and lifestyles to be adopted – was understood, from an economic viewpoint, as wise investment behaviour and, symbolically, as proof – or at least a promise – of their inclusion in the host society, as it seemed to counteract the strong discrimination they faced in the arenas of work, political rights, access to welfare provisions and the like. But, due to getting indebted upon becoming homeowners, these workers pursued their migration projects on the basis of an ethic of work and sacrifice (Terrones 2013; Palomera 2014; Sabaté 2016a); this curtailed their chances to get involved in collective mobilisations or organised claims for better living and working conditions.

Since 2009,[3] with the advent of the crisis and the emergence of mortgage indebtedness as a major social problem, movements such as the PAH have questioned the legitimacy of repossessions involving primary residences, basing their critique on the irresponsibility – and even the illegality – of predatory lending practices implied in mortgage loans (Nasarre 2011; Zunzunegui 2013), and on the disastrous social consequences entailed by the loss of the home and lifelong indebtedness, a condition that, due to the particularities of Spanish mortgage law, does not end after the eviction. The movement has succeeded in mobilising and empowering a great variety of people directly affected and others who sympathise with them (Mir et al. 2013; Mangot 2013; Sabaté 2014). Through different actions of civil disobedience against eviction attempts and protests against the involved financial institutions, it has gained force and a broad legitimacy and support in civil society.[4] Their ability to mobilise otherwise excluded groups, such as migrants or minorities, alongside non-migrants around a common identity of victims of fraudulent mortgages (irrespective of any kind of ethnic, cultural or national identification) is especially salient. However, our main object of reflection is whether this common identity has indeed encompassed and transcended other ascriptions, or whether it has rather contributed to masking existing inequalities among the different social sectors that, as several ethnographic accounts reveal (Palomera 2014; Suárez 2014), have been unevenly affected both by mortgage over-indebtedness and by home repossessions. That is, to what extent do these discursive strategies actually succeed in attracting public support and in constructing 'those affected by mortgages' as a wide identity containing heterogeneous experiences? In fact, the main question of this article is whether social movements promote a mirage of equality by omitting actual inequalities and injustices, specific to migrants or to certain ethnic groups, which would require special struggles in order to be reversed.

In order to do so, we will start out by describing the particular impacts of mortgage default and home repossessions on households with a migrant background, drawing on the ethnographic data we have collected during our fieldwork in three towns in the metropolitan areas of Girona and Barcelona where the movement has been particularly successful: Barcelona, l'Hospitalet de Llobregat and Salt (Girona). The bulk of the data analysed here comes from Barcelona, where the fieldwork has consisted of over thirty semi-structured interviews with mortgage debtors, anti-foreclosures activists, members of non-profit organisations, bank clerks, professionals of finance, real estate agents, lawyers and public notaries, representatives of the public administration. In addition, participant observation has been carried out during social movements' assemblies and mobilisations, and relevant documents – including legislation, documentary films, websites, written and graphic materials created by the anti-foreclosure movement, and so on – have been collected and analysed. These main sources have been compared with material from ethnographic fieldwork undertaken in the metropolitan area of Girona between 2011 and 2014, not specifically concerning the movement itself, but rather the incorporation of migrants into civil society (Lundsteen 2015).

Specifically, for this chapter, we analyse the ideological and material foundation and political strategies of the anti-foreclosure movement. In doing so, we mainly focus on different critical moments in their mobilisations and in their internal organisation in order to compare and thus foster a more global analysis of the economic and political circumstances entrenched in these mobilisations. We will also try to identify the possible pitfalls and/or shortcomings of the movement. Our main contention will be that, interestingly, the PAH tends to overcome the usual social divides, but they somehow stop short of an overall critique of existing racist structuring and class divides. As a matter of fact, they may end up inadvertently and involuntarily reproducing these divides.

HOUSING, THE FINANCIAL MARKET, AND MIGRANT WORKERS

After he arrived in Spain in 2004, leaving his wife and three children in Ecuador, Nelson got several jobs in the building sector and found accommodation in sub-rented rooms. He could not afford to rent a whole flat, as prospective tenants were asked for a deposit and several months' rent in advance. At some point, he met Álvaro, an acquaintance he vaguely remembered from his home town. Álvaro had divorced his wife and left her and their teenage daughter in Ecuador. Together with his new wife, Manuela, he was starting his own business, related to building activities. Unlike Nelson, he had a university degree in business administration and saw himself as an entrepreneur. In 2005, as time passed and both Nelson and Álvaro seemed to do well in their jobs, each of them started to make further plans. As Nelson's priority was to have his family settled in Spain, he started to look for more housing space and considered the possibility of renting a flat with Álvaro and Manuela. They had already found one that seemed to fit the expectations of both families when, suddenly, Álvaro and Manuela stated their preference for homeownership. As they did not meet the requirements to obtain a mortgage loan, a broker advised them to look for someone who could act as a guarantor in their contract. They started to put pressure on Nelson, who had not considered the possibility of becoming homeowner but now started to see the advantages of such condition. 'If he [Álvaro] can, then so can I', he said to himself. Initially, €600 mortgage repayments seemed more advantageous than €800 rent payments. In addition, the decision should ease the process of family reunification, as officials were said not to scrutinise the residential conditions of homeowners as they did when applicants were tenants. Once both customers agreed, the mortgage broker, who also ran a real estate agency based in a deprived, densely populated neighbourhood, offered them a financial deal in which Nelson and Álvaro would act simultaneously as guarantors for each other. This should have allowed them to obtain their mortgage loans, each of them for the whole price of each flat, to be repaid over the next thirty years, from two different savings banks within a few days' time. But, in fact, at the moment of signing, Nelson and Álvaro found out that the credit institutions would not list them as mere guarantors but as co-owners, which rendered them fully liable in case either of them went into arrears. In addition, several strangers were added as guarantors.[5]

Although they were living in the same area, for the next several years Nelson and Álvaro almost lost contact with each other, as they moved into new phases in their lives. Nelson's family arrived from Ecuador and settled in the humble forty-two-square-metre flat for which they had paid €189,000. His wife got several jobs as a domestic worker and the boys attended secondary school. Álvaro, in turn, had to deal with serious problems as, just a few months after moving into his flat, the building was declared uninhabitable by the authorities. The occupants had to move out and pay for a thorough reconstruction. In order to cope with the expenses, Álvaro had to get a new loan, while he continued to repay his mortgage. In the meantime, Nelson, worried about the implications of co-ownership, made the legal arrangements to become the sole owner of his flat and asked Álvaro to do the same – a procedure that was never completed in the case of Álvaro's flat.

Then the economic situation got worse. Nelson's wage decreased, as he was no longer offered overtime work, and mortgage repayments were on the rise. Hence he was forced to apply for a restructuring of his loan, which was then transferred to another bank. By the time Nelson could no longer meet the repayments, Álvaro had already been in arrears for several months. They met again and found out about each other's situation at a meeting of the local PAH. In Nelson's case, a long struggle awaited before he could get rid of his mortgage debt in exchange for his flat.

Unfortunately, the story we have just told is not a unique one. During the recent housing bubble experienced in Spain up to 2007, many households took out a mortgage in order to become homeowners, a widely shared aspiration across the middle and working classes. As it has been argued elsewhere (Allen et al. 2004; Palomera 2013; Sabaté 2014), the high rates of homeownership in Spain, rather than deriving from a supposed cultural trait, can be seen as an outcome of housing policies and other structural factors at play at least since the Francoist dictatorship (1939–1975): the chronic lack of social housing and the insufficient stock available in the rental market, the attractiveness of real estate investments as an antidote to the shortcomings of the welfare state, as well as the fiscal incentive scheme for the purchase of properties, among other deliberate policies aimed at the conversion of 'proletarians' into homeowners.[6] With the turn of the century, the effects of these conditions were added to those of a growing economic cycle (García Montalvo 2008; Naredo 2009; López & Rodríguez 2010), with a booming building sector, a rapid revaluation of both old and new real estate properties – which made them seem an almost perfectly liquid form of wealth – and an unprecedented availability of cheap credit, fuelled by the arrival of capital flows at the country and by a growing demand for housing (partly due to the arrival of several millions of migrants since the mid-1990s).

In this way, an atmosphere was created where, for households trying to satisfy their housing needs, the purchase of a home seemed the most sensible move. The risks entailed by heavy indebtedness, and by the need to repay mortgages over the next three or even four decades, were to a great extent disregarded. Among the bulk of housing purchasers and mortgage borrowers, households with a migrant background became a specific target for real estate agents and credit institutions. They were considered eligible for borrowing, despite the precariousness of their jobs and incomes, as they constituted a subprime market, and indeed a lucrative one from a financial viewpoint (Nasarre 2011). This explains why, in some cases, as our ethnographic account illustrates, they became the target of aggressive marketing practices that can be depicted as predatory lending, a phenomenon Dymski (2009) refers to as 'racial exploitation'.

In turn, as mentioned above, migrant households themselves – as did Spanish ones – saw the purchase of a home as a self-evident decision from the point of view of prevailing consumption patterns and of the common-sense aspirations guiding the management of working-class domestic economies. Some specific factors were at play in their case. For example, it was a widespread feeling that becoming homeowners would allow them to avoid the strong discrimination and the adverse residential conditions that, in many cases, they had suffered in the rental market as they arrived in the host country (Martínez Veiga 1999; Colectivo IOÉ 2005: 83; Terrones 2013). After some time in the country (Colectivo IOÉ 2005: 77; Onrubia 2010), as they intended to pursue their migration projects by moving to the next phase of their lifecycles, homeownership was seen as a factor that would increase their chances of obtaining permission for family reunification.[7] And, in the context of their expectations of upward social mobility, consisting of both the improvement of their material living conditions and the symbolic incorporation into the host society, purchasing a property was often understood as a crucial step to building a patrimony – proof of social and economic success (Suárez 2014) that would secure the standard of life both for the migrants themselves in their old age and for their children in the future.

Overall, migrants took part in the general atmosphere of economic euphoria, both as overworked wage workers, many of them employed in the building sector or in related activities, and as consumers, not only of housing but also of other goods and services that could be purchased, with a strong reliance on credit borrowing. In most cases, when purchasing their homes, as they did not have any savings to make a down payment, migrants had to take on mortgage loans for the whole price of the property, or even for more than 100 per cent if they intended to cover other expenses, such as the notary and broker fees. Getting heavily indebted – an action that, as we have seen, involved not only the borrower but also other members of their social networks – entailed a high risk, as it implied decades-long repayment periods over which uncontrollable factors could fluctuate, such as the availability of jobs and income, or the evolution of interest rates and real estate prices. In addition, other life circumstances, such as illness or the breakup of marriages, could also affect the ability to keep up with mortgage repayments.

As a result, with the burst of the housing bubble and the advent of the economic crisis in 2008, a spate of home repossessions hit the country, and its impact on migrants, among the weakest sectors of the population, has been particularly dramatic (Terrones 2013). They were the first to get into arrears due to the precariousness of their jobs and the lack of public and private support. Under the current rates of unemployment, their chances of obtaining new sources of income in order to meet their arrears are low. The steep depreciation of their properties, often located in deprived areas as a result of strong segregation trends already at play during the housing bubble (Martínez Veiga 1999; Terrones 2013; Palomera 2014; Lundsteen 2015), has also reduced their chances to have their debts cancelled in exchange for the housing unit. In addition, their ability to mobilise resources through their social networks has been dramatically damaged, as they tend to be surrounded by people equally affected by unemployment and insolvency. The lack of access to relevant information, due to the unfamiliarity with local markets, bureaucracies and laws, and even due to linguistic barriers, has also been a differential factor for migrants throughout the process, from the moment they decided to buy a home, up to the point where they found themselves unable to repay the mortgage.

In some cases, returning to the country of origin has been perceived as the only solution available for them. However, fleeing their debts in this way does not guarantee a real second chance, while it entails a painful renunciation of their migration project, often including a sense of failure and even social ostracism in the 'sending society'. Nelson's family, for instance, has ruled this possibility out because two of their sons are still receiving their education and, for their parents, returning to Ecuador would result in denying them prospects in the future.

As a result, many mortgage defaulters with a migrant background have remained in Spain, struggling to overcome such an adverse situation (Sabaté 2014) by means of strategies that, we contend, are largely built upon their specific legal and socio-economic conditions as migrants. This specificity includes their approach to, and participation in, social and political mobilisations, as we will argue in the next section.

THE POLITICAL MANAGEMENT OF THE 'FINANCIAL CRISIS' IN SPAIN AND 'CIVIL SOCIETY'S' RESPONSE: THE CASE OF THE PAH

The spate of repossessions that have occurred in Spain since the burst of the economic bubble has provoked a variety of reactions among the affected population and society at large. It must be taken into account that, in many cases, the feelings of shame and guilt attached to mortgage default have contributed to the invisibility of debtors in arrears. This was the norm, especially during the first years of the crisis, when many households made desperate attempts to keep up with repayments. They would often restructure their domestic economies by cutting down on their expenses, which severely harmed their living conditions. But, as time passed, the crisis became chronic, people's desperation grew, and attempts of collective organisation among mortgage defaulters started to appear progressively.

Among these forms of collective organisation, there is no doubt that the PAH emerges as the most conspicuous example. It was founded in 2009 in Barcelona by a core of housing activists with previous experience of struggle who succeeded in gathering together a considerable number of mortgage debtors in hardship. It was rapidly replicated in other towns, until the figure of about 160 PAHs across Spain was reached.

With the aim of representing the interests of households who face difficulties in repaying their mortgages, the PAH's activity shows five distinct orientations.

1. *Acts of civil disobedience against foreclosures.* Probably the most visible trait of their strategy has been their call for public gatherings against particular evictions. Through an act of civil disobedience, they try to physically detain the police and judicial representatives from carrying out the foreclosure.
2. *Regular meetings in local assemblies.* Although closely connected to the former orientation, the regular meetings that the local assemblies carry out serve as mutual support, providing an opportunity for the affected to express their worries and overcome the sense of isolation. At the same time the participants become aware of the collective dimension of their problem, and often they are able to reverse the processes of self-incrimination, attributing responsibilities instead to different agents with whom the debtors maintain unequal power relations, such as the bank or public authorities. This way the assemblies turn into a space of empowerment against isolation and social stigma, and at the same time they are useful for determining both the material and psychological needs of the members.
3. *Collective counselling and negotiation with banks.* These are in general exerted by those members who have the most experience, and in some cases by professionals – above all lawyers – who offer their services voluntarily. This way relevant expert knowledge is circulated in order to tackle the different situations of the members. The main objective of this collective counselling is to promote the agency of the affected and provide them with tools which can improve the situation of helplessness when facing banking agents or civil servants, who control the expert knowledge with regard to the laws, finance and the bureaucratic resources of social assistance. Alongside these counselling practices, the most experienced members within each local assembly accompany debtors during their negotiations with banks and other institutions involved.
4. *Promotion of political engagement by means of collective action at different scales.* The promotion of political and legal changes is a cornerstone of the objectives of the PAH, through exerting influence on public opinion and requiring the intervention of legislators, judges and other public authorities. Thus, they have promoted the People's Initiatives for Legislation (*ILPs* in Spanish), and they are promoting municipal motions which penalise the banking entities economically when they possess empty housing. Similarly, collective demonstrations are organised against

certain banks (in front of or inside some of their offices), who have played a prominent part in the multiplication of foreclosures.

5. *Collective squatting in order to offer alternative housing.* The PAH has also come up with a mechanism in order to provide already evicted domestic groups with housing. This they do by squatting and occupying flats or entire buildings which are empty and owned by the banks. This strategy is not exclusive to the PAH, but also practised individually by many of the evicted families who return illegally to their old homes, often due to the lack of alternatives. Nonetheless, in the case of collective squatting, promoted by the assemblies of the PAH and institutionalised under the name of *Obra Social de la PAH*,[8] the practice acquires a protest characteristic directed at the authorities with the aim of making them prioritise the social function of property and the effective recognition of the constitutional right to adequate housing. Overall, they have primarily succeeded in the last aspect, of making the problem visible and demanding a political response, achieving even a favourable pronouncement from the European Court of Human Rights.

All in all, the movement has been considerably successful in building a common identity for mortgage defaulters, not only empowering them at the level of their particular cases, as they face negotiations with their banks, but also turning them into a crucial social actor that has overcome its previous stigma and invisibility. The strategies and methods of the PAH assemblies are being profusely described by social scientists (Mir et al. 2013; Mangot 2013; Sabaté 2014; Suárez 2014; Azis 2016)[9] as a conspicuous example of good practice in the arena of contemporary social movements emerging from the most recent financial and economic crisis.

The universalistic inspiration of the movement, that has tended to downplay the diverse circumstances in which debtors find themselves at present, and found themselves when they took out their mortgages, implies a monolithic narrative of the economic crisis in which banks and public authorities are pointed out as those responsible for a dramatic social situation.

This does not mean, however, that the PAH has always been equally monolithic in its action, far from that. At certain stages, classifying debtors in narrower categories in order to plan specific mobilisations has proved its effectiveness. This has been the case when particular problems and situations have been detected and specifically addressed; for example, those affecting debtors with abusive clauses in their contracts, those who have been denied the assignment of payment because their mortgage had been securitised, those who have a multicurrency mortgage, and the like. Besides, debtors who have borrowed from the same bank often assemble to force collective rather than individual negotiations, and to claim equal treatment from the credit institutions. This strategy has been successful in upgrading bargaining to higher departments within the bank rather than remaining in local bank branches where less pressure can be applied.

However, both the official narrative of the movement and its strategies for struggle have avoided the public recognition of the diversity of mortgage debtors due to other important, more structural factors. This has resulted, we contend, in an invisibilisation of such diverging circumstances, due to the universalistic inspiration of the movement and the fact that they have not been considered useful to device-specific strategies of mobilisation.

Nevertheless, we argue, factors of social diversity such as gender, national origin, educational level or socio-economic background have a crucial importance for the understanding of how the current rates of mortgage default were attained in Spain, and for the resolution of the social problem entailed by this, both at the household level and on a societal scale. Indeed, members of many different social sectors became indebted in the past and are facing indebtedness at present, but, beyond their common condition of defaulting debtors, they find themselves in very unequal circumstances. Such unequal circumstances derive from particular forms of discrimination and differentiated access to resources.

In this regard, in the narratives of some activists and social analysts, some patterns have been acknowledged with regard to gender discrimination. Women's specific vulnerabilities to mortgage default are attributed to the precariousness of their jobs, their lower wages, and, whenever this is the case, to their condition of single motherhood. In addition, it is also commonplace to highlight the prominent role adopted by many of them in the struggle against the threat of foreclosure, in contrast to their partners' inability to get over the dejection they have experienced, due to their failure to uphold their role as the main supporters of their families during the economic crisis. And, finally, a typical pattern has also been unveiled regarding the entanglement of mortgage default and gender violence, as the former PAH spokesperson – and current mayor of Barcelona – Ada Colau, described in an interview in 2013[10]:

> We have a specific problem of gender violence in relation to mortgages. For an abuser, a mortgage is a very useful tool. If he stops repaying, the bank cannot determine whether it is a case of gender violence or not. To stop repaying his half [of the] repayment is a way to put pressure on his ex-wife, and it becomes more acute if this leads to default and repossession. It is a frequent situation: there is a divorce and the woman is accorded the possession of the dwelling by the judge. If husband and wife are both the formal owners, and one of them stops repaying, the bank doesn't care about them having split up. They go against the wife. It is a specific problem, the use of the mortgage as a mechanism for gender violence, and this is why we created the gender committees.

In contrast to this, and perhaps surprisingly, other crucial factors of inequality and discrimination based on ethnic and national origin that, as we have illustrated in the previous section, are key to understanding the particular circumstances faced by defaulting debtors tend to be kept invisible both in the internal organisation and in the public action and discourse of the anti-foreclosure movement.[11] In most of its dialogue, the narrative of the PAH attributes the spate of repossessions to the unsustainability of mortgage over-indebtedness for 'wide layers' of the population, a circumstance that was particularly salient among low-income households and people with temporary jobs, without regard for their ethnic background. This, at least, is the approach that emerges in the report 'Emergencia habitacional en el Estado español', published by the PAH and the *Observatori DESC*[12] (2013: 11–12):

> The indebtedness in order to access housing was a generalised phenomenon amongst the different sectors of the population although especially prominent amongst the ones with a low income. In fact, jobs characterised by a temporary nature, such as the ones related to the service or the building sectors, represented an obstacle when soliciting a rental agreement for housing. On the contrary, it presented no problem when signing a mortgage.[13]

However, in other instances, the PAH chooses a slightly different discourse, where repossessions are presented as an all-encompassing social problem that, rather than being restricted or specific to any sector of population, cuts across the whole of Spanish society. Interestingly, in a preview of the report quoted above,[14] a supposedly generalised attribution of repossessions to migrant populations or to poorly educated people was explicitly refuted on the basis of statistical data:

> The profile of the affected persons I: 82 per cent have been born in the Spanish State. Amongst the people born in other countries the most affected community is the one from Ecuador counting 4 per cent. The educational level is high: 59 per cent finished secondary education or did professional training, while 24 per cent finished university studies. These data in themselves refute the image that has been portrayed from time to time that it is a problem of 'migrant and ignorant people'. The data show the complete opposite.

In a similar vein, it is common to hear PAH members understating the importance of unequal social positions, including the ones built upon ethnic and national origins, in their accounts of the repossessions problem, as the leader of the PAH, Lleida, expressed:

> The PAH spokesperson affirms that they handle completely different cases and that the affected people range from university professors to migrant population. 'It affects all social classes', he points out. (Lijarcio 2012)

In contrast to this discursive dimension, during our observation of the PAH local assembly in l'Hospitalet de Llobregat in 2012, we could establish the distinct impacts of default and repossessions on debtors, to a great extent depending on their national origins and ethnic backgrounds. Similar to what happened to Nelson and Álvaro, many migrants got indebted as a result of the discrimination they experienced as tenants and their eagerness to get attached to the host country, to improve their legal situation and to attain upward social mobility; they then found themselves exposed to the risk of repossession as they lost their jobs – the most precarious ones within the Spanish labour market.

In l'Hospitalet, despite the majority of members having a migrant background – about one hundred people congregated every week, most of them Latin American – we witnessed the predominance of autochthonous members in the leading roles within the assembly, with the only exception being one very active and charismatic Equatorian young man who would quit his struggle and return to his country a few months later. The unequal access to resources available to autochthonous and migrant debtors – for example, as regards the possibility to access resources through supportive family networks providing financial aid and/or shelter – as well as the diverging origins and features of their default situations, such as their different levels of indebtedness and their varying ability to negotiate with bank clerks, became apparent at every weekly meeting. However, these divergences and regularities were rarely highlighted or addressed as such. The fact of having been victims of predatory or fraudulent lending practices, such as the crossed guarantees described in Nelson and Álvaro's case, and of having been sold subprime financial products was not featured as particular circumstances of migrants. It has rather been encompassed under more general descriptions of the mortgage crisis as the result of a generalised fraud perpetrated by banks. Slogans that were often heard during mobilisations, such as '*No es una crisis, es una estafa*' (It is not a crisis, but a fraud) or '*El pueblo, unido, jamás será vencido*' (The people united will never be defeated), contributed to including all defaulting debtors under a common label – '*el pueblo*' / the people – and to depicting them all as victims of the same mechanism of dispossession – '*una estafa*' / a fraud.

The most immediate question that may be raised here, whether all 'social classes' – or, more generally speaking, all social groups – are indeed *equally* affected, has an obvious answer: no. Several vulnerability factors unevenly affecting mortgage debtors have already been pointed out in previous research (Terrones 2013; Sabaté 2014; Suárez 2014) and should be taken into account in order to properly assess the impacts of mortgage default and home repossessions on specific groups.

There is, in addition, a second question to be answered: how does a social movement like the PAH cope with this uneven affectation, especially concerning key factors such as national origins and ethnic ascriptions? And, if the emphasis on job precariousness – and on a shared, post-facto self-identification as precarious workers – entails a reference to the most precariously employed of Spanish workers, migrants, then why is it preferable that it remains implicit? Or, in other words, when activists choose to emphasise the participation in the movement of members of more privileged groups, such as well-educated people and small entrepreneurs, are they trying to avoid the stigmatisation of PAH members as belonging to marginal groups?

Indeed, the ethnography reveals that the mentioned categorisations do play a role in the everyday workings of the movement itself. During the assemblies and mobilisations of the PAH, as well as when we interviewed some of its members, we could observe several regularities in the contrasts between migrants and autochthonous debtors.

First of all, in order to access housing and possibly to socially progress, a lot of migrants were led to buy a flat (often in 'degraded neighbourhoods') due to segmentation and racism in the housing markets, which kept them from being able to rent, as several authors have noted – both during and after the housing bubble (Leralta 2005; Palomera 2013; Terrones 2013; Bernat 2014: 49) – and as we could also observe in Nelson's case. In some instances, migrants who found themselves in an irregular situation were encouraged to take out a mortgage by merely showing their passport, while more constraints were imposed on them if they tried to rent an apartment. That was, according to Nelson, the case for Álvaro and Manuela.

Indeed, working-class migrants comprised a distinct subprime market that had been targeted by mortgage brokers operating in decayed neighbourhoods where the housing bubble had a great impact on real estate prices. Such brokers, using aggressive strategies, were not interested in testing the reliability of customers, but rather in offering banks the opportunity to operate in this niche market. They earned considerable fees on this basis and then, as the bubble burst, simply faded away. As a result, many migrants found themselves dealing with banks for the first time as they went into arrears; at the time of signing the mortgage, they had only dealt with their mortgage broker, who usually had also put them in contact with their guarantors (complete strangers) and even with their co-owners. Now they were considered customers of the bank and had to adapt themselves to this condition, trying to rapidly acquire a particular knowledge and a complicated language (Sabaté 2016b). An condition that the mortgage broker had shielded them from at the time they became homeowners, as their strategy included 'simplifying' – and distorting – the customer's perception of what he/she was doing: for example, propagating the 'myth of home-ownership' (Terrones 2013), comparing the monthly rent with mortgage repayments in their initial amount, and concluding that renting was 'throwing away one's money', while purchasing a property was always an advantageous investment. In contrast, most of the autochthonous debtors had taken out their mortgage directly from the bank, and had, at least to some extent, a certain familiarity with it. In many cases, their relationship with bank clerks was imbued with trust, as a result of their mutual acquaintance.

Secondly, the migrant populations were the first to arrive at the PAH, as their jobs were more precarious and they were the first to lose them, finding themselves therefore insolvent. They also tended to be more heavily indebted, as they had not been able to save before taking out their mortgage, and their options to access resources and support from their social networks ceased in a few months' time. On the contrary, autochthonous debtors were generally able to resist longer by drawing on family support. They also lost their jobs later, and in some cases they had been able to pay part of the property's price (with kin support, with savings or by selling other properties they inhabited before – often paid for by migrants who would take them over). Therefore, they did not join the PAH in great numbers until the crisis aggravated. As Esmeralda, a debtor and activist, put it:

> It can be that we Spanish people come here [to the PAH's assembly] after drying up all our family. ... You thought everything was going to improve next year. ... But, on the contrary, everything goes worse. You say, well, this month I will ask my father for help, my parents-in-law next month, then my brother ... Until you get to a point ...

In all, the lack – or the weakness – of support and reciprocity networks is perceived as a specific feature of migrants. Thus, Mayte, a Spanish informant who faced imminent repossession and whose family (she, her husband and three children) had one daily meal at her mother-in-law's, compared her situation to that of another member of the local PAH who came from Morocco and had no relatives here:

> She has three little children. She needs more than I do. So, we make a chain, I give her the clothes we don't need any more, instead of taking them to Caritas [a charitable organisation]. We do not need to go there, she does.

Thirdly, the migrant populations have the theoretical option to move back to their country, and thus out of their difficult situation. However, this is not as easy as it may seem, as, among other things, it is perceived as a social failure, as Salvador, a Catalan debtor, described:

> Migrants have the possibility to return, which we Spanish people don't have. But it is not a solution for them. Really, if you talk to them, you realise that they are not happy with it. For them it's a loss, a defeat. As they came, they thought

> about building their life here, about settling as members with every right, and they return defeated, with nothing. They have to restart their life over there, with or without aid from their family. In the case of Ecuadorians, they have the advantage that their country does not acknowledge their debt. But, if you talk to them, you realise that this is no solution. Those people do not really want to go. Many of them don't. They have their life here; they have been here for eighteen or twenty years. Their life is falling apart. It is very nice to travel once a year, or every two years, to go to Ecuador and see your family, but then they want to stay here, their life is here.

As another point of contrast, whenever migrants had guarantors in their mortgage loan contracts, they were very likely default also, as we have seen in the case of Nelson and Álvaro. Therefore, no actual properties or patrimony or even income (as soon as subsidies were exhausted) could be seized by the bank, which entailed, to a point, a certain advantage, as it might provide them some strength in front of the bank when claiming for the 'assignment in payment'.[15] On the other hand, this situation entails a real risk of homelessness that, in many cases, is coped with by living in sub-rented rooms and other low-standard housing arrangements. In some cases, debtors already evicted, or at imminent risk of being so, have benefited from the aforementioned collective squatting of bank-owned buildings. Among the squatters of these buildings, migrants have an important presence, as they are over-represented among households at risk of becoming homeless after eviction.

Autochthonous debtors, in contrast, lack the option to 'flee', and, in many cases, their defaulting situation involves those who have acted as guarantors (often their retired parents), who typically are already homeowners with paid-up properties, and who now risk losing their homes. The implications of this entanglement of moral bonds and fluxes of support have resulted in very conflictive situations, namely, the cohabitation of grown-up children (often with children of their own) with their parents in the latter's homes. Or, as Salvador told us, the resentment of relatives who had supported him acting as guarantors, and now, as their own position as homeowners is in danger, find it difficult to come to terms with the situation:

> Family meetings with my parents-in-law are no longer the same, my father-in-law is more understanding, he understands we were deceived, they were also victims of deception, but my mother-in-law's nature is more tense, and she is always like, oh, I am gonna lose my flat, look, we made you a favour and now look in what situation you have put us.

As a matter of fact, all the processes involved in the buying and selling of properties, mortgage contracts, debt restructuring and renegotiation, and the final process of repossession – in itself composed of several phases, including eviction – are in their essence built on several social encounters and social relations at different levels. In some instances, these imply a real physical encounter, while in others they do not. Hence the different people involved (such as valuation agents, real estate agents, mortgage brokers, bank clerks, public notaries, the magistrate's court or court of first instance, as well as housing activists and social movement leaders) have a certain autonomy of manoeuvre in terms of the decision to be adopted in relation to the person(s) they are dealing with. As these encounters are not neutral, it is important to acknowledge that different ideas, ideologies, interpretations, stereotypes and prejudices – racism and classism included – may influence the decision and actions adopted (as Bernat 2014: 51–53 interestingly shows).

A question that remains unanswered is whether structural inequalities and everyday racism is present in the movements themselves, where a great majority of leaders are white middle-class, educated and autochthonous. And whether their focus on specific features of mortgage defaulters – rather than on other traits – as well as the recruitment strategies and commitment requirements they enforce, are actually favouring the participation and interest of all the affected people, as they tend to claim. In fact, it could be the case that a large part of the migrant population, among other particularly vulnerable groups, needs to overcome a considerable number of setbacks in order to be fully admitted as members of the movement.

Therefore, with the aim of being as constructively critical as possible (and despite our profound sympathy for the movement), to what extent are the inequalities between PAH members of different national origins theorised within the movement? And, if such theorisation is not being addressed, could it be the case that certain existing inequalities are in fact being reinforced inadvertently? As our data reveals, although the dominant narrative states that everybody is equal within the assembly, this is not always the case. Social inequalities (historically fraught social relations) are also present in the PAH; they do not simply cease to exist with the stroke of a magic wand. Why is it, then, such a problem to acknowledge that people are different, some poorer and some richer, some with more cultural capital, others with more social capital, but each of them, from their own particular social position, united against a common problem? Why is it so important to overcome or to downplay these divides discursively?

The indistinct focus on 'those affected by mortgages' might equally be ignoring what might be seen as a classist and racist attack from the capitalist banking and financial elites, the brutal dispossession (Harvey 2003) and expropriation (Lapavitsas 2009) of the economic resources that the working classes – migrant workers perhaps being its most vulnerable fraction – had been able to earn. This fact has led to a brutal impoverishment of the weakest party involved in the transaction, which might be interpreted as an actual class struggle, or perhaps rather as the defeat of a subordinate class whose lives – and not only their homes – have been the object of financialisation, indeed have been 'mortgaged' themselves (García-Lamarca and Kaika 2016).

ALL EQUAL AND LIKE A FAMILY? CITIZENISM AND ORGANICISM IN THE PAH'S DISCOURSE AND PRACTICE

There is little doubt that one of the main successes of the PAH is the attainment of a mobilisation which transcends typical divides. The strategy of the movement has led to a visibilisation of the migrant communities as political agents for social change, challenging the hegemonic perception of migrants as passive subjects. That is, they have succeeded in incorporating the migrant subjects as part of the public. They have altered their perception as a burden for the welfare state during the economic crisis, integrating them into a shared narrative of victimisation – due to the social effects of the crisis – enabling a social (virtual) space of commitment and sharing, of communication across the usual divides among workers. Indeed, the PAH might actually be the political actor who has most successfully achieved a certain erosion of the social segregation between autochthonous people and migrants in the Spanish context.

Interestingly, the PAH aims to overcome structural differences by means of educating about and facilitating access to important information on legislation and ways to handle foreclosure threats. Nonetheless, although information – and thus social and cultural capital – is circulated, the actual pre-existing inequalities, as we have showed in the previous section, are not recognised as such. Rather, they are attempted to be overcome mainly through discursive means, if not simply put aside. But ignoring these socio-economic differences might actually end up reinforcing the same racist arguments that they have tried to avoid (remember the quotation where they reject the idea that foreclosures are a 'migrant thing'). It seems as though they believe that, by ignoring socio-cultural stratification, this will lose importance.

The citizenist discourse employed by the PAH is bound with a certain avoidance of existing inequalities and an idealist view of the performative effects of new discourses. So, it seems that, by simply 'forgetting' about historically constructed ethno-racial categories, these seem to fade away. In a similar vein, they seem to downplay the material inequalities between people who have lived in the terrain for more years and people who have just recently arrived. People who had lived in Spain before the boom of the real estate sector have generally been more protected – either because they relied on more consolidated support networks or because they already owned other properties that were also revaluated, thus reinforcing their financial situation. In contrast, people who came later and purchased their properties when prices were at their highest, lacking any social safety net as they got into hardship, have generally been more severely affected.

These are the two phenomena we have intended to investigate in this chapter. The main shortcoming of the anti-foreclosure movement, as far as we see it, is that the already existing inequalities between people, be they migrant or non-migrants, are somehow blurred and ignored, or not given the attention that might be needed, while, when outsiders observe the movement, they are struck by the great presence of migrants in the assemblies (although often not in the leading positions). This is probably due to the devastating social effects of the economic situation on these social sectors, due to their lack of effective social networks or of previous experience in making collective claims.

The fact is though, that, as should be clear from what we have seen until now, the 'crisis' did not have equal effects on 'people'. Hence the prevailing question is how this difference, if recognised, is understood and acted upon. For instance, during its everyday functioning, the movement is often described as a 'family' by its members. One of our informants, Sonia, even made a word game of it: she talked about her 'PAHmilia', expressing that she felt intimately bound together with her fellow members in a family-like manner. Another member, Celia, told us: 'Here is a great family'. But, when talking about the PAH as a 'family', are they not in fact referring to a latent organicist view, according to which everybody is equal in their difference and despite their inequalities?

As a possible interpretation, this blurring of social divides could be understood as a result of the urgency of the repossessions problem, and of its harsh social consequences, due to the fact that housing satisfies a basic need. Given these circumstances, to what extent are we in fact observing a process of incorporation of migrants as full members of society? The question is whether the PAH has succeeded, or will in the future, in recognising the role of migrants in the process of reclaiming rights for all (with or without citizenship, nationality, etc.). That is, does the PAH acknowledge the importance of the total inclusion of migrant subjects in the social body?

We argue that the ideological foundation of the PAH and their actual political mobilisation runs into several shortcomings which mainly have to do with structural factors. As we have shown, one refers to their rather sui generis way of understanding the financial crisis and its roots, and the other to the stratified social consequences of this. Now one might argue that these are part of an overt strategic way of mobilising people around a common identity that would transgress the typical boundaries of class, race, gender and so on in a similar way to nationalism, a strategy which seemingly succeeds.

However, recent literature on the making of the working classes and the poor shows that class, at least in late-modern/liberal/capitalist societies, is intrinsically ordered and socially structured by ethno-cultural and racial factors (Harvey 1996; Anderson 2014; Goldberg 2015; Virdee 2015). As Goldberg states:

> The postracial makes it possible to ignore, avoid, or fail to attend to the spiralling disparities between the deraced privileged and the racially de-faulted disprivileged (in short, the racial default). So the postracial becomes not just the cover-up, the ideological 'racializing' rationalization after the fact. It is the constitutive ordering that enable extension of the disparities from the racial default. Not only do blacks remain poor, the poor are made to be black. As David Starkey remarked, 'Britain's white looters became black'. And for Newt Gingrich, only blacks are the beneficiaries of food stamps. ... The postracial accordingly, embeds an epistemology of deception. Things are not as they appear to be. The nonracial, to which postraciality is conceptually wedded and out of which historically it has grown, is the refusal to acknowledge the structures of race ordering the social. (Goldberg 2015: 92–93)

In fact, it is surprising that, while the great majority of the members of the local PAHs both in Salt (Girona) and l'Hospitalet were actually foreign nationals, who have experienced a distinct discrimination throughout the whole mortgage-borrowing process, the ones in charge were almost always Spanish nationals.

Thus, when examining this literature in the light of our ethnographic case study one might come to the conclusion that the PAH's citizenist discourse and its corresponding 'organicist organisation' are part of the hegemonic belief in the contemporary societies of the Global North, according to which the problem of racism has already been overcome. In fact, it seems that some of the patterns of the political mobilisation of the PAH are quite clear examples of a tendency to consider that social stratifications bound in ethno-cultural and/or racial factors, historic-geographically situated and (re)produced, have lost their significance, or, at least, that their importance is considered less relevant. The question though remains whether this is due to the strategy employed or, as the data of the ethnographic cases seems to point out, whether it might have more to do with the original inspiration of the movement. Be that as it may, our main contention is not that the movement should abandon the struggle for an all-encompassing identity, but rather that this should not prevail over others. The economic crisis has been racial (in its broad sense) and gendered from the start exactly because that is how Spanish society has been forged historically and geographically. A strong unifying identity might be able to mobilise a major portion of the affected working-class populations in Spain, but, as long as most of these populations still experience numerous other interpellations and discriminations, which will not simply vanish due to discursive and performative actions, there is an urgent need to tackle these, both within social movements and in society at large.

NOTES

1. This can be translated as 'Coalition of People Affected by Mortgages'.

2. Between 2007 and the third trimester of 2015, 656,839 repossession processes were initiated in Spain, according to the General Council of the Judiciary (*Datos sobre el efecto de la crisis en los drganos judiciales. Datos desde 2007 hasta tercer trimestre de 2015*, http://www.poderjudicial.es/cgpj/es/Temas/Estadistica-Judicial/Informes-estadisticos-periodicos/Datos-sobre-el-efecto-de-la-crisis-en-los-organos-judiciales---Datos-desde-2007-hasta-tercer-trimestre-de-2015).

3. In 2009, the first PAH assembly was created in Barcelona.

4. For example, in 2012–2013 the PAH and other activist organisations collected 1,402,854 signatures to support a modification of mortgage law in the Spanish Parliament. However, the opposition of the main political parties could not be overcome.

5. Nelson now suspects that these people were paid a certain amount in exchange for their service.

6. This turning of *proletarios* (proletarians) into *propietarios* (owners), as a minister put it – that is, the political de-mobilisation of a formerly subversive working class – was a central aspiration of Franco's regime.

7. This was a widespread belief among our informants, even if, in fact, official regulations did not include the obligation to be homeowners, but to prove the ability to house family members under one's roof, even if this was done in a rented flat.

8. A name which ironically refers to the work that banks, and especially savings banks, have traditionally presented as the social, philanthropic aspect of their activities.

9. To our knowledge, there are several publications on this issue about to appear in the coming months, including some Masters and PhD dissertations, as well as a journal special issue including the contributions of scholars that took part in the panel 'The Spanish mortgage crisis: social impacts and reactions', AIBR Conference, Madrid, July 2015.

10. http://www.feminicidio.net/articulo/ada-colau-%E2%80%9C-la-pah-hay-claro-protagonismo-las-mujeres%E2%80%9D (accessed 1 September 2016).

11. A seeming exception to this can be found in Madrid. There, the PAH sued the *Central Hipotecaria del Inmigrante* (CHI), a mortgage broking firm disguised as an NGO, that operated specifically with Equatorian borrowers, for predatory lending practices. Their victims participate in a specific assembly within the PAH where this criminal process is dealt with. Still, despite the blatant targeting of victims with a migrant background, taking advantage of their vulnerability, CHI is only being prosecuted for economic fraud, and not for racial discrimination.

12. The *Observatori dels Drets Econòmics, Socials i Culturals* (Observatory for Economic, Social and Cultural Rights) is an organisation based in Barcelona whose

research and reports have contributed to inspire social movements working in several fields, the PAH in the housing arena among them, from a human rights viewpoint. It has also been key to the rise of the popular movement that has been governing the city since May 2015, called Barcelona En Comúo (Barcelona In Common), with Ada Colau, former PAH spokesperson, as mayor.

13. This quote and the following: our translation.

14. AVANCE: Nuevo informe con datos sobre ejecuciones hipotecarias, desahucios y derecho a la vivienda con datos inéditos de la Plataforma de Afectados por la Hipoteca, 08/07/2013 (http://afectadosporlahipoteca.com/2014/12/23/avance-del-informe-emergencia-habitacional-e-impacto-en-el-derecho-a-la-salud-e-infancia-en-la-crisis-hipotecaria/).

15. The assignment in payment, in Spanish *dacióaciish ni*, entails the cancellation of the debt after handing back to the bank the keys of the property. Unlike other legislations, the Spanish mortgage law does not include this possibility: debtors are responsible for the remaining debt after the property's auction. Therefore, only some debtors are accorded the assignment in payment after putting much pressure on the bank. The acquiescence of the credit institution on a case-to-case basis is a necessary condition.

REFERENCES

Allen, J., J. Barlow, J. Leal, T. Maloutas and L. Padovani. 2004. *Housing and Welfare in Southern Europe*. Oxford: Blackwell.

Anderson, B. 2014. *Us & Them? The Dangerous Politics of Immigration Control*. Oxford: Oxford University Press.

Azis, G. 2016. 'Rising up against the subordination of life in Barcelonès: an ethnography of the struggle of the "afectadas" for a future without debt chains'. MA diss. Uppsala Universitet, Institutionen För Kulturantropologi Och Etnologi (http://www.diva-portal.org/smash/get/diva2:903456/FULLTEXT01.pdf).

Bernat, I. 2014. 'Eviction and immigrants: Ethnography in a damaged community'. *Revista Crítica Penal y Poder* 7: 35–63.

Colectivo IOÉ. 2005. 'Inmigración y vivienda en España'. Documentos del Observatorio Permanente de la Inmigración, Ministerio de Trabajo y Asuntos Sociales (http://www.colectivoioe.org/uploads/0eaefc67da03a40d6be2755eecf2e5b3c284198b.pdf).

Doñate, M. 2013. 'El movimiento 15-M en un pueblo del maresme: la asamblea oberta de Cambrils'. In *Economías cotidianas, economías sociales, economías sostenibles*, edited by S. Narotzky. Barcelona: Icaria.

Dymski, G. 2009. 'Racial exlusion and the political economy of the subprime crisis'. *Historical Materialism* 17: 149–179.

García-Lamarca, M. and M. Kaika. 2016. '"Mortgaged lives": The Biopolitics of Bebt and Homeownership in Spain'. *Transactions of the Insitute of British Geographers* 41 (3): 313–327.

García Montalvo, J. 2008. *De la quimera inmobiliaria al colapso financiero*. Barcelona: Bosch.

Goldberg, D. T. 2015. *Are We All Postracial Yet?* Cambridge & Malden, MA: Polity Press.

Harvey, D. 1996. *Justice, Nature and the Geography of Difference.* Cambridge (Mss): Blackwell.

Harvey, D. 2003. 'Chapter 4: Accumulation by dispossession'. In *The New Imperialism.* Oxford: Oxford University Press.

Lapavitsas, C. 2009. 'Financialised capitalism: Crisis and financial expropriation'. *Historical Materialism* 17: 114–148.

Leralta, O. 2005. 'Ser inmigrante: Factor de riesgo en el acceso a la vivienda'. *Documentación Social* 138: 157–171.

Lijarcio, A. 2012. 'La Plataforma de Afectados por la Hipoteca de Lleida atiende 50 casos en cuatro meses'. La Vanguardia 28 March 2012. Available at: http://www.lavanguardia.com (accessed 16 February 2016).

López, I. and E. Rodríguez. 2010. *Fin de ciclo. Financiarización, territorio y sociedad de propietarios en la onda larga del capitalismo hispano (1959–2010).* Madrid: Traficantes de sueños.

Lundsteen, M. 2015. *Conflicts and Convivencia: An Ethnography of the Social Effects of 'The Crisis' in a Small Catalan Town.* PhD Thesis in Anthropology, Departament d'Antropologia Social, Universitat de Barcelona, Spain.

Mangot, L. 2013. 'La Plataforma de Afectados por la Hipoteca. De la Crisis a la Estafa. Del Prozac al Empoderamiento'. *Clivatge* 2: 56–88.

Martínez Veiga, U. 1999. *Pobreza, segregación y exclusión social. La vivienda de los inmigrantes extranjeros en España.* Barcelona: Icaria.

Mir, J., J. França, C. Macías and P. Veciana. 2013. 'Fundamentos de la Plataforma de Afectados por la Hipoteca: activismo, asesoramiento colectivo y desobediencia civil no violenta'. *Educación Social* 55: 52–61.

Naredo, J. M. 2009. 'La cara oculta de la crisis. El fin del boom inmobiliario y sus consecuencias'. *Revista de Economía Crítica* 7: 313–340.

Nasarre, S. 2011. 'Malas prácticas bancarias en la actividad hipotecaria'. *Revista Crítica de Derecho Inmobiliario* 727: 2665–2737.

Observatori DESC & Plataforma de Afectados por la Hipoteca. 2013. 'Emergencia habitacional en el Estado español: la crisis de las ejecuciones hipotecarias y los desalojos desde una perspectiva de derechos humanos' (http://afectadosporlahipoteca.com/wp-content/uploads/2013/12/2013-Informe_habtitatge-17Dic.pdf).

Onrubia, J. 2010. 'Vivienda e inmigración en España: situación y políticas públicas'. *Presupuesto y Gasto Público* 61: 273–310.

Palomera, J. 2013. 'How did finance capital infiltrate the world of the urban poor? Homeownership and social fragmentation in a Spanish neighborhood'. *International Journal of Urban and Regional Research* 38 (1): 218–235.

Palomera, J. 2014. 'Reciprocity, commodification and poverty in the era of financialization'. *Current Anthropology* 55 (9): 105–115.

Romero, P. 2013. 'Autonomía política y el 15-M: una reflexión sobre el movimiento desde Barcelona'. In *Economías cotidianas, economías sociales, economías sostenibles*, edited by S. Narotzky. Barcelona: Icaria.

Sabaté, I. 2014. 'Del país de los propietarios al país de los sobre-endeudados. Reciprocidad, solidaridad y proyectos de transformación sistémica en tiempos de crisis'. *Ars & Humanitas* 8 (1): 167–187.

Sabaté, I. 2016a. 'The Spanish mortgage crisis and the re-emergence of moral economies in uncertain times'. *History & Anthropology* 27 (1): 107–120.

Sabaté, I. 2016b. 'Mortgage indebtedness and home repossessions as symptoms of the financialisation of housing provisioning in Spain'. *Critique of Anthropology* 36 (2): 197–211.

Suárez, M. 2014. 'Movimientos sociales y buen vivir: Ecuatorianos en la lucha por la vivienda en la plataforma de afectados por la hipoteca (PAH)'. *Revista de Antropología Experimental* 14 (6): 71–89.

Terrones, A. 2013. 'Segregation, housing market segmentation and the origin of over-indebtedness. The access to homeownership by foreign migrants based on over-indebtedness'. Paper presented at the 25th European Network for Housing Research Conference, Tarragona, Spain.

Virdee, S. 2015. *Racism, Class and the Racialized Outsider*. Houndmills, Basingstoke & New York: Palgrave Macmillan.

Zunzunegui, F. 2013. 'Over-indebtedness and mortgage lending'. *Revista de Derecho Bancario y Bursátil* 129: 35–76.

Chapter III.3

Obstacles Before Struggles

Freedom of Movement and the Conditioning of Collective Response

Raia Apostolova

The most glaring image of captivity in liberal thought, from the early nineteenth century onwards, is the one that depicts the chained, immobilized body of a slave (see Figure III.3.1). The image positions the 'free' subject as a moving, mobile subject. Liberal thought makes physical movement imperative for freedom. This has greatly informed our contemporary political context and, in a similar manner, one of the main principles behind the implementation of the 'European project' contains the notion of freedom, on the one hand, and movement as a constitutive element, on the other.[1]

What does it mean to have the right to free movement? What is the relation between collective struggles and freedom of movement? Is it one of secured liberation or of unexpected limitation? This chapter engages with some of the contradictions in the notion of freedom of movement and the emerging hurdles that confront anti-capitalist movements. I invite the reader to think of freedom of movement not as the antithesis to unfreedom of movement. I break out of such binary definitions. Instead, I look at freedom of movement's implications for labour subjectivities and its productive power under capitalism. Political groups that are organized around issues of asylum and anti-racism denounce the border violence imposed on refugees, often invoking the construct of freedom of movement as their main political and ethical claim. I attempt to enter into a dialogue with refugee movements as well as with EU (migrant) labour movements. In this last analytical thread, I reject the emancipatory potential of the notion and convey that freedom of movement is a liberal notion bringing liberal freedoms which in turn work within and with the logic of capitalism and not against it. This chapter exemplifies one possible response to the processes of labour flexibilisation, exclusion and inclusion as identified in the previous chapters. I seek to portray how

Figure III.3.1 Picture: 'Am I Not a Man and a Brother?' Year: 1835. *Source*: Picture History.

the contemporary expression of flexible, mobile, deskilled labour strives to identify its opposing forces.

Freedom of movement is not external to the workings of capital but rather represents its very fluctuation. So-called migrants' struggles are not necessarily or only struggles against immobility but also against accelerated mobility. Such accelerated mobility shelters in the space created by the increased movement of capital and the continuous need to shorten the temporal gap between the potential to gain and the reality of employing labour power; the transformation of labour power into value. Freedom of movement allows for such a shortening. In our current historical moment, where we can witness the continuous remaking of the EU, we can see that the struggle for movement is also a struggle against movement. This, we could say, is also the case with asylum seekers' struggles against the infamous Dublin Regulation.[2] The moment their arrival in the desired destination becomes a reality, their struggle turns into a struggle against deportation, that is, against a return movement. In contrast to asylum seekers, the movement of the EU migrants is framed as 'voluntary'. However, the EU migrant is, in actuality, mobilized by capital through mediators in supply chains and in this sense her flight from place to place is not necessarily voluntary, that is – of her own will. Its involuntariness is disguised by the liberal notions of freedom and equality, yet it is travel stirred by the possibility of exchanging the only commodity she has – her capacity to work. At the same time, however, what these travelling labourers dream of is to remain home with families and friends. Their struggle is against their accelerated mobility as a labour power constantly on the move. My analysis is organized around the relation between capital and labour and the state, and the radical limitations to the collective response of migrants when they encounter the simultaneous workings of free movement, the demand for their potential as captured in their labour power and the valuation process.

Freedom of movement is a demand that has been granted to Eastern European workers in the post-socialist context and it is central to the current transformations in Europe's division of labour. I demonstrate how it slows down and often obscures emerging struggles. This chapter emerges from encounters with EU migrants' struggles during fieldwork in Germany between October 2013 and March 2014, and in November and December 2014. The overall stability of the German labour market produces a space where the dialectic between freedom of movement and securitization of movement – so prominent in Europe – is nicely captured. This dialectic has a tremendous impact on the way (social) movements are organized as well. The conclusions drawn here are based on close examination of numerous other forms of resistance against overexploitation. However, the central argument is informed primarily through two concrete instances of migrants' struggles. Here, Balibar's (2013) insight that overexploitation represents the normalization of capitalism and that the consequent class struggles over the (re)establishment of exploitation, over the 'fair' contract, is of particular importance as it shows precisely the limitations to the collective response and the necessity to organize in respect to a long-term vision.

To demonstrate, I engage with two instances of (attempted) political organization on the part of migrant labourers in Munich and Berlin. The first one describes a violent imposition of fear among Bulgarian labourers. Police checks at Munich's day-labour market, a radius of a couple of blocks close to the central train station, became a daily occurrence between October 2013 and January 2014, scaring both employees and potential employers in the process. I point out the ways in which the organizational attempts of both supporters and labourers failed to bring about a full-fledged campaign against such violence. The analysis of the second case is situational and it concerns Romanian labourers who worked at the Mall of Berlin's construction site. Their struggle, which started in October 2014 and continues to this day, was organized around the issue of unpaid wages. Unlike the Munich struggle, the Romanian one won the public's sympathy and brought about a strong political formation. As Bulgarian and Romanian workers are EU citizens, their stay in Germany is legal and hence they are not necessarily subject to deportation. Their ability to remain in Germany does not undergo the same pattern of state strategies for illegalization as is the case with asylum seekers and third-country nationals. It is important to keep this in mind when we think of their response to state and capital violence. Both (attempted) mobilizations took place within a similar policy context (i.e. the legal status of the actors and being subject to the same border and labour regulations in the framework of the EU). Both ended in a territorial dispersal of the main protagonists. The composition of the labour force involved in these struggles is similar, as they were both built by men from different age groups. All of them came from either Bulgaria or Romania, where the so-called structural adjustment programmes following the 1990 changes ended in the capitulation of public sectors and the creation of 'unproductive labour'.

I separate the chapter in three major sections. The first addresses the structural importance of freedom of movement in the current reorganization of labour markets at the EU level. The second section speaks to the difficulties connected to political organization and critiques the attempts to portray the right to move in its emancipatory capacity. The final section looks at the challenges facing the collective resistance of these labourers and raises questions about the possible strategic points where we could organize a stronger and unified response.

DIAGNOSING FREEDOM OF MOVEMENT

In 2013, for the first time in several years, the notion of freedom of movement – one of the main pillars behind project Europe – was under serious threat, posed by major political figures such as David Cameron (UK), Angela Merkel (Germany) and, implicitly, by representatives of the European Commission itself. The threat transpired because of the impending opening up of all EU labour markets to Bulgarian and Romanian workers scheduled to take place in January 2014. During the international conference held by the Confederation of German Trade Unions (abbreviated DGB in German) in April 2014, Annelie Buntenbach, a member of the executive board of the union, insisted that freedom of movement had to stop serving the needs of markets and start serving the needs of people. 'Equal pay for everyone in Europe', demanded Buntenbach. The name of the conference, 'Free movement for workers in Europe – the fair way', holds two presuppositions: that free movement is an unresolved political demand within European space, and that, if fair, it will contribute to the well-being of workers.

Human immobilization has informed much of the scholarly work in relation to regimes of deportability (De Genova 2002), 'gradation' of statuses (Goldring, Berinstein and Bernard 2009), its role in constituting new ways of 'being political' (Isin 2002), enactment of citizenship by non-citizens (Andrijasevic and Anderson 2009), production of 'first- and second-class citizens' (Nyers 2010), and indeed its role in sustaining binaries such as legal/illegal migrants (Squire 2010). I would like to shift the attention placed on migrants' struggles as always expressing and being oriented towards citizenship and immobilization, however. The AoM approach, which shifts the often taken-for-granted power of regulation to the excess of this regulation and the ways this excess in fact shapes institutional practices (inter alia, Papadopoulos, Stephenson and Tsianos 2008; Mezzadra 2010; Mezzadra and Neilson 2013), inhabits a similar contradiction. Some of the accounts of AoM (inter alia, Papadopoulos and Tsianos 2013; Casas-Cortes, Cobarrubias and Pickles 2015), however, tend to engage solely with (attempted) immobilization as a terrain of struggle. The latter approaches within the AoM stem from the way the subject of research is chosen – namely, the one who is a subject of border controls; the non-citizen, the non-European, and so on. Such an approach risks turning the immobilized subject into an outsider or as someone surplus to struggles within and against capital. I believe having a critique of freedom of movement can help us go beyond this. I argue that by analysing the break, the void that exists between the presence and the absence of (the right to) movement, we can push forward a radical discussion on political potentialities within this framework. In the void between the presence and the absence of movement is where we can find the space to connect the struggles against capital.

Kotef (2015) attaches a foundational significance to the notion of freedom of movement in liberal thought. She demonstrates that the liberal terrain is configured by bodies, whose liberty, and hence free movement, must be protected by all means possible (i.e. citizens and property owners), and by the other racialized, classed, foreignised bodies, whose motion is perceived as a security problem. The egalitarianisation of liberal societies prohibited the differentiation in governance of different categorical identities (e.g. blacks, women), however, and instead focused on patterns of mobility in order to punish these identities. Movement 'mediates freedom and violence to the degree that in some contexts they can barely be distinguished' (139). It is not solely the absence or the imposed restriction on movement that could be thought concurrently to lead to violence; it is also the movement itself, as practised by inclusion in liberal democracies which goes hand in hand with violence.

In 1951 the right to move freely within European space was conceptualised as being based on the expanding production in the coal and steel industries that led to a demand for skilled workers. As European market integration deepened, the demand for free labour increased. The 1951 Paris Treaty provided for the right of skilled labourers to be employed in the steel and coal industries of the member states. It prohibits any discrimination in wage and working conditions as based on the distinction between national and migrant workers (article 69, paragraph 4). Furthermore, the Treaty called on member states to ensure that 'social security arrangements do not inhibit labour mobility'. As De Genova and Peutz (2010: 58) point out, 'the unbounded mobility of capital … demands [the] parallel freedom of movement of labouring humanity'. The signing of the Schengen agreement in 1985, which began the dismantling of internal borders within Europe, heralded this notion as a constitutive part of what is now known as the EU. The Union was organized around an articulation of an internal and common market, where the freedoms to move (of goods, services, capital and people) formed a seemingly harmonious entity.[3] Behind such an appearance we can recognize the work of deeply antagonistic relations, where (the battle over) freedom of movement plays a major role.

The transition from state socialism to liberal democracy in Bulgaria and Romania, which commenced officially in 1990, was based on an overall political consensus that the future must be oriented towards a Euro-Atlantic partnership. Economic and political reforms followed the so-called shock therapy.[4] For Bulgarian labour, European integration was an inseparable part of the transition, where freedom of movement was a prioritized political demand. Such demands stemmed from the very material reality of thousands affected by previously unseen rates of unemployment and sweeping social insecurity. By achieving the right to travel freely, the Bulgarian and Romanian integration into Europe, and arguably East European integration in general, encountered a contradiction. Free movement both threatens and protects (potential) labourers. It protects them because it provides them with the right to escape the social situation in Bulgaria and Romania and is subsequently a channel for reproduction. It threatens them because it creates the conditions for an extensive and intensive overexploitation.[5] And here, with this contradiction, I bring the discussion forward.

In regards to movement, European integration for Bulgarians and Romanians involved a few stages. After the immediate fall of the Berlin wall, travelling from Romania and Bulgaria was very similar to what asylum seekers now experience at the borders of Europe: risky and fractured into numerous possibilities of being caught. Moreover, such travelling was often quite creative and worthy of the entrepreneurial spirit we breathe under neoliberalism. Ivan, for example, one of the most persistent young men in the mobilization in Munich, remembers that he flirted with the idea of working for the cleaning company responsible for the Bulgarian-Serbian border in the mid-1990s.

Eventually, this idea materialized, and one night he crossed the border dressed as a cleaning mate on the back of the trash truck, 'showing them [the Bulgarian authorities] the finger' (interview November 2013). Conversely, this type of 'illegal' crossing into European countries resulted in a settled migration precisely because of the risk one was undertaking when engaged in criminalized travelling.[6] The situation eased after a while, however. The decision for the two countries' accession into the EU was taken in 1999 and ratified in 2000, which gave their citizens the right to travel to the EU without a visa for a period of ninety days, with the exception of labour- and study-related visits. Access to social security was part of these restrictions. Certainly, as borders are always penetrable (Papadopoulos et al. 2008), thousands found their way into the EU for labour purposes.

The year 2007 brought about a peculiar situation for Bulgarians and Romanians. On the one hand, it simplified travelling, as visas were no longer a requirement, but, on the other, it did not bring about the final stage of European integration. According to EU law, there is a seven-year-long gratis period for established member states until they are obliged to fully open their labour markets to new members. What that meant for Bulgarian and Romanian citizens who worked in Germany is that, despite their status as EU citizens, they still had to apply for a work permit in order to be regularly employed. Alternatively, they could acquire a self-employed status or work irregularly. Such a situation can be described as one of putting regular labour on hold, where irregularity and self-employment became the main aspects of what De Genova (2005: 234) describes as 'an active process of inclusion through illegalization'. Such processes, in the case of labourers in Germany, involved a falling-off of the regular status as many workers could become 'false self-employed' overnight. Yet they are still actively involved in the accumulation of capital.

Furthermore, employers and municipalities actively promote irregularity. The falling-off of the self-employed status – which prior to January 2014 meant losing the right to employment and hence fit the framework of irregular labour – often happens because of the immense bureaucracy involved in keeping it, which is often complicated by workers' lack of German language skills and lack of awareness of their rights. Where the promotion of irregularity on the part of employers is explained by the general desire to save taxes, the municipal role is linked to the growing impossibility of meeting the increased need for space in homeless shelters and other social costs. Additionally, municipalities felt increased pressure from the Federal authorities to deal with migrants coming from the two Eastern European countries.[7]

The EU's freedom of movement is premised on a normative division between the 'inside' and the 'outside'. It fragments the subjects enabled by it. As Aradau, Huysmans and Squire (2010) show, some EU citizens are rendered more deserving based on their economic activeness and low potentiality of becoming a burden on the welfare state. The authors define freedom of movement as a regime that '[governs] cross-border movement in the EU, which operates at the interstices between individual citizenship rights that facilitate movement and security and welfare policies that restrict these rights'. Yet, such analysis does not take into account the productive part of freedom of movement which makes a specific type of labourer: a labourer, we might say, who traverses Europe at a gallop in order to find the next subcontracted job. As Samaddar points out (2014), 'transit labour occupie[s] a crucial place in capitalist production'. There is nothing novel behind such a statement; in our contemporary political conjuncture, however, the speed with which such transit labour travels has vastly accelerated. The movement of this labour force is eased by the notion of freedom of movement in a way that does not necessarily guarantee the 'regular' status of its subjects.[8] In fact, EU labour has been immensely fragmented as expressed in differentiated discursive statuses. These statuses are not necessarily a part of a legislative framework. Their existence may be only discursive; yet they do bear material consequences for the people who are racialized by them. In the post-2008 constellation and a year after Bulgaria and Romania's accession into the EU, we witnessed a proliferation of migratory categories: 'poverty migrant', 'fake self-employed', 'social benefit tourist', 'beggar Mafioso', and so on. Such racialization, produced on both municipal and state levels, leads to differential inclusion in the labour market and legitimizes practices of (over)exploitation.

FREEDOM OF MOVEMENT: IN THE CRIB OF OVEREXPLOITATION AND EXODUS

A year before the opening up of EU labour markets to Bulgarians and Romanians, a fully fledged campaign took place against them on a European scale during which freedom of movement was redefined discursively by political figures. From being considered a right to strive for and one of the main strongholds against nationalism, it came to be associated with its potentiality to enable abuse of nation states' social security systems.[9] Although the campaign was directed towards the new discursive category of the 'benefit tourist', day labourers and the self-employed in Germany also became objects of state repression.

Munich saw unprecedented police raids on the so-called day-labour market, where migrants gather and wait to be offered employment. Such employment opportunities vary greatly but for the most part migrants are employed in the construction and cleaning sectors, where subcontracting has become a must and low wages normalized. Between October and December 2013, daily police checks took place, usually early in the morning, scaring away both employers and labourers. Nikola, a Bulgarian in his late sixties who worked for a lead factory between 1974 and 1987, but could not get a pension because of the 1997 reforms, was one of those frequently checked[10]:

> It was humiliating. I am an old man. [The police] looked into my pockets. [They] strip us naked sometimes even on the street, before the eyes of all. If they want to strip me naked, they should do it in the police department. This is what I call shame.

One of the most vivid examples of a police check took place on 21 October at about 8 o'clock in the morning, when thirty Bulgarian day labourers were pushed into a backyard near the central train station by twenty police officers. The workers had to sign documents that they could not understand and the officers intimidated them through spreading false information that they would be charged €1,000 if they were caught working.

Yet the most atrocious police tactic came just before the release of the labourers, when they were made to wear neon green bracelets, effectively becoming branded labourers. Over the next couple of days, one could see marked Bulgarians wandering around the neighbourhood. 'Humiliation', 'fear', 'anger', 'frustration' were just some of the words used by them to describe this act of branding. According to a press release issued by the police department, the neon bracelets served to indicate the people who were already checked so that no double checks would occur. The labourers, however, feared that the bracelets contained electronic chips that would track their physical movement; despite this, they did not want to remove them. The city used other tactics as well. Blacklisting addresses to prevent further registration of Bulgarians in Munich, intimidating German citizens who helped with address registration and having special memos on 'how to behave with Bulgarian and Romanian citizens' spread through social services offices were just some of the daily reality for day labourers and citizens and personnel employed by the city.[11]

This was not the last raid. Such practices became commonplace in the months before January 2014. People often found themselves in situations where they were not paid for their labour, placed in prison because of unpaid public transportation fees, and unlikely to find shelter because of below 0°c admission policies.[12] 'Many left. They took the buses', Radoy told me. Radoy is a single man in his forties who came to Munich in the early 2000s and who managed to get a working permit. Radoy told me this as we were walking down the street in search of people to join the upcoming meeting, where a protest was to be decided. Despite numerous efforts by 'Civil Courage', a local group which provides legal and political support, and some of the labourers to organize around the issue of police raids, a visible struggle against them never took place. Fear and the possibility of escape are among the reasons behind the inability to establish a response to the actions of the city. As Mladen, a young man in his mid-twenties who came to Munich three months prior to the beginning of the police raids and who was a regular at the day-labour market, told me: 'I am going to Frankfurt now. It is obviously written on my forehead that I am a Bulgarian and Munich cannot offer anything anymore for me. I will go to find job elsewhere, but I cannot stand the humiliation here'. The right to move freely spreads labour territorially and tames political organization.

The normative status of freedom of movement prohibits its suspension by nation states.[13] Yet, repression often avoids the normative to touch its object in seemingly indirect ways. The city had to somehow suspend the legal right to freedom of movement by secondary measures, that is, to prevent further movement, on the one hand, and make the city unattractive by using repressive measures that effected labourers' social and physical security, on the other. One has the choice, however, to escape such repression by exercising her right to move freely, to escape. And many did. We see that escape has become inseparable from freedom of movement. This continuous escaping reproduces a certain type of labour. One that is constantly on the go, escaping. Freedom of movement oscillates between possibilities of escape and opportunities for exploiters.

This notion has enabled a spatio-temporal dimension of travelling labour power, where it has become increasingly easy (and necessary) to leave one site for another. In this conjuncture, it compresses time and space as the discharge of (cheap) labour power from one site leads to a fast gain of labour at another site. Europe has become a miniature space for travelling labourers. The visa requirement, or the border check, the insecurity of travelling and the dependence on a smuggler are not there to slow such travelling. In my frequent travelling by bus to different European cities, I encounter precisely such labourers. They traverse the European space depending on where subcontractors call them to be. Two labourers I met in November at Frankfurt's international bus station hectically drew a picture of their travelling during the past months – from construction sites in Spain to agricultural fields in the Czech Republic and Italy to fields in England. They never stayed in one place for more than three months. Often such 'calls to job' end in disappointment, as promises are broken and men and women are forced to leave. Some go to the next European country and to the next subcontracted job. Others go back to their home countries to wait for yet another call so they can stay awhile with their families. And yet, when a job does indeed exist, this does not necessarily mean one will make a living out of it.

Wages are rarely being paid anymore. Such is the story of the labourers who came to be known as the Mall of Shame workers. These are Romanians who worked on the construction site of the Mall of Berlin in August 2014. This infamous mall was built in the fast-developing quarter around Leipziger Platz, an area which increasingly resembles Times Square in New York City. The multi-block-long massive edifice cost approximately one billion euros, making it the most expensive extravagance in mall construction. The story of the Romanian workers is almost identical to the tens of other stories I have heard elsewhere in Germany and on my bus travels. A friend of a friend contacted one of the eleven men and offered them a job. That friend also had a friend who was looking for more labourers, possibly from Bulgaria and Romania, as they faced no travel restrictions. The deal was a contract, good payment and €150 rent for accommodation in a shared flat. Arriving in Berlin, it turns out that there was no contract, the payment was €5 per hour as compared to the lawful €10.25, and the apartment was a phantom. The Romanian workers found themselves frequently sleeping rough on the streets. In the next three months, they would often experience what they described as humiliating behaviour from the subcontractors: ranging from changing promised pay to unrealized accommodation opportunities, to eventually no payment of wages at all. The workers changed one subcontractor due to unpaid wages and ended up in the same situation with the second. As it turns out, 'hundreds of Romanians left the [construction] site without being paid just before we came'.[14] Not knowing that wages are not being paid is perhaps explained by the fact that all eleven had come to work in Germany for the first time. Unpaid wages have become the norm. Despite the many assurances uttered by their Bulgarian and Turkish colleagues that '[they] will not resist for more than a month', the Romanians decided to stage a protest.

On 2 October 2014, fifteen Romanian workers unfolded a banner in front of the office of one of the subcontractors. The banner read, 'Metatec Fundus GmbH, slavery is protected by law in Germany'. Thirty-three people were willing to protest if their wages were not paid. The number of people willing to participate in a collective action scared the subcontractors, and every two or three days a portion of the wages was in fact being paid back – €200 one day and €300 the next. Yet, the amount paid was not even close to what was owed. 'Soon' was what the Romanians heard each day. Within four days workers started going back to Romania. The pressure between the workers and the subcontractors intensified as the latter stopped paying even the small portions of wages. The labourers decided to strengthen the scale of the protest and gathered in front of the main entrance of the mall, where hundreds of thousands pass by on a daily basis. In a few days, a fellow worker put the protestors in touch with the FAU – the Free Workers' Union, an anarcho-syndicalist union.

The union supported the protest by finding night shelter when possible, applying for demonstration permits, and strategy building. My conversations with the Mall of Shame workers, as well as with members of the FAU, led me to the conclusion that one of the hardest limitations such struggles are faced with is building the possibility for continuation. The participants have to manage differences in political contexts. It is important to understand that FAU members work primarily within the Berlin context, where political life blooms. Yet, at this stage of building the collective struggle, at its very beginning, it seems that finding the means to sustain and reproduce the very physicality of the body in order to continue the struggle – to find shelter, to find food, to find medical supplies if needed – is a major preoccupation, which often makes strategic and political conversations secondary. The culmination of the protest came on 6 December 2014, when, with the support and networking capability of the FAU, around 400 people joined a three-hour demonstration. Despite the large turnout and the media and public pressure exercised in favour of the Romanian labourers, most of them went back to Romania; only two were still there at the beginning of 2015.[15]

The concept of freedom of movement needs to be looked at both in its temporal and spatial dimensions. Evoking the image of a 'decompression chamber', Mezzadra and Neilson (2013:149) point to the link between the administrative detention of third-country national border crossers and the labour market and describe a temporal vacuum in which delays and deceleration stratify the movement of these subjects into national labour markets. Here, we have a taming of the labour movement. Yet, where the European right to move freely is concerned, we have the opposite process. A process, which resembles CERN's speed accelerators and which guarantees the expediting and dispatching of a constant and timely supply of labour power.[16]

Reducing restrictions on movement allows EU nationals to follow capital wherever it goes. There is a sharp contrast in the ways in which labour and capital are organized based on their free movement in a post-Fordist context (see Moody 1997). Where capital tends to consolidate in transnational companies, in the process concentrating power, the movement of labour often leads to dispersal and to the impossibility of organizing politically as expressed both in the decreased presence of unions and in the freedom to escape. These, in conjunction with the demising welfare state, have direct consequences on the reproduction of a travelling labour power and the political struggles of EU migrants. As Mezzadra and Neilson (2013: 95) show, analysing the possibilities of translation between struggles and subjects can only happen by addressing 'the complex ways [in which the heterogeneity of global space] crisscrosses the production and reproduction of labour power'.

Above I addressed some of the productive spatial and temporal aspects of freedom of movement that speak to such re/productions.

To move rapidly and widely is one of the intrinsic characteristics of EU labour.[17] The principle of freedom of movement, in conjuncture with flexibilization of labour and strong reliance on subcontractors as the primary recruiting force, has brought about a continuously migrating workforce. These workers are often brought directly to work locations, in bulk. They rarely have direct contact with the primary employer and their struggles, as their hiring, are, seemingly, with the mediators in the labour-capital relation. Of course, as is the case with the workers in Munich, the labour market still relies on recruitment that is individualistic in its nature. This type of workforce does not have the job security as offered by employers in settled jobs, for example, incentives aimed at preserving, training, conserving or bettering the workforce.[18] On the contrary, the fragmentation of the labour market by numerous subcontractors needs an easily disposable labour force and movement which is neither hesitant nor slowed by barriers to leaving or arriving. Usually, such workers do not get attached to the workplace and they go through cycles of de- and re-skilling since hopping from town to town, country to country, and sector to sector requires speedy adaptation. The type of worker that is being created is not one that identifies with a workplace or a skill but with the ability to move.

FREEDOM OF MOVEMENT: TO ESCAPE A HABIT

Having a job does not necessarily mean settlement. The struggles from above are confronted by a double-bind logic. On the one hand, they are at the forefront of capitalism, 'the legitimate sets of commercial and productive relations', and, on the other, at the backend of capitalism, 'the shadowy markets, unpaid work of all sorts, and irregular recruitment and hiring practices' (Rajaram 2015: 68). If the decision to leave a place for another is itself a social movement (Mezzadra 2004; Papadopolous et al. 2008), then freedom of movement has the potential to multiply these social movements and to radicalize them. This, however, is only a present possibility insofar as it overcomes its embeddedness in the making of capitalism and turns its power precisely against such makings. This is hidden in its spatio-temporal character, which enables the rapid and widespread physical movement of people who are subjects of the double bind of accumulation by dispossession and accumulation by exploitation (see Harvey 2005; Mezzadra and Neilson 2013: 232–242). Political organizing needs to take place along the crisscrossing points of this labour. As we learn from Bologna (1972: 8), at the turn of the twentieth century the labour movement in the US was well equipped to face the challenge of the 'mobile proletariat'. The IWW, in particular, organized the latter by means of placing agitators who '[swim] within the stream of proletarian struggles, move from one end to the other' (ibid.). We also have to realize that what we have here are mobility-based struggles.

In the struggles described above, a dimension comes forward that is not celebratory; there is nothing heroic about it. It is the failure to struggle further, to continue. Continuity has been interpreted as the umbilical cord between immediate demands and general ends (Panzieri 1958, 2014) and as such affirming it is an immediate task.[19] The interruptions from above largely take place as labourers lack activist networks, but often, even if such networks exist, they can rarely ensure shelter, food supplies, new jobs or the reproduction of labour power. People move on to the next opportunity in order to meet such basic needs. One of the spatial dimensions of the EU workers struggling in both Berlin and Munich is that they take place literally blocks away from the proliferating refugee movements in and beyond these two cities. I have heard of short-lived instances where participants of these differentiated struggles have crossed paths; however, to my knowledge, there has not been a persistent organizational endeavour to combine efforts. And even when and where such efforts took place, they failed. In fact, according to many of my interlocutors, the possibility of such efforts would be too tedious, or impossible to achieve as the rights held by EU migrants are too great compared to those of the third-country national.[20] Deportability is perhaps the most cited reason behind the impossibility of translating EU labourers' struggles into the structures of the refugee and anti-racist movements. 'You know, this is all great, but then these [economic migrants] can at least stay here. They don't face deportation', I am sometimes told.[21]

We see how the break I spoke about in the beginning of the chapter, the void between the absence and the presence of the right to move, has grown wider. Perhaps the latter comes about because of the strong, albeit not the only, focus on border controls in refugee movements and the theoretical construction of freedom of movement as being an outstanding demand. In the meantime, such presuppositions leave conceptions of class aside and erase possibilities for relating the struggles at hand. Moreover, they erase the heterogeneous, yet common aspects of many of these movements. To create radical possibilities of collective response, we must first decentre the political habit in which we recall freedom of movement. This is not to say that the millions of migrants who are struggling with violent border controls, often dying at sea, or those who have already made it to peripheral Europe and still struggle to reach the 'core' of European capitalist societies have to abandon this demand. But we need to denaturalize the liberation potentialities of freedom of movement and interrogate its material and conceptual instabilities.

NOTES

1. Freedom of movement is guaranteed by the Council Directive 2004/38/EC. It is governed in a way so as to 'encourage Union citizens to exercise their right to move and reside freely within Member States, to cut back administrative formalities to the bare essentials, to provide a better definition of the status of family members, to limit the scope of refusing entry or terminating the right of residence and to introduce a new right of permanent residence'. EU citizens are not required to obtain a visa in order to reside in another EU state. http://europa.eu/legislation_summaries/education_training_youth/lifelong_learning/l33152_en.htm (accessed 11 March 2015).

2. The Dublin Regulation stipulates that asylum seekers have to remain and apply for asylum in the EU country, where they first entered the EU. As the crossing happens primarily on the periphery of Europe, many escape and travel to countries such as Germany and Austria, where they immediately become object of return deportation to the first country of entry. As a response, many activist groups within the German anti-racist movement and asylum seekers have organized against such deportations. Prevention of return movement (deportation) is the primary goal. For a detailed discussion see Hristova, Apostolova, Fiedler (2015).

3. Throughout the chapter I speak of the freedom of movement of people.

4. 'Shock therapy' basically stands for the structural adjustment programmes as facilitated by the IMF and the World Bank. Today, these programmes are known as 'austerity measures', which have swept throughout Europe resulting in major political struggles. The shock therapy involved liquidation and subsequent privatization of industries and resulted in a humanitarian catastrophe that beholds the countries to this day.

5. Here I implicitly refer to Balibar's (2002) notion of the 'real universal' which scrutinizes globalization in its extensive and intensive character.

6. Many Bulgarian labour migrants in Germany told me this. One can also add the previously more or less stable economic situation in western and southern countries such as Germany, Spain, Italy, Greece and the Netherlands – the main destination of Bulgarians and Romanians.

7. In the case of EU migrants, deportation is not a (legal) option.

8. Having the legal right to remain in Germany, and hence being considered a 'legal' as opposed to an 'illegal' migrant, prior to opening of the labour markets, did not guarantee regular working status. Regularity is contingent and constantly being reinvented.

9. And in the past against socialist regimes.

10. In fact Nicola was not able to receive his pension to guarantee his reproduction minimum as he had fallen prey to the reforms in the Pensions law. In 1997, the Kostov cabinet changed the methodology according to which pension coefficients were being calculated. According to experts in the National Social Security Institute, the new methodology (the methodology is too complex for me to do it justice in the present work) has resulted in a decrease in individual pensions and moreover, has been detrimental for people with low incomes (interviews conducted August 2014).

11. Employment in Germany and acquiring self-employment status depend on address registration.

12. The city of Munich used to open the homeless shelters only if the temperature was below 0°c. The warm winter of 2013/2014 forced many to sleep under bridges as the shelters did not open regularly. This policy has now been revoked.

13. With the exception of a threat to national security and when illegal appropriation of social benefits is proven.

14. Interview 7 December 2014.

15. Social media conversation February 15, 2015.

16. The acronym CERN stands for *Conseil Européen pour la Recherche Nucléaire* (European Council for Nuclear Research).

17. This is not a characteristic peculiar to 'cheap' labour.

18. Certainly, I would not want to dismiss the fact that such 'protection' is minimized under the ethos of flexibility and versatility for the so-called settled workers.

19. The notion of continuity implies a process which is not defined simply in time boundaries but it is related to the developing of consciousness about one's role in the production process, development of institutions and uniting different sectors of production.

20. Such interlocutors include both German citizens and non-citizens who have been involved in the anti-racist movement.

21. Conversation with a refugee supporter, September 2014. In fact, not all EU citizens are exempted from deportation. To this we can recall the infamous deportations of Bulgarian and Romanian citizens from France in 2010 and also of Italian citizens.

REFERENCES

Andrijasevic, R. and B. Anderson. 2009. 'Conflicts of mobility: Migration, labour and political subjectivities'. *Subjectivity* 29 (1): 363–366.

Aradau, C., J. Huysmans and V. Squire. 2010. 'Acts of European citizenship: A political sociology of mobility'. *JCMS: Journal of Common Market Studies* 48 (4): 945–965.

Balibar, E. 2002. *Politics and the Other Scene*. London and New York: Verso.

Balibar, E. 2013. 'Exploitation'. *Political Concepts* Issue 3.3 (Winter). http://www.politicalconcepts.org/balibar-exploitation/ (accessed 13 March 2015).

Bologna, S. 1972. 'Class composition and the theory of the party at the origin of the workers councils movement'. *Telos: Critical Theory of the Contemporary* 13 (Fall): 4–27.

Casas-Cortes, M., S. Cobarrubias and J. Pickles. 2015. 'Riding routes and itinerant borders: Autonomy of migration and border externalization'. *Antipode* 47 (4): 894–914.

De Genova, N. 2002. 'Migrant "illegality" and deportability in everyday life'. *Annual Review of Anthropology*: 419–447.

De Genova, N. 2005. *Working the Boundaries: Race, Space, and 'Illegality' in Mexican Chicago*. Durham, NC: Duke University Press.

De Genova, N. and N. Peutz, eds. 2010. *The Deportation Regime: Sovereignty, Space, and the Freedom of Movement*. Durham, NC: Duke University Press.

Goldring, L., C. Berinstein and J. K. Bernhard. 2009. 'Institutionalizing precarious migratory status in Canada'. *Citizenship Studies* 13 (3): 239–265.

Harvey, D. 2005. *A Brief History of Neoliberalism*. Oxford: Oxford University Press.

Hristova, T., R. Apostolova and M. Fiedler. 2015. 'On some methodological issues concerning anti-Dublin politics'. *Movements* (1): 1. http://movements-journal.org/issues/01.grenzregime/10.hristova,apostolova,fiedler--dublin-methodology.html (accessed 11 April 2015).

Isin, E. F. 2002. *Being Political: Genealogies of Citizenship*. University of Minnesota Press.

Kotef, H. 2015. *Movement and the Ordering of Freedom: On Liberal Governances of Mobility*. Durham, NC: Duke University Press.

Mezzadra, S. 2004. 'The right to escape'. *Ephemera* 4 (3): 267–275.

Mezzadra, S. 2010. 'The gaze of autonomy: Capitalism, migration and social struggles'. In *The Contested Politics of Mobility: Borderzones and Irregularity,* edited by V. Squire, 121–142. London: Routledge.

Mezzadra, S. and B. Neilson. 2013. *Border as Method, Or, The Multiplication of Labour*. Durham, NC: Duke University Press.

Moody, K. 1997. *Workers in a Lean World*. London: Verso Books.

Nyers, P. 2010. 'Forms of irregular citizenship'. In *The Contested Politics of Mobility: Borderzones and Irregularity,* edited by V. Squire, 184–198. London: Routledge.

Panzieri, R. 1958. 'Seven theses on Worker's Control'; translated by Asad Haider *Viewpoint Magazine* 2014 (4). https://viewpointmag.com/author/raniero-panzieri/ (accessed 11 March 2015).

Papadopoulos, D., N. Stephenson and V. Tsianos. 2008. *Escape Routes. Control and Subversion in the 21st century*. Ann Arbor, MI: Pluto Press.

Papadopoulos, D. and V. S. Tsianos. 2013. 'After citizenship: Autonomy of migration, organisational ontology and mobile commons'. *Citizenship Studies* 17 (2): 178–196.

Rajaram, P. K. 2015. 'Common marginalizations: neoliberalism, undocumented migrants and other surplus populations', *Migration, Mobility, & Displacement* 1 (1): 23–39.

Samaddar, R. 2014. 'Why should we go back to the histories of immigration of late andearly twentieth century? Expanding the margins: migration, mobilities, borders'. International Summer School. http://www.expandingthemargins.net/?p=91 (accessed 13 March 2015).

Squire, V., ed. 2010. *The Contested Politics of Mobility: Borderzones and Irregularity*. London: Routledge.

Chapter III.4

Precariousness in Unlikely Places

The Role of High-skilled Migrant Worker Networks in Resisting and Reproducing Precarity

Chibuzo Ejiogu

Research on changes to work and employment in the EU has highlighted the increase in precarious forms of work (ILO 2012; McKay et al. 2012) especially among migrant workers (Anderson 2010; Potter and Hamilton 2014). However, precariousness has traditionally been conceptualised as affecting migrants in low-skilled, low-status and low-wage jobs (Ahmad 2008; De Lima and Wright 2009) and undocumented migrants (Bloch 2013). This chapter argues that high-skilled migrant workers are increasingly experiencing precariousness resulting from changes to immigration policies in the UK. The precarisation of high-skilled migrant workers is not merely an issue of changing legislation but occurs within the context of, and is driven by, neoliberal economic transformations. This raises the question: how do high-skilled migrants respond collectively to precariousness? Migrant networks are increasingly recognised as important sites for the collective agency of high-skilled migrants in their attempts to resist precarity; the complex dynamics of migrant collective agency are explored in this chapter as well as the shadow cast by the 'dark side' of migrant networks: the social reproduction of the very things migrant networks aim to resist – the control, potential for exploitation and segmentation of high-skilled migrants in work and employment.

This chapter is organised into five sections. After this introduction, the next section sets the conceptual grounds for understanding high-skilled migrant workers, migrant networks and precariousness. The third section discusses the research methodology and the research findings are analysed in the fourth section. The final section concludes and identifies directions for future research.

PRECARIOUSNESS, HIGH-SKILLED MIGRANT WORKERS AND MIGRANT NETWORKS

Contextualising Migration: Flexibilisation of Employment and Non-EU Migration

The rise in precarious work through increasingly insecure and unstable employment arrangements and the contraction of standard forms of employment has become the dominant feature of employment relations within the EU (Kalleberg 2009; McDowell and Christopherson 2009). There has been a shift from relatively stable forms of full employment to more flexible forms of (under)employment (such as fixed-term work, temporary agency work, zero-hour contracts, part-time work, posted work, etc.) as a result of the neoliberal economic transformations in national economies (McKay et al. 2012; Standing 2011). According to Rubery (2015), one hallmark of recent changes to work and employment is the increasing flexibilisation of employment systems. However, there is an underlying paradox in the employment policies within the EU at the national and supranational levels regarding the flexibilisation of employment; on the one hand, greater flexibility is encouraged in response to the business and economic interests of capital and employers, while, on the other hand, there has been an attempt to marry flexibilisation with greater employment security for workers through the EU's flexicurity policy agenda (Viebrock and Clasen 2009). The European Commission promoted flexicurity as a flagship policy in the mid-2000s (EU 2013), and it is a crucial element of the Employment Guidelines, European Employment Strategy and the Europe 2020 Strategy (European Commission 2015).

Flexicurity is a forced marriage between labour market flexibilisation and social security provisions for workers. The flexibilisation of employment has proceeded rapidly across the EU with the deregulation of labour markets and the growth of non-standard employment arrangements, leading to increasing levels of precarious employment (EU 2013). The security provisions consist of comprehensive lifelong learning strategies, effective active labour market policies and modern social security systems (European Commission 2015). However, this forced marriage has been under threat, the global economic crisis has resulted in higher unemployment levels, decreased and in some cases even negative real GDP growth, and scaled-back income security policies. Although 'flexicurity' is a term rarely used in UK policy discourse, the essential elements of the flexicurity policy agenda can be found within the UK employment system. The UK has one of the most flexible and lightly regulated labour markets in the EU; UK government policy focuses on active labour market policies to encourage participation in employment rather than dependence on social security (Simms 2009). However, the UK's active labour market, lifelong learning and social security provisions are largely restricted to UK and EU citizens, as a result non-EU migrants are excluded from accessing these labour market security measures. Therefore, non-EU migrants are in the unique position of suffering the detriments of the increasing flexibilisation of work in the UK without enjoying the concomitant security provisions. This places them in a particularly precarious position within the UK labour market.

The growth of flexible and atypical employment arrangements within the EU has been supported by increasing levels of migration to meet the demand for a flexible, mobile and disposable workforce. There are an estimated 232 million international migrants globally (ILO 2014; United Nations 2013), while 22 per cent of international migrants are highly skilled migrants (Dumont, Spielvogel and Widmaier 2010; IOM 2013). According to Shachar (2006), nation states engage in 'targeted' or 'managed' high-skilled migration programmes in order to retain or gain competitive advantage in the new global economy and this often takes the form of inter-jurisdictional competition in a 'race for talent' using legal and policy tools to attract the 'best and the brightest' (Shachar 2006: 153). Countries in the EU are in a 'regime competition' with other EU countries and other 'knowledge economies', like the USA, Australia and Canada, for highly skilled migrants in a 'global war for talent' (Guo and Al Ariss 2015). In 2004, the EU High Level Group chaired by the former Dutch prime minister, Wim Kok, identified selective migration focused on attracting and retaining highly skilled non-EU migrant workers as an important factor in ensuring an adequate knowledge workforce (EU 2004). The exodus of high-skilled migrants such as doctors, engineers, scientists, academics and other professionals from developing countries outside the EU to industrialised economies such as the UK has been characterised as a 'brain drain' of university-educated workers (Castles and Miller 2009; OECD 2007).

The recent changes to employment and migration are interrelated, capitalism endeavours to reduce the wages of workers by increasing the supply of cheap labour through international migration (Freeman 2006) from developing countries outside the EU. According to Ruhs and Anderson (2011), UK employers are attracted to recruiting migrant workers because of their lower expectations of wages and employment conditions; in addition, new migrants may be prepared to accept jobs whose skill requirements are lower than their actual skills and qualifications enabling employers to profit from a high-skilled migrant workforce without paying for the true level of skill provided by migrant workers. A case in point is the UK health sector, a third of all doctors in the UK are foreign-trained migrants (OECD 2007) and the British National Health Service (NHS) is heavily dependent on trained staff from outside the EU particularly from Asia and Africa (Alkire and Chen

2006). Migrant health workers provide a flexible workforce which is essential in providing continuity of healthcare services at night and on weekends to patients (OECD 2007).

The global economic crisis which started in 2007 has resulted in the tightening of state regulation in relation to migrant labour and the externalisation of borders (Casas-Cortes et al. 2015), imposing new restrictions on the stock and flow of migrant labour in several EU countries (Shachar 2006; Tilly 2011; Rienzo and Vargas-Silva 2014). In the UK, in particular, there have been greater restrictions placed on the entry and conditions of stay of both low-skilled and high-skilled migrants. The introduction of the points-based system (PBS) of visa control in 2008 has restricted skilled migrant workers within the UK labour market and increased the precariousness of non-EU migrant workers; for instance, it places restrictions on their occupational mobility as well as making it difficult to change employer because the employer acts as the 'sponsor' to the migrant's visa. One major difference between EU and non-EU migration to the UK is that non-EU migrants are more likely to be from ethnic minority groups which occupy precarious positions in the labour market due to racial and ethnic discrimination (Healy and Oikelome 2007; Kirton and Greene 2010; Martínez Lucio and Connolly 2010; Alberti et al. 2013).

According to Rienzo and Vargas-Silva (2014), the two main policy changes to highly skilled migration in the UK in recent times are the introduction of the PBS, which regulates high-skilled immigration, and the commitment made by the coalition government in 2010 to reduce net migration from the 'hundreds of thousands' to the 'tens of thousands'. They argue that both of these policy changes were driven by key economic events such as the global economic crisis and the Eurozone crisis. The increase in UK unemployment during the global financial crisis led to the call by Prime Minister Gordon Brown for 'British jobs for British workers' (Barnard 2009) and subsequent policy changes tightened restrictions on non-EU migration. The crisis in the Eurozone could potentially increase the supply of EU migrant workers (including highly skilled migrants) and the UK government is virtually powerless in restricting flows of EU migrants; therefore, the policy commitment to reduce migration to the 'tens of thousands' would in reality have to be focused on tightening restrictions on non-EU migration.

While work is increasingly becoming more precarious due to the high degree of flexibilisation of the UK labour market, non-EU migrant workers do not enjoy the security provisions conceived as part of the common principles of flexicurity within the EU. This high level of precarity of non-EU migrants is further exacerbated by tighter immigration controls resulting from the global economic crisis (originating from a crisis in major neoliberal capitalist economies), UK immigration policy and discrimination experienced by ethnic minorities in the UK labour market. This raises important questions regarding the extent to which high-skilled migrant workers can be conceptualised as experiencing precariousness. It also questions the scope for collective responses by migrant workers given the individualisation of employment relations resulting from flexibilisation of economies.

High-skilled Migrant Workers and Precariousness

According to the ILO, precarious work is a multifaceted, context-specific and complex issue that is vague and difficult to define; in a general sense, it is characterised by various degrees of uncertainty and insecurity in the objective legal status and subjective feelings of workers (ILO 2011). According to Anderson (2010), low-skilled and low-wage migrants experience precarisation from the legal and social categorisation of migrants by UK immigration policies and the resulting institutionalisation of uncertainty. This chapter extends the concept of precarious migrant status to high-skilled migrant workers who experience precariousness as a result of their legal and socially constructed status as skilled migrant labour. The categorisation of migrants according to skill, as well as the definition and measurement of skill, is problematic. According to McGovern (2012) and Csedo (2008), the concept of highly skilled migrant workers is socially constructed and 'highly qualified' does not necessarily equate to 'highly skilled'. Skills are socially constructed and legitimated along occupational, gender and ethnic dimensions (Steinberg 1990; Rigby and Sanchis 2006). There are many definitions of highly skilled migrant workers because 'high skill' is a relative concept (MAC 2009; Cerna 2011; Ruhs and Anderson 2011). The MAC was set up by the UK government to provide independent advice to the government on migration issues; it defines a high-skilled worker as a person who 'may be equipped to do a relatively challenging and difficult job, or perform in a job to a particularly high standard against the relevant success criteria' (MAC 2009: 14). This definition is vague and ambiguous, with no firm criteria for assessing 'high skill'.

The problem with defining 'high skill' in relation to migrants is intimately linked with the lack of recognition of educational, vocational and professional qualifications obtained in the country of origin (Martínez Lucio et al. 2007; OECD 2007), which may lead to their exclusion from active participation in the labour market and result in precarious circumstances. The state (through its immigration selection procedures and agencies) and employers (through their recruitment and selection practices) prefer 'Western qualifications' over qualifications obtained in non-Western countries. Many non-EU high-skilled migrants to the UK experience precariousness as a result of the lack of recognition of their non-Western qualifications which keeps them out of employment in their professional occupations (Cerna 2011).

After the global economic crisis the UK government sought to reduce the number of high-skilled migrants coming to the UK (Rienzo and Vargas-Silva 2014). The Highly Skilled Migrants Programme (HSMP) visa and its successor, the Tier 1 (General) visa, are now closed to new entrants. They were replaced in 2010 by the Tier 1 (Exceptional Talent) visa which is capped at 1,000 migrant visas per year (down from over 10,000 visas under the Tier 1 General visa). This marks a shift in UK high-skilled immigration policy from attracting the 'best and brightest' under the HSMP and Tier 1 (General) visas to attracting a more restricted Exceptional Talent migrant workforce, the 'crème de la crème' of high-skilled migrant workers (Cerna 2011). This also highlights the precarious nature of high-skilled migrant labour in the UK. The categorisation of migrant labour as 'highly skilled' or as an 'Exceptional Talent' is a legal construct. The real differences between various categories of visa are based on the demand and supply of migrant workers in certain occupations, the use of earning targets in regulating and selecting migrant workers and their inclusion or exclusion from the UK labour market. During periods of economic recession, the UK government redefines the meaning of 'high-skilled migrant' in order to restrict and select migrant workers for the UK labour market. This arbitrary change in the legal and social categorisation of high-skilled migrants places migrant workers in precarious positions, as they are in a constant state of uncertainty regarding their legal status to work and reside within the UK. The malleability of UK immigration policy regarding the categorisation of high-skilled migrant workers and their right to work in the UK institutionalises uncertainty by creating a psychological state of insecurity and enforces a high degree of temporariness in the lifestyle of migrant workers (Anderson 2010). High-skilled migrant workers experience precarity as the absence of the right to plan one's future with a minimum of security, predictability and job certainty.

The normative characteristics of the employment relationship under which many high-skilled migrants work contribute to the precarisation of skilled migrant labour. Recent changes to employment norms, especially the impact of financialised capital in fragmenting work, restructuring firms and the flexibilisation of employment practices (Rubery 2015), have made work more precarious for high-skilled migrants in a number of ways. First, many high-skilled migrants are under-employed or experience long-term unemployment in the UK. There is evidence to show that highly skilled migrants have resorted to low-skilled employment in the UK in significant numbers despite the rhetoric of a skills shortage (Aldin et al. 2010; Rienzo 2012; UK Home Office 2010). This may be due in part to issues of social exclusion and institutionalised ethnic discrimination within labour market institutions.

Many employers fail to recognise non-Western educational qualifications and work experience gained outside the UK (Martínez Lucio et al. 2007). Consequently, high-skilled migrants from outside the EU experience the precariousness of long-term unemployment and under-employment within the UK.

Second, high-skilled migrants in the UK are excluded from access to many government-sponsored skills training and social security provisions. Low levels of social security protection and skills training designed to enhance employability are normative characteristics of precarious work (Tangian 2007). By excluding skilled migrants from access to social security provisions that provide alternative income during periods of unemployment, skilled migrant workers are placed in precarious positions should they lose their job as a result of sickness, redundancy, and so on. Third, the normative dimensions of the employment relationship governing migrant workers include changes in employment arrangements which have been linked with precarious work (Vosko 2006; Fudge 2011) such as changes to employment status (from paid employment to self-employment) and forms of employment (growth in temporary and part-time employment). Research on high-skilled knowledge workers, such as software developers who focus on Apple and Google platforms, has shown that they are not immune to the precarisation of working conditions through shifting employment arrangements and uncertainty in labour markets resulting from changing market structures (Bergvall-Kareborn and Howcroft 2013). Skilled migrant workers are not immune to the growth in non-standard employment practices, and many 'knowledge workers' are migrants working on fixed-term contracts (Guest and Clinton 2006; Hopkins and Levy 2012).

Fourth, the degree of employer control over employees and work processes is an important factor in the precarisation of employment (Rodgers and Rodgers 1989; Fudge 2011). There is a significant link between the legal status of high-skilled migrants and the greater degree of control the state has provided to employers who act as 'sponsors' of work visas (Ruhs and Anderson 2011).

Fifth, an important norm in the employment relations of high-skilled migrant workers is the relatively low level of trade union protection for migrant labour. The absence of trade union protection is considered a characteristic of precarious work (Rodgers and Rodgers 1989). Research suggests that there may be a degree of self-policing by migrants, as they may not join trade unions even when they have the opportunity to do so because they perceive that many employers prefer non-union workers and workplaces (Anderson 2007, 2010). Migrant workers are less likely to belong to a trade union (Grunell and Van Het Kaar 2003) and high-skilled workers (who are predominantly in professional occupations and the service sector) are less likely to work in unionised organisations (Korczynski 2002; Waddington 1992). Therefore high-skilled migrant workers are doubly at risk of not benefiting from the collective representation of trade unions. The situation may be worse for female highly skilled migrants due to the gender dimensions of migration, unionisation and knowledge work (Healy, Brown and Heery 2004; Healy, Bradley and Mukherjee 2004).

There is a major concern with trade union responses to migration and precarisation (see the discussion by Aziz, Egan and Polkowski, Chapter III.1 in this book). Trade unions have generally engaged with migrant workers in the UK as part of a wider Black, Asian and Minority Ethnic (BAME) equality and diversity agenda (Fitzgerald 2007; Martínez Lucio et al. 2007; Fitzgerald and Hardy 2009); unfortunately this has tended to focus on low- and semi-skilled migrant workers to the exclusion of highly skilled migrant workers. According to Virdee (2000), over time trade unions have evolved from policies of exclusion regarding migrants to inclusive policies. There has been a growing recognition of a 'crisis in representation' of migrant workers in employment relations (Martínez Lucio and Perrett 2009) and a 'gap in the voice and representation' of migrant workers (Martínez Lucio and Connolly 2010). This gap may be filled by alternative institutions of worker representation such as skilled migrant networks. Therefore, migrant networks need to be recognised as important actors in understanding the complex dynamics of collective agency among high-skilled migrant workers in the UK.

Migrant Networks and the Dynamics of Collective Agency

Neoclassical economics and institutional analysis of labour migration is limited by the paradigm of the *Homo economicus* – the assumption that economic migrants are rational, self-seeking, amoral agents (McGovern 2007). A more nuanced and realistic view of labour migration is open to the role of social, psychological and historical factors in understanding labour migration. The social network perspective emphasises that 'networks migrate' (Kearney 1986; Tilly 1990; Portes 1995; Vertovec and Cohen 1999; Brettell 2000; Poros 2001). According to Tilly (1990), the effective units of migration are neither individuals nor households but sets of people linked by acquaintance, kinship and work experience. Networks connect migrants across time and space through flows of information increasingly facilitated by the internet and social media (Boyd 1989; Koser and Salt 1997; Aneesh 2001; Vertovec 2002).

Networks are made up of nodes, ties and flows. Nodes are distinct points connected by ties, flows pass along ties on their way to other nodes and ties forming the network (Castells 1996; Barney 2004). Flows such as information, money and goods pass through ties which are often transportation systems or information and communication technology systems (such as the internet and social media) to nodes (such as computers, humans, organisations, etc.).

Migrant networks can be distinguished by the different structural and functional configurations of ties resulting in different outcomes (Poros 2001). 'Open' networks are characterised by relatively heterogeneous membership and members do not all know each other while 'closed' networks have a homogenous and exclusive membership structure and members usually know everyone else in the network (Antcliff, Saundry and Stuart 2005).

Migrant networks enable the collectivisation of migrant workers and the exercise of agency in complex and varied ways. Informal social networks developed by migrants themselves usually engage in 'chain migration' (Price 1963) to facilitate the international movement of migrants through social connections. Social and cultural capital (Bourdieu 1986) within migrant networks play an important role in supporting international migration and encouraging the flow of skilled migrant workers along 'beaten paths' (Stahl 1993). Information, knowledge, and resources are accessed by migrants through their social networks to enable them to navigate legal requirements, organise travel, obtain information regarding destination countries, access work and adapt to new environments (Bauder 2006). Migrant networks also facilitate the process of settlement and community formation in the destination country. Migrant networks develop their own social and economic infrastructure (Castles and Miller 2009) such as the provision of professional services (e.g. doctors, lawyers, accountants, etc.), shops, restaurants, places of worship, cafes, educational services, community associations and cultural services. Migrant networks engage in recruitment activities by providing employers and recruitment agents with a readily available and cheap source of skilled labour; there is growing evidence that employers prefer recruiting migrants because migrant networks provide a self-regulating and self-sustaining supply of labour (Rodriguez 2004; Ruhs and Anderson 2011).

According to Putnam (2000) the decline in trade union membership and rise in contingent employment have resulted in increased isolation of workers. Social networks are simultaneously the site for self-seeking individual behaviour as well as collective agency fostered by common identities, interests and a greater sense of community (Antcliff, Saundry and Stuart 2005). Networks that organise the collective representation of worker interests in promoting social inclusion, equality and diversity can either be in competition with trade unions or complementary to existing union structures (Healy and Oikelome 2007). Social networks are therefore important 'new actors' in employment relations which are largely under-theorised and under-studied (Heckscher and Carre 2006; Heery and Frege 2006). This chapter proceeds to discuss the methodology underpinning the empirical research followed by a discussion of the findings regarding the relationship between migrant networks of high-skilled workers and precarity.

RESEARCH METHODS AND CASE STUDIES

This research is part of a wider research project on the inclusion and exclusion of migrants within the UK in work and employment conducted by the author. This chapter draws on the phase of research conducted in 2015 and 2016. The principle research objective of this phase was to examine the collective responses of migrant networks in resisting and reproducing precarity.

For the purposes of this study, migrants were defined following the 'country of origin' approach (Castles and Miller 2009) as persons born outside the UK. This includes persons who have naturalised (taken on the nationality or acquired the citizenship of the receiving country). This approach was adopted because skilled migrants often continue to experience exclusion or inclusion in labour markets based on ethnic identity and social capital linked to ethnicity or nationality. Furthermore, this is the approach used by the UK government in regulating immigration policy (Rienzo and Vargas-Silva 2014). This study defines skilled migrants as possessing at least a university degree in line with both government policy and academic literature on high-skilled migrant workers (McLaughlan and Salt 2002; Martin 2003; Cerna 2011; Cerdine et al. 2014). The focus of the research was on non-EU highly skilled migrant workers to enable greater understanding of ethnicity-based inclusion or exclusion.

Four case studies were selected from a population of migrant networks in the UK, following an internet search of migrant organisations and anecdotal evidence from members of immigrant community groups in the UK. The case studies were chosen because they were actively engaged in resisting or reproducing precarity among high-skilled migrant workers and as such comprise leading or critical cases (Williams et al. 2011). They were also chosen because their membership and regulatory focus centred on non-EU skilled migrant workers. Members of the four networks were drawn from private and public sector organisations and were all in employment; the main professional occupations in the sample were doctors, engineers, managers, lawyers, accountants, human resource professionals and university academics.

The four case study networks examined were the Migrant Doctors Network in Scotland (MDNS), the Nigerian Community in Diaspora Network (NCDN), The Global Nigeria Forum (TGNF) and the Association for Black and Minority Ethnic Engineers UK (AFBE-UK). MDNS is an informal 'open' network of migrant doctors which campaigned for change to visa regulations affecting migrant General Practitioner (GP) trainees in Scotland. It was formed in 2011 and its core membership base was approximately twenty migrant doctors, mostly from Nigeria, with a minority from other (mostly African and Asian) countries.

NCDN is an informal 'closed' network of skilled migrants from Nigeria; most of its members have undertaken postgraduate education and are employed in a range of professions (e.g. doctors, lawyers, accountants, etc.) and are spread across the UK. They are a faith-based and alumni network which started officially in 2013 although members share close pre-migration links. They are an informal network with the aim of providing mutual support in diaspora, including career and migration support. Membership fluctuates between approximately twenty to thirty members. They hold a major annual event which emphasises diaspora support and they have close links with other migrant networks in popular destination countries for skilled Nigerian migrants such as the USA, Canada and Finland.

TGFN is a formal network of skilled Nigerian migrants working in the UK oil and gas sector, it has over 200 members mostly based in Aberdeen and a coordinating team which provides leadership. Members do not all know each other because of the size of the network despite its 'closed' and exclusionary membership to Nigerian professionals working in the UK oil and gas industry. Its members work in a range of professions in the oil and gas industry with a predominance of engineers and managers. It was officially started in 2013 and aims to promote greater participation in the Nigerian oil and gas industry by Nigerian professionals in diaspora; influence the regulation of the Nigerian oil and gas industry especially as regards indigenisation and local content policies; promote the transfer of best practices in the oil and gas sector and knowledge exchange to improve the Nigerian oil and gas industry; and to provide opportunities for learning and development to Nigerians working in the oil and gas sector. It launched an online portal in 2014 to facilitate these objectives and its networking activities.

AFBE-UK is a formal 'open' network of BAME professionals working in engineering and allied professions in the UK. It is an inclusive network and has a core base of members who are non-EU skilled migrants, predominantly from Africa, although it also includes membership from Asia, the UK and Europe (migrants and non-migrants; BAME and non-BAME backgrounds). Its objectives include promoting the participation of people of BAME origin in engineering and providing career support for people in engineering and allied professions targeted at migrants and persons of BAME origin. Its approach is inclusive, although it targets its activities at skilled migrants and others of BAME origin, it also provides such services to persons from non-migrant and non-BAME backgrounds. It was formed in 2007 and although its membership is largely made up of engineers, it includes members of other professions who work in engineering firms such as managers, human resource professionals and lawyers. AFBE-UK has its headquarters in London and chapters in Birmingham and Aberdeen. However this research focused on the Aberdeen chapter because high-skilled migrants constitute most of its membership.

The study draws on twenty-four interviews across the four case studies, pseudonyms are used for interview respondents to protect anonymity. The informal networks are not officially registered organisations and members use a variety of labels in lieu of officially designated organisational names, the network names used here are provided by the leadership of such informal networks. A multiple case study enables theoretical analysis based on contrasting findings (Bryman 2008) while a small number of intensive case studies allows for 'depth' in data collection (Yin 2009). The aim of the case studies is not to arrive at findings that can be generalised across all migrant networks but rather to obtain rich insights into the complex reality of the selected cases (Yin 2009). Although no claim of generalisability is made regarding the findings, there is scope for the transferability of findings and recommendations in ways that can be adapted to different contexts (Lincoln and Guba 1985; Bryman 2008). An initial purposive sample was used to select key respondents possessing a rich insight into each network's activities (Kumar et al. 1993; Easterby-Smith et al. 2012; Creswell 2013). The key informant approach is useful in examining the structural mechanisms which influence policy development (Ackroyd 2009; Williams et al. 2017). Additional interview respondents were also obtained using a snowball sampling technique (Bryman 2008; Saunders et al. 2009).

Interviews lasted an average of one hour and were carried out either face to face, by video conference or over the telephone. The interviews were recorded and transcribed. The interviews were semi-structured, with main questions and probing questions covering the regulatory role of migrant networks and the attraction, development and retention of skilled international migrants. Interviews were based on the interviewees' perspectives and experiences in order to gain an understanding of how migrant networks operate (Antcliff et al. 2007). Interviews were coded and analysed using a template analysis to develop themes from initial codes and identify patterns and relationships in the data (King 1998). The initial findings of a tentative nature are presented in the next section.

FINDINGS AND DISCUSSION

Resisting Precarity: Power and Voice

The precarisation of skilled migrant labour through the legal and social construction of a precarious migrant status and the increasing precarisation of the norms of employment relations governing skilled migrant labour are to a large extent dependent on state and employer control of migrant mobility. According to Vicki Squire (2011), the state engages in *politics of control* while migrants engage in *politics of mobility*; the interplay of both types of politics is a useful starting point in analysing recent migrants' collective responses through social networks. According to Smith (2010), the mobility power of migrant workers is central to the balance of power between capital and labour in neoliberal capitalist economies. By enhancing their ability to move across geographical, occupational and workplace boundaries, migrants can choose employment regimes that are less precarious in terms of migrant status and employment norms. In order to attract the highly skilled migrant labour necessary for economic productivity, the state and employers will need to respond with policies that reduce the precariousness, insecurity and uncertainty of migrant labour or risk losing out in the 'global war for talent' (Guo and Al Ariss 2015).

This research suggests that a common practice within migrant networks is the sharing of information about opportunities to move to another country after using the UK as a 'stepping stone' on global mobility pathways. This was a response to a perceived tightening of the UK immigration policies and the UK becoming increasingly 'unfriendly' to high-skilled migrants. This practice was illustrated by the following quote from an interview respondent:

> If I do eventually leave the UK it would be because of the perception of the UK as a welcoming or not welcoming society for migrants ... and the UK policy ... it would also be my sense of opportunity ... we don't make those kind of moves without migrant networks, basically you need the network ... it's not just enough what you read about ... you need it [the network] for the move ... to connect me with the opportunities and people I need ... and to understand what's going on, if the country is welcoming or changing. (Victor, NCDN)

This research highlights the transnational agency exercised by migrant networks. Migrants not only shared information about possible destination countries, comparing these to the UK to enable skilled migrants make decisions based on their personal circumstances; they also connected skilled migrants to opportunities and support networks in potential destination countries for career mobility in order to reduce the precarisation experienced by skilled migrants as illustrated in the quote below:

> I have quite a number of friends now who've migrated from Nigeria to Canada, Nigeria to Australia and Nigeria to the USA. Also, I have a few friends who've migrated to the UK first, and then migrated again from the UK to say Canada and some are in the process. … I have all these friends or people [in the network] there, and if I really want to take the step to move then I have the support network there. I have access to the information I need. I have a place to stay if I need to, for the initial period I need to settle down … some of the migrant doctors in my network are considering moving to Canada because there is a possibility of entering a partnership with other migrant doctors there from part of the network or that kind of support. (Amara, NCDN)

The foregrounding of the agency of migrants in managing their mobility across borders (rather than state-centric approaches) has been highlighted by the AoM approach to understanding international mobility (Moulier-Boutang 1998; Papadopoulos and Tsianos 2013; Casas-Cortes et al. 2015); of interest in the quotes above is the collectivisation of such agency among skilled migrant workers across international geographical locations through migrant networks. Migrants are not passive victims of state migration and border control but engage in activities and strategies which necessitate new forms of state action in response.

Migrant networks resist precarisation by actively enhancing the employability of skilled migrants within such networks; in effect, migrant networks act as an alternative service provider to the state and employers in enhancing the employability of migrant labour denied them under the 'security' provisions of flexicurity. One formal skilled migrant network (AFBE-UK) organised training seminars delivered by experienced professionals and experts on technical aspects of engineering thereby giving its members an edge in their career progression. A member of this network stated that

> the quality of the [migrant network] training is really good, I mean excellent. I don't usually get this kind of development at work, not only me, many people, they come because they may not get this level of knowledge exchange at work. Sometimes the seminars are on very niche topics so unless you work in that area you may never get to learn about it except through [the migrant network] … but we can then apply this knowledge at work and it helps progress our careers. (Irene, AFBE-UK)

Another method used by migrant networks to develop the employability skills of members and resist precarisation was for more experienced members of the networks to act as mentors to younger skilled migrant workers in the same professional occupation; such mentoring usually occurred 'beyond the workplace'. Migrant networks also supported the careers of high-skilled migrant workers by developing their social capital. Career networking and training programmes were designed specifically to develop the social and cultural competencies of network members; one interview respondent stated:

> I used to feel like I stuck out like a sore thumb, the culture is so different from Nigeria ... then he [a member of the network] showed me ... [how] to pick up the [social] cues because they are so subtle here. (Chiamaka, NCDN)

These 'soft' skills, network of contacts and 'employability' skills transferred through social networks in the form of social capital (Bauder 2006; Raghuram, Henry and Bornat 2010; Healy and Oikelome 2011) are often the difference between a successful job application and being unsuccessful in 'breaking into' the job market. As one high-skilled migrant observed:

> These are the things we lacked when we first came to this country, we wanted to give the newcomers the knowledge we wished we could have had back then so they don't have to go through what we went through ... it's the kind of knowledge you don't get taught in school. I had to pick it up the hard way over the years but it's what makes you stand out from the rest of the crowd at the job interview. (Ade, AFBE-UK)

The development of employability and social capital by migrant networks enhanced migrants' knowledge and such knowledge can be viewed as a power resource that improves migrants' career progression (French and Raven 1968; Abbott, Heery and Williams 2012). Therefore, skilled migrant networks alter the balance of power between individual migrant workers and employers in the employment relationship. They enhance the mobility power within internal and external labour markets by empowering migrants to bargain for a better deal within organisations or manoeuvre their careers more successfully within the external labour market by securing better jobs.

At the macro level there was evidence of migrant networks articulating the collective voice of migrants in order to resist the precarisation of highly skilled migrant workers. One illustrative case concerns the precarious position resulting from the visa policy governing non-EU doctors working in Scotland in post-qualification training roles. Non-EU migrant doctors undergoing post-qualification GP training were required to work under a sponsored work visa, the 'sponsor' being their employer. This is a legal requirement for all high-skilled migrant workers in the UK working under that category of visa. The nature of GP training is such that trainees rotate placements every six to twelve months, each rotation involves changing hospitals and medical specialisms to achieve the required broad range of experience and training required to qualify as a GP. The policy in Scotland was that each rotation required a new sponsor (i.e. the new hospital the trainee was posted to), which caused a significant amount of detriment to non-EU GP trainees (EU trainees did not require a visa); one GP trainee described the precariousness resulting from their migrant status:

> Our place of work would change every six months or every twelve months, depending, so we had to apply for a visa each time we move from one place of work to another, so for a family of three or four, you're looking at two or three thousand pounds every six months as visa fees ... it was very difficult ... some of the stories were eyewatering ... our salaries were stretched to the very limit just to pay for visa fees. (Ifechukwu, MDNS)

In the absence of effective trade union representation on the issue, a few GP trainees got together to form an informal network (MDNS) to campaign to change the regulation through lobbying the UK Borders Agency (UKBA was the UK state agency responsible for migration, it was restructured in 2013 to become UK Visas and Immigration – UKVI). They also lobbied NHS Education Scotland (the public sector agency responsible for GP trainees) and a Member of the Scottish Parliament. They sought to change the policy to have a single sponsor (NHS Education Scotland) throughout the four years of their training programme. The situation in England was that GP trainees had a single visa sponsor (the equivalent body to NHS Education Scotland) throughout their training. The migrant network sought to replicate this model in Scotland based on knowledge obtained from their interaction with networks of migrant doctors in England. The effectiveness of the campaign organised by the skilled migrant network is discussed in the quote below:

> So what we then did was that we got together … and looked for our MP [member of parliament] in the area and itemized all these problems and also had to find out that these are the other reasons why it is [a] trouble to get trainees who are not from EU to come to Scotland because they have to face a special difficulty which will cost them an extra 12,000 pounds … so we wrote the letter to the MP ... but he thankfully took us seriously, he wrote to NES [NHS Education Scotland] also [to] the UKBA ... but fortunately, it was resolved towards the end of our training … the NHS Education for Scotland, it has now agreed to become the sole sponsor throughout the training which is [what] should have happened since [the start of our training]. (Ifechukwu, MDNS)

Migrant networks can harness the collective power of migrant labour in resisting precarisation. By articulating the collective voice of skilled migrant workers, the migrant network was able to influence state regulatory bodies and employment practices that reduced the precarious financial position of migrant doctors in Scotland. This research suggests that migrant networks are involved in resisting precarity among high-skilled migrant workers, primarily outside the workplace, through the development of mobility power and the articulation of collective worker voice. There was very little evidence of resistance within the workplace, highlighting the continued requirement for workplace-level collective agents such as trade unions in representing worker (migrant and non-migrant) interests. Nevertheless, the exercise of collective agency by migrant networks was not unproblematic and evidence of a 'dark side' emerged from the study.

Reproducing Precarity: The 'Dark Side' of Migrant Networks

The 'inclusion' of migrants is complex and contested, inclusion goes beyond a simplistic binary contradiction to 'exclusion'. De Genova (2013) highlights processes of 'inclusion through exclusion' where the very process of inclusion of migrants is a form of subjugation. Similarly, this research suggests that the exercise of agency by migrant networks in facilitating the access of skilled migrants to job and career development opportunities includes a 'dark side' – the marginalisation of high-skilled migrants into less desirable and more precarious segments of the UK labour market.

Migrant networks actively support their members to secure jobs by sharing information on job adverts, advising network members on selecting potential employers, providing support in writing resumes, coaching applicants to prepare for job interviews and assessment centres, and sharing information on pay rates, terms and conditions of employment to enhance members' negotiating power over a contract of employment. This shows a remarkable breadth of collective agency in the attempt by migrant networks to exert power by resisting ethnic discrimination and overcoming a lack of social capital which exclude skilled migrants from entering and progressing within the UK labour market (Bauder 2006).

Bourdieu's work on various forms of capital shows how social and cultural capital serve as processes of distinction, differentiation and social reproduction (Bourdieu 1984, 1986). Migrant networks play an important role in developing and socially reproducing social and cultural capital by providing access to social networks and by enhancing the employability and skills of highly skilled migrant workers. There was a remarkable variation in the way agency was exercised among the three networks which provided support services to facilitate the inclusion of high-skilled migrants in the UK labour market. NCDNS prioritised members in the provision of support services to access job and career development opportunities. Members were also able to facilitate non-members (primarily from BAME backgrounds) to access such services. In contrast, AFBE-UK explicitly made available its services to members and non-members alike, it targeted migrants from BAME backgrounds in advertising its services, while the delivery of support services was provided to workers irrespective of ethnicity or nationality and it therefore provided services to a wide range of migrants including workers from CEE. TGNF provided access to job vacancies advertised on its online discussion forum exclusively to members, who were all originally from Nigeria. All organisations provided support services free of charge.

However, this research suggests that there are complexities and contradictions in the agency of migrant networks in relation to precarity, by enhancing the social and cultural capital of high-skilled migrant workers the networks produced and reproduced labour market segmentation. One interview respondent talked about the segmentation of migrants occurring along geographical lines resulting partly from the activities within his migrant network:

> Geographic clusters also … people tend to want to be where their friends are … yes … but [there is] also the economic push. For migrants, most of them will

> go where the jobs take them … and this is often to locations the UK citizens do not like to work or live in so migrants find it easier to get jobs in places like that because no one else wants to work there … some of them would make specific effort to find jobs around where their friends [in the migrant network] or families are … so I work here and I know the job opportunities and I can pass them on to other migrants. So, you have other migrants begin to cluster around [here] because they are more aware of the job openings here … there's a bit of network in it … so there's that kind of information passed around [in the migrant network]. (Amara, NCDN)

Another interview respondent commented on how the mentoring and career networking support from older and more established members of his migrant network influenced the career choice and occupational segmentation of skilled migrants at the early stages of their careers:

> Those that moved to the UK first are helping the newer highly skilled migrants … they get a lot of guidance and direction … encourage them to go into certain occupations and specializations because a few people have found themselves in there and have the experience … these tend to be specialisations that may be considered unattractive [to the non-migrants] … they can tell them what they need to do to get in and progress … that sort of dynamic around access to information and support … I think that's the way we sort of help ourselves. (Victor, NCDN)

The 'dark side' of social capital (Portes 1998; Navarro 2002; Raghuram, Henry and Bornat 2010; Uribe 2014) simultaneously results in the exclusion of migrant workers from more desirable and less precarious segments of the labour market. This research suggests that the unintended consequences of the development of social and cultural capital within migrant networks results in the occupational and geographical segmentation of high-skilled migrant workers in the UK.

Another aspect of the 'dark side' of migrant networks is the way they socially reproduce precariousness by enhancing the normative control and potential for economic exploitation of high-skilled migrants by employers. Therefore, there are complex and contradictory dynamics involved in the exercise of collective agency through migrant networks.

Migrants workers are regarded by many employers as 'good workers' exhibiting greater levels of effort, productivity and performance; migrant labour is preferred by employers because they are regarded as possessing superior work ethic, attitudes and dispositions (Rodriguez 2004; CIPD 2005; Dench et al. 2006; MacKenzie and Forde 2009). The stereotyping of migrants as 'good workers' is related to greater levels of control and exploitation by employers over migrant workers. This reflects the level of dependence migrants have on their employers for jobs and 'sponsored' visas underpinned by UK immigration policies (Anderson 2010; Thompson et al. 2013). This research provided evidence that the stereotype of migrants as 'good workers' was not limited to employers, but was internalised by high-skilled migrants as a strategy to respond to perceived discrimination. Skilled migrants believed they needed to be 'good workers', regardless of whether or not specific employers will discriminate against them or require significant amounts of discretionary effort from them as a result of a supposed superior work ethic and motivation levels. A common theme among the high-skilled migrants interviewed was the belief they needed to 'go the extra mile' and 'work twice as hard' as non-migrants workers to advance their careers as reflected in these quotes by interview respondents:

> My name is not John Smith or any other English name … once they [employers] hear a foreign name the doors automatically shut … with an African name I have to work twice as hard if I want to get anywhere with my career. (Chidi, NCDN)
>
> You know, it will always be everywhere because your name in the first place tells people that you are not a home based [local] … you have to work extra hard to let people know that you are capable and you are competent … and putting that in mind, remember that this is the reality of life, there are some people that won't like you because of the fact that you are an IMG [international medical graduate]. I have also been particularly a victim of that on few occasions, I remember one supervisor telling me that 'do I know how many people are eyeing the seat I am seating on?' ... in one of my hospital training posts people would raise issues and say 'oh you didn't do this and you didn't do that' but I would see the same mistakes made by locals and nobody would say anything about it. I remember one day that I particularly pointed this problem out to the matron and she didn't say anything about it. So, these are the things that are there in the system and everybody knows. (Seyi, MDNS)

Being a 'good worker' is normatively embedded in migrant employment relationships, often in implicit rather than explicit ways. High-skilled migrants attempted to secure jobs and advance their careers by internalising the attitude of a 'good worker', making them more amenable to employer control and exploitation. This research suggests that migrant networks are complicit in socially reproducing the stereotype of migrant workers as 'good workers' thereby providing employers with an extra lever of control and exploitation at the workplace. This research shows that migrant work ethic and dispositions to work stem from self-policing and control *within* migrant networks. One interview respondent described how his identity as a 'good worker' was socially constructed through the social interactions occurring within his migrant network:

> When I came [to the UK] my friends in the network told me I had to work twice as hard as the locals … it makes me definitely want to go the extra mile to prove

> myself. Generally, makes me feel like I don't have any room for errors. I don't have any room to make a mistake [at work], because the mistake I make would not be interpreted the same way if a local [non-migrant] makes the same mistake . . . I will not be forgiven if I make a mistake. (Victor, NCDN)

The stereotype of the migrant being a 'good worker' is subtly strengthened by the social interactions within migrant networks. The networks studied suggest that not only are recent arrivals to the UK informed that they need to 'work twice as hard' as non-migrants by older members of the migrant networks but new members are actively encouraged to make use of the support and mentoring offered within the networks for their career development. This involves identifying ways to improve performance at work by a mentor to help the recent arrival 'get recognised' at work as a high-performing employee. Furthermore, members are often introduced to jobs in firms and recruitment agencies through older members of the networks on the condition that they maintain the reputation of being 'hard workers' so they don't jeopardise subsequent recruitment from the network through poor performance at work. This acts as a form of normative control *within* the migrant networks that perpetuates the stereotype of the 'good worker' by subtly pressuring members to keep open the access to recruitment into organisations on the basis of their reputation for 'working twice as hard' as non-migrant workers.

Neoliberal capitalism constantly seeks new and more effective ways to control labour (Sturdy, Fleming and Delbridge 2010) and migrant labour is considered more complaint and amenable to control (Anderson 2010). The stereotype of the migrant as a 'good worker' preferred by employers needs to be understood in terms of self-disciplining by migrants which gives employers an extra lever of normative control and economic exploitation over migrant labour. The high degree of control by employers over skilled migrant workers contributes to the precarious status of high-skilled migrant workers and increases the imbalance of power in the employment relationship in favour of the employers. One interview respondent described the way being a 'good worker' was related to greater levels of employer control:

> I felt I was caged. I had to 'behave myself' because if I didn't like the employer I couldn't just tell them or leave … they have the control so I have to be good and not have any issues with my employer … If you feel you have any grievances [against the employer] you just keep quiet and shut up … you just take it all in. It feels restricted … you don't have the freedom to work wherever you want to work or whatever you want to do. (Victor, NCDN)

The quote above indicates that the migrant 'good worker' stereotype, when combined with the uncertainty resulting from employer control over the employment and legal status of migrant workers (e.g. the requirement that employers act as a 'sponsor' of the visa of migrant workers), induces a significant degree of precarity among highly skilled migrant workers. This opens up the possibility of the exploitation of high-skilled migrant labour by some employers if migrants are restricted in their ability to change employers and there is a normative expectation that migrant labour exerts more effort than non-migrant labour in the workplace. The response by highly skilled migrants to the excessive degree of power and control employers have over migrant labour, as evidenced in the quote above, is to conform to (and reproduce) the 'good worker' stereotype. In essence, this involves the provision of high levels of work effort and productivity by highly skilled migrants that may be exploited by employers for no additional reward to the migrant workers. Furthermore, employers may take some liberties in the employment relationship with migrant workers if they know that migrant workers are unlikely to raise a grievance or exit the employment relationship (e.g. degrading terms and conditions of employment or exploiting migrant workers by paying lower wages for the same or higher skills), although this would likely occur only among unscrupulous employers. Nevertheless, the evidence shows that the employment relationship between highly skilled migrants and their employers may be considered exploitative when it involves a significant degree of 'extra effort' on the part of the migrant workers and if there is no commensurate payment for such extra work effort. This is the case particularly when the expectation of high-skilled migrants conforming to migrant work ethic stereotypes is normalised within the employment relationship.

The collective agency of migrant networks is problematic in that it is intimately involved in the social reproduction of the 'good worker' stereotype. While this may help the careers of individual migrants, it nevertheless contributes to the social reproduction of collective precarity and the psychological insecurity which migrants experience in their employment relations. Migrant networks are complicit in developing normative rules for the concertive control (Barker 1993) over their labour process; therefore, the collective agency of migrant labour has a 'dark side' – the social production and reproduction of precarity through self-disciplining processes that manufacture consent and compliance (Burawoy 1979) to employer control, which may potentially result in economic exploitation.

CONCLUSION

The increasing flexibilisation of the UK economy (Rubery 2015) in line with the EU's policy of flexicurity (Simms 2009; Auer and Chatani 2011) and the imposition of a more restrictive regime of immigration regulation as a result of the global economic crisis (Tilly 2011; Rienzo and Vargas-Silva 2014) have resulted in the increasing precarisation of migrant labour within the

UK's neoliberal capitalist economy. Precarious work is usually analysed in terms of low-skilled, low-status and low-wage migrant labour. However, this chapter has argued that high-skilled migrant labour has increasingly become precarious through the legal and social construction of a precarious migrant status and the precarisation of the employment norms that characterise the employment relations of high-skilled migrant workers in the UK. Migrant networks are involved in resisting precarity by enhancing the mobility power of skilled migrants and articulating their collective voice in order to influence the precarious policies of the state and employers. However, the collective agency of skilled migrant networks is complex and contradictory, the very processes of resistance to precarity have the unintended consequences of socially reproducing precarity among high-skilled migrant workers.

The collective agency of migrant networks has a 'dark side'; migrant networks are involved in the manufacture of normative control and compliance to employer stereotypes of migrants as 'good workers' who 'go the extra mile' over and beyond non-migrant labour, providing an extra lever of control and economic exploitation to employers. The social capital developed by migrants to enhance their mobility power within social networks also has a 'dark side' (Portes 1998; Navarro 2002; Raghuram, Henry and Bornat 2010; Uribe 2014) as social capital inadvertently results in the segmentation of skilled migrant labour into less desirable and more precarious work along geographical and occupational lines. Furthermore, there was very little evidence of resistance within the workplace by migrant networks, highlighting the continued requirement for workplace-level collective agents such as trade unions in representing worker (migrant and non-migrant) interests.

This study raises a number of implications for future research. First, broader empirical analysis needs to be undertaken regarding the scope and nature of precariousness among high-skilled migrants from countries within and outside the EU that was beyond the focus of this study. Second, there is a gap in our understanding regarding the relationship between migrant networks and trade unions; research that examines how migrant networks may complement, compete with, replace or reinforce trade unions is required. Third, this chapter calls for research regarding the impact of proposed legislative changes in the UK, on high-skilled migrant workers, particularly the extension of precarisation to the social sphere (outside the workplace) in ways which will negatively impact on the work–life conditions of skilled migrants.

REFERENCES

Abbott, B., E. Heery and S. Williams. 2012. 'Civil society organisations and the exercise of power in the employment relationship'. *Employee Relations* 34 (1): 91–107.

Ackroyd, S. 2009. 'Research designs for realist research'. In *The Sage Handbook of Organisational Research Methods*, edited by D. Buchanan and A. Bryman. London: Sage.

Ahmad, A. 2008. 'Dead men working: Time and space in London's ("illegal") migrant economy'. *Work, Employment and Society* 22 (2): 301–318.

Alberti, G., J. Holgate and M. Tapia. 2013. 'Organising migrants as workers or as migrant workers? Intersectionality, trade unions and precarious work'. *The International Journal of Human Resource Management* 24 (22): 4132–4148.

Aldin, V., D. James and J. Wadsworth. 2010. 'The changing shares of migrant labour in different sectors and occupations in the UK economy: an overview'. In *Who Needs Migrant Workers? Labour Shortages, Immigration and Public Policy*, edited by M. Ruhs and B. Anderson. Oxford: Oxford University Press.

Alkire, S. and L. Chen. 2006. '"Medical exceptionalism" in international migration: Should doctors and nurses be treated differently?' In *Globalizing Migration Regimes*, edited by K. Tamas and J. Palme. Aldershot: Ashgate.

Aneesh, A. 2001. 'Rethinking migration: On-line labour flows from India to the United States'. In *The International Migration of the Highly Skilled*, edited by W. Cornelius, T. Espenshade and I. Salehyan. La Jolla: Centre for Comparative Immigration Studies, University of California, San Diego.

Anderson, B. 2007. *Battles in Time: The Relation between Global Labour and Mobilities*. Centre on Migration, Policy and Society Working Paper No. 55. Oxford: University of Oxford.

Anderson, B. 2010. 'Migration, immigration controls and the fashioning of precarious workers'. *Work, Employment & Society* 24: 300–317.

Antcliff, V., R. Saundry and M. Stuart. 2005. *Networks, Collectivism and Representation of Workers Interests: The Case of the UK Television Industry*. Paper presented at the 7th European Sociological Society Conference, Torun, Poland, September 2005.

Antcliff, V., R. Saundry and M. Stuart. 2007. 'Networks and social capital in the UK television industry: The weakness of weak ties'. *Human Relations* 60 (2): 371–393.

Barker, J. R. 1993. 'Tightening the iron cage: Concertive control in self-managing teams'. *Administrative Science Quarterly*: 408–437.

Barnard, C. 2009. '"British jobs for British Workers": The Lindsey oil refinery dispute and the future of local labour clauses in an integrated EU market'. *Industrial Law Journal* 38 (3): 245–277.

Barney, D. 2004. *The Network Society*. Cambridge: Polity Press.

Bauder, H. 2006. *Labour Movement: How Migration Regulates Labour Markets*. Oxford: Oxford University Press.

Bergvall-Kareborn, B. and D. Howcroft. 2013. '"The future's bright, the future's mobile": A study of Apple and Google mobile application developers'. *Work Employment and Society* 27 (6): 964–981.

Bloch, A. 2013. 'The labour market experiences and strategies of young undocumented migrants'. *Work Employment and Society* 27 (2): 272–287.

Bourdieu, P. 1984. *Distinction: A Social Critique of the Judgement of Taste*. Translated by R. Rice. Cambridge, MA: Harvard University Press.

Bourdieu, P. 1986. 'The forms of capital'. In *Handbook of Theory and Research for the Sociology of Education*, edited by J. Richardson. New York: Greenwood.

Boyd, M. 1989. 'Family and personal networks in international migration: Recent developments and new agendas'. *International Migration* 23 (3): 638–670.

Brettell, C. 2000. 'Theorizing migration in anthropology: The social construction of networks, identities, communities and globalscapes'. In *Migration Theory*, edited by C. Brettell and J. Hollifield. London: Routledge.

Bryman, A. 2008. *Social Research Methods*. 3rd edition. Oxford: Oxford University Press.

Burawoy, M. 1979. *Manufacturing Consent: Changes in the Labor Process Under Monopoly Capitalism*. Chicago: University of Chicago Press.

Casas-Cortes, M., S. Cobarriubias and J. Pickles. 2015. 'Riding routes and itinerant borders: autonomy of migration and border externalization'. *Antipode* 47 (4): 894–914. http://onlinelibrary.wiley.com/doi/10.1111/anti.12148/pdf (accessed 25 February 2016).

Castells, M. 1996. *The Rise of the Network Society: The Information Age. Economy, Society and Culture Vol. 1*. Oxford: Blackwell.

Castles, S. and M. J. Miller. 2009. *The Age of Migration: International Population Movements in the Modern World.* 4th edition. Basingstoke: Palgrave Macmillan.

Cerdine, J.-L., M. A. Dine and C. Brewster. 2014. 'Qualified immigrants' success: exploring the motivation to migrate and to integrate'. *Journal of International Business Studies* 45: 151–168.

Cerna, L. 2011. *Policy Primer: Selecting the Best and the Brightest*. Migration Observatory Policy Primer. Oxford: COMPAS, University of Oxford.

CIPD. 2005. *Quarterly Labour Market Outlook*. London: Chartered Institute of Personnel and Development.

Creswell, J. 2013. *Research Design: Qualitative, Quantitative, and Mixed Methods Approaches*. 4th edition. London: Sage.

Csedo, K. 2008. 'Negotiating skills in the global city: Hungarian and Romanian professionals and graduates in London'. *Journal of Ethnic and Migration Studies* 34 (5): 803–23.

De Genova, N. 2013. 'Spectacles of migrant "illegality": the scene of exclusion, the obscene of inclusion'. *Ethnic and Racial Studies* 36 (7): 1–19.

De Lima, P. and S. Wright. (2009) 'Welcoming migrants? Migrant labour in rural Scotland'. *Social Policy and Society* 8 (3): 391–404.

Dench, S., J. Hurstfield, D. Hill and K. Akroyd. 2006. *Employers' Use of Migrant Labour.* Home Office Online Report 04/06, London: Home Office.

Dumont, J-C., G. Spielvogel and S. Widmaier. 2010. *International Migrants in Developed, Emerging and Developing Countries: An extended profile*. OECD Social, Employment and Migration Working Papers No.114. Paris: OECD.

Easterby-Smith, M., R. Thorpe and P. Jackson. 2012. *Management Research.* 4th edition. London: Sage.

European Commission. 2015. *Flexicurity*. Brussels: European Commission, Directorate-General for Employment, Social Affairs and Inclusion. http://ec.europa.eu/social/main.jsp?catId=102 (accessed 25 February 2016).

European Union. 2004. *Facing the Challenge: The Lisbon Strategy for Growth and Employment.* Report from the High Level Group chaired by Wim Kok. http://ec.europa.eu/research/evaluations/pdf/archive/fp6-evidence-base/evaluation_studies_and_reports/evaluation_studies_and_reports_2004/the_lisbon_strategy_for_growth_and_employment__report_from_the_high_level_group.pdf (accessed 25 February 2016).

European Union. 2013. *Flexicurity in Europe.* Final Report. Brussels: European Commission, Directorate-General for Employment, Social Affairs and Inclusion.

Fitzgerald, I. 2007. *'Working in the UK'. Polish Migrant Workers Routes into Employment in the North East and North West Construction and Food Processing Sectors.* London: TUC.

Fitzgerald, I. and J. Hardy. 2009. '"Thinking outside the box"? Trade union organizing strategies and polish migrant workers in the United Kingdom'. *British Journal of Industrial Relations* 48 (1): 131–150.

Freeman, R. 2006. 'Labour market imbalances: shortages, or surpluses, or fish stories?' *Boston Federal Reserve Economic Conference, Global Imbalances – As Giants Evolve, Chatham Massachussetts*, June 2006. http://flash.lakeheadu.ca/~mshannon/freeman_global_labour_imbalances.pdf (accessed 25 February 2016).

French, J. and B. Raven. 1968. 'The bases of social power'. In *Group Dynamics*, edited by D. Cartwright and A. Zander, 256–269. New York: Harper & Row.

Fudge, J. 2011. *The Precarious Migrant Status and Precarious Employment: The Paradox of International Rights for Migrant Workers.* Metropolis British Columbia Centre of Excellence for Research on Immigration and Diversity Working Paper Series No. 11–15. https://www.isv.liu.se/remeso/konferenser-och-workshops/labour-rights-as-human-rights/proceedings/commissioned-papers/1.342814/JudyFudgePrecariousMigrantStatusandPrecariousEmployment.pdf (accessed 25 February 2016).

Grunell, M. and R. Van Het Kaar. 2003. Migration and Industrial Relations. European Industrial Relations Observatory On-Line (EIROnline). http://www.eurofound.europa.eu/eiro/2003/03/study/tn0303105s.htm (accessed 15 December 2012).

Guest, D. and M. Clinton. 2006. *Temporary Employment Contracts, Workers' Well-Being and Behaviour: Evidence from the UK.* Department of Management Working Paper No. 38, Kings College London. https://www.kcl.ac.uk/sspp/departments/management/research/papers/theme/hrm/hrm/temporary.pdf (accessed 25 February 2016).

Guo, C. and A. Al Ariss. 2015. 'Human resource management of international migrants: Current theories and future research'. *International Journal of Human Resource Management* 26: 1287–1297.

Healy, G., W. Brown and P. Heery. 2004. 'Inspiring union women – Black and minority ethnic women in trade unions'. In *The Future of Worker Representation*, edited by G. Healy, E. Heery, P. Taylor and W. Brown. London: Palgrave.

Healy, G., H. Bradley and N. Mukherjee N. 2004. 'Individualism and collectivism revisited: A study of black and minority ethnic women'. *Industrial Relations Journal* 35 (5): 451–466.

Healy, G. and F. Oikelome. 2007. 'Equality and diversity actors: A challenge to traditional industrial relations'. *Equal Opportunities International* 26 (1): 44–65.

Healy, G. and F. Oikelome. 2011. *Diversity, Ethnicity, Migration and Work: International perspectives*. Basingstoke: Palgrave Macmillan.

Heckscher, C. and F. Carre. 2006. 'Strength in networks: Employment rights organisations and the problem of co-ordination'. *British Journal of Industrial Relations* 44 (4): 605–628.

Heery, E. and C. Frege. 2006. 'New actors in industrial relations: Position and prospect'. *British Journal of Industrial Relations* 44 (4): 601–604.

Hopkins, L. and C. Levy. 2012. *Simply the Best? Highly-Skilled Migrants and the UK's Knowledge Economy*. London: The Big Innovation Centre.

International Labour Organisation. 2011. *From Precarious Work to Decent Work. Policies and Regulations to Combat Precarious Employment*. Geneva: ILO.

International Labour Organisation. 2012. *From Precarious Work to Decent Work: Outcome Document to the Workers' Symposium on Policies and Regulations to Combat Precarious Employment*. International Labour Office, Bureau for Workers' Activities. Geneva: ILO.

International Labour Organisation. 2014. *Labour Migration: Facts and Figures* (ILO Factsheet). Geneva: ILO.

International Organisation for Migration. 2013. *World Migration Report 2013: Migrant Well-Being and Development*. Geneva: IOM.

Kalleberg, A. 2009. 'Precarious Work, insecure workers: Employment relations in transition'. *American Sociological Review* 74 (1): 1–22.

Kearney, M. 1986. 'From the invisible hand to visible feet: Anthropological studies of migration and development'. *Annual Review of Anthropology* 15: 331–361.

King, N. 1998. 'Template analysis'. In *Qualitative Methods and Analysis in Organisational Research*, edited by G. Symons and C. Cassell. London: Sage.

Kirton, G. and A-M. Greene. 2010. *The Dynamics of Managing Diversity*. 3rd edition. Abingdon: Routledge.

Korczynski, M. 2002. *Human Resource Management in Service Work*. London: Palgrave Macmillan.

Koser, K. and J. Salt. 1997. 'The geography of highly skilled international migration'. *International Journal of Population Geography* 3: 285–303.

Lincoln, Y. and E. Guba. 1985. *Naturalistic Inquiry*. Newbury Park, CA: Sage Publications.

MacKenzie, R. and C. Forde. 2009. 'The rhetoric of good workers versus the realities of employers' use and the experiences of migrant workers'. *Work, Employment and Society* 23 (1): 142–159.

Martin, P. 2003. *Highly Skilled Labour Migration: Sharing the Benefits*. Geneva: ILO.

Martínez Lucio, M. and H. Connolly. 2010. 'Contextualising voice and stakeholders: Researching employment relations, immigration and trade unions'. *Journal of Business Ethics* 97: 19–29.

Martínez Lucio, M. and R. Perrett. 2009. 'The diversity and politics of trade union responses to minority ethnic and migrant workers: The context of the UK'. *Economic and Industrial Democracy* 30 (3): 324–347.

Martínez Lucio, M., R. Perrett, J. McBride and S. Craig. 2007. *Migrant Workers in the Labour Market the Role of Unions in the Recognition of Skills and Qualifications*. Research Paper 7, Unionlearn Research Series. London: Union Learn.

McDowell, L. and S. Christopherson. 2009. 'Transforming work: New forms of employment and their regulation'. *Cambridge Journal of Regions* 2 (3): 335–42.

McGovern, P. 2007. 'Immigration, labour markets and employment relations: Problems and prospects'. *British Journal of Industrial Relations* 45 (2): 217–235.

McGovern, P. 2012. 'Inequalities in the (de-)commodification of labour: Immigration, the nation state, and labour market stratification'. *Sociology Compass* 6 (6): 485–498.

McKay, S., S. Jefferys, A. Paraksevopoulou and J. Keles. 2012. *Study on Precarious Work and Social Rights Carried Out for the European Commission.* Final Report (VT/2010/084). London: Working Lives Research Institute, Faculty of Social Sciences and Humanities, London Metropolitan University.

McLaughlan, G. and J. Salt. 2002. *Migration Policies Towards Highly Skilled Foreign Workers.* Report to the Home Office. London: Migration Research Unit, University College London.

Migration Advisory Committee. 2009. *Analysis of the Points Based System: Tier 1.* London: Migration Advisory Committee.

Moulier-Boutang, Y. 1998. *De l'esclavage au salariat. Economie historique du salariat bride´.* Paris: Presses Universitaires de France.

Navarro, V. 2002. 'A critique of social capital'. *International Journal of Health Services* 32 (3): 423–432.

Organisation for Economic Cooperation and Development. 2007. *International Migration Outlook: Annual Report 2007.* Paris: OECD.

Papadopoulos, D. and V. Tsianos. 2013. 'After citizenship: Autonomy of migration, organisational ontology and mobile commons'. *Citizenship Studies* 17 (2): 178–196.

Poros, M. 2001. 'The role of migrant networks in linking local labour markets: The case of Asian Indian migration to New York and London'. *Global Networks* 1 (3): 243–259.

Portes, A. 1998. 'Social capital: Its origins and applications in modern sociology'. *Annual Review of Sociology* 24: 1–24.

Potter, M. and J. Hamilton. 2014. 'Picking on vulnerable migrants: Precarity and the mushroom industry in Northern Ireland'. *Work Employment and Society* 28 (3): 390–406.

Price, C. 1963. *Southern Europeans in Australia.* Melbourne: Oxford University Press.

Putnam, D. 2000. *Bowling Alone: The Collapse and Revival of American Community.* New York: Simon and Schuster.

Raghuram, P., L. Henry and J. Bornat. 2010. 'Difference and distinction? Non-migrant and migrant networks'. *Sociology* 44 (4): 623–641.

Rienzo, C. 2012. *Migrants in the UK Labour Market: An Overview.* Migration Observatory Briefing, COMPAS. University of Oxford.

Rienzo, C. and C. Vargas-Silva. 2014. *Highly Skilled Migration to the UK 2007–2013: Policy Changes, Financial Crises and a Possible 'Balloon Effect'?* Migration Observatory Report. Oxford: COMPAS, University of Oxford.

Rigby, M. and E. Sanchis. 2006. 'The concept of skill and its social construction'. *European Journal of Vocational Training* 37: 22–33.

Rodgers, G. and J. Rodgers, eds. 1989. *Precarious Jobs in Labour Market Regulation: The Growth of Atypical Employment in Western Europe*. Geneva: International Labour Organisation.

Rodriguez, N. 2004. '"Workers wanted": Employer recruitment of immigrant labour'. *Work and Occupations* 31 (4): 453–473.

Rubery, J. 2015. 'Change at work: Feminisation, flexibilisation, fragmentation and financialisation'. *Employee Relations* 37 (6): 633–644.

Ruhs, M. and B. Anderson. 2011. *Responding to Employers: Labour Shortages and Immigration Policy*. Migration Observatory Policy Primer. Oxford: COMPAS, University of Oxford.

Saunders, M., P. Lewis and A. Thornhill. 2009. *Research Methods for Business Students*. 5th edition. Harlow: FT Prentice Hall.

Shachar, A. 2006. 'The race for talent: Highly skilled migrants and competitive immigration regimes'. *New York University Law Review* 81: 148–206.

Simms, M. 2009. *United Kingdom: Flexicurity and Industrial Relations*. European Observatory of Working Life EurWORK. http://www.eurofound.europa.eu/observatories/eurwork/comparative-information/national-contributions/united-kingdom/united-kingdom-flexicurity-and-industrial-relations (accessed 25 February 2016).

Smith, C. 2010. 'Go with the flow: Labour power mobility and labour process theory'. In *Working Life: Renewing Labour Process Analysis*, edited by P. Thompson and C. Smith. Basingstoke: Palgrave Macmillan.

Squire, V. 2011. 'Politicising mobility'. In *The Contested Politics of Mobility: Borderzones and Irregularity*, edited by V. Squire. Routledge Advances in International Relations and Global Politics. Abingdon: Routledge.

Stahl, C. 1993. 'Explaining International Migration'. In *Global Population Movements and their Implications for Australia*, edited by C. Stahl, R. Ball, C. Inglis and P. Gutman. Canberra: Australian Government Publishing Service.

Standing, G. 2011. *The Precariat: The New Dangerous Class*. London: Bloomsbury Academic.

Steinberg, R. 1990. 'Social construction of skill gender, power, and comparable worth'. *Work and Occupations* 17: 449–482.

Sturdy, A., P. Fleming and R. Delbridge. 2010. 'Normative control and beyond in contemporary capitalism'. In *Working Life: Renewing Labour Process Analysis. Critical Perspectives on Work and Employment,* edited by P. Thompson and C. Smith, 113–135. Basingstoke: Palgrave Macmillan.

Tangian, A. 2007. *Is Flexible Work Precarious? A Study Based on the 4th European Survey of Working Conditions 2005*. Paper presented at the Conference of the European Foundation for the Improvement of Living and Working Conditions together with the Hans Bockler Foundation Flexicurity: Eine Perspektive fur flexible Arbeitsmarkte und soziale Sicherheit? Berlin, July 2007.

Thompson, P., K. Newsome and J. Commander. 2013. '"Good when they want to be": Migrant workers in the supermarket supply chain'. *Human Resource Management Journal* 23 (2): 129–143.

Tilly, C. 1990. 'Transplanted networks'. In *Immigration Reconsidered*, edited by Yans-V. Macloughlin. New York: Oxford University Press.

Tilly, C. 2011. 'The impact of the economic crisis on international migration: A review'. *Work, Employment and Society* 25 (4): 675–692.

UK Home Office. 2010. 'Highly skilled work for highly skilled migrants'. *UK Home Office News*, 27 October 2010. http://www.homeoffice.gov.uk/media-centre/news/migant-jobs (accessed 15 December 2012).

Uribe, C. 2014. 'The dark side of social capital re-examined from a policy analysis perspective: Networks of trust and corruption'. *Journal of Comparative Policy Analysis: Research Practice* 16 (2): 175–189.

United Nations. 2013. Population Facts (No. 2013/2). United Nations Department for Economic and Social Affairs Population Division. http://esa.un.org/unmigration/documents/The_number_of_international_migrants.pdf (accessed 25 February 2016).

Vertovec, S. 2002. *Transnational Networks and Skilled Labour Migration*. Paper presented at the Ladenburger Diskurs 'Migration' Gottleb Daimler- und Karl Benz-Stiftung, Ladenburg, February 2002.

Vertovec, S. and R. Cohen. 1999. 'Introduction'. In *Migration and Transnationalism*, edited by S. Vertovec and R. Cohen. Aldershot: Edward Elgar.

Viebrock, E. and J. Clasen. 2009. *Flexicurity – A state-of-the art review*. Working Papers on the Reconciliation of Work and Welfare in Europe REC-WP 01/2009. Edinburgh: RECWOWE Publication, Dissemination and Dialogue Centre.

Virdee, S. 2000. 'A Marxist critique of black radical theories of trade-union racism'. *Sociology* 34 (3): 545–565.

Vosko, L. 2006. *Precarious Employment: Understanding Labour Market Insecurity in Canada*. Montreal: McGill-Queen's Press.

Waddington, J. 1992. 'Trade Union Membership in Britain'. *British Journal of Industrial Relations* 30 (2): 287–324.

Williams, S., E. Heery and B. Abbott. 2011. 'The emerging regime of civil regulation in work and employment relations'. *Human Relations* 64 (7): 951–970.

Williams, S., B. Abbott and E. Heery. 2017. 'Civil governance in work and employment relations: How civil society organisations contribute to systems of labour governance'. *Journal of Business Ethics* 144 (1): 103–119. https://doi.org/10.1007/s10551-015-2812-0

Yin, R. 2009. *Case Study Research: Design and Methods*. 4th edition. London: Sage.

Conclusions

Olena Fedyuk and Paul Stewart

Located at the interdisciplinary intersection of migration studies and critical sociology of labour, this edited book focused on the overlap of work, employment and migration regimes with the intention of creating a more constructive debate on the forms of exclusion and inclusion of migrants in the EU. Drawing on the notion of the politics of mobility (Squire 2011) we sought to investigate processes in which both states, as policy defining bodies, and migrating individuals, as mobile individuals navigating often more than one state system, have political agency. Moreover, the chapters explored in various ways and registered how individuals and states collide and challenge each other in the world of work and migration. We sought to step beyond the archetypal social science debate of structure versus individuals to locate a collective politics of mobility emerging in migration practices, regulation and experience. Here we turned to the AoM perspective (Papadopoulos and Tsianos 2013; Casas-Cortes et al. 2015) that sees migratory flows as uncoordinated, apolitical, yet concerned with collective action. A starting point was to see migration as a social reality that despite its lack of internal organization powerfully challenges national attempts to manage migratory flows. However, as Section III (on collective responses) suggests, political positions often become central to drawing solidarity lines between migrants, workers and citizens. We conclude therefore that the importance of the political should not be underestimated.

Methodologically, the book goes beyond simple policy analysis or case study exploration but makes a vertical cut through what we describe as macro, micro and meso levels of the social reality of migration. The three sections of the book reflect this structure. They consequently investigate the political economy of regimes (Section I), place individual life stories in the latter (Section II), but also, again, imagine individual experiences in terms of possibility of collective struggles and search for alternatives (Section III). In Section I, the challenge was to set up a macro perspective illustrating the overlap between work and migration regimes bringing recent trends of both on to one plane, where they can be seen as mutually affected transformations. One of the central questions of this section was concerned with the nature of neoliberalism, that is, what is neoliberal about the ways in which employment and migration are structured and managed today. The main finding of all three chapters of Section I points out that we should pay closer attention to the repositioning of the role of the state in relation to capital and its citizens, including a closer exploration of the shifting principles of the citizen–state contract. Chapter I.1 (by James Woodcock) kicks off by painting a broad picture of the reconfiguration of the role of the state in managing employment regimes from the 1970s. The aim of the author's investigation is to show that through seeming liberalisation and withdrawal of the state from direct management of employment, it has effectively and powerfully sided with capital's interests, opening the way to a further deterioration in workers' rights. In so doing we can see that the state features more as an agent of the market economy than as a guarantor of citizens' rights.

Chapter I.2 (by Ben Egan) sets out to discuss what he describes as 'migrational institutional relations'. In so doing he poses several important conceptual questions: why does the migrant labour force, while increasingly incorporated side by side with the local labour force, and often in the same workplace, experience a gap in terms of remuneration, rights, provisions and recognition? Moreover, if we are to halt the fragmentation of the migrant labour force in terms of its use as a temporary, transitory state of exception to industrial relations, to what extent might we include it fully in the analysis of neoliberal changes to contemporary industrial relations? Finally, if we are to integrate migration into the institutional analysis of employment relations, what would these employment relationships look like? Egan articulates a similar finding to that in Chapter I.1, arguing that in a context in which bargaining between capital and labour is pushed into the domain of an individual worker's space for negotiation, migrant workers face a multiplication of barriers to access to social rights equal to those of other (non-migrant or different migrant status) workers. The final chapter, I.3, of the section (by Nina Sahraoui, Radosław Polkowski and Mateusz Karolak) takes this latter point in order to explore the character of the fragmentation of a migrant's status that allows for profound degradation of workers' rights. Here, the nature of the state–citizen contract returns to the centre of the debate. Specifically, by formally withdrawing its regulatory power, the state de facto sides with the interests of capital in such a way as to undermine the basis of a rights-based citizenship contract. With the description of these broader tendencies, the book moves on to explore the ways in which these changes translate into the experiences of mobile individuals, particularly at the sites of their employment per se or in relation to their particular experiences of employment as migrant workers.

An intriguing addition of the contributions in Section II to the burgeoning literature on how work is experienced by mobile populations is a focus on the ambiguous personal perception of migration as a social and personal opportunity for advancement despite frequent experiences of deskilling and downward employment mobility. All chapters indicate that migration (especially, though not only, in the case of internal EU mobility) is not merely an economic project but rather involves a complex system of personal and perceived gains and losses in the process. Thus, as highlighted in Chapter II.3 (by Karima Aziz), Polish women often see themselves as winners in migration, even while experiencing professional deskilling, insofar as their perception is based on the experience of liberation from suffocating gendered pressure in which marriage and raising a family are expectations which they leave behind in Poland. In their experience, migration represents a significant improvement by simply leading to material independence that allows them to carve space for their private lives on their own terms. Similar themes were echoed by respondents cited in Chapters II.1 (by Radosław Polkowski) and II.4 (by Mateusz Karolak). The former explored how mobility allows migrants to embody new ideals such as the development of a proactive, self-sustaining, flexible individual, who earns enough in order to purchase services, including health and social security. This ideal became a new ideological standard in the context of the neoliberal ideals of economic utility-based citizenship constructed in opposition to the state paternalism characteristic of Poland's socialist past.

In research by Polkowski (Chapter II.1) and Karolak (Chapter II.4), a failure to achieve the desired level of affluence, or an inability to meet the perceived standard of living and working conditions on the way to their dream, is often perceived by mobile individuals as a personal failure rather than a systemic problem. In such circumstances, individuals experience a sense of shame and apathy; collective action against tough working conditions or injustices is sorely missing. The chapter by Karolak speaks of similar mechanisms of individualization of employment and migration pathways, in search of the promised success under conditions of liberalization and the adoption of proactive individual positions. Moreover, Karolak argues that many mobile workers chose paths of repeat migration, or exit into self-employment rather than challenging the system with an attempt at collective action. In this context, Sahraoui's chapter, II.2, stands out as it addresses the experience of work in care homes in Greater London by non-EU and non-white workers. While the chapter details the ways in which race and migration status directly translate into division of work tasks, ability to negotiate hours and security behind employment contracts, it also speaks of migrants' coping strategies. Re-focusing on the acquired ability to help families back home or focusing on the temporariness of their employment in the care sector were cited as the most common strategies, despite the fact that most respondents were effectively trapped in care jobs as the only form of employment available to them.

Overall, Section II thus tackles what can be seen as the political apathy of migrating individuals: the neoliberal promise of self-reliance and flexibility, coupled with a complex system of fragmented rights granted on the basis of an individual's utility and contribution often turns mobile individuals into willing and faithful agents of this system (Ong 2006; Somers 2008). And yet, a mobile workforce presents an increasingly more visible and powerful challenge to the state's migration and employment deals with capital, which is visible in the increase of migrants' strikes across Europe in, for example, the logistics industry, the agriculture sector, as well as at border crossings and at the increasingly outsourced and privatized detention facilities. Section III of this book moves to various sites of such mobilizations, seeking to locate the nature of migrants' solidarities based upon the search for common ground on which collective responses might develop.

With our focus on work and employment, Section III opened with discussion of trade unions' responses to the migrant labour force, as the authors felt strongly that solidarity should arise from more traditional forms of workers' struggles. Chapter III.1 (by Karima Aziz, Radosław Polkowski and Ben Egan), which looked at selected cases of trade unions in Italy, Northern Ireland and the UK, however, indicated that the presence of migrant labour re-enforced dilemmas for unions' identity politics, with class, gender and race being at the core of the dilemmas. The following two chapters turned to the analysis of emerging solidarity movements in which migrants became a visible force and were able to articulate agendas relevant for mobile populations. Chapter III.2 (by Martin Lundsteen and Irene Sabaté) considered the case of the anti-repossessions movement PAH in Catalonia that emerged after the economic crisis that hit homeowners, many of whom where migrants previously encouraged to take loans and invest in housing as a successful integration model. The authors observed that the movement gained wide legitimacy since it consciously capitalized on inclusion of previously marginalized groups (including migrants and minorities); however, here, it fell short of genuinely overcoming those divisions. Thus, the authors concluded that bridging the gap between natives and foreigners is insufficient without tackling the divides of race and class already existing within both Catalan and migrant communities. Chapter III.3 (by Raia Apostolova) was a sharp critique of the ways in which the ideal of freedom of movement has been appropriated by EU politics and policies in order to create a de-based, unattached and docile, mobile labour force of posted workers and temporary agency workers. By examining the course and outcome of the struggles of Bulgarian day labourers in Munich and Romanian construction workers in Berlin, Apostolova argued that the very intra-European mobility that creates opportunities for workers' employment outside their national economies fragments their rights and capacity for collective bargaining to the degree that these workers often remained unpaid while working in substandard conditions fully within EU labour regulations. Apostolova attributes the failure of both campaigns (in Munich and Berlin) for fair payment to the workers' forced hypermobility. As both struggles picked up supporters and visibility, none of the workers could afford to stay to see it through to conclusion, eventually moving away to their next employment within the framework of European labour mobility.

Chapter III.4 (by Chibuzo Ejiogu) addressed the so-called high road of mobility – employment of high-skilled workers. He explored the national-based professional networks of Nigerian high-skilled workers in the UK considering the extent to which they provided solidarity and support against the insecurities of non-EU migrants' status or, on the contrary, embraced the legitimacy of the migrants' fragmented employment status seeking case-by-case situational relief for individuals. Ejiogu concluded that the position of these networks is 'complex and contradictory'. While they provided individual support, often they also subjected members to peer surveillance along stereotypical lines anticipating flexible, hard-working and obedient migrant professionals.

One of the initial challenges of the book was to remove the experience of mobile workers from the framework of migration per se, and focus on their role and inclusion or exclusion as workers. The book thus contributes to both established and more recent literature indicating the critical prominence of work and employment for migrants whatever their legal status (Sayad 2004; Wills et al. 2010; De Genova 2013). Abdalmalek Sayad, in his classic text *The suffering of the immigrant* (2004), argues that a migrant 'is also the only worker who, not being a citizen or a member of the social and political body (the nation) in which he is living, has no other function but work' (204). The research presented here demonstrates that while institutionally and socially migrants are often tolerated in the receiving states due to their ability to work, often individuals themselves see their ability to work as justifying their mobility (all chapters in Section II). Our book also highlighted the disparities in treatment, including the precarity, facing migrants in their mobility which cannot be attributed either to their migratory status alone or to their difference in origin to local, native workers. On all three levels (macroeconomic transformations of regimes, individual experiences of migration and collective responses) their difficulties are specifically situated within larger transformations: principally of labour and citizenship regimes affecting non-mobile workers and impacting them unevenly as a result of their class and gender.

The main findings of the book thus point to the fact that mere similarity in the experience of precarity within a broad and diverse body of mobile individuals, and increasingly among migrants and non-migrant workers, is not enough for a collective response to increasingly precarious employment. Collective responses remain limited due to the persistence of class, gender and ethnic divisions, which create hierarchies among precarious workers wherever they are. Another important finding of this book was the role played by neoliberal ideologies in workforce governance. These ideologies, and in particular those promoting the ideal of the self-sustaining individual, a client of the state who can earn and purchase state services, in addition to the idea of free movement, as an ultimate means of achieving such ideals, are criticized in several chapters (Chapters III.3, II.4 and II.1). Crucially, these are understood as ways of thinking that hinder solidarity and collective struggle.

With these conclusions, we felt that it was important to encourage the authors to articulate their position on these main findings beyond the format and scope of their individual and collective chapters. Our research has highlighted the fact that an experience of common oppression does not automatically lead to emerging solidarities, though certainly an active political position does. To explore the nature of the relationship between migration and political engagement, we organized a two-day workshop on the findings of the book. The workshop was premised on the possibility of exploring the political dynamics of the relationship between migrants' experiences, political economy and collective action(s). Due to its methodological specificity, we decided to include this discussion as a transcript of the round-table debate that took place at the end of the workshop. The format of the final chapter presented here, while not exactly traditional for a publication of this type, nevertheless is intriguing in that it allowed space for articulating more politically engaged opinions and conclusions by the authors and several external readers who were participants in the debate. For us, as editors, it was an important means by which we were able to consider a range of political and academic perspectives beyond the usual protocol requiring disciplinary rigidity. We also see it as a starting point for drawing lessons from the cases elaborated in the book and a chance to speak to an audience of activists more directly. While in some respects these findings bring us back to the classical struggles of the last several centuries, we see this book as making an important and timely contribution given the political climate of the so-called European migration crisis, which includes a rising intolerance of mobile people around the globe.

REFERENCES

Casas-Cortes, M., S. Cobarriubias and J. Pickles. 2015. 'Riding routes and itinerant borders: Autonomy of migration and border externalization'. *Antipode*, Early View (online version of record published before inclusion in an issue), http://onlinelibrary.wiley.com/doi/10.1111/anti.12148/pdf (accessed 19 December 2015).

Ong, A. 2006. *Neoliberalism as Exception: Mutations in Citizenship and Sovereignty*. Durham, NC: Duke University Press.

Papadopoulos, D. and V. Tsianos. 2013. 'After citizenship: Autonomy of migration, organisational ontology, and mobile commons'. *Citizenship Studies* 17 (2): 178–196.

Sayad, A. 2004. *The Suffering of the Immigrant*. Blackwell, Cambridge: UK Polity Press.

Somers, M. 2008. *Geneaologies of Citizenship: Knowledge, Markets, and the Right to Have Rights*. Cambridge: Cambridge University Press.

Squire, V. 2011. 'Politicising mobility'. In *The Contested Politics of Mobility: Borderzones and Irregularity*, edited by Vicki Squire, 1–16. Routledge Advances in International Relations and Global Politics. Abingdon: Routledge.

Round-Table Debate

Is Collective Response from a Mobile Workforce Possible? In Search of New Analytical Paradigms

Olena Fedyuk and Paul Stewart

This book appears during a period in which, we argue, migration has been picked up by political elites across the EU to mask the crisis of democratic accountability and capital accumulation as well as a moment of precarity experienced by a progressively growing population across class and social status. We see the 'migration crisis', which most prominently captured the public imagination of 2015 in Europe, as a critical moment punctuated by various events related to, and including, migration, but also as a time of political unrest related to new and emerging structures of inclusion and exclusion for both mobile and non-mobile people.

This chapter aims to tackle these shifting forms of inclusion and exclusion in a contextualised but nuanced manner. It is based on a transcript of a round-table debate that gathered many contributors of this book and some external readers in an intensive two-day long workshop dedicated to collective writing. We aimed to create a common paradigm beyond the authors' individual contributions. In doing so – in addition to concluding our book with a section dedicated to collective response (Section III) – we also wanted to make a methodological point about the importance of face-to-face dialogue and the collective production of knowledge. Each contribution to the book was peer reviewed by other contributing authors and three invited external readers. Our external readers were Marek Čaněk (Multicultural Centre Prague NGO, Prague), Frances Pine (Goldsmith's University College, London) and Francesca Alice Vianello (University of Padova). The following text is the edited version of the discussion around the themes, as well as political positions of the authors and an attempt to collectively map out further research directions and critical interventions.[1]

18 OCTOBER 2015, ROSS PRIORY, SCOTLAND

Olena Fedyuk (moderator): Welcome all to the round-table debate 'Inclusion and exclusion in Europe: migration, work and employment perspectives'. In the following hour we hope to discuss some of the common themes arising from this edited book. In particular, I want us to focus on finding more critical and productive paradigms to explore the potential for collective struggles to emerge from the overlap of the experiences of migration and precarisation of working lives. We can start by speaking about some of the issues that you found interesting or innovative in this book and move on to some of the remaining puzzles and questions.

Marek Čaněk: One point I would like to make that connects many of contributions in this book is the definition of citizenship and precarious work 'here' and 'there' [as in home country and migration country]. I think it was exemplified in Chapter II.4, by Mateusz Karolak, and also in Chapter II.1 by Radosław Polkowski where you have competing understandings of mostly neoliberal citizenship in Poland and then in the UK. These readings are mostly from the perspective of work, but also larger social and family concerns. Then from these chapters you then go into Section III, where you deal with the protests and reactions of the trade unions and other organisations. The big question for me to the authors is the issue of equality and common interest; and how, out of these different contexts of very temporary kinds of migrations and different understandings, emerges a shared interest of the workers? Dealing with this question for me is the main contribution of the book. The second is the larger picture of EU citizenship. I find it important that though most of chapters deal with intra-EU migration, where there is no longer a question of migration control and migration policies, you maintain a migration framework, emphasising the inequalities that separate new EU citizens from more established EU members. To me, it becomes not so much a matter of citizenship but a question of poverty migration.

Frances Pine: One of the things that is really interesting to me about this book is the way that you've structured it into three parts. You've got the methodological section at the beginning which involves quite a lot of sophisticated conceptual problems, which all authors keep linking back to the more local and ethnographic material in the later sections. Then you've got this very detailed ethnographic work in the middle that really feeds back into the first section. Then the one that looks at the collective; I think that that tripartite organisation makes the book very interesting and innovative. One of the things that you are all doing, all the way through, is looking at quite a meta-level of analysis of locating problems, trying to grapple with concepts and the theory while dealing with some qualitative data. Because you have this very detailed ethnographic work on people who are moving around or living migrant lives in one place, you are continually having to move backwards and forwards between all three levels. The things that are coming up very frequently are concepts around structure and agency or the local and global. These seem to me still to be the most difficult and challenging conceptual problems in social science.

Francesca Alice Vianello: What is present in the background of many chapters is the co-existence between the intra-EU migrations and the extra-EU migrations [in the EU space]. It is a very tricky but at the same time a very important point. If we don't deal with this issue, it will be very difficult to think about citizenship in the first place. The difference and inequality between people that have the freedom to move, for me, the main characteristic of the EU citizenship, and those who start from basic restriction to enter EU makes a basic division among the workers. In order to discuss inclusion and exclusion of migrant workers, it is very important to find a way to deal with simultaneous presence of these two kinds of migrant workers within the same economic space. It is important also because it allows us to better understand the relation between international migrations and capitalism. How these two kinds of migrations fit within the EU economic space, for instance, how the companies, the entrepreneurs use differently these two kinds of labour migrants. Ones the new citizens, as we see in Chapter III.3, by Raia Apostolova, they can move and leave and find another work, go back to their original or other country. The others are much more immobilised and fixed in one place or if they can move it is with much more difficulties. It is a central point.

There are two other red lines running through the book. They are the links between the transformations of employment relations, specifically the preacarisation, and flexibilisation of workers' and migrant workers' employment. These we have to understand – as was already told by Marek – in connection to what is happening in migrants' original countries, because the process of precarisation of workers is taking place in both sending and receiving places. This is connected to the third red line, that is migrant activities and unionisation, which also have to be framed within the transnational perspective. Particularly for the EU migrant workers, who move a lot between the two spaces and different regimes of employment if they experience more unionisation in – say London or in Paris, as discussed in this book – maybe they will continue to be active and organised in other contexts and places. Those migrants that have the experience of activism in their original country, when they go abroad they seem to continue to be active. I think that it is very interesting how you manage to synthesise these different issues in the different sections of the book; the transnationalism, the existence of different kinds of citizens with the different kinds of freedoms to move and the transformation of employment relations in different EU contexts.

Radosław Polkowski: To follow up on Francesca's comment, the division between the EU and non-EU migrant seems to be a very important line dividing solidarities. But there are also serious implications for the European citizenship, as the latter emerges as a kind of failed promise for many EU citizens as well. Just as we show in Chapter I.3, new EU members can enjoy EU citizenship, but it is contingent and migrants can lose it in a moment, as we have seen in case of Roma people. One problem is that European citizenship is so much tied to the notion of productive activity of waged labour. Then add to this the dimension of the national citizenship and different value, so to say, of the national citizenships within the EU that have further implications, not least in terms of gender, and we then get to Francesca's earlier point that the only benefit mobile people get from the EU citizenship is their toleration of being in the territory of the other state but limited opportunity to exercise rights, participate in the society and so on. All this speaks of fracturing within EU citizenship. These points make 'citizenship' a complex terrain with various fragmentations and aspects to consider.

Karima Aziz: To pick up on the point Radosław just raised about the gendered dimension of citizenship – in terms of European citizenship there is of course the explicit exclusion of all non-EU citizens, but also a more implicit inclusion–exclusion based in the gendered division of work. This is rooted in the construction of the ideal citizen as an economically 'useful' or productive man. Parallel to this the European citizenship is more about the free movement of labour than of people. The separation of public and private spheres and the under-valued gendered caring responsibilities can then lead to a form of exclusion. Gendered expectations can then inhibit migrant women in using their European citizenship rights as well as in accessing them. However, among the non-migrant population tendencies of granting full rights only to the 'good' citizens can also cause this inequality for women.

Paul Stewart: So we need to keep asking what is of importance for our inquiry. For me, it is about concretising around the social aspect of labour as a form of capital, really. Our inquiry makes sense to me as a way of looking at neoliberal processes today. 'Neoliberal' is often used in a very incoherent manner these days; it could mean anything you want it to be. The way I would see migration is a specific example of pinpointing that; it is citizenship today that is being challenged. If you took migration out of the period, just since 2004 citizenship has been eroded, been assaulted all the time. We don't even need to talk about migration, talk about changes within the British political class, assaulting peoples' citizenship rights, and it's already been mooted, that people who don't work shouldn't be allowed to vote. In the north of Ireland, there was something a little bit like that for fifty years. It wasn't if you didn't work, you couldn't vote but if you didn't work, you couldn't have a house and if you didn't have a house, you couldn't vote in the local elections. In the contemporary environment you can see citizenship becoming a problem. You have to add into that people coming from outside the particular polity and then you can see labour, their position as people working, as part of that change in society including our economy. I think we can still talk about the AoM but maybe be a little bit different and talk about the *relative* AoM. We can certainly talk about the interaction of migrant experience in the context of the changing political economy.

Frances Pine: I wanted to raise an issue around diversity. I think that obviously there are all sorts of real, grounded differences between people outside the EU and people within the EU in terms of movement and borders and what possibilities you have. But what is really important here is to point out that EU membership at the moment is creating a kind of double- or triple-tiered system. We've got a lot of people who are from the former socialist states and are very much excluded from the rights that nationals have. We need partly to look at the difference in the original EU countries' policies and policies of benefit, policies of access to movement, housing, education, health and length of stay. We need to look at how people from the different periods of accession are treated, what kinds of possibilities they have. On the one hand, particularly because of the current refugee crisis, it is incredibly important to say there is a difference between people who are coming in with no EU rights and people who have EU rights. I think that hides myriad differences and hidden exclusions which it is important to pay attention to. That leads to a critique of each member state's internal economy and how it is being managed. I think in the way it came out in some of the chapters, that also feeds back to the way that people who are part of local populations are also being excluded on the basis of non-deservingness or non-compliance or different kinds of being, different ways of being less than would-be citizens. Those are things that are very easy to hide if we go for the big binaries.

Nina Sahraoui: My comment follows what Frances was saying. As much as this dual, external–internal boundary is important, we do need to nuance it. I would argue that we need to relate it to racialisation processes. After some time many non-EU migrants might apply for an EU citizenship in the country they reside. Some of them will obtain a European citizenship but it doesn't mean that it is going to solve all the problems so that's why we need to relate it to racialisation processes and to the concept of temporal border.

For example, part of the CEE migrants won't apply for European citizenship because they are within the EU and maybe that's not part of their long-term plan to apply for, let's say, French or British citizenship. As EU citizens and migrants, they will nevertheless find themselves in a different position as compared to non-EU migrants who accessed the citizenship of the country they reside in, for instance, France or the UK. So, we also need to be attentive to how some initial differences between various group of migrants, that serve to construct categories, evolve with time. This exclusion on the basis of national citizenship is not only about the legal and administrative dimensions because citizenship legislations enact divisions that have long-lasting effects and affect migrants in differentiated ways beyond the legal dimension.

Karima Aziz: This post-enlargement migration, however, is still a rather new phenomenon and precarious in its conditions. In my fieldwork I actually found that many Polish women I talked to were either considering or had already got active in applying for UK citizenship, if not for themselves, then at least for their children. With the EU in constant crisis talks and the threat of a 'Brexit' lurking around the corner, many migrants will try to stabilise their status and avoid future loss of rights.

Jamie Woodcock: I wanted to follow up a little bit on what Paul was saying because, for me, the central contradiction identified in the book is about how we understand Europe as a political and economic project. In the post-2008 crisis period, what we have with so many of the contradictions of the Eurozone coming to the fore, the relationships between the core and periphery or, various peripheries in Europe and southern Europe. The project of German capital accumulation driving the European project to the point of potential collapse with particular countries thinking about leaving and so on. The understanding of migration within that is the challenge we have in a sense, and this is something that will become, I think, more and more live as Britain comes closer to a referendum on Europe. So, what is the basis of Europe? We can see two things emerging from it; there is a Europe from above – a project of allowing free movement inside for the needs of capital, of allowing particular export-driven markets to benefit. We also have a Europe from below: a sense of European community of shared values, people should be able to travel and settle in different places. What's important about this book is we lay out the framework at the beginning of how you operate and particularly the different constructions of Fortress Europe and how these things work out in practice. The way that the AoM comes up in this, I think, is very useful. To say that actually, despite what we see in the media in the moment, that is, people's hardships trying to enter EU, in a way that flow of migration shapes Europe as the potential corrective to some of the more elite projects and a hope for European project from below. Working these things out in practice is both empirically and academically important but also a very important political dimension will be worked out over the next months and years.

Olena Fedyuk (moderator): What seems to be really coming up in all of these discussions is the issue of various levels and degrees of fragmentation. We keep talking about fragmentation of statuses and citizenship, roles and rights. What the third section of this book is asking is where do we go from here? In particular, the question of solidarity. We often use 'solidarity' as based on common identities but maybe it's time to move on beyond understanding solidarity as identity based but think in a more post-colonial way as solidarity based on the experience of common oppressions rather than common identities. I think this is the main struggle that we see in Chapter III.1 and the struggles that trade unions face. This is the hope that we see in other movements, such as anti-eviction, anti-austerity movements that we see rising up. Frances mentioned the notion of precariat, which also pops up a few times in our book. Despite all this fragmentation, can we talk about the struggle of migrants as a class struggle? Can we talk about this as the solidarities that a migrant can build with another migrant despite the diversity of their mobility, goals and aspirations? If it is not a class struggle, then what is the nature of this struggle emerging? What type of emergent solidarities are they and how are they possible? Maybe we can brainstorm a bit around these questions.

Mateusz Karolak: When we look at some research or media that speaks of the fears that the 'non-migrant' people voice, we can say they are basically scared of turning into 'migrants in their own country'. This is particularly strongly linked to the situation on the labour market, let's say, the precariousness of their working lives. The fear is the same across the migrant/ non-migrant divide, so I think the solidarity should not be among migrants exclusively but spill out to the native workers. Importantly, when we say 'migrants' we don't think about the cosmopolitan class of financiers, traders or even international researchers, who also travel around the world, but they are also migrants. Maybe it is more productive to look for solidarity around common economic interest rather than identity – in this case understood simply as being migrant. An exploited member of British working class has more in common – in terms of interest – with a vulnerable Polish migrant than with a banker in the City of London and it doesn't matter if the latter is migrant or not. I think that the class struggle perspective makes more sense for solidarity. Maybe we should try not to essentialise migration as a process but look at the economic conditions of what accompanies it.

Now going back to citizenship and this change that the citizenship is linked directly to one's ability to exercise work which is narrowly understood only as a paid work, mainly employment or self-employment. Following on what Jamie said – that migrants can be seen as a potential for the Europe-from-below project – there is one point which I find quite puzzling; that is, that migrants themselves are the guardians of many neoliberal values. Migration might be a potential for upcoming struggles and solidarity but when we look into our fieldwork and when we talk to people then it emerges, and it shows really well in Radosław's chapter, that intra-EU migrants often self-exploit in attempt to fully comply with neoliberal values. The question for me, and I don't know how to answer it, is linked to the process of creating the subjectivity. Many – if not the majority of – migrants tend to adjust and in practice realise those values that somehow undermine the potential for the struggle. While there are groups of migrants who do want to struggle, who want to fight, there are many of those who do not. The question is how can such struggle be organised?

Jamie Woodcock: Can I say something very quickly on that? I think, particularly the research on CEE migrants was fascinating in the book. I don't want to project a political subjectivity on to people without having very empirical evidence to hand, but you have a number of failed revolutions across the world with which you have people then fleeing these situations. They've already been through a process of political struggle. I think we've already seen there has been some research in Italy on people from North Africa becoming involved in struggles in logistics. You can hear in the cadence of the chants on the demonstrations the echoes of anti-government protests elsewhere. I think, while it's certainly true that it's not an automatic thing, we are already starting to see some of those ripples of previous struggles re-emerge inside the European context which I think is very exciting.

Paul Stewart: The complexity is bewildering, isn't it? Just as the border is being pushed out of the EU, beyond the EU, now the borders rise within the fleeing migrant communities, as in both 'real' and 'non-real' Syrians. We shouldn't be idealising people fleeing or people in oppression. The split within stigmatised groups is very common, so to say, 'I am Syrian but I am OK but she isn't and she is potential security risk'. It's about essentialising: 'You're Polish or Irish or Lithuanian but it's not you that thinks you're a Paddy, it's the others'.

Frances Pine: I think it's really important to unpack continually the categories that we might think are contained. If you look at the research on different waves of migration, and the ones I know best are from the former Soviet states or eastern Europe, you have people who came before or immediately after the Second World War and then people who were new wave, at different times of political crises and then post-1989. The way that earlier migrants closed ranks and said 'these people who are coming in now, they are the wrong kinds of people. We've made a community here'. These are discords that are coming up in your research too in this book. Rather than assuming that there is such a thing as a Pole migrating to the UK or the Russian migrant in France, you've got these very split communities where people are establishing boundaries, partly to keep other people out.

Francesca Alice Vianello: What I think is really puzzling for me, that if I think about Italy and migrant struggles in Italy, it seems to me that non-EU migrants are struggling much more and are more conflicted than intra-EU migrants in Italy. They are more involved in the unions, they are more involved in different kinds of political groups or migrant organisations fighting for better working conditions. Let's think about the experiences of migrant organisations in Southern Italy, among African tomato pickers. Or for example, in the logistics sector, where non-EU migrants from Morocco are very active. On the other side intra-EU migrants – I don't know why, and it is a lot of time that I am thinking about it – are less conflicted. They are less involved in struggles, maybe because they can leave. They think that if there is no work here, they can go to Germany, 'I can go to the UK where there are better work conditions, better wages', and so on. This question is very connected with Chapter III.3, by Raia Apostolova, in this book. What is the impact of mobility on migrant workers' struggles or capacity to organise themselves and carry on struggles for a medium or long period of time? I think that this issue is connected also with the problem of the political subjectivity of migrant workers so the question is: 'In what conditions does this political subjectivity take shape and in what place?' What are the spaces of solidarity among migrant workers? I am thinking in a group of Latin American women[2] [Territorio Domestico, Madrid] that are very active in fighting and struggling for better work conditions in the domestic and care sector. While in Italy domestic workers, who are mainly European women (EU citizens and non-EU citizens), are not very active in claiming more rights. The women from Territorio Domestico are not EU citizens – they are coming from very different contexts, on the other side of the ocean – but they are much more active than EU citizens that are working in the care domestic sector in Italy or in other European countries. I don't know, it is my puzzle and I don't know how to deal with it.

Mateusz Karolak: Let's go back to Chapter II.1, by Radosław, because I think it might shed some light on your question. There is a stream of literature about the way in which members of post-socialist societies have internalised the so-called capitalist values.[3] In a nutshell, after the transformation of the Socialist Block system in the early 1990s, the reliance on the state has been linked ideologically to being *Homo Sovieticus* and only those who can maintain themselves by their own work and salary can feel as a 'proper man of the twenty-first century'. My hypothesis is that this hyper-neoliberal development was caused by the shock therapy, both in economy and in ideology and it is still so much internalised and embedded in central Eastern European workers that they tend to accept it without resistance. There is no obvious pressure for that but they do bring an idea of a self-dependent man wherever they go. And of course, the possibility to leave and move on to another place is also contributing to the weakening of the need to struggle.

Francesca Alice Vianello: About this, I think that in the next years it will be interesting what happens with the new waves with internal migrations from Southern Europe, from Spain, Italy and Greece. These new internal migrants, what kind of value and what kind of political activity will they have?

Nina Sahraoui: It also made me think about the trans-locational positionality of migrants, notably along the lines of what Floya Anthias wrote on this topic. As we all need to make sense of our own lives and stories, very often listening to migrants' narratives we hear very positive stories. Even in the case of downward mobility on the labour market or for domestic workers in live-in caring arrangements, they will often say, 'I'm actually really lucky because I don't even have to pay for rent and I can send money back home'. I know it doesn't mean that there is no problem, but maybe that is also something that we need to take into account when we think about how people get mobilised and what are the struggles that can mobilise them? The frame of reference that people go back to, at least for a certain period of time, is mainly the country of origin and not the country of destination.

Olena Fedyuk (moderator): We had this discussion with Frances quite a lot. We need to be aware that, in a way, what we study is always a successful migration. As researchers of migration, we need to look at the failures to migrate. I think Chapter II.4, by Mateusz, goes to the very heart of the categories of who is a migrant and when do you start or stop being one, when he talks about the returnees and re-migrants. Maybe among people with that experience we can find more critical perspectives.

Radosław Polkowski: To follow up on what Nina and Olena said, I'd like to add that every migration story which on the surface appears or is narrated as a success story is in fact often haunted by some form of hidden injuries which subvert the apparent success narrative. This is what I try to show in my chapter [Chapter II.1] when I speak of, for example, the sense of shame and fear of social failure. I think these experiences are maybe one of the factors that can bring people together. Guy Standing[4] talks about the shared emotional sense of failure and anger of what he calls the precariat and I think it is useful to look at such lived experiences of migrants I think the problem is that these feelings or these emotions can give rise to some disapproval of the situation and can be easily manipulated into a wrong direction, maybe towards right-wing movements, for instance.

Olena Fedyuk (moderator): I think it is a very important point; shame is a feeling that is very difficult to build solidarity around. It is a possibility of giving somebody dignity or giving somebody pride, this is what the right-wing is often based on; so, to say, 'even if you are downtrodden you still have the national, you have to remember the history of your ancestors and who you are'. It seems that the experienced commonalities in the ways of exploitation do not necessarily lead to the rise of solidarity or to the movements of response. We've been talking about the necessity of rethinking activating class struggles as one of the ways. What is coming out in our discussion of this book is reactivating of a class struggle, re-drawing the boundaries of that.

Radosław Polkowski: Yes, on the one hand, you have nationalist pride but, on the other, many other social movements, Gay Pride, Black Pride, Mad Pride have developed ways of working with feelings of shame and pride to build solidarity and mobilise people.

Frances Pine: When you have these kinds of exclusion it goes back to your discussion of Bridget Anderson. If we take the UK context, for instance, you've got people who are long-term, several generation unemployed, who live on the same estates and who are viewed as 'the shameless'. In some ways they are more excluded than people who come in as migrants but are considered to hold pride in what they do. I think that that becomes more and more a forgotten category; that if we are talking about considerations of class, we have to consider what happens to the people who are pushed out, and though I hate the concept of underclass, I think that the ideas behind it are the ideas that are being used to stigmatise and exclude those categories of people and to keep them out of any discussion in a way.

Ben Egan: Is that not because of the legitimisation? You were saying about the different types of pride. It's because they have become legitimised in a kind of public shaming discourse. Just thinking about Francesca's question, about why is it that people with more to lose, if you like, are more active in social movements. I think part of that is because of a breakdown of any kind of coordination from the trade unions or from other bodies within society. In Italy, you have seen several amnesties for undocumented workers since the 1980s which you've never seen the likes of in Britain. I think each and every one of those campaigns, even if it doesn't directly give the apparatus for the next campaign, it creates a sense of what's legitimate in society and what's not. For example, the idea of 'because it's chavs' in the UK, it's legitimate to stigmatise those defined by this term. It reminds me of the first week in the university. I got there and I found it bizarre that there are so few working-class people on university campus. On the first week there was a Chavs Party where loads of upper-middle-class people put on tracksuit bottoms and pretend that they were unemployed. It was a fancy dress thing. You wouldn't be able to do that for any other group.

Frances Pine: It's insignificant in a way. It becomes a caricature.

Ben Egan: That is true of class discussions generally. Only among Marxists and academics do you really talk about class because, even at trade union meetings, it's the delegitimised subject to discuss. If you look at anything the trade unions will say, they will say 'working people', they don't say 'working class' because it's no longer a legitimate thing to discuss.

Olena Fedyuk (moderator): I wanted to follow up on Francesca's question, more on the need to historicise some of these processes and also on the paradoxical way in which ideologies use certain rhetoric. Mateusz was talking about the neoliberal citizen who only can legitimise her or his existence by contributing and being active in economic sense, so to say. It just came to my mind from the onset of the Soviet state, one of the main slogans of the Soviet state was 'Those who don't work, don't eat'. We talked today about the *Homo Sovieticus* as being opposite to the proactive neoliberal citizen. It is very interesting because actually the Soviet state was promoting a very similar idea; you had to work even if you were not really effective but you absolutely had to work, in order to be a deserving citizen. The question is: What is neoliberal about the specific conditions that we see now? When we talk about work, I think we have a much clearer understanding; it is linked to precariousness, to being lean and all that. When we talk about citizenship, what is it that is new that is emerging out of this?

Mateusz Karolak: The self-entrepreneur is the new man the neoliberal hegemony is expecting to have. That other slogan in the Soviet times was 'Everyone contributes as much as they can but everyone gets as much as they need'. Nobody will say that the Soviet Union was actually implementing that. In many ways it was simply another way of keeping monopoly held by the state, and party bureaucracy which was a privileged class.

Frances Pine: The ideology behind the period of the Soviet state was that labour establishes the values of the person. You realise your value through labour and labour gives you entitlement. Without labouring you are no longer a social person in a way and you are no longer an entitled person.

Mateusz Karolak: That is actually the basis of Marx's assumption that you became a human through work but it doesn't necessarily mean paid labour.

Frances Pine: The values change to monetary values.

Mateusz Karolak: Nowadays work is understood narrowly only as paid labour which excludes reproductive labour, or unpaid labour. When we were discussing these as lines for potential mobilisation and I thought: 'Can precariat be useful for mobilising?' I see a big problem here because when we say about Gay Pride, Black Pride and so on, could precariat be proud? People in precarious work, they don't want to be precarious, they don't want to have these insecure jobs. To be proud in this case would be to legitimise the situation.

We need to think about what value we could mobilise, not only for migrants but for various other exploited workers. We often forget that different migrant groups are played off against one another. I can see it in my research that intra-EU, Polish and Central Eastern European migrants in the UK, they often express racist views, especially about non-EU migrants. They became racists by moving to the UK. That is something that was striking and that is something that we need to understand because they play with the anger against other exploited groups.

Frances Pine: If you are going to talk about unity and grounds for emerging solidarity, you've got to talk about divisions. If you don't talk about them, you're papering over things because they are the main obstacles for creating solidarity.

Olena Fedyuk (moderator): We open the book with a quote from Papadopoulos and Tsianos[5] (2013: 187): 'The spectre of migration will never become a new working class'. It's about what Mateusz says about finding common interest, and I wonder, can there really be a common interest in migration? What can it be, if not essentially dismantling the nation states and their borders? In this way, intra-EU mobility really stands out in the sense that that has been achieved and yet we see all the other many fragmentations within it in many other ways. What can be the common interest for mobile workers? Maybe gaining the same level of freedom for mobility as that enjoyed by capital globally?

Mateusz Karolak: Exactly. Among migrants there are those who exploit and those who are exploited. They have different interests. I would draw rather the conflict line between classes and I put it really simply that on one side are those who exploit and on the other those who are exploited. Migrants could find themselves in one or in the second group.

Nina Sahraoui: I would like to add a consideration about how we can mobilise around precarious employment. We have mentioned Standing earlier, who has a list of criteria of how we can define precarious employment. What comes out from my interviews is that the notion of precariousness is something very difficult to grasp. I think it was in your chapter, Mateusz, I remember writing on the margins of a quote you give, that it's about a subjective understanding of stability. In my interviews this perception of stability was not connected at all to the type of contract that respondents held. It's not enough to have a figure about the share of atypical contracts in the labour market to measure the extent of precarious employment, the meanings that are attached to such indicators are fundamental in order to understand who is affected by precarious employment and what these experiences are. This, I think, relates to the question of subjectivities and that's why Radosław's chapter is crucial to shed light on these dynamics. In some of the interviews I conducted, the idea of not relying on anyone was a source of pride and collective action or organisation was perceived in negative terms. If people had very different perceptions around precarious employment and its causes, what would be their common interests after all? If people who find themselves in exploitative relationships derive a sense of pride from the fact that 'they have made it' I think it illustrates that there is no easily identifiable common interest in migration. In relation to the nation state and borders, for example, several works within diaspora studies argue how diasporas contribute to reinforcing the narrative of the nation state; they do not work towards the cosmopolitan idea of the global world but rather contribute to strengthening national divides. So, are we in a dead end?

Mateusz Karolak: If I can answer Nina. The question is the trick about the migration narratives; we need to ask how those narrations are constructed and from what resources and what are the discursive ways of talking about something. The first layer are the discourses which are internalised and help create subjectivity. What could be the answer to a situation of migration? To start with a new language, new narrations, upon which individuals can also draw and through which they can see their situation and explain it in different ways, not the one which is imposed by the mainstream and the ruling discourse. Maybe that could be the first step, to have a new common language to speak about migration, exploitation, and so on. I think it's necessary to have a common struggle for a new narration which will be opposite to the dominant one in common discussion. However, it shouldn't be researchers who come in and say, 'Oh listen, you can look at your situation from this perspective'. It should be a grassroots movement that encourages it.

Olena Fedyuk (moderator): And that's what we explore in detail in the Section III of this book. Thank you very much everyone for your thoughts and discussion.

NOTES

1. Participants of the round-table debate (in the order of speaking): Olena Fedyuk, Marek Čaněk, Frances Pine, Francesca Alice Vianello, Radosław Polkowski, Karima Aziz, Paul Stewart, Nina Sahraoui, Jamie Woodcock, Mateusz Karolak and Ben Egan.
2. A blog entry by Nina Sahraoui about 'Territorio Domestico' at *Changing-Employment Blog*, http://www.changingemployment.eu/Blog/ViewPost/tabid/3428/articleType/ArticleView/articleId/5186/Feminisms-fragmentation-vs-collaboration--A-reflection-from-fieldwork-in-Spain.aspx.
3. See, for example, Buchowski, M. 2006. 'The Specter of Orientalism in Europe: From Exotic Other to Stigmatized Brother'. *Anthropological Quarterly* 79 (3): 463–482; Dunn, E. C. 2004. *Privatizing Poland. Baby Food, Big Business, and the Remaking of Labor*. New York: Cornell University Press; Sowa, Jan. 2012. 'An Unexpected Twist of Ideology. Neoliberalism and the Collapse of the Soviet Bloc'. *Praktyka Teoretyczna* (5): 153–180. http://www.praktykateoretyczna.pl/PT_nr5_2012_Logika_sensu/13.Sowa.pdf.
4. Standing, G. 2011. *Precariat. The New Dangerous Class*. London and New York: Bloomsbury Academic.
5. Papadopoulos, D. and V. Tsianos. 2013. 'After Citizenship: Autonomy of Migration, Organisational Ontology, and Mobile Commons'. *Citizenship Studies* 17 (2): 178–196.

Index

About the Contributors

Raia Apostolova obtained her doctoral degree in sociology and social anthropology from Central European University, Budapest. Her dissertation (Moving labor power and historical forms of migration) looks at the formation of three major categories: the internationalist socialist worker, the social benefit tourist and the economic migrant. The author argues that we need to exceed the legal frameworks of migration that are readily available to us and interrogate the very spaces (historical, ideological, and socio-political) of their making in order to understand the relation between migration and capitalism.

Karima Aziz holds a Mag. phil. in political science and a Mag. phil. in Polish studies from the University of Vienna and was a Marie Skłodowska Curie Early Stage Researcher in the 'ChangingEmployment' Initial Training Network. Her PhD thesis at the London Metropolitan University examines the experiences of female Polish migrant workers in the UK. Her academic interests lie in the field of migration, gender and work.

Ben Egan has since 2013 been a PhD candidate at the Catholic University of Leuven in Belgium, working on employment relations in multinational companies and diversity management in Belgium, France and the UK. He is a policy advisor at the European Trade Union Confederation, advising on labour market and employment issues. He has previously worked as a trade union official in the UK, working mostly as a campaign organiser in the education sector.

Chibuzo Ejiogu is a lecturer in Human Resource Management (HRM) and employment relations at Coventry University, UK. He is a PhD candidate at the University of Strathclyde, Glasgow. His teaching and research draws on his industry experience including roles in sustainable development, HRM and hospitality management as well as his involvement in social movements and worker activism. He was part of a team at the University of Strathclyde that pioneered the 'scenes and sounds of migration' seminar series that utilises documentary films, dialogue and music to explore and innovatively engage with the complex dynamics of migration. His multi-disciplinary research interests include changes to work and employment, migration, sociology of work, political economy, postcolonialism, regulatory and institutional change, organisational analysis, global governance, corporate governance, CSR, reward management, performance management, human rights, worker activism, networks and social movements.

Olena Fedyuk currently enjoys her maternity leave and parallel to that works in several projects exploring work conditions of the non-EU citizens employed as temporary agency workers in the EU. Between 2014 and 2016 she was a postdoctoral researcher in the Marie Curie 'ChangingEmployment' network at the University of Strathclyde, Glasgow. As a Marie Curie SocAnth doctoral scholar, she obtained her PhD degree from the department of Sociology and Social Anthropology at the Central European University, Budapest. Her dissertation is an ethnographic examination of transnational moral economies and distant motherhood through the cases of Ukrainian female labour migrants to Italy. Her recent work dealt with transnational migration, overlap of gendered employment and migration policies as well as transformations in care and labour regimes. Since 2012 she has directed two documentary films dealing with the issues of migration, church and gender.

Martin Lundsteen is an independent researcher, currently working on a project studying the tension between urban and national scales1 of belonging, and an assistant professor at the Universitat Autònoma de Barcelona. In 2015, he obtained his PhD with a thesis on social conflicts and convivencia in Salt, a small Catalan town ('Social Conflicts and Convivencia. An Ethnography of the Social Effects of "The Crisis" in a Small Catalan Town'). As a postdoctoral researcher, he has worked in several research projects on Islamophobia in Catalonia and, specifically, in Barcelona. He has been a member of the Grup d'Estudis sobre Reciprocitat (GER) since 2009, the Observatori d'Antropologia del Conflicte Urbà (OACU) since 2013 and Stop Als Fenòmens Islamòfobs (SAFI) since 2014. His research interests include political and economic anthropology, informal economy, urban anthropology, the political management of the poor, Islamophobia and racism, and, lately, nationalism and diversity.

Mateusz Karolak is a research assistant and PhD candidate at the Institute of Sociology at the University of Wroclaw (Poland). From 2013 to 2016 he worked as an Early Stage Researcher in the Marie Curie Initial Training Network 'ChangingEmployment'. His research interests include the political economy of Central-Eastern Europe, reproduction of inequalities, consequences of precarisation of work and intra-EU migrations with a particular focus on causation, consequences and subjective experiences of returning migrants. He is member of the editorial board of the academic journal *Praktyka Teoretyczna.*

Radosław Polkowski works as a researcher at the Scottish Government. From 2013 and 2016, he was a fellow in the FP7 Marie-Skłodowska Curie 'ChangingEmployment' programme and obtained his PhD in 2017 from the University of Strathclyde for a thesis on East-West migration in Europe with a focus on new immigration destinations: Northern Ireland, Scotland, and Poland. He has an extensive expertise also in relation to migration in East Asia, and in particular South Korea, which he gained through a post-doctoral research at the Academy of Korean Studies (2017). Moreover, he taught about political economy of East Asia and South Korea as a visiting lecturer at the University of Wroclaw (2016-2017), wrote articles for major newspaper media in South Korea and runs an analytical blog focusing on social affairs in this country. Of additional special interest both within the academy and in the policy community is his media work which embraces both photographic exposure and video presentations. His photographic work has received two awards, and he has completed a documentary film called *Our Kingdom* about migrant workers in Northern Ireland.

Irene Sabaté is a researcher in Social Anthropology and a lecturer at the Universitat de Barcelona. In 2009 she obtained her PhD with a dissertation on housing provisioning in East Berlin (*Habitar tras el Muro. La cuestión de la vivienda en el este de Berlín*, 2012). As a postdoctoral researcher, between 2009 and 2012 she took part in the 7th FP European project MEDEA (Models and their Effects on Development Paths), on industrial work and economic models, and, since 2012, she has been investigating mortgage indebtedness and home repossessions in the Barcelona metropolitan area, with a Post-PhD Research Grant from the Wenner Gren Foundation in 2014. She has been a member of the Grup d'Estudis sobre Reciprocitat (GER) since 2005, and she teaches Economic Anthropology, Anthropology of Consumption and Urban Anthropology. Her research interests include political economy, reciprocity, provisioning, work and social reproduction, housing, debt and credit relations, and financialization.

Nina Sahraoui is Postdoctoral Research Associate at the Robert Schuman Centre for Advanced Studies at the European University Institute within the ERC project EU Border Care. Nina received her PhD at London Metropolitan University supported by the Marie Curie ITN 'ChangingEmployment'. Her doctoral research focused on a gendered political economy analysis of the articulation of migration, care and employment regimes through the study of migrant and minority ethnic workers' experiences in older-age care in London, Paris and Madrid.

Paul Stewart is a Professor of Sociology of Work and Employment at the Department of Human Resource Management, University of Strathclyde in Glasgow. He is also a Coordinator of the Marie Curie Initial Training Network ChangingEmployment. He is a non-Executive Director of CAIRDE teo, a social economy organisation in Armagh City providing social and cultural services in the medium of the Irish language. His areas of expertise are the fields of employment, labour market change and economic restructuring. He has been working in the field of labour transformation and employment relations in the automotive industry in Britain, Brazil, Canada and Japan since the 1990s and, more recently, in the field of migration in Ireland and Poland. The area of industrial and employment change has now drawn focus on the development of global commodity chains in the automotive and ethanol sectors in Brazil and Europe and the consequences for employment, local and national economic change.

Jamie Woodcock is a fellow at the LSE. He is the author of *Working the Phones*, a study of a call centre in the UK inspired by the workers' inquiry. His current research involves developing this method in co-research projects with Deliveroo drivers and other digital workers in the so-called gig economy. He is on the editorial board of *Historical Materialism*.

www.ingramcontent.com/pod-product-compliance
Lightning Source LLC
Chambersburg PA
CBHW021809270326
41932CB00007B/116

* 9 7 8 1 7 8 6 6 1 3 1 2 7 *